SCOTTISH HISTORY SOCIETY

FOURTH SERIES

VOLUME 21

The Jacobean Union

Six tracts of 1604

The
Jacobean Union

Six tracts of 1604

edited by Bruce R. Galloway, PH.D.
and Brian P. Levack, PH.D.

★

★

EDINBURGH
printed for the Scottish History Society *by*
CLARK CONSTABLE, EDINBURGH AND LONDON
1985

ISBN 0 906245 06 0

Printed in Great Britain

PREFACE

While doing research on separate projects concerning Anglo-Scottish union, Bruce Galloway and I discovered a number of manuscript treatises regarding the efforts of King James VI and I to strengthen the regal union of 1603. Recognising the richness of this material, which historians have rarely used, we decided to collaborate on an edition of six of these treatises. We completed our work before Dr Galloway's untimely death in 1984.

For permission to publish and consult the various manuscripts used in the edited texts, acknowledgement is made to: The British Library; The Trustees of the National Library of Scotland; The Master and Fellows of Trinity College, Cambridge; The Curators of the Bodleian Library, Oxford; The Treasurer and Masters of the Bench of Lincoln's Inn; and the Public Record Office. For generous financial support at different stages of my work on this project I wish to thank the John Simon Guggenheim Memorial Foundation and the University Research Institute of the University of Texas at Austin. I also wish to express my gratitude to Revd Albert J. Loomie, SJ, for helping me to solve a number of problems connected with Sir Henry Savile's treatise, and to Dr Thomas I. Rae for his encouragement, advice and editorial assistance in preparing this volume.

BRIAN P. LEVACK

University of Texas at Austin
May, 1985

*A generous contribution from the
Carnegie Trust for the Universities of Scotland
towards the cost of producing this volume
is gratefully acknowledged by the
Council of the Society*

CONTENTS

INTRODUCTION

THE REGAL UNION of England and Scotland, often referred to as the Union of the Crowns, took place in March 1603, when James VI of Scotland acceded to the English throne. Although this union constituted a dramatic dynastic achievement, attributed by many to divine intervention, the long-term prospects of this conjunction appeared highly questionable. The two kingdoms over which James now ruled exhibited similarities in religion, language and manners, but they formed two distinct nations which had in the past regarded each other as enemies. Formal peace and a common Protestant bond had brought about an improvement in Anglo-Scottish relations in the late sixteenth century, but a host of differences still prevailed between the two countries. In order to strengthen the regal union James set out to reduce these differences, with the ultimate goal of creating a united British nation. This was patently a project of great scope and importance, thrilling to some and daunting to more. As a result, a large number of tracts were written on 'the union' in both countries. A few have already appeared in modern print, notably the two discourses of Sir Francis Bacon and Sir Thomas Craig's *De Unione Britanniae Tractatus*.[1] Many more remain available only in their manuscript or pamphlet originals. The main purpose of this volume is to expand the amount of readily accessible material by printing six of the more important treatises: those by Robert Pont, John Russell and an anonymous author from Scotland and by John Doddridge, Sir Henry Spelman and Sir Henry Savile from England. Before examining each of these tracts, however, it is

---

[1] *The Letters and Life of Francis Bacon*, ed. J. Spedding, iii (London, 1868), 89-99, 217-47; Sir Thomas Craig, *De Unione Regnorum Britanniae Tractatus*, ed. C. S. Terry (Scottish History Society, 1909)

necessary to discuss the political developments that inspired them and the terms of the broader literary debate to which they contributed.

THE POLITICAL BACKGROUND

i. *Before the Parliaments of 1604*

The history of the union project during James's first year as king of England has received a considerable amount of historical attention.[2] Most accounts of this early phase of the project stress the eagerness of James to abandon Scotland, his vainglory as a motive force behind the union project, his precipitate speed in pressing his design against the plain wishes of England and the cautious advice of counsellors such as Cecil, and his excessive favour to the Scots. The last theme has provided the foundation for the argument that the Scots supported the union because it tended to their particular advantage.

In general these accounts present a false picture of the union project. Nevertheless, each of the themes they emphasise contains an element of truth. James did complete his arrangements in Edinburgh very quickly and hurry south. The assumption of many historians that the king was overwhelmed by his good fortune and that this explains his sudden departure and the rash of honours he bestowed in both countries is, however, questionable. James's speed is surely the natural reaction of a new king distant from his capital and anxious to secure his crown. Political insecurity can also be used to justify the knighthoods and honours bestowed *en route*; all new monarchs were expected to show 'liberality', while James in particular needed to build up very quickly a party of greater and lesser men bound to him by favour. The second allegation, of vainglory, is unanswerable. James received many panegyrics praising himself and the union as examples of divine providence. He encouraged such sentiments, as we shall see, even inserting passages suggestive of a personal mission and a link with God into his

---

[2] See esp. D. H. Willson, *King James VI and I* (London, 1956) and 'King James I and Anglo-Scottish Unity', in *Conflict in Stuart England*, ed. W. A. Aiken and B. D. Henning (London, 1960), 43-55

speeches on the union. It is however impossible to tell how far these suggestions influenced royal thinking, and how much they constituted mere propaganda to further the project itself. The general interpretation of the project included here makes more of other elements also to be found in James's writings and speeches: the resolute rejection of ideas of 'Empire', the determination to have the project implemented by Parliament, and above all the continual emphasis on the need for a union in the hearts and minds of the two peoples. This suggests a much more likely motive for the project; namely, a desire to establish firmly the hold of the Stuarts over two traditionally hostile nations, by eliminating the hostility. The desire for a 'union in hearts and minds' explains the king's great concern with propaganda, his desire to create an outward show of union through unification of the royal style, the seals, and the flags, and his emphasis on the need for the union to proceed gradually, by the will of the two peoples.

It is here that the conventional interpretation of the project is most inadequate. There is in fact very little evidence suggesting a headlong rush by James towards union in 1603. Bacon's famous remark, that he 'hasteneth to a mixture of both kingdoms and nations, faster perhaps than policy will conveniently bear' is inconclusive.[3] Besides coming very early in the reign, the remark could have referred to a mixture of nationalities at court, rather than to progress on union itself. What is most notable about 1603 is, after all, the absence of substantive action on the project. James restricted his activities to those few areas where he could use his prerogative powers without prejudicing discussion by either parliament. Thus, he set out to establish peace, order and brotherhood among his two peoples, to reconcile their commercial and economic systems, to settle the government of Scotland from London, and to establish a mixture of English and Scots at court.

James was active and insistent in the first of these areas. In the proclamation of Scotland announcing his accession to the English throne, James ordered Scots to acknowledge Englishmen 'as thair deirest bretherein and freindis, and the inhabitantis

[3] Spedding, *Letters of Bacon*, iii, 77

of baith his realmes to obliterat and remove out of thair myndis all and quhatsumever quarrellis ... with ane universall unanimitie of hartis' – a theme repeated in his later 'Proclamation for the Uniting of England and Scotland', issued in May.[4] One area where such pious sentiments were made action was the Borders. The suppression of dissident Border clans, notably the Grahams, and the rundown of the large but now superfluous garrison at Berwick reflected partly a desire to keep order and cut expenditure. Such actions also, however, reflected James's insistence that English and Scots here be one people, enshrined symbolically under the name of the 'middle Shires'. His policy was 'utterlie to extinguishe as well the name as substance of the bordouris, I mean the difference between thaime and other pairts of the kingdome. For doing quhairof it is necessarie that all querrellis amoungst thaim be reconcyled and all straingenes between the nations quyte removed'.[5]

Commercially, the first year saw some major steps towards union. A proclamation in April quickly established the relative values of Scots and English currency, as an encouragement to mutual trade. Englishmen trading in Scotland were exempted from outward and inward customs laid on aliens, and allowed to transport forbidden goods like cloth. This was tantamount to a free trade in domestic commodities. How far such relaxations were mutual, and effectuated, is uncertain; the English government in November proclaimed against the unlawful conveyance of goods into and from Scotland, seeking to restrict trade to the customs posts at Berwick and Carlisle.[6]

The final area of activity lay in the settlement of government and the court. It is difficult here to separate measures taken to promote union from those made necessary by the exigencies of

[4] *Register of the Privy Council of Scotland (RPCS)*, vi (ed. D. Masson, 1884), 553, 558; *Stuart Royal Proclamations*, ed. J. Larkin and F. Hughes (Oxford, 1973), i, 18-19

[5] Historical Manuscripts Commission (HMC), *Calendar of Salisbury Manuscripts Preserved at Hatfield House (HMCS)*, xvi, ed. M. S. Giuseppi (London, 1933), 405. See also S. and S. J. Watts, *From Border to Middle Shire: Northumberland, 1586-1625* (Leicester, 1975), 133-4

[6] National Library of Scotland (NLS), Advocates MS 34.2.2, ii, fos. 321, 328; T. Keith, *Commercial Relations of England and Scotland, 1603-1707* (Cambridge, 1910), 9-19; S. G. E. Lythe, 'The Union of the Crowns and the Debate on Economic Integration', *Scottish Journal of Political Economy*, v (1958), 219-28

governing two kingdoms, and one *in absentia*. The significant question is whether the measures were intended as an interim or permanent arrangement. Professor Lee has shown that many initial measures in Scotland for the education of the prince and management of the Queen's estates appear temporary. The Scottish bureaucracy, however, was generally retained intact, as Scots who had accompanied James to London either returned quickly or resigned their Edinburgh posts.[7] The new features were rather those necessitated by absentee government: the establishment of an efficient post between the capitals, and the division of the Scots Privy Council into London and Edinburgh groups. The post was of great importance. By it, the king received each year over sixty public (and many more private) letters, while it acted also as the principal communications system between London and Edinburgh Scots. In this early period, the function of these groups can be identified very accurately. The Edinburgh Council became primarily executive, handling everyday affairs like the Borders but submitting major questions, with advice, to the king. The London group – Lennox, Mar, Kinloss, Sir George Home and Sir James Elphinstone – formed a coterie of trusted advisers to James on his Scots policy. Other London Scots could be used as unofficial channels to the king, Sir Thomas Erskine in particular maintaining a lively correspondence with Scotland.

In all this, there was very little to suggest a precipitate rush towards union. English complaints concentrated instead on the allied question of the mixture of the two nations at court. There was much resentment felt at the number of Scots in England, and a belief that they were monopolising the royal favour. The Venetian Ambassador reported that 'the supreme offices are bestowed upon Scots ... every day posts are taken from the English' in a 'highhanded manner', causing great 'chagrin'.[8]

Before examining these allegations, one must recognise that there were very good reasons why Scots favourites should have

---

[7] M. Lee, Jr., 'James VI's Government of Scotland after 1603', *Scottish Historical Review*, liv (1975), 41-53

[8] *Calendar of State Papers Venetian (CSPVen), 1603-1607*, ed. H. F. Brown (London, 1900), 33, 44-45

received preferential treatment. Besides being men whom James knew he could work with and trust, old servants, they were also the people who had done most to establish the unprecedentedly efficient government of Scotland during the previous decade. In that time, they had received very few rewards in cash or honours,[9] and it was only reasonable they should expect to share James's fortune. They were also the people on whom James would be relying to maintain Scots government during his absence. The creation of obligations now might obviate the danger of political alienation later.

This special pleading is partly valid, but obscures the most important truth: namely, that there was no 'flood of Scots' into English government. The number of Scots who travelled south was small, especially after James's proclamation against unlicensed passage.[10] The number who secured official positions in London was smaller still. Overwhelmingly, James rewarded his Scots servants with pensions and cash rather than offices – sometimes to their chagrin, as the French Ambassador made clear.[11] Having bestowed these rewards, the king then required the recipients to return home and resume their posts in the Scots government. The residue of 'official' Scots in London made up three groups. The first were a small group of men who were advanced into government posts and denizated.[12] The second were the five close friends who formed James's inner ring of counsel on Scots affairs. These were likewise denizated and admitted to the English Privy Council.[13] This did not entail any takeover of policy on English affairs. The Scots members were occasionally appointed to Council committees, but did not

---

[9] G. Donaldson, *Scotland: James V to James VII* (Edinburgh, 1971), 218. See also Craig, *De Unione*, 430 ff. For James's lavish farewell distribution of honours see *RPCS*, vi, p. liv

[10] *RPCS*, vi, p. lxiv

[11] British Library (BL), King's MS 124, fos. 27-28. The Venetian Ambassador also notes the return of the Scots home, rationalising that they were 'bought off' by the English Council: *CSPVen, 1603-1607*, 70. For an example of such gifts see BL, Additional MS 12497, fos. 153-60

[12] Alexander Douglas, for example, was admitted Keeper of the Council Chamber with Humfrey Rogers on 13 May 1603. *Acts of the Privy Council (APC), 1601-1604*, ed. J. R. Dasent (London, 1907), 498. For James's later proclamation against such appointments see Public Record Office, State Papers Domestic (S.P. Dom.), 14/10/40

[13] 4 May 1603, *APC 1601-4*, 496-7

form part of the quadrumvirate (Cecil, Worcester, North-ampton and Suffolk) generally considered to have had most influence on royal policy in England. They were outnumbered not only by established Privy Councillors, but by Englishmen raised to the Council during James's first years of rule. Of the five, only Home received a governmental position, and that briefly. The admission of the Scots can be seen either as a means of giving them a recognised standing at court, or as a symbol of the united, 'British' Council which James hoped in time to create.[14] The third and numerically largest group were Scots given places in the royal Household, most notably in the Bedchamber and Privy Chamber. The number concerned was again small, but sufficient to establish a definite Scots presence, particularly in the Queen's service.[15] Two factors apply here. It was entirely natural that the king and queen should wish to continue in their immediate entourage personal servants who had shown loyalty and goodwill. Equally, the king and queen could in practice have only one such entourage; any separate establishment or Household maintained in Edinburgh would be superfluous, and a sham. Since James was king over both countries, it would have been a gross insult to Scotland if his entourage had been entirely English. This basic principle of union surfaces in Beaumont's report of James's intention to make up his Bedchamber from seven of each nation.[16]

Nevertheless, the presence of Household Scots in England caused much discontent, as the same report showed. D. H. Willson considers this discontent justified, claiming that the Scots acted as major sources of patronage. This is at best un-proven.[17] Certainly, some Englishmen must have been dis-placed, and others disappointed. What is more significant is the

[14] For Scottish fears of this, see *CSPVen 1603-1607*, 106-8
[15] P. R. Seddon, 'Patronage and Officers in the Reign of James I' (unpub. Ph.D. thesis, University of Manchester, 1967), 155-72
[16] BL, Add. MS 30640, fo. 97
[17] The reference cited in Willson is R. Winwood, *Memorials of Affairs of State*, ii (London, 1725), 57. This however concerns discontent at court over the excessive deference of Sir Thomas Lake. The only hints of Scottish dominance at court appear in PRO, S.P. Dom. 14/7/59 and 'Advertisements of a Loyal Subject', in *Somers Tracts*, ii, ed. W. Scott (London, 1809), 144-8. See also the apology of John Burgess in S.P. Dom., 14/8/85

spread of the resentment to groups within English society whose own chances of favour were non-existent. It is clear that the allegation of Scots monopolising the royal favour became a rallying-cry for the residual hostility, suspicion and prejudice held by the two nations against each other.[18] Any account of the union during 1603-4 which does not chart this dark side would be guilty of grave imbalance. That such prejudice existed is unsurprising. The two nations had centuries of hostility to overcome. Englishmen consistently appear in 16th-century Scots literature as haughty, superior and overbearing, while the corresponding Scots stereotype in England was that of a poor, lazy, grasping, quick-tempered buffoon. English and Scots writers on the union relate almost word for word the methods used during their childhoods to reinforce these prejudices. Correspondingly, evidence for friction in 1603 is considerable. French and Venetian Ambassadors are for once united on this point. The historian Arthur Wilson later recalled that 'the streets swam night and day with bloody quarrels' between Englishmen and Scots.[19] James was forced in July 1603 to issue a proclamation against Scottish insolencies, and in April 1604 to order the arrest of 'Swaggerers' who were ambushing Scots in London.[20] In Scotland, there were already signs of discontent with their legacy of absentee government, and fears that future 'union' would be an unequal settlement.

In short, it was amply clear by March 1604 that union would be a contentious subject. To James, this contention was itself proof of the project's necessity. To others, it merely made the prospect of union more repellent.

ii. *The Parliaments of 1604*
Discussion of the union project during the English session of March-June 1604 has long been affected by the controversy

[18] See esp. A. Wilson, *The History of Great Britain* (London, 1653), 25-26
[19] *CSPVen, 1603-1607*, 4; BL King's MS 124, fos. 27-28, 73; Add. MS 30640, fos. 24-25
[20] For other actions of James against insults from either side see S.P. Dom. 14/8/85. In 1605 James imprisoned two of the authors of *Eastward Ho* for their remarks against the Scots. See George Chapman, Ben Jonson and John Marston, *Eastward Ho*, ed. R. W. Van Fossen (Manchester, 1979), 4-8

over relations between the early Stuarts and the House of Commons. Historians have traditionally interpreted the session in a 'whig' manner, emphasising the importance of parliament, of the Lower House within parliament, and of those in the Commons who spoke against what were conceived to be royal interests. Politics therefore appeared to be a battle between a 'Court Party' of dependants and a relatively well-organised 'Opposition' seeking to rectify grievances, secure parliamentary privileges, and expand the scope and effectiveness of the House. According to this interpretation the most significant issues of the session were the debates on wardship, purveyancing, the Merchant Adventurers and the Goodwin–Fortescue election dispute. These questions of grievance and privilege allegedly led to strident conflict with a king unused to and unsuited for the patient management of long, powerful English parliaments. The session's climax was therefore the Commons' Apology, 'a bold declaration of right, a lecture to a foreign king upon the constitution of his new kingdom'.[21]

Whig ideas about the rise of parliament under the early Stuarts have come under heavy fire. Scholars have emphasised the relative unimportance of the institution at the time and the ideological consensus that prevailed within it. When 'opposition' did surface, it often reflected divisions and factions within the Privy Council and the court. This general reassessment of Stuart parliaments has led to a radical reinterpretation of the session of 1604, particularly on grievances and privilege.[22] The Buckinghamshire election has been relegated to a dispute between Commons and Privy Council, James himself showing strict impartiality. His 'high-handed' and 'dictatorial' com-

[21] Willson, *James VI and I*, 249; W. Notestein, *The House of Commons, 1604-1610* (New Haven, Conn., 1971)

[22] See esp. R. C. Munden, 'James I and "the Growth of Mutual Distrust": King, Commons and Reform, 1603-1604', in *Faction and Parliament*, ed. K. Sharpe (Oxford, 1978), 43-73. For a general reinterpretation of the role of parliament see C. Russell, 'Parliamentary History in Perspective', *History*, lxi (1976), 1-28. For criticism of such revisionism see J. H. Hexter, 'Power Struggle, Parliament, and Liberty in Early Stuart England', *Journal of Modern History*, l (1978), 1-50, and T. K. Rabb and D. Hirst, 'Revisionism Revised: Two Perspectives on Early Stuart Parliamentary History', *Past & Present*, xcii (1981), 55-99

mand to the Commons to confer with the judges, and subsequent decision to admit neither candidate without fresh elections, appears as a compromise enabling the Commons to back down without losing face. Similarly, the programme of grievances put forward by Wroth on 23 March is considered a *royal* initiative, to secure regular composition of the feudal purveyancing and wardship dues.[23] Purveyancing and the 'monopoly' of the Merchant Adventurers survived mainly because of internal divisions in the Commons, while the failure to agree on wardship reflected only the deteriorating relations of king and Commons during May 1604.

Any independent discussion of the union in this session must both take account of and affect these rival interpretations. In this, two cardinal features stand out. First, the union was undoubtedly intended as the major issue of the session, and in fact occupied more parliamentary time than any other subject. Second, modern insistence on general cooperation between king and Commons cannot obscure the very real exasperation, even acrimony on both sides by June 1604. The 'Apology' may never have been submitted to James. The king may have been more careful in his final speech to distinguish between the well-affected majority and knavish minority in the Commons than is generally believed. Nevertheless, that speech remained a blistering admonition, and contemporary records leave no doubt about the royal disfavour.[24] The same sources clearly show the main reason for that disfavour, and for 'the growth of mutual distrust' generally, was the union.

It is at first sight difficult to understand why the union programme should have been so contentious. Many historians believe that James originally intended to force a substantive union through the 1604 session but as a result of parliamentary pressure accepted a preparatory commission as a second best. In fact, the reverse is true. The central plank of the royal programme for the session had always been just such a commission, 'with pouer onlie to reporte to the nixt parliamen-

---

[23] N. Tyacke, 'Wroth, Cecil and the Parliamentary Session of 1604', *Bulletin of the Institute of Historical Research (BIHR)*, 1 (1978-9), 120-4

[24] For the speech see S.P. Dom. 14/8/93

tis'.[25] The other main union proposal for the session was similarly limited: a change in the royal style from 'King of England, Scotland, France and Ireland' to 'King of Great Britain'. Its purpose was symbolic and emotive, to mark the unity and equality of his two peoples. It was also a change which James *could* carry out without parliament, by proclamation; his desire for parliamentary ratification reflected his wish to have 'a display of goodwill towards a general idea' by the highest public representatives in either nation. The royal speech of 19 March opening the session was a blatant appeal for just such a show of solidarity. It also established many of the themes reiterated in the tracts: the comparison of this union with that of York and Lancaster under Henry VII and its achievement by divine providence, manifested in their long peace and existing unity in language, religion, continent and manners. It displayed James's belief in a direct personal relationship between himself and his island. 'What God hath conjoined then, let no man separate. I am the husband, and all the whole isle is my lawful wife; I am the head and it is my body; I am the shepherd and it is my flock'.[26]

Surprisingly, the speech was followed by a month of silence on the union. On 13 April, however, replying to a Commons vote of thanks for his handling of the Goodwin-Fortescue case, James set out his union programme both for this session and later years. 'His wish, above all things, was at his death to leave: one worship to God: one kingdom, intirely governed: one uniformity in laws'.[27] For the present, however, he asked only for a preparatory commission and a change in style. These proposals were elaborated in joint conferences of Lords and Commons on 14 April. In the ensuing fortnight, debate concentrated entirely on the style. This was a confused affair, often acrimonious, producing a flurry of different arguments in the Lower House. Those supporting the change, including

[25] *RPCS*, vi, 596-7. James adopted this programme almost certainly on Cecil's counsel: *HMCS*, xv, 228. See Beaumont's report of 21 April 1604, BL, Add. MS 30640, fo. 63
[26] *Constitutional Documents of the Reign of James I*, ed. J. R. Tanner (Cambridge, 1961), 26. For a novel interpretation of this speech see M. J. Enright, 'King James I and his Island: An Archaic Kingship Belief?', *Scottish Historical Review*, liv (1975), 29-40
[27] *Journals of the House of Commons (CJ)*, i, 171

Bacon, predictably emphasised the proclamatory power of the king, the antiquity of Britain, divine providence, and the symbolic importance of the name in securing a union of hearts and minds.[28] The arguments against the change were many and various. A number of these dealt with the question of England's precedency and superiority. Sir Maurice Berkeley urged that Scotland, as the 'less honourable' kingdom, should seek the change in style. Nicholas Fuller used the historical precedent of the Henrician union with Wales to argue for a commission examining the laws of Scotland before agreeing to any union. Sir Edwin Sandys spoke of English precedency in the existing style, believing that Scotland should yield and take the famous name of England.[29]

Some of the objections to the proposed change were of a constitutional and legal nature. Sandys, an enigmatic figure whose precipitate rise in the Commons came during these debates, argued that a parliament commissioned to discuss English affairs could not resolve on the wider matter of 'Great Britain'. He also insisted that a change in the royal style would legally mean changing the name of the kingdom itself for all purposes, thus invalidating laws, oaths, legal instruments and institutions (including parliament) running currently under the name of England.[30] This line of resistance involved no offence to James or Scotland, and it found support among MPs who had previously based their opposition on more emotive grounds. For all these reasons the Commons decided on 20 April to oppose any change in the name before the question of a union in government had been resolved.

The reaction of James and his supporters to this resistance came on 20-21 April, both in debate and in a royal audience in St James's Gallery. James underlined the moderate and limited nature of his project, even excluding from the scope of the Commission the 'fundamental laws' by which the two kingdoms were governed. Legal union would thereby be restricted

---

[28] *Ibid.*, 176; Spedding, *Letters of Bacon*, iii, 191
[29] *CJ*, i, 177-8
[30] 'The Name urgeth and inwrappeth the Matter: – We shall prejudge the Matter', *CJ*, i, 177-8; PRO, S.P. Dom. 14/7/75

to an abolition of laws in which the two kingdoms expressed mutual hostility, and to 'a participation of such lawes as were good in each and defective in the other'. After answering a number of general objections to the new style he said that he would forego the change if any confusion in the laws was thereby entailed. To make his position clear beyond any doubt, he also delivered a statement of intent in the form of a draft Act.[31]

This royal intervention did not prevent increasingly confused and heated debates during the following week; nor did a further royal message on 24 April guaranteeing freedom of speech and referring the legal question to the judges appreciably cool the situation. After further debate the Commons set up a committee under Bacon to compile a list of objections to the change in style, in preparation for a conference with the Lords. MPs competed with each other to add arguments to this compilation. The most important speech again came from Sandys, who restated his earlier arguments in a manner similar to the later tracts. Distinguishing between unions by marriage, election and conquest, he argued that only the last normally brought reconciliation in laws, offices or styles. The adoption of 'Great Britain' would not only abrogate existing English and Scots laws, but would also impede the ability of the two parliaments to legislate in the future. Neither assembly could pass laws for all 'Britain', or for part of an indivisible new kingdom. The change, therefore, entailed automatically an entire union, by which James alone would possess constitutional authority. No proviso could avoid this. The oath between king and subject, treaties running in the name of England, and the diplomatic precedency of the king abroad would all be affected.[32]

The list was completed on 27 April and reduced to a scheme for the conference. Despite its later importance, the compilation did not have any decisive importance at the time. Although used in the conference of 28 April, the objections were rendered unnecessary by the opinion of the judges, which supported the

[31] Spedding, *Letters of Bacon*, iii, 194; S.P. Dom. 14/7/75. For copies of the 'Act' see BL, Harleian MS. 292, fo. 131; Lincoln's Inn Library, Maynard MS 83, item 4
[32] *CJ*, i, 186; S.P. Dom. 14/7/63

petition of the Commons. The new style, if taken by Act, would entail 'an utter extinction of all the laws now in force', affecting 'all processes, all writs, all executions of justice, yea the very recognition of the king in this parliament to be lawful possessor of the crown of England'.[33] James therefore agreed to abandon his proposal for a statutory change.

The fortnight of debate on the name, and the list of objections arising from it, showed that the Lower House had very little desire to make any public show of goodwill towards the union. While the legal pretext was from James's viewpoint an entirely valid argument, many of the other objections raised had been profoundly offensive – either implying distrust of his own purposes, or depreciating Scotland. The latter was particularly unfortunate, as likely to alienate the Scots just as they were called upon to show their whole-hearted support for union. It is in this context that one must see the king's sharp message of 1 May to the Commons, accusing them of 'jalousie and distruste, ather of me the propounder, or of the maitter by me propounditt'.[34] The Commons' reaction was a motion to make reply to the king. This was headed off into committee by Bacon, Hastings, and Sir Richard Leveson, but from here grew 'The Form of Apology and Satisfaction'. Again, the union played a central role in the growth of poor relations between king and Commons, the debate on the name providing the immediate occasion of the Commons' protest as well as the background of mutual dissatisfaction.

By contrast, the remaining part of James's union programme, namely the Act for a preparatory Commission, passed with great ease. Outlines were agreed in conference with the Lords on 2 May. The Commission was to be established by Act, framed (most unusually) by a joint subcommittee of the two houses, with nine Lords and twenty MPs. The number and nomination of Commissioners was to be decided by each House, but the number was to be 'competent' and was to include a mixture of common and civil lawyers, government

---

[33] PRO, S.P. Dom. 14/7/85
[34] See Winwood, *Memorials*, ii, 20-21 and W. Cobbett, *The Parliamentary History of England*, i (London, 1806), 1021-2

officials, and merchants. It would sit between parliamentary sessions, starting on 1 October in the Painted Chamber at Westminster, with power only to prepare proposals to be submitted to the next sessions of either national parliament. By 10 May, the number of Commissioners had been agreed (30 MPs and 14 Lords) and a draft bill submitted by the subcommittee to the Upper House. The same draft reached the Commons two days later, and a list of Commissioners agreed over the following days. The Lower House did find 'certain doubts and differences' in the Bill, and established its own committee on 22 May to examine these – the first union committee on which Sandys actually sat. The result was a conference with the Lords on the inclusion of a 'provision or restriction', and an agreement that Commissioners should not be bound on their return to parliament to support any of the proposals. The amended Bill was finally engrossed by the Lords on 28 May, and passed by the Lower House five days later.

In all this, only two areas of substantial disagreement between king and Commons may be seen. The first lies in the phraseology of the Act. The original draft had been a fulsome commendation of the union, containing long references to divine providence and geographical unity, dismissing the 'shadows and fears' of those concerned about the dangers to existing privileges with a brief pledge not to alter fundamental laws, and anticipating a union of 'such points of incongruity and disconvenience as the several laws and customs . . . may bring forth'.[35] It was also couched in petitionary form. The final Act by contrast included a lengthy preamble on the pledge (this is probably the 'restriction' desired by the Commons), while reducing the commitment to further legal union to cover only the elimination of hostile laws. The petitionary form and references to divine providence were excised, leaving it altogether a more grudging and half-hearted document.

The second area of disagreement concerned the first of the tracts on union produced in response to parliamentary debate. This was John Thornborough's *Discourse* (see the Appendix), a detailed answer to the Commons' objections of 27 April to the

[35] Spedding, *Letters of Bacon*, iii, 204-6

change in style. The *Discourse* was already in print by 26 May, when a complaint was raised in the Lower House that Thornborough, who sat in the Lords as Bishop of Bristol, had breached parliamentary privilege and 'discovered the secrets' of parliament. The book was formally examined by both Houses, and its author required to apologise on June 5 for any breach of privilege of which he might have been guilty. Sir John Holles believed that this comparatively lenient treatment reflected royal favour and intervention.[36]

The development of the union project in the English session raises many questions of general interest. To an extent, it confirms the traditional 'whig' thesis of an innate and organised opposition to the king in the Lower House. The resistance of the Commons was undoubtedly coordinated, and moreover successful on the proposal to change the style. Nevertheless, the feeling remains that the union was very much a special case, which cannot safely be used for generalisations about the relationship between King and Commons. Many of the MPs speaking against the name, or against the union *per se*, appear in 'whig' histories as 'government men'. Considerable evidence exists to suggest covert support for the opposition from within the Upper House and Privy Council.[37] It is clear that the English reaction against the union project ran wider and deeper than feelings on other issues before parliament. The extraordinary mistrust of the 1604 session thus reflected an extraordinary issue.

The union project in 1603-4, and indeed in 1603-8 generally, has traditionally been treated as an episode in English parliamentary politics, with Scottish attitudes being generally overlooked. Some historians have portrayed the Scots as highly motivated towards the union, hoping to obtain the rich lands, benefices and offices of England. This is to accept the Commons' propaganda at its face value.[38] Manuscript evidence for Scotland is poor, except in the tracts. Nevertheless, enough survives to show not only the ambivalence of Scotland to the project, but

---

[36] *Journals of the House of Lords (LJ)*, ii, 306; *HMC Portland MSS*, 13
[37] See for example, *HMC Portland MSS*, 12-13; *CSPVen, 1603-1607*, 151; BL, Add. MS 30640
[38] For English beliefs see *CJ*, i, 361

her influence on political developments in 1603-4. By Autumn 1603, the French and Venetian Ambassadors were for example reporting the same things: increasing hatred and discontent between the two countries, the Scots' decision to have representatives at the English parliament to report on proceedings there, and the agitation of leading political figures in the northern kingdom against any union involving a change in their ancient laws and privileges.[39] Thus, in March 1604, even as the English parliament met, we learn that the earl of Mar assured James of Scotland's good affections to the union – provided that a saving on such changes were to be made.[40] The same source speaks of Englishmen opposing Scottish access to English offices and privileges unless Scotland also accepted English common law. Several Commons speeches after 18 April groped rather tentatively at this idea, the main theme of opposition to the union in 1606-7. This throws into sharp relief the assurance by James on 21 April that he intended no change in fundamental laws at this stage. Rather than being an answer to English fears about the change in name abrogating all the laws of England, as it is traditionally regarded, it reflected crown policy adopted before the parliament sat, at least partly under Scots influence.

Scots wariness before the English parliament turned to bitter resentment during the session. The progressive prorogations of the Scots parliament necessitated by the long Commons debates delayed the first substantive day of debate from 10 April to 3 July, exasperating many Scots. A more important factor in alienating the northern kingdom was of course the nature of the arguments used in the English Lower House. Both ambassadors report the righteous indignation of the Scots at the English references to the poverty and inferiority of Scotland.[41] The growth in acrimony is also traced in the letters of those

---

[39] *CSPVen, 1603-1607*, 94, 106-8; BL, King's MS 124, fos. 27-28, 53, 73, 148. Scaramelli, the Venetian ambassador, is unreliable. He identifies Huntly, Errol and Angus as leading opponents, but Huntly and Angus were both later to write to James protesting their good affections towards the union. NLS, Advocates MS 33.1.1, i

[40] BL, Add. MS. 30640, fos. 63, 71

[41] *CSPVen, 1603-1607*, 153-5; BL, Add. MS 30640, fo. 126. Beaumont also notes Scottish fears regarding English claims that 'l'Ecosse peur et doit estre adioustee et comprise soubz la domination d'icelle ainsi qui l'Irlande'

statesmen working hardest to counteract it – Cecil, Mar and Balmerino. On 3 May, Cecil urged Balmerino 'in no sort to suffer bruicts unanswered, so to possess the mynds of that parliament there (which may be collected out of some particular and idle speaches comon in multitudes)'.[42] His concern was justified. Subsequent letters from Balmerino and Mar speak of 'malicious speechis sentt heir and spred in this cuntrie', and of the English debates 'exasperat[ing] some sores that the best physicians of both our states will be troubled to cure . . . most of us all could be rather content in our wonted condition nor to match with so unequal a party'.[43] The ambassadors show the Scots parliament resolving to have nothing to do with any union involving changes in their ancient laws or the French alliance, proposing York or even Berwick as a site for the Commission, and opposing certain names on the king's list of Commissioners as being too closely associated with English interests.[44]

It was to this resentment that James addressed himself, in an admirable, soothing letter to the Scots parliament on 12 June. Reporting the passage in England of the Act of Commission, he swore on his royal honour that 'als wele in all the speichis as actionis of this oure parliament heir, nothing . . . [wes] utterit or done whiche mycht tend ather to the reproche in honour or the prejudgeing of the liberteis and freedomes of that our ancient and honourable realme'.[45] He would always consider the honour and weal of Scotland as equal to that of England. Eye-witnesses were sent with the letter to confirm this peaceful view of the English debates.

The Scots Act of Commission was passed by 11 July; but there remain echoes of this acrimony and resentment in its passage. Firstly, a list of Commissioners submitted by the king was rejected, and replaced with one drawn up by parliament.[46] Secondly, and more significantly, the Scots Act included a

---

[42] Scottish Record Office (SRO), GD 156/6/3 (Elphinstone Papers)
[43] PRO, S.P. Dom. 14/8/9-10; *HMCS*, xvi, 86, 98-99
[44] *CSPVen, 1603-1607*, 153-4; BL Add. MS 30640, fos. 98ff, 126, 157, 166
[45] *RPCS*, vii, 457-9
[46] *Ibid.*, 461. See also D. Calderwood, *The History of the Church of Scotland*, vi (Edinburgh, 1845), 262-3

saving on fundamental laws not only in the preamble (where it did not legally bind the Commission) but also in the main text. The effect was drastically to reduce the scope of discussion available to the Commissioners. This change was the more notable as James had required the parliament to match the English Act 'worde be worde'. Even more notable was the success of the earl of Morton and his followers in securing a supplementary Act excluding changes in the Kirk from the scope of discussion available to the Commissioners. These were almost certainly reactions to the political developments in England. James's attitude is uncertain. He was already pledged against alterations in fundamental law at this stage, and did not upbraid the Scots for this or the religious caveat. Nevertheless, the king must have been disturbed to find Scotland too ready for resistance on the union, and so unenthusiastic, even in show. Certainly, there are indications of disfavour to nobles sitting in the parliament, for their attitude on the union.

The political background to the union tracts was therefore ambiguous. On the one hand, machinery had been established to continue discussion of the project, and to produce proposals for the first stage in a long-term consolidation of the two nations. Tracts were therefore free to discuss union in broad terms. On the other, James's project had already encountered prejudice and resistance in both nations, endangering its long-term prospects. Underlying fears and assumptions in both nations had surfaced, affecting the union: England fearing Scots monopoly over the royal favour and asserting ancient superiority, Scotland fiercely repudiating all claims to precedency and making the maintenance of ancient laws and the kirk a touchstone of nationhood. The tracts, of course, reflect these feelings, but also indicate a more complex series of attitudes on either side of the border than that apparent in the dry political records.

TRACTS AND TREATISES ON THE UNION, 1603-5

The six treatises reproduced in this volume provide a substantial and varied body of opinion regarding the union, but they form only a part of a much wider literary debate. Between 1603 and 1605 no fewer than twenty-eight tracts were written on the union – eighteen by Englishmen, nine by Scots and one by an Italian resident in England. The six treatises in this volume receive detailed discussion below, while brief descriptions of the other twenty-two appear in the Appendix. Of the entire twenty-eight, eleven found their way into print during this period, while many others appear in sufficient manuscript copies to suggest a considerable circulation. Two of the printed treatises, Pont's *De Unione* and Cornwallis's *Miraculous Union*, were published both in Edinburgh and London. The size and circulation of this body of literature, and the survival of many other works that deal only in passing with the union confirm contemporary references to the union as a major subject of public discussion. 'There is nothing more in the mouthes of men', wrote one commentator in 1604, 'then discoursing the Union of England and Scotland'.[47]

The tracts vary greatly in length, purpose and attitudes towards the union. Nevertheless, they shared a common set of assumptions about the union and the way in which it should be debated. Generally they addressed the same questions, and in so doing often employed the same arguments, used the same examples and cited the same sources. The three themes that received the most sustained treatment were the general principle of unity in Britain, the name of Great Britain, and the advisability of further union in law, government, religion and trade.

i. *The Principle of Unity in Britain*

A great majority of the tracts on the union declare their support, at least in passing, for the general principle of British unity. These statements frequently celebrate, either explicitly or by strong implication, the already accomplished Union of the Crowns, but they do not specify what type of union their authors wished to see established. These discussions of unity, therefore, engendered little controversy, attracting only occasional criticism on the grounds of triviality and irrelevance.

[47] BL, Stowe MS 158, fo. 34

Even those tracts that adopted a negative stance on the question of further union, such as Spelman's 'Of the Union', had little difficulty declaring their support for the general principle. In many cases, however, these discussions of British unity served as a preface to more substantial proposals and therefore possessed considerable value as propaganda.

In providing support for the general principle of unity, the authors of the tracts adopted both secular and religious approaches. The central theme of the first was that unity brought prosperity, division misery. Several tracts, including Russell, used Livy's comparison between human and politic bodies to illustrate this point, while Bacon employed a more sophisticated analogy between political union and unity in nature. Most writers cited numerous historical precedents in support of the general proposition, showing that united kingdoms achieved fame and fortune, while disunited territories fell prey to invasion, sedition and malaise. Many of these precedents came from British history. Craig dedicated a long section to prove that 'the separation of the crowns of the island is the cause of all the calamities that have befallen Britain'.[48]

The religious approach to the question of unity in Britain occurs less frequently than the secular, but it had deeper implications for 'the union'. The writers who adopted it used Christian theology and scripture to establish unity as a divine principle, emphasising the unity of God himself, of His universe, and of God with man before the Fall and after the Redemption. Consequently division itself – manifest in the separation of man from God by original sin, of Adam's family after the expulsion from Eden, and of the Heavenly Host itself through Lucifer's rebellion – became the mark of Satan. This commonplace equation of God and unity required little supporting material. Gordon, however, did invoke the cabala, analysing the Hebrew word for union into three letters meaning knowledge, life and door. Thus Union became 'the door whereby we enter by knowledge to life and eternal felicitie'.[49]

Religious arguments in favour of unity, especially when

[48] Craig, De Unione, p. xii
[49] J. Gordon, A Sermon of the Union of Great Brittanie (London, 1604), 7

supported by the biblical precedent of the union of Israel and Judah, encouraged the belief that the Union of England and Scotland was the work of God, a reward for the maintenance of the true religion in the two kingdoms. This belief had a bearing on attitudes toward the union project, for if the union were God's work, then James was His tool, and to oppose James in his efforts to perfect the union would be to oppose God's will. Gordon and Russell carried this argument further by attributing to James and to Britain itself a divine mission to purify all of Christendom. In establishing the ancient (and now restored) unity of Britain, a common theme in the literature of this period, these two authors concentrated on the mythological King Lucius, allegedly the first Christian king, to whom the Pope gave complete ecclesiastical jurisdiction over Britain. Lucius symbolised the religious purity of Britain. Gordon explicitly represents British churchmen like Bede and Wycliff as zealots struggling on behalf of the true religion against Roman tyranny, while James himself becomes, in Russell's words, a 'vive Lucius'. Britain was touched with divinity: the very name, in cabalistic lore, meant 'Covenant of God There'. Effectively, Gordon is trying to do for Britain what Foxe's *Book of Martyrs* did for Elizabethan England: create a belief among the inhabitants that they constituted an Elect Nation, singled out for great deeds and salvation.[50]

ii. *The Name of 'Great Britain'*

The proposed adoption of the name of 'Great Britain' provoked more discussion than any other single aspect of the union project in the tracts of 1603-5. Most of the writers who tackled this issue commented specifically on the list of objections produced by the English Commons on 27 April 1604. This is unsurprising. The list was widely copied and circulated in manuscript, and was given added publicity by its reproduction in Thornborough's *Discourse*.[51] Five other tracts (Hayward,

[50] See W. Haller, *The Elect Nation* (New York, 1964); A. H. Williamson, *Scottish National Consciousness in the Age of James VI* (Edinburgh, 1979)
[51] Several copies have survived, including BL, Harleian MS 292, 58 and 60; PRO, S.P. Dom., 14/7/58 and 76; Bodleian Library, Tanner MS 75, fo. 44; San Marino, Calif., Huntington Library, Ellesmere MS. 1226

Clerk, Craig, 'Pro Unione' and the Trinity College manuscript) answered the list in full, while many others singled out a
few objections for reply and generally commended the change.
The objections under the first of the four major headings,
entitled 'Matter of Common Reason', alleged that the change
had (a) no 'general necessity or evident utility' justifying such
an innovation and (b) no precedent. The tracts achieved near
unanimity in replying to the first objection. Names are seen as
potent things, holding the imaginations of the people. To
maintain separate names would continue their longstanding
connotations of hostility, risking new hatred. By contrast, the
new style would 'imprint and inculcate into the hearts and heads
of the people, that they are one people and one nation'.[52] The
Greeks and Swiss were frequently used here, as polities united
by a common name. The objection on precedent resulted from
three distinct arguments used in the Lower House: that 'Britain'
was itself harsh, foreign and unknown; that there was no
precedent for such a change by Act of Parliament; and that there
was 'no president at home nor abroad, of uniting or contracting
of the names of two several kingdomes or states into one name
where the union hath growne by marriage or bloode' rather
than conquest. The third argument was that on Bacon's list, and
was answered by the five main tracts with examples of just such
unions. Many also took the opportunity to recite precedents for
'Britain' itself, including Brutus, Roman Britannia, and the use
of 'Rex Britanniae' by Anglo-Saxon kings like Athelstan. Here,
the tracts were on solid ground. Professor Hay has shown that,
by 1600, the name was widely used to comprehend England and
Scotland. Its considerable diplomatic heritage included use by
Edward I, by the Council of Constance in 1414-18, by Edward
IV in his marriage negotiations with Scotland, and most
importantly by Protector Somerset during his propaganda
campaign of 1548. James's own mother had assumed the title
'Queen of Great Britain' in 1584, at the Bishop of Ross's
suggestion. Alongside this ran a powerful literary tradition,
drawing particular strength from the Arthurian legends, and

[52] Spedding, *Letters of Bacon*, iii, 227

including as diverse sixteenth-century works as John Major's *Historia Majoris Britanniae* and Cervantes' *Don Quixote*.[53] To these objections, the tracts' answers were convincing. It was in the second section, 'Matter of State Inward', that their position was weakest. The central principle here was 'that the alteration of the name of the king doth inevitably and infallibly draw on an erection of a new kingdome or estate'. This would extinguish in law the separate nations of England and Scotland, and threaten a range of government instruments and institutions (parliamentary summons, acts, seals, Crown offices, laws, customs, privileges, oaths and courts) currently existing under the authority of the 'King of England'. The laws governing the succession might even be affected, with England conceivably passing to a new Scots dynasty.

Many contemporaries expressed frank scepticism that a change in style should have such an effect in law. Savile defined these objections as 'trickes and sharpness of wit to overthrow that by wresting of law and wrangling which they had no liking should go forwards'.[54] Two factors, however, made counter-argument more difficult. The first was the judges' opinion upholding the objection. The second was its own lack of absolute clarity. The danger of extinction arose only by taking the new style by Act. This was unprecedented, and would have the force of new law, superseding all done under the English style. James *might* take the name by proclamation, safely, since this had no power to make new law.[55] This distinction did not appear in the objection, perhaps because the Commons majority opposed any change, however achieved. Consequently, writers could easily misunderstand the real issue. Certainly, their answers to the legal technicality are often inadequate. Thornborough, Clerk and Craig referred to 'Great Britain' as a restitution, not an alteration, Craig also arguing that it 'encompassed' the existing names. Unfortunately, no *legal* doctrine of 'restitution' or 'encompassment' existed. Only Hayward and

---

[53] D. Hay, 'The Term "Great Britain" in the Middle Ages', *Proceedings of the Society of Antiquaries of Scotland*, lxxxix (1958), 55–67
[54] Below, p.208
[55] See esp. BL, Add. MS. 38139, fo. 27v

Clerk tackled the pretext directly, denying that the change would erect a new estate. Hayward dismissed the judges' opinion as having no legal force, and compared the question to that raised under Mary Tudor whether laws passed under the name of a king remained in force. Even Hayward, however, advised the inclusion of a caveat in the Act stating that the change should not be construed to affect the validity of existing instruments or institutions. The 'Discourse on the Proposed Union' advised a similar caveat (notwithstanding the Commons' assertion 'that no explanation, limitation or reservation can clear or avoid that inconvenience'), while Thornborough desired a clause retrospectively changing all previous references in laws and instruments to the separate national names.

The tracts show particular confusion over the lesser objections in this section, notably concerning the king judging English cases in Scotland and England passing to a Scots dynasty. The Trinity College manuscript was quick to show the English chauvinism implied here, but totally missed the point in its belief that under international law, the failure of the Stuart line would return Scotland to a Scots dynasty, England to an English. The best answer here was that of Russell and 'Pro Unione', pointing simply to James's wealth of progeny – by divine providence.

The two remaining groups of objections came under 'Matter of State Foreign' and 'Matter of Honour and Reputation'. The first objection in the former exported the legal pretext, arguing that the change threatened all leagues and treaties, giving nations wishing to escape their diplomatic ties an opportunity.[56] Craig and the Trinity College manuscript again missed the legal point with their talk of 'encompassment', while Thornborough and 'Pro Unione' lamely argued for a new initiative to establish alliances under the altered style. It is again Hayward who tackled the legal question, pointing out that treaties relied for their force only on 'bona fidei'. Princes using this pretext to escape a treaty would lose their reputation in other countries. The second objection here, relegating Britain to the lowest diplomatic rank, elicited a varied response. All respondents

---

[56] For this possibility see *CSPVen 1603-1607*, 195

surprisingly accepted that the antiquity of a kingdom rather than its greatness determined precedency; but while Hayward and the Trinity College manuscript simply denied that a new name would be held to imply a new kingdom, Thornborough and Craig alleged further that the restoration of so ancient a name as Britannia should actually elevate her rank. As 'A Briefe Replication' said, this was unlikely to impress envious foreign courts.

Answers to the remaining objections were more cogent. The final objection under state foreign, that the glory and good acceptance of the English name would be diminished, provoked few tears. Thornborough alleged that the name of Great Britain would thereby shine the more strongly, while the Scots Trinity College manuscript remarked more sourly that 'I wish it [i.e., the name of England] were such as they do esteme of it'! This objection connected logically with the four under 'honour and reputation': that there was nothing dearer than a name, that the new style would consign 'England' and 'Scotland' to oblivion, that England would lose her precedency over the northern kingdom, and that the change was unpopular. The tracts answer these consistently. Several point to the numerous changes in name by foreign nations and condemn the Commons' example of fathers disinheriting their daughters to maintain their name. This answered the first objection. Hayward, the Trinity College manuscript and the 'Discourse on the Proposed Union' prophesied that popular and literary use would save the old names from oblivion. The argument about precedency produced from Craig a revealingly reflex denial that Scotland had ever admitted such – although the objection clearly referred to the precedency 'England' had in the royal style. Other writers condemned this precedency, Hayward pertinently asking whether England should 'contend for general precedence with them, with who we intend, or at least pretend desire to be one'.[57] All the five main respondents saw time and usage as the answer to the alleged unpopularity of 'Great Britain'.

As this summary implies, the tracts provided argument for rather than against the change. Only 'A Briefe Replication'

[57] J. Hayward, *A Treatise of Union* (London, 1604), 54

openly supported the Commons against their critics. Four other English tracts showed less than enthusiasm for the change. Doddridge merely commented that a change in name was 'the moost absolute unyon of kingedomes', to follow union in other fields. Savile, Spelman and the 'Discourse Against the Union' concentrated on demonstrating the truth of one objection, that the change was unprecedented save in unions by conquest. Savile gave this eight of his thirty-three chapters, and. wished 'with all my heart his Majesty could be pleased the names of England and Scotland might still continue'.[58] This said, he then denied that the change would be impossible or inconvenient. Spelman was much more reluctant, referring to the Britons as 'an obscure and barbarous people' whose memory was best forgotten.[59]

iii. *Discussion of Further Union*

All but a few of the union tracts made recommendations, at least in passing, regarding further union in specified areas of public life. These included the law, the institutions of government, offices, religion and trade. The first of these, the union of laws, attracted the most discussion but by no means the most widespread support.[60] The idea of legal union appealed both to King James and to a number of law reformers, but even those who endorsed the plan in principle recommended caution and restraint in implementing it. No writer or public figure of this period – not even James himself – advocated complete legal fusion; at the very least a union of laws would exclude local custom and in the minds of most it would not embrace private law.

The reluctance of English writers to support a programme of legal union reflected prevailing attitudes towards the common law. Most Englishmen of this period regarded their law with reverential conservatism. Believing that the common law had survived without change from immemorial antiquity to the

[58] Below, p.148
[59] Below, pp.205-6
[60] See B. Levack, 'English Law, Scots Law and the Union', in *Law-making and Law-makers in British History*, ed. A. Harding (London, 1980), 105-19

present, they considered it to be superior to Roman law, more conducive to liberty and ideally suited to England. They paid particular reverence to fundamental law, an ill-defined term roughly equivalent to 'the constitution' and used variously to describe the law governing the royal succession, the powers of the king and the rights of the subject.[61] While all but a few accepted the mutability of the common law by statute, all forms of legal innovation remained suspect.

English beliefs in the superiority, immemoriality and quasi-immutability of their law inevitably affected their attitudes towards legal union. A reluctance to allow change in English law, coupled with a view of Scots law as debased common law, Roman law or a mixture of the two prevented most Englishmen from even considering a genuine reconciliation or fusion of the laws. For those who thought in such terms the only tolerable form that legal union could take would be a Scottish submission to English law, a proposal that emerged explicitly in the English parliamentary session of 1606-7.[62] The assumption, however, that legal union, if possible at all, would involve the Scottish acceptance of English law underlay most of the English tracts of 1603-5.

The prospect of this type of union was clearly apprehended in Scotland and met predictable resistance. Although Scots generally had a more utilitarian, less reverent view of their law than the English and had in the past incorporated large amounts of both English and Roman law into the substantive law of their kingdom, they naturally feared a reception of English law under the present circumstances. In arguing against the proposed union they occasionally adopted quasi-English attitudes, expressing distrust of *any* new law, but they based their case mainly on patriotism. As Russell pleaded, 'Sall all this be lost in ane day, and be our auin voluntar consent? Sall ane frie kingdome, possessing sua ancienne liberteis, become ane slave?'[63]

The danger of a Scottish submission to English law led those few who favoured legal union to qualify their support for such

---

[61] For one statement of James's views see S.P. Dom., 14/7/75
[62] See Willson, 'King James I and Anglo-Scottish Unity', 52-53
[63] Below, p.89

an undertaking. Pont supported legal union on the grounds that the laws were 'almost the same in substance' but also defended the retention of the ancient customs of each nation when they differed.[64] Hume called for the appointment of a ten-man commission drawn from both nations to consider a union of laws but recommended in the meantime that no change take place. The most famous Scottish advocate of legal union, Sir Thomas Craig, actually retreated from the position he had previously taken. In *Jus Feudale* Craig had challenged the immemoriality of the common law, tracing its origin to a medieval feudal code already adopted by Scotland in a purer form. He then proposed legal union by return to these feudal roots.[65] In *De Unione* Craig again illustrated the similarity of the two laws but argued merely that their union was possible, while in the final section of this work he recommended against the adoption of any such scheme. In taking this position Craig may have felt constrained to justify the verdict of the Commission, which did not recommend legal union. More probably, the alienation of Scots opinion from England in 1604 had influenced his views, inducing a nationalistic reflex similar to Russell's.

The combination of English immemorialism and Scots patriotism left little prospect for legal union. George Saltern tried to establish a common, antique origin of the laws of both kingdoms in the law of God, which the British King Lucius had adopted, but his proposal had little practical value.[66] John Cowell proposed the codification of both English and Scots law on the basis of the civil law as a means to facilitate legal union, but English suspicion of both Roman law and codification prevented his plan from attracting any widespread support.[67] John Hayward, who like Cowell had training in the civil law, proposed a gradual and equitable union of public law, arguing that the fundamental laws of the two kingdoms already stood in agreement and that other 'laws of government' possessed

---

[64] Below, p.24
[65] Sir Thomas Craig, *The Jus Feudale*, ed. J. A. Clyde (Edinburgh, 1934), i, p. ix
[66] G. Saltern, *Of the Antient Laws of Great Britaine* (London, 1605)
[67] J. Cowell, *Institutiones Juris Anglicani* (Cambridge, 1605), ded.

sufficient conformity.[68] Hayward's treatise, however, involved a full-scale challenge to the alleged immemoriality and immutability of English law and therefore offended English sensibilities. In some respects Hayward's proposal reflected the more cautious position of Bacon. In the 'Discourse' Bacon claimed that a successful union required uniformity in the principal and fundamental laws, both ecclesiastical and civil, but he presented no specific programme for achieving unity. A year later, however, in his 'Certain Articles', Bacon developed his proposal, calling for the repeal of the hostile laws, the establishment of a Border court which would administer a mixture of English and Scots law, and the reconciliation of the criminal statutes. By restricting his programme in this way, and by insisting on the necessity of a gradual process of uniting the laws, Bacon gave a certain respectability to the case for legal union. His emphasis upon a union of public but not private law later served as an inspiration of early eighteenth-century plans for minimal legal union.

While legal union became the subject of a broad literary debate, only a few of the early Jacobean tracts considered union in the institutions of government, and those which did concentrated exclusively on the parliaments and the councils of the two kingdoms. Hume's 'Tractatus Secundus', Bacon's 'Certain Articles' and 'Pro Unione' all favoured parliamentary and conciliar union. The latter called for immediate implementation of the plan, advising James to summon Scots to the next session of the English parliament and to elevate members of each nation to the council of the other. Bacon approached the problem more cautiously, leaving the question of conciliar membership to the King's discretion and counselling a united parliament in which Scots would have one third of the seats. To achieve this proportion the small number of English peers would have to be drastically increased. Hume, with his strong Scots sympathies, favoured a British parliament at York and a council comprising equal numbers of Scots and Englishmen. All seem to have viewed the proposed parliament in an English light, although Bacon did advise importing the Lords of the Articles as a

[68] Hayward, *A Treatise of Union*, 14-15

preparatory commission. A different, federal approach emerged from Doddridge and 'The Divine Providence'. Both favoured three parliaments, the third being a joint British assembly to handle matters of common concern.

On the need for unity in outward marks of government – seals, coins, crowns, weights and measures – the tracts reflected wide agreement. Bacon and Craig in particular saw such union as a means of instilling a sense of unity in the two peoples. Concerning the eligibility of one nation to the governmental offices of the other the tracts displayed a greater range of views. Spelman, predicting a deluge of Scots into offices of power throughout England, reflected the full strength of English fears. Hayward spoke of these English jealousies, scornfully condemning those of 'dazzled judgement' whose entire case against the union was 'that all the sweete of the land will hereby be drawne from the auncient inhabitants of the same'.[69] He believed this prejudice to be so deeply ingrained as to make participation of offices impossible until the bond of union became indissoluble. He also followed 'The Divine Providence' in referring to the dangers of promoting Scots to positions requiring knowledge of English law. Other writers expressed less ambivalence in their support of participation. All the Scots writers favoured it, as did Cornwallis, Thornborough, *Rapta Tatio*, and 'Pro Unione'.

A great majority of the tracts commented in one way or another on the question of religious unity. Although all spoke of it as essential, the greatest of all possible bonds between the two peoples, few advanced proposals to strengthen it, mainly because they believed unity in this regard to have already been achieved. All of the tracts assumed broad agreement in doctrine, while some argued that at least general uniformity prevailed even in matters of church government and discipline. A few writers, however, recognised that in the latter regard significant differences did exist, and two of them proposed that the churches be brought into greater conformity. Doddridge recommended a gradual anglicisation of the Scottish kirk, a proposal that reflected James's attempts to reinvigorate the Scottish episcopacy. Hume, on the other hand, proposed the

[69] *Ibid.*, 23

exportation of presbyterianism to England. Neither of these
writers, however, specifically called for the establishment of
joint ecclesiastical institutions. Indeed, the only proposal for
actual church union, as opposed to the achievement of
ecclesiastical uniformity, came from 'The Divine Providence',
which advised a federal ecclesiastical union, with clerical
assemblies for each nation, a joint synod for common concerns
and a union of ecclesiastical law.

The reluctance of the tracts to advance specific schemes for
church union reflected not only a recognition that such steps
were unnecessary, but the existence of strong sentiment in both
nations against changes in ecclesiastical government. Both
parliaments took steps in 1604 to guarantee the integrity of their
'fundamental ecclesiastical laws', which James himself promised he would preserve. Many of the Scots clergy opposed the
union mainly out of fear of English influence in their church,
while both Russell and Hume included passages supporting the
integrity and independence of their church. In England Hume's
plan for reconstituting the Anglican church on the Scottish
model caused such great consternation that the publication of
his 'Tractatus Secundus' was stayed, on the grounds that it tried
to establish Scotland's superiority over England.[70]

The idea of a commercial union received widespread praise
but little development in the literature of 1603–5. Only Bacon
and Craig outlined concrete proposals for a union of this type.
De Unione merely advocated exemption from alien customs,
not even including the other recommendations of the Anglo-
Scots Commission. Bacon, however, proposed mutual eligibility for membership in the great commercial companies and a
single system of imports and customs throughout Great Britain.
Opposition to any such scheme came entirely from England,
most notably in Spelman and the 'Discourse on the Union as
being Triple-headed'. Both allege that free trade would empty
the royal treasury and that goods would in the future enter
Britain through Scots ports, where duties were cheaper. Spelman advanced a number of unconvincing but often repeated
arguments to show that the Scots would come to dominate

[70] PRO, S.P. Dom., 14/57/100 and 104

British trade. All of these arguments, as well as Savile's concern over the inequity of Scottish trading privileges in France, reappeared in the debates of 1606-7.

Closely related to the question of commercial union, and also to that of offices, was the issue of naturalisation. This of course became a major concern in the negotiation of the Commissioners and in the subsequent debates of 1606-7. In the tracts, however, naturalisation did not emerge as a major consideration. Doddridge and Bacon recognised the naturalised status of the *post-nati* and the right of the king to grant individual acts of denization or naturalisation to the *ante-nati*, while Bacon called attention to the problem of the remaining *ante-nati* who did not receive such grants. Spelman, taking the negative side of the issue, painted a dire picture of the consequences of such action, but did not deny the king's authority in this regard. In most of the other tracts, with the exception of Russell, the issue did not even arise. Either they assumed that naturalisation had already taken place or that no impediment to its realisation existed. A great majority of the tracts, however, did recognise the necessity of creating a lasting social union, a 'union of love'. Like James they realised that the union would not endure unless Scots and Englishmen could be melded into one people, a united British nation. In order to foster such a union a number of writers, especially Craig, Bacon, Doddridge and Hume, proposed a variety of measures to encourage assimilation, including the encouragement of intermarriage and the education of the aristocracy of one nation at the universities of the other.

In discussing the possibility of further union, the tracts made frequent use of historical precedents, thus adopting a method of political disputation that English politicians customarily employed in the early seventeenth century. In the case of the union the reliance upon precedent was especially strong, for the simple reason that the union was new and therefore no tradition of argument had developed during Elizabethan times. It was also a project whose ultimate scope was unclear, making an appeal to history, as an independent authority, the more attractive. The precedents used in the tracts were notably more Continental than British, both because Europe provided more plentiful examples of the union of kingdoms and because the various British unions that had occurred in the past did not appear to be analogous to the present situation. Thus the unions of Castile and Aragon, Spain with Portugal, Poland with Lithuania, and France with Brittany figured more prominently in the tracts than the union of England with Wales.

Many of the tracts cited precedents incidentally and indiscriminately in order to support specific points, but a few conducted extensive and systematic surveys of large numbers of precedents in order to discover the basic principles that governed the union of states. When the tracts marshalled and analysed precedents in this way, they generally reached negative conclusions regarding the desirability of further union, especially with respect to laws and institutions. And when the tracts focused specifically, as did Savile, on precedents of sovereign states that had entered into peaceful union, the historical case for a limited union became even more compelling.

iv. *The Significance of the Tracts*

The union tracts of 1603-5 provide a considerable amount of information regarding the union project of the first year of James's joint reign. Their number alone confirms the importance of the subject both within and outside parliament. The willingness of Bacon, Russell and Savile to present very different proposals to the king suggests that James was not openly committed to a single programme. Indeed, Savile's opposition to parliamentary union may have contributed to James's apparent abandonment of that objective as even a distant goal in 1604. The arguments used by so many tracts to justify the 'urgent necessity' of the change in name, as fostering a sense of unity in both peoples, provides a credible alternative to the allegations of royal vainglory. The answers of the writers to the Commons' objections highlight the diversity of the latter, showing the many different strands in the 'opposition' of the Lower House. Finally, the bitterness roused by the English session, both between king and Commons and between the nations, is echoed in the widespread condemnation of the Lower House by the English and more particularly the Scots tracts.

It is more difficult to prove that the tracts influenced later political developments. The proclamation of the change of names, the issuing of the 'Unite' coinage in October 1604 and the other measures to achieve unity in the 'outward marks of government' in 1604-5 strongly recall the advice of Bacon and other authors. By contrast, the Anglo-Scots commission ignored most of the proposals for further union, being bound in scope by the Scottish statutory restriction on the discussion of the fundamental civil and ecclesiastical laws. Since subsequent debate followed the Commission's recommendations, the proposals in the tracts might at first seem irrelevant. Nevertheless, the enormous overlap between the arguments in the tracts and in the Commons in 1606-7, implies a considerable indirect influence on political debate. Questions like the Scots trading privileges in France and the legal reconciliation of sovereign states, first fully stated in the tracts, became major elements in the parliamentary opposition to enactment of the Commissioners' proposals.

After 1607 the tracts continued to have some influence on the history of 'the union'. Thornborough's two discourses appeared in a new, combined edition in 1641 to strengthen the renewed hopes for religious and social union at that time.[71] In the early eighteenth century a number of the tracts, including the unprinted works of Doddridge, Bacon, Craig and Savile, received frequent mention in the furious pamphlet war that preceded the negotiation of an incorporating union in 1707. In some instances the early Jacobean tracts became the target of serious criticism, such as when James Hodges labelled Bacon's proposals as 'so many Castles built in the Air, being only fair imaginary Superstructures, having no solid bottom on which they can subsist'.[72] In other cases, however, early eighteenth-century pamphleteers appealed to the arguments of their predecessors. An opponent of incorporating union, for example, alluded to Doddridge's plan for a federal union, while

[71] J. Thornborough, *The Great Happiness of England and Scotland by Being Reunited into one Great Britain* (London, 1641)
[72] [James Hodges], *The Rights and Interests of the Two British Monarchies ... Treatise I* (London, 1703), 23

George Ridpath used Doddridge's collection of precedents to buttress his case against the union.[73] The occasional reliance of early eighteenth-century writers upon the tracts of 1603-5 should not surprise us. The circumstances of the union debate of the early eighteenth century may have differed considerably from those of the previous century, but the basic issues were the same. Even the question of adopting the name of Great Britain arose again, since the Treaty of 1707 proposed to extend the use of that term to those areas of public life where the proclamation of 1604 had no impact. Most of the arguments advanced in the great debate of 1700-7 first appeared, at least in tentative form, in the union tracts of the early seventeenth century. The tracts and treatises of 1603-5 stand therefore not only as products of a particular political and intellectual milieu but as documents that defined the terms of a debate which lasted more than one hundred years.

ROBERT PONT – 'OF THE UNION OF BRITAYNE'

i. *The Author*

Of the three selected Scots tracts, the dialogue 'Of the Union of Britayne' has by far the best-known author.[74] The treatise from Trinity College, Cambridge, is in fact anonymous, while John Russell remains a shadowy, at most secondary figure. By contrast, Robert Pont (otherwise known as Kylpont or Kynpont) was a man of considerable importance, more so even than John Gordon or Sir Thomas Craig – the other major writers of Scots tracts on the union. Pont was primarily a churchman, but had also during his long life held legal positions and written books on a variety of subjects. Born at Culross between 1524 and 1530, educated at St Leonard's College in St Andrews and possibly studying the civil law thereafter at one of the Continental universities, he made his first mark during the 1560s as an elder and minister firmly allied to the Protestant

---

[73] *Vulpone* (n.p., 1707), 14; [George Ridpath], *Considerations upon the Union of the Two Kingdoms* (London, 1706), 3, 20

[74] For the details of Pont's life see *Dictionary of National Biography*, xvi, 91-94; R. Chambers, *A Biographical Dictionary of Eminent Scotsmen* (Glasgow, 1835), iv, 117-19

interest. His first major publication, in 1566, was a translation and interpretation of the Helvetian Confession. In 1571, his work in the General Assembly won him both the provostship of Trinity College in Edinburgh and the vicarage of St Cuthbert's church. At the same time, he was the leading figure in the excommunication of the Bishop of Orkney (who had married Bothwell to Mary Queen of Scots), and was elected by the Regent as a Senator of the College of Justice – a position he kept until the Act of 1584 depriving clergy of civil appointments. During the 1570s and 1580s, Pont achieved the difficult feat of being acceptable to the reformed kirk and the Scots government at all times. He took part in the famous protest of clergymen against James VI's Act making it criminal to decline the jurisdiction of the Privy Council or to hold Assemblies without royal permission. This led briefly to self-imposed exile in England, until the victory of the party of the earl of Angus. Yet in 1587, James raised him to the see of Caithness – a position, however, which the Assembly would not permit him to take. During the remaining nineteen years of his life, he remained a trusted servant of the government, first on the short-list of possible bishops. His duties included work as moderator and public spokesman of the kirk, commissioner on many commit-tees (e.g., for suppression of papacy and trial of beneficed persons), being appointed as late as 1597 to a commission to discuss with the King 'all matters concerning the weal of the kirk'. At the same time, his literary career was burgeoning. Much of the work produced by him was religious, following commissions by Assemblies of the Kirk. Such were his three sermons on Sacrilege (1599) and his revision of the Psalms (1601). His *New Treatise on the Right Reckoning of Yeares and Ages of the World* (1594) also served directly a religious purpose – to show that 1600 was not the jubilee or day of reckoning, as many Scots supposed. Other works were more literary in nature, including a translation of Pindar's *Olympic Odes*, a *Dissertation on the Greek Lyric Metres*, a *Lexicon of Three Languages* and a *Collection of Homilies* – most now lost to posterity. *De Unione*, composed after his retirement from most official duties and within sight of his death in 1606, is his nearest approach to political writing. In short, Pont was (like Craig) a man of considerable religious and political importance, possessed of great scholastic experience and literary pretensions as well.

ii. *The Manuscript*

The full title of Pont's treatise is 'Of the Union of Britayne, or conjunction of the kingdomes of England and Scotland, with the bordering Brittish Ilands into one monarchie, and of the manifold commodities proceeding from that Union. A Dialogue'. Unlike the other English and Scots tracts selected for publication in this volume, Pont's 'Dialogue' was actually printed in a contemporary edition. Copies of a Latin version of the tract, which was published in Edinburgh and London, have survived in the National Library of Scotland, the British Library, and the Bodleian Library. It is therefore reasonable to assume that of the six selected tracts, the 'Dialogue' reached the widest audience, even though it probably had less of an impact on men of power than that, for example, of Savile or even Russell. An English version of the tract, registered together with the Latin tract by the Stationers Company on 22 March 1604, apparently never appeared in print.[75] The only English copy that has survived is Royal MS 18.A.XIV in the British Library. This manuscript might very well be the English copy referred to in the *Stationers' Company Register*. The prefatory description, 'A dialogue composed in Latin by R.P.', confirms that the manuscript constitutes a translation rather than a vernacular draft and suggests that Pont himself did not prepare the translation.

The manuscript consists of about 11,000 words, covering 24 folios. It provides a translation of almost the entire printed treatise, omitting only the preface, '*Candidis Lectoribus*', and two concluding poems, '*Unionis Britanniae Elogium*' and '*Ad Omnes Britannicarum Insularum Habitatores*'. These omissions, which are reproduced in appendices to the text, comprise 1500-2000 words of Latin text. In length, therefore, the 'Dialogue' is

---

[75] *A Transcript of the Registers of the Company of Stationers, 1554-1640*, ed. E. Arber, iii (London, 1876), fo. 106v

marginally the shortest of the three selected Scots tracts. It is written, as has been noted, in English rather than Scots dialect, its spelling and (often inconsistent) punctuation again being closer to English usage. The hand is in the Italian style and is neat and continuous throughout, with very few alterations or additions. This again suggests a translation rather than a draft. The manuscript is, with one exception, completely legible.

The translator has clearly set out to render the spirit of the original, Latin text, rather than to produce an exact verbatim translation. By these standards he has done a more than adequate job, rarely straying beyond the strict meaning of the passage translated. Given this free approach to the original text, the editors have avoided detailed comparisons of the two in the footnotes. Major solecisms have, however, been footnoted.

iii. *Contents and Themes*

Pont is the only writer on the union who adopted the difficult and sometimes cumbersome fiction of a classical 'dialogue' as the format for his tract. However, this is not a genuine dialogue between people of different views, reaching a synthesis of ideas. Of the three characters, one serves only to introduce the conversation and to make occasional interjections in support of the main themes, while the second briefly propounds objections in which he himself never professes belief. Both therefore serve the function only of priming the main speaker, Polyhistor, whose domination of the exchange brings about a tract or monologue similar in approach to that of other writers.

The tendency of writers commending the union to visualise it and speak of it in religious terms was particularly strong in Scots treatises. With Pont, as with Russell and Gordon, the tendency becomes extreme. The first half of the 'Dialogue', after a brief discussion of the merits of mixed monarchical and aristocratic government, deals with little more than the advancement and maintenance of religion in the united commonwealth of Britain. The formal justification for this concentration is a link drawn between political stability and union in true religion. Thus 'distraction of religion commonly followeth the separation of kingdomes, and contrarywise the uniting of them doth confirme it'.[76] This is seen both as a political truth – unity in religion being a prime cause of civil obedience – and as part of God's will, Israel and Judah under Solomon and his successors being invoked to show divine punishment by division. It follows that Pont should strongly emphasise the hand of God in the union, and also consider the two countries already united in religion. This, and the long passages on the need to abolish idolatry, the wickedness of tolerating papists, and the covenant with God possessed by the kings of Israel bring Pont close to the Gordon/Russell theme of a divine mission vested in James for the union and purification of Christendom. Pont however on this occasion avoids apocalyptic argument, and notably denies Gordon's picture of antique religious purity in Britain. Instead, he sees the plague raging in London as proof positive of grave sins lurking among the people – a far cry from the Elect Nation.

The second half of the 'Dialogue', examining the civil commodities of union, contains more material directly relevant to the political development of the project. Pont sets out firstly to prove the advantages of unity as a principle. Unity enlarges the dominions, brings greater strength and security, not only to the king but to all his loyal subjects, against foreign enemies and internal seditions. Pont identifies the same domestic opponents of the union as Russell: papists, Irish, Borderers and High-landers, and 'fierce and insolent governours and pettie princes possessing large territories in the places most remote and abandoned of justice'. Union will bring an end to such lawlessness, and to the tyranny of the great over their tenants. It would also create a royal court where the nobles and learned men of both nations vied with each other to serve God and the king. Pont briefly touches on the need for a mutual participation in trade and offices, and then addresses a number of specific objections made against the union. The English (i.e., Parsons) had urged the incompetency of James, before his accession – but such calumnies were now repeated only by enemies of the union. The allegation that the two nations were too diverse in language and manners to be united is dismissed out of hand. The

---

[76] Below, p.6

other two most important objections both reflect the English
debates on the name: that union must involve an alteration in
the laws, and that 'it ill becometh the valarous and conquering
nation of the English to stoope to the government of an inferior
power, but rather that the Scots submit themselves to them, as
often they have done by the testimonies of their owne chronicles'.[77] The English fears of a flood of Scots and of unequal royal
favour were also cited. Pont is notably less concerned about
legal union than Russell or the Trinity College manuscript.
'The lawes of England and Scotland are almost the same in
substance; and if any small differences arise, a parliament of each
kingdome being summoned, they wil be by sage counsel easily
reconcyled. Or the ancient customes may be retayned . . . for
many nations under the Romaine Empire, using different lawes
and customes persevered in peace and obedience'.[78] The
'Dialogue' reacts much more temperately to English claims to
precedency than other Scots tracts. Pont points to the *de facto*
advantage to England by the union, Scotland being essentially
(as Henry VII had prophesied) an accessory dominion. Nevertheless, Pont clearly desires an equal union, like other Scots
writers, and like them he uses the offers made by Protector
Somerset in 1548 as the basis of his proposed settlement. 'Thus
far went they then; which if now the English would call to
minde and approve by their deedes their mindes' consent, the
fears which possesseth the hearts of many Scottish would be soone
voyded, and they assured that the English seek not to have the
Scots in thrall and subjection, but with them to live in brotherlie
concord'.[79] As for favour, the king is British and will distribute
his posts and rewards indifferently to Britons according to their
virtue. There remained only the need to patch over the deadly
feuds and centuries' legacy of hostility between the nations for a
true unity in affections to be achieved. Here would operate the
providence of God, in uniting the two nations in true religion –
the tract seeing human sin and idolatry as the prime causes of the
previous discord between England and Scotland.

[77] Below, p.27
[78] Below, p.24
[79] Below, p.31

'A TREATISE ABOUT THE UNION OF ENGLAND AND SCOTLAND'

i. *The Author*

If this manuscript ever did contain an indication of its authorship, it has been lost together with the opening page or pages of the text. The only thing clear about the author is his Scots nationality. His use of Scots spelling and words, his consistent support for Scotland against English claims to primacy, and his explicit identification with the Scots[80] make this evident.

ii. *The Manuscript*

The manuscript currently exists in a single copy in Trinity College Library, Cambridge (R5.15, No. 10). Since the title page, as well as the opening part of the manuscript, is lacking, the original title of the work remains unknown. The front of the manuscript volume contains the description 'A Treatise about the Union of England and Scotland, to King James the Ist', but there is no reason to consider this designation original or even contemporary.

Like the title and authorship of the manuscript, its provenance is unclear. It was probably given to the library by Sir Henry Puckering (alias Newton), one of the library's major seventeenth-century benefactors. Born Henry Newton in 1618, the younger son of Sir Adam Newton and Katharine (daughter of Lord Keeper Sir John Puckering), Puckering changed his name in 1654 after inheriting the estates of his maternal uncle, Sir Thomas Puckering. Puckering was a noted Royalist, with Catholic sympathies, and was Paymaster-General to the Forces after the Restoration. Tracing the manuscript back beyond Puckering is, however, entirely a matter of speculation. It is possible, though unlikely, that it may have come from his maternal grandfather, the Lord Keeper. More possibly, he may have inherited it directly from his father, who had at various times been tutor to James VI and I's eldest son, Prince Henry, and Secretary to the Council.[81] In the latter capacity, at least, he

---

[80] 'Is their name more deir to them then ours to us?' Below, p.72

[81] M. R. James, *The Western Manuscripts in the Library of Trinity College, Cambridge* (Cambridge, 1922-53), ii, p. vi

might have had contact with a treatise of this type. In date, the manuscript is on internal evidence a work of May–October 1604. Again, the criteria are those of the proposal to change the royal style. The treatise gives much of its time to answering the English parliamentary objections to this change, produced in late April 1604. At the same time, in supporting 'the imposition of one name to both the nations, such as should be thoght meetest, by renewing the ancient appellation either of Albion or Great Brittaine',[82] the author strongly implies a date before the royal proclamation in October 1604 effectively closed the issue.

The surviving portion of the manuscript comprises fourteen folios, or about 13,000 words. Given that the missing fragment probably made up only a single folio, an overall length of 14,000 words seems likely for the original. The tract is written throughout in a single hand, following the secretary style. This hand differs from any other to be found in the volume, implying that this is an original rather than a later seventeenth-century copy by Sir Adam Newton or Sir Henry Puckering. The hand is neat and legible, with only occasional alterations of individual words, and a few additions. Nevertheless, the number of words underlined in later ink for possible correction or alteration makes it clear that this was in the nature of a draft, though possibly a final draft ready to be made over into a fair copy. It is noteworthy that many of these underlined words are Scots in spelling or usage, and we may therefore conclude that the author was attempting to anglicise his text before its final submission. The text itself is typical of its period in the inconsistency and confusion of its punctuation, spelling and grammar. Even more than Russell, the author is given to writing enormously long sentences broken up by colons (often in the wrong places), and to sentences that do not in fact contain any verbs. These tendencies have been moderated or obscured by editorial modernisation but nevertheless remain fairly evident. The author also has particular difficulty with plurals, consistently rendering 'were' as 'was' even in the most obvious of circumstances. This occasional lapse into illiteracy is all the

---

[82] Below, p.61

more startling for the neat and sometimes telling nature of the arguments being advanced.

iii. *Contents and Themes*

Given the very fragmentary nature of the tract – anonymous, incomplete, untitled, and without a clear provenance – it may be surprising to find it considered worthy of reproducing here. Nevertheless, the contents and arguments of the Trinity College manuscript make it an important contribution to the debate of 1604 on the union. The tract is significant above all as the only Scottish treatise to use as its basis the historical approach most tellingly employed by Savile. Thus the first part of the manuscript divides the union of kingdoms into a number of different categories, each with its own historical precedents and lessons. These categories basically concern the method of union – by election, by marriage or succession, and by conquest. The author is very concerned with the permanency of each type, unions by marriage or succession being particularly subject to dissolution at the will of the reigning prince.

From here, the argument shifts to examine a perfect union in laws, name, language, religion and institutions. After citing many ancient precedents for such a union – and the author is impressive in the range of historical precents used, from classical antiquity to contemporary Continental and British experience – he demonstrates from history the dangers of such incorporation. 'For there be many realmes and monarchies, whereof the souvereignities being confused or annexed, the bodys of the commonwealthes wold not, yea might not well suffer any either mixture or alteration of their ancient laws and customes, or of their privileges of estate ... without a great hurt to the common-wealth and discontentment of the whole people – who other-wise may be induced to an uniformitie of name, language and habilites or freedomes of a naturall subiect'.[83] Such a partial union, related to the Roman municipal agreements, is shown to have been that most commonly used in Europe since the fall of the Roman Empire. It is also, unsurprisingly, the type of union

---

[83] Below, p.44

which the author considers most suitable for England and Scotland.

Like other Scots writers, and in contrast to the other proponents of the historical philosophy, the author includes a section praising the principle of British unity, and describing the union (after so many centuries of dissension and blood) as the work of God. The themes here are very familiar: the miserable divisions of Britain exposing her to foreign invasion, the ingratitude of the English in cavilling at a union for which they had striven so hard in medieval times and under Protector Somerset, the increase in strength occasioned by union and its effect in subduing both the foreign enemy and the dissident, especially Border and Highland elements at home.

Unity duly praised, the treatise then continues to answer three principal objections alleged by England against the union. These are the dangers of alteration to the English estate, of a flood of Scots seeking royal favour, and of English wealth being drained away through union with a poor and barren land. The first is ruled out by reference to the partial union, while Scots participation in English offices is 'justified' by a long and impassioned description of the woes facing England in 1603, from which James's accession had rescued her. 'Since we ar the instruments of their peace and enriching, and by us they have received so many great benefits, shall they not be ashamed to thinke us unuorthie to be parttakers of their wealth?'[84] This is followed by a more conventional description of James's 'aequitie, like favor and magnificence in rewarding such of both the nations who have deserved of him'.[85] The charges of poverty are dismissed at some length, with arguments very similar to those of Russell and of Craig's *De Unione*.

Having dismissed these objections, the author examines what is necessary to cement the union. Logically, given his previous comments on the impermanence of unions by succession, the first necessity cited is a law indissolubly uniting the crowns in the same line of succession. The second returns to the theme of the partial union. An incorporation is dismissed at some length,

[84] Below, pp.52-53
[85] Below, p.55

in the same terms as those of Russell. Alteration of laws and privileges is seen as dangerous, akin to servitude. 'As to the subiecting of the one of those kingdomes to the other, then equalitie of power and love of naturall libertie will not suffer it'.[86] Instead, there should be mutual participation in commerce, offices and rights of naturalisation, and a common name not only for Britain but also for the Borders. In this last recommendation and in the allied proposal for the abolition of laws of hostility the author comes close to royal policy.

With these recommendations, the substance of the treatise is almost complete. The long remaining section merely provides answers to the objections of the English House of Commons on the changing of the royal style. Throughout the answers, the author comments very clearly on the inequity of English assumptions, notably (and inevitably) on precedency. His comment on the loss of the glory and good acceptation of the English name ('I wish it were such as they do esteme of it')[87] is especially apt. The writer consistently defends the honour of Scotland, as an older nation, never conquered, and the first of James's dominions – although the reference to England as an 'accessory' kingdom appears really only as a passing thought. He is entirely willing to see the separate names of England and Scotland die away, as marks of jealousy, and again employs an impressive array of historical scholarship both to justify the necessity of the change and to provide ample precedents. Thus on the name as on the other parts of the union, the Trinity College manuscript is remarkable as an example of an 'English' historical approach being used to justify a 'Scots' political position.

'ANE TREATISE OF THE HAPPIE AND BLISSED UNIOUN' BY JOHN RUSSELL

i. *The Author*

The John Russell who wrote 'Ane Treatise of the Unioun' is probably, although not certainly, the lawyer John Russell who

---

[86] Below, p.58
[87] Below, p.72

pursued a career as an advocate in the central courts at Edinburgh from the 1590s until his death in 1613.[88] This Russell is the only individual by that name known to have been active in the public life of Scotland in 1604. Married to Mariote Carmichaell, and the father of John, who also served as an advocate, Russell lived at Granton, just to the northwest of Edinburgh.[89] In 1602 he was charged before the Privy Council with the 'wrongous detention' of a number of individuals who burned down his house at 'Wester Grantoun'.[90] Russell's will was proved in the Commissary Court at Edinburgh on 22 July 1613.[91]

ii. *The Manuscripts*

The full title of Russell's treatise is 'Ane treatise of the Happie and Blissed Unioun betuixt the tua ancienne realmes of Scotland and Ingland, eftir thair lang trubles, thairby establisching perpetuall peace to the posteriteis of baith the nationes, presentlie undir the gratious monarchie and impyir of our dread souerane, King James the Sixt of Scotland, First of Ingland, France and Ireland'.[92] The work survives in two manuscripts, one in the National Library of Scotland (Advocates' MS 31.4.7) and the other in the British Library (Royal MS 18. A. LXXVI). As will be shown below, there exist significant differences between the two, both in presentation and content. They are, however, basically the same tract. The provenance of neither manuscript is clear. The Edinburgh manuscript, as its notation implies, came from the library of the Faculty of Advocates, and was purchased by the Faculty in 1723 at the sale of the manuscripts of the antiquary Sir Robert Sibbald. The London manuscript has no history. However, a comparison of the two manuscripts and the introductory address or letter written by

---

[88] *The Register of the Great Seal of Scotland*, ed. J. M. Thomson (Edinburgh, 1882-1914), vi, 318; *RPCS*, vi, 612, 624, 627, 738, 767; vii, 554, 584, 653; viii, 80, 282, 653, 756; ix, 164, 171, 560

[89] *Register of the Great Seal*, vi, 539. For the activity of John, junior, see vii, 424 and *RPCS*, ix, 164

[90] *RPCS*, vi, 388

[91] SRO, CC8/8/47, fo. 294

[92] The manuscript in the British Library has a slightly different title

Russell does suggest the likely relationship and origin of the two texts. Russell's treatise was clearly written by a Scot, whose language and spelling betrays heavy Scots influences, and whose emotions are very much bound up with the welfare of Scotland. It is therefore probable that the tract was written in Scotland itself. At the same time, it was written for the king in London. The date of the two manuscripts is reasonably clear. The Edinburgh tract was written explicitly after the Commons' objections to the change in the royal style, and before either the Proclamation changing the style or the first meeting of the Anglo-Scots Commission; that is to say, between May and October 1604. The London tract, however, uses James's new style as 'King of Great Britain', omits references to the Commission and speaks of ratification by the parliaments of the two realms. This would date it after October 1604, and probably to 1605.[93] Provisionally, therefore, the Edinburgh manuscript may be treated as the original, contemporary version, from which the eventual submission to James was produced. This conclusion is supported by a detailed examination of the two texts. The omissions and alterations (see below) often suggest second thoughts or a desire to tighten up the argument, while the consistent 'anglicisation' of the spelling in the London text should also be noted. The London manuscript is therefore likely to have been Russell's submission to the king, and it probably found its way into the Royal manuscript collection by that route.

The two manuscripts are superficially identical. They are in the same, very neat Italian hand, with a remarkable absence of visible alterations or additions. This suggests the use of working papers and drafts which have not survived. The length of each is the same: 24,000 words, covering 22 folios in the London text and 20 in the Edinburgh. In each case, this includes the introductory letter or address to the king. Appended to each manuscript is a short second tract, 'contiening the deuty and office of ane Christiane prince, resclving in the conclusioun thairof in ane faithfull *paraenesis* to his Maiestie, in the

<hr>

[93] The London manuscript refers to James's speech being given in April 1604. See below, p.103

administratioun of his Imperiall Crounes'. This tract has been omitted from the text, because of its lack of relevance to the Union. Russell's treatise is therefore the longest included in this volume, and indeed is one of the longest of all the tracts on the union. Both tracts demonstrate considerable Scots influences in spelling, punctuation and vocabulary, the London manuscript however showing a conscious attempt at anglicisation. Sentences are long and punctuation haphazard even by seventeenth-century standards – although the text in this volume incorporates a general modernisation of punctuation wherever possible. Spelling, by contrast, is remarkably consistent, and occasionally modern. The London tract, interestingly, contains few of the side-notes and classical or biblical references to be found in the Edinburgh manuscript.

iii. *A Note on Transcription*
The Edinburgh and London manuscripts of Russell's tract cover the same ground but vary very considerably in the order of certain passages and in detail throughout the text. To cover all these variations fully would require several hundred footnotes and the use of bold, faint and italic types. This makes neither economic nor academic sense. The text presented here is therefore that of the earlier, Edinburgh manuscript, with major variations in the London manuscript identified in the footnotes. In transcribing the text, the editors have modernised punctuation, extended abbreviations and avoided obvious archaisms, such as the use of 'z' for initial 'y'.

iv. *Contents and Themes*
Russell's treatise is a long, discursive piece containing many digressions and many rhetorical, patriotic expostulations. Consistently, the London manuscript attempts to cut down these wilder flights of intellectual or nationalistic fancy. Thus, the long digression in the Edinburgh tract attacking popery and justifying the antiquity of the reformed church in Britain is replaced by a slightly shorter passage justifying from history the author's contention that union brings happiness to a commonwealth. The author also eliminates many of the passages of

advice to James, counsel that is invariably contentious in tone, antagonistic to England and (arguably) impinging suspiciously on the impartiality and intentions of the king.[94] Extraneous and repetitive material is also frequently excised, leaving the London text more taut and relevant in its argument than the original.

Russell's 'Treatise' demonstrates more clearly than any other tract the apprehensions of Scotland in 1604 and her determination not to engage in any union that would admit England's precedency or involve alteration in the ancient laws and privileges of the kingdom. It was an open appeal to James not to allow anything to the dishonour of his first dominion. The author clearly had major reservations about the effect of the existing union on Scottish sovereignty. Notwithstanding this, he begins his long work with a startling commendation of unity as a principle, recalling Gordon. After centuries of misery, Britain had been returned to a golden age – 'our sacred and royall king send down from Heaven with ane triumphant maieste, bringand uith him peace, joy and tranquillitie to this ile forevir'.[95] Her blessings were beyond those of any other country, as James's abilities exceeded those even of the antique heroes. The hand of God and James's divine mission are explicitly stated: 'The aeternall God hes raysit his Majestie in this age to be the vive image of Lucius and Constantine, and to be successor to his predecessoris and contreymen, to banisch paganisme and idolatrie furth of this Impyir... Certanelie... sall we not hoip the same God sall imploy his Majestie to the unitie of the Christiane and universall kirk, and to abolisch idolatrie forevir'.[96] Correspondingly, Russell condemns Englishmen who opposed the project, claiming they were 'cariet away with thair proposterous opinions' and notably with disesteem for Scotland. In this first section all the main themes and attitudes of the author are shown, especially his insistence on equality in the union: 'The said unioun to be mutuall and reciproque, not the translatioun of the estait of ane kingdome in ane uther, not

---

[94] Below, p.104
[95] Below, p.78
[96] Below, p.80

of Scotland as subalterne to Ingland, quhilk is not unioun bot
ane plaine discord, the ane to be principall, the uther accessor,
the ane to command, the uther to obey – thairby ancienne
Scotland to loss hir beautie for evir! God forbid!'[97]

At length, Russell sets out a format for the tract, dividing it
into sections giving the arguments against and then for the
union, the decision between them, and the measures and
conditions necessary for the project. After a discursive and
largely irrelevant attempt to define union philosophically,
Russell presents the main objection to union: that it would
involve alteration of laws and estates, which would be dangerous and difficult to achieve. This theme is elaborated at
prodigious length, a wealth of supporting material being
deduced from classical philosophy (Plato, Aristotle, Isidore),
ancient history, and individual historical precedents from all
parts of Christendom. Scotland's religious and political estate is
seen as at least the equal of England's, so that alteration thereof
must be for the worse. A section defending the honour and
wealth of Scotland is included. Laws are given reverential
treatment; those commonwealths are most happy where laws
are obeyed as tyrants, men being their subjects and not their
masters. The fundamental laws of any commonwealth should
never be changed even in the slightest detail, for to do so was
servitude. Russell also laments in passing the *de facto* results of
the existing union, and particularly the absence of the king from
Scotland. By contrast, England had received great advantage
by the union.

Russell's treatment of the arguments for union is notably less
whole-hearted than the previous section, and received considerably more alteration in the London manuscript. The themes
included are fairly conventional. Unity is praised as a principle:
divine in origin, approved by classical philosophy, central to
every branch of human affairs, the source of prosperity. This
union brings peace, love, an end to the raids of Borderers and
Highlanders. It entails an increase in power, using Solomon's
proverb about the king's strength residing in the multitude of
his subjects. This done, however, Russell's argument loses

[97] Below, p.84

direction, with a long section attacking idolatry and papism –
the only relevant purpose of which is to prove, like Pont, that
distraction of religion is intimately connected with distraction
of kingdoms. A mass of material is used, notably the precedent of
Edward VI and the example of ancient Israel and Judah. The latter
is used to reinforce the link between divine providence, union as
a reward for true religion and prosperity as the result. Russell
clearly had second thoughts on this section, making many
changes and replacing entirely the four-page assault on the Pope
with a long passage (Appendix I to the text) proving that
disunion in empires entails misery. In general, Russell contents
himself with an unconvincing assertion that the commodities of
unity are so self-evident as to need no proof. The enemies of the
union were therefore contraverting God and Nature and must
be activated by self-interest. They are the same opponents
identified by Pont – foreign enemies, papists, Borderers and
Highlanders, and lawless princes. Russell affects to believe the
English incapable of real opposition, since they are to gain so
much from the union. Henry VII's prophecy is brought into
play, and a long section included reciting the offers of equal
union made by Protector Somerset, and urging James to carry
out the same.

His 'case' for the union made, Russell proceeds to the
decision. This is already abundantly clear from the previous
sections: great praise for union, condemnation of its opponents,
but an emotional insistence on the need to maintain Scots laws
and privileges intact. The objections to the union are 'answered', Russell indulging in much high-flown analogy with
union in the animal world, the universe and the triple Godhead
to justify his contention that perfect union involves no alteration
of the things united. The answer in the Edinburgh manuscript
to allegations that the union could not be perpetual is unpersuas-
ive, arguing merely that the unity in affections would continue
even if the end of the royal line split the kingdoms. This was
replaced in the later, London manuscript with a sharp rebuke,
and reference to the wealth of progeny given James – by divine
providence.

The proposals of Russell follow on logically from the general position taken. Russell approves the change in name, mutual participation in offices and commerce, and reciprocal naturalisation. Measures must be taken to cement the union in hearts and minds between the peoples, and to secure the same in perpetuity. On the other hand, provisions are also included to make the union more palatable to a Scots taste: her laws and privileges to be invoilable, her public revenues to be kept for the betterment of the king's estates in Scotland, and the king to reside in Scotland for a due proportion of his time.

'A BREIF CONSIDERACION OF THE UNYON' BY JOHN DODDRIDGE

i. The Author

John Doddridge's 'Breif Consideracion' is the work of a lawyer, MP, and scholar who had just embarked upon a career at Court. Born at Barnstaple, Devon, in 1555, Doddridge received his BA from Exeter College, Oxford, in 1577 and then entered the Middle Temple, where in 1585 he was called to the bar.[98] Possessing a deep scholarly interest in law, history, and politics, he became one of the original members of the Society of Antiquaries and also took an active part in the intellectual life of the Inns of Court.[99] In 1588 he was elected to Parliament from Barnstaple but was not returned to any subsequent Elizabethan parliament. At the accession of James I, Doddridge began his career at Court, receiving appointments as Serjeant for Prince Henry and member of the Queen's Council at large.[100] He also re-entered Parliament at this time, sitting for Horsham, Surrey, and on 14 April 1604 he was named to serve on the large committee for the union.[101] On 28 October 1604 he was appointed Solicitor-General. Sir Francis Bacon replaced him at that post in 1607, but Doddridge became the King's principal

[98] For the details of Doddridge's life see DNB, v, 1062-3; A Collection of Curious Discourses, ed. T. Hearne (London, 1771), ii, 432; J. Foster, Alumni Oxoniensis (Oxford, 1891-2), i, 410
[99] Regarding Doddridge's status as one of the original members see Sharpe, Cotton, 17n; L. Van Norden, 'Sir Henry Spelman and the Chronology of the Elizabethan College of Antiquaries', Huntington Library Quarterly, xiii (1950), 151
[100] J. Nichol, The Progresses . . . of King James the First (London, 1828), i, 268; ii, 135n
[101] CJ, i, 172

serjeant and also received a knighthood. In 1612 he was
appointed justice of the King's Bench, a position he held until
his death in 1628.

The activities of Doddridge, both in Parliament and on the
bench, have earned him a reputation for subserviency to the
King. Identified as a member of the 'royal faction' in the first
parliament of James, he spoke 'over bitterly' in favour of supply
in 1606 and in 1610 he used a large number of historical
precedents to justify the King's right to levy 'reasonable'
impositions.[102] The only time he apparently went against the
wishes of the King was in the famous conference regarding the
naturalisation of the Scots in February 1607, when he joined
four other common lawyers in declaring that allegiance was to
the laws, not the King, and that therefore the *post-nati* were not
naturalised.[103] The fact that he took the opposite position in his
treatise on the union more than two years earlier suggests that he
might not have held his new views very strongly. And since
there is no record of Doddridge's own words in that conference,
it is possible that his individual position was misrepresented. In
any event, on becoming a judge Doddridge acted as a 'lion
under the throne', yielding quickly to royal pressure in the case
of *Commendams* in 1616 and supporting the right of the King to
imprison without cause in The Five Knights' Case in 1627.[104]

Doddridge's writings include not only two manuals for law
students and judges, *The Lawyer's Light* (1629) and *The English
Lawyer* (1631), but also antiquarian studies, such as *The History
of the Ancient and Modern Estate of the Principality of Wales,
Dutchy of Cornwall, and Earldome of Chester* (1630) and a short
tract on the office and duties of heralds. As both common
lawyer and antiquary he was concerned primarily with English laws and institutions, but he displayed a broad knowledge
of Continental European law and history. His manuscript

[102] D. H. Willson, *The Privy Councillors in the House of Commons 1604-1629* (Minneapolis, Minn., 1940), 106, 215; *The Parliamentary Diary of Robert Bowyer*, ed. D. H. Willson (Minneapolis, Minn., 1931), 80-81; *Proceedings in Parliament, 1610*, ed. E. R. Foster (New Haven, 1966), ii, 201-21; Notestein, *House of Commons*, 164, 377-8, 390, 467
[103] *Cobbett's Complete Collection of State Trials*, ed. W. Cobbett, T. B. Howell, et al. (London, 1809-28), ii, 566-8
[104] See W. J. Jones, *Politics and the Bench* (London and New York, 1971), 70-73

treatise on the King's prerogative cites the work of numerous French and Italian lawyers,[105] while in his union treatise he demonstrated more than a passing acquaintance with both the sources and literature of French and Spanish political and constitutional history. Other members of the Society of Antiquaries, most notably Sir Henry Spelman but also Sir Robert Cotton, possessed similar, if not deeper and broader, interests in Continental European culture and politics.[106]

ii. *The Manuscripts*

The full title of Doddridge's treatise is 'A Breif Consideracion of the Unyon of the Twoe Kingedomes in the Handes of One Kinge'. The only complete copy that has survived is preserved in the British Library, Sloane MS. 3479, folios 59r-67r. This manuscript, which is written in a secretary hand and comprises approximately 6500 words, forms the basis of this edition and will be referred to henceforth as manuscript A. It is bound with three other works by Doddridge: *The History of Wales*, a short tract on maritime law, and 'A Treatise Concerning the Nobilitie'. The volume also contains papers regarding the revenues of Windsor College, parsonages in the King's gift, fees of royal offices, and the commitment of Prince Edward to the care of Earl Rivers and the Bishop of Worcester. How the manuscript came into the possession of Sir Hans Sloane is unknown. The front flyleaf of the volume bears the notation: 'This MS is of Sir John Doderidge, one of his Majesties judges in the Court of King's Bench and is printed in 4° in the year 1630 to p. 44 inclusive'. The ambiguity of this inscription, which could refer either to authorship or mere possession, has led to some uncertainty regarding the authorship of the various items in the volume.[107] There is little doubt, however, that Doddridge is the author of the union treatise. Indeed, he was recognised as such as

---

[105] BL, Harleian MS. 5220

[106] See Sharpe, *Cotton*, esp. 84-110

[107] See S. Ayscough, *A Catalogue of the Manuscripts preserved in the British Museum hitherto undescribed* (London, 1782), i, 70, 77, 97, 110, 121, 302; ii, 703, and the manuscript notes in the British Library's re-arranged copy of this volume, fo. 179. See also E. J. L. Scott, *Index to the Sloane Manuscripts in the British Museum* (London, 1904), 146

early as 1706, when George Ridpath, the Scottish journalist, quoted extensively (and inaccurately) from it in one of his treatises on the union.[108] Further evidence regarding Doddridge's authorship comes from other copies of portions of the tract. Lincoln's Inn Library, Maynard MS 83, item 2 (manuscript B), which duplicates the contents of folios 63r-67r of A, bears the endorsement 'Union Mr Soliciter'. A copy of B in the Public Record Office, SP 14/7/80 (manuscript C), carries the endorsement 'J.D.' The two remaining copies of portions of the tract, British Library, Cottonian MS. Titus F IV, folios 33-37 (manuscript D) and Lansdowne MS. 486, folios 63-67 (manuscript E), both of which have the title of A but duplicate only folios 59r-61v of that manuscript, provide no indication of authorship.

Manuscript A indicates that the treatise was written in 1604, but it is difficult to establish a more precise date of composition. The endorsement 'Mr Soliciter' in B suggests a date after 28 October, the day of Doddridge's appointment to that office, but the endorsement could easily have been made after B was joined to the other papers regarding the union with which it is now bound. Other evidence points to an earlier date of composition. The discussion of the assumption of the name of Britain as if it were a possibility rather than accomplished fact proves that at least the first portion of A was composed before the royal proclamation of 20 October. The inclusion of D and E in collections that are primarily of parliamentary interest suggest a date of composition at the time of Parliament's discussion of the union in April 1604. We know from the postscript to B and C that Doddridge wrote at least the last portion of the treatise at the request of Sir Walter Cope, who was not only a member of the Society of Antiquaries but also an MP in the Parliament of 1604.[109] Both Cope and Doddridge served on the Committee of One Hundred named on 14 April 1604 to confer with the Lords on the matter of the union, and Cope may have sought

---

[108] [G. Ridpath], *Considerations upon the Union of the Two Kingdoms* (London, 1706), 3, 20-21, 24-26
[109] See M. McKisack, *Medieval History in the Tudor Age* (Oxford, 1971), 157-8 for a discussion of Cope's membership in the Society

Doddridge's scholarly assistance either during or after that conference.[110] Certainly the material Doddridge gathered regarding other unions in Europe was the type of information that proved to be useful during the parliamentary debates on the union. It is perhaps for this reason that the *Calendar of State Papers Domestic* offers the possible date of 27 April 1604 for C. The entire problem of dating the treatise is compounded by the fact that its components may have been written at different times in 1604. The only complete version, A, is an imperfect copy that is based either on an unlocated original or on a number of separate pieces written by Doddridge. Since the description of the contents of the treatise on folio 1r of A refers only to the contents of that portion of the treatise duplicated in D and E, the latter alternative is probably the correct one.

If in fact the material in B and C was composed independently of the remainder of the tract, we cannot be certain that the entire treatise was written for the benefit of Cope. Since Doddridge wrote *The History of Wales* in order to establish the financial prerogatives of the Prince of Wales and dedicated the work to King James, he might very well have written the first part of his union treatise with the specific intention of pleasing the King. Certainly the support that the tract gave to a number of features of James's union project, especially the union of parliaments and the intermarriage of Scots and Englishmen, ensured that it would receive royal approval. It is even remotely possible that the tract was commissioned either by the King or some member of the Court, such as Henry Howard, Earl of Northampton. Northampton, who was both a patron of the Society of Antiquaries and a firm advocate of Anglo-Scottish union, later commissioned Sir Robert Cotton to draft a similar treatise in support of the union.[111] Even if Cope was the inspiration of the entire treatise, we cannot discount the possibility of some sort of official commission. Cope had not yet

[110] In the postscript Doddridge refers to 'the conference we had', which could have been either a parliamentary or a personal conference. Doddridge's reference to his leisure being 'interrupted with the business of my vocacion' does not provide any indication of the date of composition, since Doddridge's legal practice and service at Court would have made heavy demands on his time during the entire year

[111] See Sharpe, *Cotton*, p.116

received a position at Court in 1604, but he was a friend of Cecil and, like Doddridge, indebted to Northampton for his patronage. Cope, therefore, would have been a likely intermediary of either a royal or some other official request. In any event, the status of Doddridge at court and the nature of the arguments advanced in the treatise place it in the same 'royal' category as the tracts composed by Savile, Bacon and Thornborough.

iii. Contents and Themes

Although Doddridge's treatise was written to support the union and probably to please the King, it did so in a most tentative and inconclusive fashion, and it displays the objectivity of a serious scholar. Of all the union tracts it is the least polemical, and the support it provides for the union is balanced by a number of serious reservations. Indeed, Ridpath used sections of the treatise to support his decidedly anti-unionist cause in the early eighteenth century. The tract begins with a statement of the commodities that the union would bring to the entire island. These include peace, greater civility and political stability among the Scots, and the more efficient administration of justice along the Borders. The discommodities against which such benefits are balanced do not by themselves constitute arguments against union. They are merely difficulties that would attend the implementation of any such union and which therefore could not be neglected. Doddridge uses one of these difficulties, the danger of subversion of the state because of extensive legal change, to advance his own negative recommendations regarding legal union. Another difficulty on which he comments, however, emerges from his most positive and imaginative proposal – a federal union of parliaments of a Swiss model.[112] The difficulty existed not so much in the idea of parliamentary union, which very few writers or statesmen besides King James and Sir Francis Bacon were willing to advance at this time, but in the establishment of equal representation in the joint assembly. In this particular instance, and in many places throughout the text, Doddridge appears to be

---

[112] Below, p.146. For the use of Doddridge's ideas on this subject in the early eighteenth-century union debates see *Vulpone*, 14

more eager than other English writers on the union to prevent the establishment of a union in which Scots and Englishmen would stand in an unequal relationship. After enumerating both commodities and discommodities, Doddridge considers the type of union that is to be established. In discussing the first of three possible kinds of union, the union of 'denization', Doddridge endorses the policy James advocated in 1604: mutual naturalisation of the *post-nati* on the basis of allegiance at birth to the same king and naturalisation or denization of the *ante-nati* by virtue of the royal prerogative. In dealing with the second type of union, a union of laws and justice, Doddridge restates his conservative and cautious position, noting that swift action along such lines could be achieved only in cases of conquest. The third kind of union, the acceptance of a common name, Doddridge curiously regards as the most absolute. He did so probably because he believed that the adoption of a new name would create an 'imperial crowne' and perhaps even one monarchy. In fact the assumption of a new style by the King did neither; only in 1707 were the crowns and the monarchies of the two countries united in the fullest sense of the word. Doddridge tends to support the proposed change of name, but he implies a reservation by noting that some kings, especially the kings of Spain, often considered the assumption of a common name to constitute a diminution of their power.

In the following section Doddridge advances the most specific recommendations for bringing about closer union. These include religious and ecclesiastical union, intermarriage, the education of Scots in England, and 'transplantacion'. The treatise concludes with 'Certayne examples of unyted king-edomes moost famous of kingedomes of Europe'. These 'presidents' provide the most substantial basis for Doddridge's previously stated recommendation for slow, minimal legal change.

iv. *Note on Transcription*

In transcribing the treatise the editors have modernised capitalisation and punctuation. The letters u and v and the letters i and j have been interchanged, where appropriate, to conform to modern usage. All abbreviations, including initials designating proper names and places, have been extended, except in the notes. The text includes a number of words and phrases supplied by manuscripts B, C, D, and E. When the words in A are defect in copy, the words from the other manuscripts have been inserted with mere notation. When the inferior manuscripts supply words omitted in A, these words are set within square brackets. Conjectural readings appear in italics within square brackets. Marginal notes have been relegated to the footnotes. Manuscript A also includes a few isolated marginal headings and summaries. Since these do not appear consistently throughout the treatise, they have not been reproduced in this text. The editors have, however, introduced Roman numerals to designate section headings.

'OF THE UNION' BY SIR HENRY SPELMAN

i. *The Author*

When Sir Henry Spelman (1564?-1641) wrote his treatise on the union he was in the very early stages of what was to become a most distinguished literary career. After receiving his BA from Trinity College, Cambridge, in 1583, he spent a year or two as a student at Furnival's Inn. In 1586 he entered Lincoln's Inn and about the same time became one of the original members of the Society of Antiquaries. Within a few years he left London and returned to his native Norfolk, where he managed the lands he had inherited from his father as well as those inherited by his wife. He played an active role in the life of his county, securing election to Parliament from Castle Rising in 1597 and serving as High Sheriff of Norfolk in 1604. During this period Spelman also managed to pursue his scholarly interests. Although he did not remain very active in the Society of Antiquaries, he did compose a dialogue on the coin of the kingdom that he probably read to the Society in 1594. About the same time he also produced a Latin treatise on coats of armour. It was not until 1612, however, when Spelman and his family moved to London, that he was able to devote the greatest part of his energies to scholarship. His writings between then and his death in 1641 display a broad range of interests but deal primarily with legal, ecclesiastical, and historical subjects.[113] More than any one Englishman he was responsible for discovering the feudal basis of the common law and thereby exploding the myth of its immemorial character.[114]

Unlike his fellow antiquary, John Doddridge, Spelman never sought or obtained a position at Court. Knighted in 1604, he served on a number of royal commissions throughout his life and in 1620 became a member of the Council for New England, but he never found it either financially necessary or otherwise desirable to seek permanent employment in the King's government.[115] Although he had a deep interest in political and constitutional matters, he did not function well in a political environment. After serving as MP for the City of Worcester in the Parliament of 1625, he concluded that he was 'no Parliament man'.[116] Spelman was first and foremost a scholar, and it was mainly in that capacity that he wrote his union treatise.

Spelman's interest in the union certainly received stimulation from his large circle of scholarly associates. Long before the Union of the Crowns his fellow antiquary William Camden had written *Britannia* (1586), and many sections of Spelman's tract reflect Camden's views.[117] As the death of Elizabeth approached, the Society of Antiquaries devoted considerable attention to the forthcoming succession, and in 1604 four papers read before the Society dealt with names of the isle of Britain.[118] Two members of the Society, Doddridge and Cotton, wrote treatises on the union, while others, such as Cope, debated the

---

[113] For the details of Spelman's life see *DNB*, xviii, 736-41; *The English Works of Sir Henry Spelman, Kt.* (London, 1723), ed. E. Gibson, i, sigs. A1-C1v; F. M. Powicke, 'Sir Henry Spelman and the "Concilia"', in *Studies in History*, ed. L. S. Sutherland (Oxford, 1966), 204-37
[114] See J. G. A. Pocock, *The Ancient Constitution and the Feudal Law* (Cambridge, 1957), 91-123; A. B. Ferguson, *Clio Unbound* (Durham, N.C., 1979), 303-11
[115] Spelman did receive £300 as an 'occasional remembrance' for his services on the commission to inquire into oppressive fees. His son later claimed that his father's estate suffered as a result of his services in that capacity. Gibson, *Works of Spelman*, i, sig. A1v.
[116] *DNB*, xviii, 738
[117] See especially his discussion of Scottish 'lawland-men', below, p.166
[118] Sharpe, *Cotton*, 199-203; Van Norden, 'Spelman and the Antiquaries', 149

matter in the Parliament of 1604. Spelman's friend, the Scot James Maxwell, also wrote about the union.

If Spelman's treatise should be considered mainly as the work of a scholar who belonged to the Society of Antiquaries, the composition of the treatise might help to explain some of the difficulties the Society encountered in the early seventeenth century. Between 1598, when the Society became especially active, and 1607 or 1608, when it was disbanded, its members became increasingly interested in affairs of state. Discussion of such matters created internal divisions within the Society and also incurred the King's displeasure.[119] One of the most controversial matters that came under consideration was the antiquity and power of Parliament. Another might well have been the union. Certainly the remarkably different approaches of Spelman and Doddridge to the union suggest that the subject could have been a source of internal friction, while the anti-Scottish and anti-unionist views of Spelman might easily have influenced the attitude of the King toward the Society.

ii. *The Manuscript*

Spelman's treatise on the union, entitled simply 'Of the Union', exists only in one holograph in the British Library, Sloane MS. 3521. It has not been included, or even alluded to, in any edition of Spelman's works, and it has attracted very little scholarly notice.[120] The absence of any extant copies, the failure of any late seventeenth- or early eighteenth-century writer on the union to refer to it, and the lack of a dedication to any member of the King's government suggests that it had a very limited audience. By the time Sir Hans Sloane acquired it in the early eighteenth century it had become detached from the main body of Spelman's work and probably appeared to have value only as a 'curious discourse'. The front flyleaf bears the inscription 'Of the Union etc.', while the final folio consists of notes taken in a different hand. These notes, which summarise some of the main points of the treatise, are not included in this

---

[119] Van Norden, 'Spelman and the Antiquaries', 135, 149-50, 156; Sharpe, *Cotton*, 31-32

[120] Powicke, 'Spelman and the *Concilia*', 230

edition. The manuscript, which consists of approximately 8,500 words written in a secretary hand, stands in a very rough state of preparation. Large sections, sometimes covering entire folios, have been deleted or inserted, and the order of five paragraphs has been rearranged by symbol. Folios 2r-3r clearly constitute an introduction, although Spelman did not designate them as such. Some of the parts of this introduction are duplicated almost verbatim in the body of the text.

iii. *Contents and Themes*
   Spelman's treatise deals with two central features of the proposed union: the union of the crowns under one title and monarchy and the union of the subjects of the two countries in 'conformity of lawes, manners and immunityes'.[121] To the first, by which Spelman simply means the proposed establishment of one common name for the two kingdoms (and not the creation of one inseparable monarchy as was proposed in 1604, 1670 and 1707),[122] Spelman is only moderately opposed. He presents a number of precedents showing that annexations to the monarchies of France, England and Scotland resulted either in no change of either kingdom's name or the extension of the title of the larger kingdom to the smaller. He also asserts that if the King wished simply to 'bury' Scotland within the title of England, as Wales already was, he would be within his right to do so. On the other hand, Spelman recognises that James, being of Scottish birth, might not be so disposed to bury the ancient and noble name of his kingdom, and in that case a common name would be devised for both. Although Spelman enters a strong plea for preserving the names of both kingdoms, thereby leaving the honourable name of England intact, he recognises that the assumption of a common name was the undoubted prerogative of the King. In choosing between Britannia and Albion as the name of the joint kingdom, Spelman prefers the latter because of its greater precision, and he recommends that any use of the

---

[121] Below, p.161
[122] See PRO, SP 14/9A/35; SP 104/176, fo. 157; *The Treaty of Union of Scotland and England 1707*, ed. G. S. Pryde (London and Edinburgh, 1950), p. 83, art. II

term Britannia carry the specific connotation of two Britains according to ancient usage.

The second part of Spelman's treatise consists of a series of arguments against a perfect union, i.e., one that would involve free trade, mutual naturalisation, freedom to hold office in either kingdom, and a union of laws. Of all the authors of union tracts in 1604, Spelman devotes the greatest amount of attention to economic factors. Showing that the Scots had greater need of English commodities than the English did of Scottish goods, he argues that English merchants had little to gain from an exemption from English tolls, tributes, and customs. If free trade were to be established, the loss of customs revenue, both in England and Scotland, would be positively damaging to the King, while naturalisation of the Scots would reduce the revenues the King received exclusively from denizens. The images that Spelman conjures up of naturalised Scots soaking up offices and benefices in England, of Scottish ships stealing away English commercial traffic, of Scots draining the country of corn and other commodities, of poor and idle Scots seeking places of abode and service in England manifest as much xenophobia as any of the intemperate speeches made in the English Parliament of 1606-7.[123] Spelman insists, however, that the English would not be the only ones harmed by the union, for Scotland itself, by losing its aristocracy and most learned men to the enticements of the south, would soon degenerate into barbarity.

Spelman also argues that the union cannot be accomplished without a change in the 'lawes and auncyent usages' of Scotland.[124] The assumption underlying this argument is that Scotland, not England, would bear the burden of any legal change. Such a process would cause innumerable difficulties because of the predominantly Continental, and particularly French, nature of the Scottish legal system. In similar fashion changes in the manners and language of Scotland could not easily be introduced because in those respects the Scots were

---

[123] See, for example, the speech of Nicholas Fuller, BL, Harley Papers, Loan 29/202, fos. 93-94
[124] Below, p.180

more similar to the Irish than the English. Spelman recognises that Parliament (by which he probably had in mind a parliament of Great Britain dominated by England) had the power to change laws, but he warns against any such imposition of English law on the Scots because it might lead to rebellion. At the very least, legal change had to be accomplished slowly, an argument that even committed unionists like Doddridge and Bacon espoused. A seven-year moratorium on any such changes would give the Scots time to consider the English laws they would be acquiring, while the English could use the same time to reflect on the implications of Scottish 'fellowship'. In the conclusion Spelman states his willingness to enter into a covenant of peace and an invoilable league with the Scots, but not an incorporating union. He mitigates the force of his statement only by deference to the superior wisdom of the King.

iv. *Note on Transcription*

In transcribing the treatise the editors have followed the same rules for modernisation of capitalisation and punctuation as they used in the transcription of Doddridge's tract. All abbreviations, a few of which are peculiar to Spelman, have been fully extended.[125] Owing to a very tight binding, a number of characters have been lost in the gutter of the manuscript. The editors have placed these concealed characters within square brackets only when they cannot be supplied with reasonable certainty. In the case of speculative readings italics have been used. The paragraphs on folios 2r-3r and 9r have been rearranged without notation in accordance with the author's symbolic instructions. Section headings have been introduced to separate the Preface and the Introduction from the two main parts of the treatise. The amount of deleted material is so great that its transcription in the notes would be cumbersome. Marginal reference notes in the manuscript appear in the footnotes of the

---

[125] Spelman used 'SS' for the 'Scots', 'firnant' for 'firmament' and 'k' with a single abbreviation mark for 'kingdome'

edited text. Other marginalia have been incorporated into the body of the text or, where appropriate, relegated to the footnotes.

'HISTORICALL COLLECTIONS' BY SIR HENRY SAVILE

i. *The Author*

Sir Henry Savile (1549-1622), Warden of Merton College and Provost of Eton, was one of the great scholars of the English Renaissance. Educated at Merton, where he received the degrees of BA in 1566 and MA in 1570, he devoted himself mainly to the study of classical and Christian antiquity. He translated the *Histories* of Tacitus, produced an eight-volume edition of St Chrysostom, and composed a treatise on Roman warfare. Knowledgeable in mathematics and astronomy as well as literature, he gained a reputation as 'the magasine of all learning'.[126] He did not, however, receive any legal training or engage in legal studies. Nor did he, like Spelman and Doddridge, undertake antiquarian research or become a member of the Society of Antiquaries. A historian in an earlier humanist tradition, he viewed history mainly as a branch of literature and a source of moral philosophy. As he wrote in the preface to his edition of Tacitus, 'there is no learning so proper for the direction of the life of man as Historie'.[127] Nevertheless, he was an associate of the antiquaries Camden, Cotton and Cope, who belonged to a somewhat different humanist tradition. With these men Savile shared an interest in medieval English chronicles, a number of which he edited in 1596.[128]

Although Savile did not pursue a career at Court, he did rely upon court patronage, mainly from the Cecils but also from the Earl of Essex, to obtain his positions at Merton (1585) and Eton (1596). He gained the favour of James I, who knighted him in 1604, perhaps at the same time that Savile presented his union treatise. In 1609 Savile received a commission to assist in the

---

[126] For the details of Savile's life see *DNB*, xvii, 865-8
[127] *The Ende of Nero and Beginning of Galba, Fower Bookes of the Histories of Cornelius Tacitus; the Life of Agricola* (Oxford, 1591), 'A. B. To the Reader'. For a discussion of this early humanist tradition see Ferguson, *Clio Unbound*, 3-27; Sharpe, *Cotton*, 2
[128] *Rerum Anglicarum Scriptores* (London, 1596)

preparation of the Authorised Version of the Bible. As a beneficiary of court influence, Savile had cause to be subservient, but he displayed considerable independence of thought and action throughout his career. He refused to follow the King's wishes regarding the reading of a sermon at Merton, and in his union treatise he opposed a number of the King's designs.

ii. *The Manuscripts*

Savile's tract has survived, in whole or part, in six manuscript copies. The most complete, British Library, Harleian MS. 1305, folios 1r-23v (manuscript A), is the text upon which this edition is based. The full title of this particular copy is 'Historicall collections left to be considered of for the better perfecting of this intended union between England and Scotland set down by way of discourse'. Unlike the other extant copies, A includes a table of contents and supplies English translations of almost all the material quoted from Latin and foreign language sources. The manuscript, which comprises approximately 19,000 words, does not identify Savile as author. It does, however, contain a dedication, lacking in the other copies, to Edward, Lord Wotton, the Comptroller of the Household and a member of the Privy Council. The dedication bears the signature 'Al. Hekineden' and it indicates that the tract 'happened into' Hekineden's hands 'in a state of confused chaos'. Whether the manuscript Hekineden used was one of the other extant copies of the tract or an earlier draft that is now lost cannot be determined.

Manuscript A is bound with a short anonymous tract, written in the same 'mixed' hand, entitled 'A Discourse upon marriage to be made between the three kingdomes of France, Spain and great Brittany'.[129] This tract, which on the basis of internal evidence appears to have been written in 1606 or 1607, was also apparently intended for the benefit of Wotton, who served on a number of diplomatic missions. Despite its title, the tract does not argue for a British alliance with France and Spain. It is extremely hostile to France, and although it sees possible advantages to a Spanish alliance, it concludes that for religious

[129] BL, Harl. MS 1305, fos. 24-27v.

reasons Britain must remain unaligned with both powers. The tract is not unrelated to the subject of Savile's treatise, since the author claims that the union had deprived France of its traditional ally against England and that consequently the King of France could only expect 'his antient sword drawn against his brest'.[130] Although Savile expressed similar sentiments in his treatise, there is no evidence that Savile wrote the second tract. It is unlikely, moreover, that Savile would have attributed to the Scots the hope 'that in the next age they may rule, subdue and in time supplant the English nation'.[131]

A second complete copy of Savile's treatise, Bodleian Library MS. e Museo 55, folios 93r-123v, provides the only certain indication of Savile's authorship and a clue to the date and circumstances of its composition. The manuscript (B), which is written in three different hands and includes a duplication of a few folios, bears the heading 'A Treatise of the Union by commandment written by Sir H. Savile Knight, Provoast of Eaton College and Warden of Merton College, his Majestie being at Windsore Anno [blank]'.[132] Although the year is omitted, internal evidence reveals that it was written after the conclusion of 'our late treaty' with Spain on 19 August 1604 and almost certainly before the King's adoption of the name of Great Britain on 20 October 1604. Since the King was at Windsor on 15 September 1604, when he issued his proclamation regarding the meeting of the Commissioners of the Union, and then knighted Savile at Eton on 30 September, we can be fairly certain that Savile wrote the treatise sometime in September of that year.[133] Whether the 'commandment' to write it, which Savile refers to again in the last sentence of B,[134] came directly from the King or from one of his courtiers cannot be determined.

[130] *Ibid.*, fo. 25
[131] *Ibid.*, fo. 26
[132] Fo. 93. The heading is written in a different hand
[133] Larkin and Hughes, *Stuart Royal Proclamations*, i, 92-93 (no. 43); *Calendar of State Papers Domestic, 1603-1610*, 149
[134] Savile concludes B, C, and D with a reference to himself as 'a foole by commandment'. In A, however, he merely states that he has 'raved enough and too much'. See below, p.239

A third relatively complete copy of this treatise is preserved in Lincoln's Inn Library, Maynard MS. 83, item 3 (manuscript C). This manuscript lacks only some of the quoted material and a few isolated words in A, but it contains numerous errors in transcription. It is bound with Doddridge's tract and a number of other materials regarding the union that Lord Ellesmere apparently used at the time of *Calvin's Case*.[135] A fourth, partially mutilated copy, Public Record Office, SP 14/7/70 (manuscript D), begins only at Chapter 9 of A and also lacks a few pages in the latter section of the treatise. Manuscript C, however, may have at one time been joined to SP 14/7/72 (manuscript E), for together they constitute a nearly complete copy. C and D were not, however, written in the same hand. A short excerpt from Chapter 9 of A, SP 14/7/73 (manuscript F), is endorsed 'The Sovereignty of the Kings of England'.

Manuscript A differs from all the other copies of Savile's treatise in a number of respects. In addition to supplying English translations of material quoted in foreign languages, it contains a number of unique stylistic variations and in some cases includes entire phrases not found in any of the other manuscripts. It is possible that Savile made these alterations on a copy of the treatise from which A was copied and which is now lost. The substitution of a few words that obscure the sense of the text, however, suggests that Savile did not prepare this particular version of his work. In the absence of any evidence to the contrary, one should regard Manuscript A as a later revision of Savile's treatise by another hand, probably Hekineden's.

iii. *Contents and Themes*

The first part of Savile's treatise consists of a systematic study of the different ways in which states had been (and therefore could be) united. The inquiry initially takes the form of an objective academic exercise, but it soon acquires a polemical tone when it addresses the question whether Scotland was a

---

[135] Ellesmere's notes on two loose sheets are included within the manuscript. Ellesmere's notes on a series of arguments against the union in the Huntington Library, San Marino, California, Ellesmere MS. 1215, fo. 1r-2r, do not refer specifically to Savile's treatise, as suggested in L. Knafla, *Law and Politics in Jacobean England* (Cambridge, 1977), 231n

subject or sovereign state. Having shown that Brittany had paid homage to the King of France for 600 years before the union and was not, therefore, a sovereign state, Savile makes a similar claim with respect to Scotland, arguing that their kings had in like fashion paid homage to the King of England. He then retreats from this position, stating that if his arguments be not 'receivable', then both states should be considered sovereign. This question of sovereignty has direct relevance to the problem whether the union could be made perpetual. Savile believes that although a subject state could be inseparably united to a superior by the authority of the parliament of the latter, a sovereign state could be perpetually united to another sovereign state only by conquest.

Conceding that a union of two sovereign states 'must be our principal butt',[136] Savile embarks upon a detailed discussion of the ways in which the union of England and Scotland could be perfected. The *sine qua non* of any such union was obedience to the same sovereign, but such a union in the head could admit many distinctions in the body. Following Vergil, Savile considers these matters under the topics of name, language, apparel, religion and law. To a discussion of the name Savile devotes the most attention (eight chapters). He states a clear preference for the preservation of the traditional names of both kingdoms and is unable to find a single precedent for the adoption of a new name for both. Nevertheless, he does not believe that it would be either impossible or inconvenient to establish a new name, and he has little patience with the objections of the common lawyers against such a policy. As far as language, apparel and religion are concerned, Savile appreciates the fact that the foundations of union have already been established. Regarding a union of laws and customs, however, he recognises that union would not be easy. After an extended investigation of the terms by which other states had been united he recommends strongly against a union of both laws and parliaments, appealing not only to the lack of precedent but also to the differences between the two legal systems. Savile also insists upon the preservation of the customs and burdens of each nation, recommending in parti-

---

[136] Below, p.198

cular that the Scots continue to pay customs in England as long as they receive preferential treatment from France. The cogency with which he presents such arguments can easily lead to Savile's identification as an anti-unionist. Savile, however, defies easy classification in this regard. Wary of legal and parliamentary union he may have been, but he was genuinely committed to the perfection of the union and in the reduction of animosity between the two nations, and like Bacon, Hume, and the authors of 'Pro Unione' and 'Divine Providence', he did recommend English and Scottish representation on the council of each country. Although he took the English side in the homage controversy, he did not base his recommendations for further union upon the implications of such an argument, nor did he exhibit the hostility to the Scottish nation that was so evident in Spelman's treatise. His final recommendations did not in fact differ greatly from those of Craig. The treatise might not have been exactly what James was looking for, but it apparently did not diminish the respect James had for Savile, and it certainly merits classification as a royal tract.

iv. *Note on Transcription*

Since the dedication to Wotton was not written by Savile, it has not been included in this edition. This edition also omits the Table of Contents, which appears at the end of A. The individual chapter titles from that Table, however, have been included at the appropriate places in the text. Variations between A and the other manuscript have been noted only when they significantly affect the meaning of the text. The individual who prepared A made a number of errors in transcription, especially in quoting Spanish and Italian sources. The editors have used the other manuscripts to correct these errors and have indicated the manuscript source of the corrected text in the footnotes. In a number of instances, however, Savile quoted rather freely from his sources. He occasionally rearranged the words of the text, failed to use ellipses when omitting phrases and clauses, and in some cases merely paraphrased the source he claimed to be quoting. These changes have been preserved in this edition, but the notes indicate where accurate quotations can be located. Savile's marginal references to his sources appear verbatim in the footnotes only when more complete or more accurate references cannot be supplied. Marginal headings, which appear only occasionally in the various manuscripts, have been omitted in this edition. Capitalisation and punctuation follow the same rules used in editing the other treatises in this volume.

OF THE UNION OF BRITAYNE
by ROBERT PONT

OF THE UNION OF BRITAYNE

or conjunction of the kingdomes of England and Scotland, with the bordering Brittish Ilands into one monarchie, and of the manifold commodities proceeding from that Union.

A dialogue composed in Latin by R. P., dedicated to the most excellent prince, James, of England, Scotland, France and Ireland, King.

The persons of the dialogue:
    Irenaeus[1]
    Polyhistor
    Hospes.

[Irenaeus].[2] God save you, good and worthy men. You cheifly, Polyhistor, whose very name is reverend, and not unfittinglie given you, being a man enriched with the knowledg and remembrance of so many excellent things. As by yester-daye's conference with you and Hospes I did finde, when dis-coursing of the most perfect forme of a commonwealth, you breifly described what Aristotle setteth downe at large, and shewed that of the three formes of government, monarchicall, aristocraticall, and democraticall, the cheif and principall is μονοκρατία, or princely power, and cometh nearest to the

---

[1] The translator misrepresents the name throughout as 'Iraeneus'. The editors have used the correct form, 'Irenaeus', which is supplied by the printed text
[2] The initial speaker is identified neither in the manuscript nor the printed text

administration of the universe³ (onely proper to God). Which caused Homer, the mirror of poets, to saye:⁴
οὐκ ἀγαθὸν πολυκοιρανίη· εἷς κοίρανος ἔστω
'The rule of many is not fitt,
In royal throne let one kinge sitt.'
And likewise the Latine:
Nulla fides regni sociis omnisque potestas
Impatiens consortis erit —
'Fayth is forlorne where many rule the state,
Competency in all men breedeth hate'⁵
Yet did you not so praecisely commend and praefer the monarchicall rule before others, but that you wished, nay thought meet their should be joyned to it the moderation of another government, which the Graecians call 'ἀριστοκρατία', aristocracy, that of this towfold kinde a sweet and pleasant harmony of governing might be composed.

Both Aristotle and Plato commend this mixt kinde of rule, and by good proofes shew it to excell all other.

You did farther prase even for this amongst other the Britons' commonwealth (I meane that of Great Britaine), and proved it to take place with the very first entrance of those nationes that peopled the country, and to be confirmed by the lawes, English and Scottish: the ancestors of both in this to be admired, that they laid the foundation of their commonwealth upon such a ground, where one kinge by the counsell of his nobility ruled all. For a prince, unlesse he be guided by the holesome and sage advice of his counsellors, easily slideth into a tyranny; and one the other side a government by authority of many is most what [sic] cause of discord and division,⁶ and falleth into a timocraty⁷ where men are preferred and wayed by their wealth not vertue or wisdome, and swarveth at length to a dicostary or faction

---

³ 'quod haec proxime ad universi administrationem'
⁴ *Iliad*, Bk. II, line 204
⁵ The translation into English is of course not to be found in the printed text
⁶ 'Et ex adverso multorum pari authoritate sine Rege gubernatio diffidiorum plaerumque causa est'
⁷ In Greek in the printed text. Timocracy has two meanings: government by those of property, and a political system in which love of honour is considered the key principle. In this case the former is clearly meant

thorowgh the sting of envye, whilst each one seekeing to rise by an eminency hunteth after and pursueth all occasions of dissention. For these and such like reasons you did very wisely praefer the custome of consecrating kings to the managing of the estate, in these realmes long since embraced, from whom all under-magistracy receaved the life of their authority, as prudent and discreet moderators of the commonwealth. Againe, you did note it as a thing worthy remembrance, that the people of ether kingdome lived under a prince of succession, not elective; and although these are not to be disavowed where such custome prevaileth (God of His wisedome approoving such elections), yet when kings attayne a government successorie by right of inheritance, besides many other, it hath this speciall favour, that the branches of dissention springing from the root of election are by this meanes cut of, and the tempests that arise by a vacancy of interraigne calmed. Againe, vassals to the government of one race or stock cannot lightly shake of the yoake of obedience, it being a quaestionles truth that the enjoying of princes by succession of blood is the most sacred anchor to fasten kingdomes too, and an appeasing of all strifes whatsoever may arise. Once, the order of succession cometh nearest unto nature, whence it may be termed the rule of naturall right. These and such like matters I call to minde, which you uttered in yesterdaye's discourse.

Poly[histor]. You remember well the cheif heades of those thinges we yesterday disputed; but if you thinke me for this not unaptlie to answer my name of Polyhistor, I may well stile you by the surname of Remembrancer,[8] having of so many divers matters so exact remembrance.

Iren. Nay, if allusion to names be not uncomely, I will also terme our freind Hospes 'Polytropus', as Homer calleth Ulisses[9]

ὃς πολλῶν δ᾽ ἀνθρώπων ἴδεν ἄστεα καὶ νόον ἔγνω

'Who many men's condicions knew,
And did their townes and cities view.'

---

[8] 'Polymnemona' in the printed text

[9] *Odyssey*, Bk. I, line 3. The manuscript here departs briefly from the printed text, which includes after the Greek quotation the following: '*Vel ut vertit Horatius.*/"*Qui mores hominum multorum vidit et orbes*"'. The English translation, therefore, arose from the Latin

So he, as I have heard him say, hath travelled many countreys, hath seen or rather seene into[10] the manners and customes of many nations, and thereby understandeth and remembreth the divers fashions of governing commonwealths. But you, Polyhistor, of love, forgett not yesterdaye's promise to intreat of the now moderne state of Brittish affayres, and of the profitt that to this our Great Brittaine, Ireland and the adjoyning Brittish isles undoutedlie happen, in that they are now reduced to the monarchicall obedience of one emperor; whereof I would gladlie, may it please you, heare a continued discourse, unless it seeme otherwise to our worthy freind Hospes.

Hosp[es]. I yeild with all my heart, least happily with too much quaestioning I break the thred of Polyhistor's speach and be counted a curious and uncivill stranger.

Polyh. Pardon me, sir. He were of a crabbed condicion, that would take in ill part the diligence of an ingenuous and vertuouslie affected stranger, desirous to be informed in the state of commonwelths where he sojourneth; and I have alreadie sufficient proofe of your curteous and gentle disposition, hating all vayne and unseasonable interruptions. Wherefore, it is free both for you and Irenaeus so often as it seemeth good to cutt of my talk, if peradventure I swarve from the marke or that any obiection is to be answered.

Iren. This charge we will undertake (if you think meet) as occasion is offered. In the meanewhile forget not to dischardg your promise.

Poly. I confess that in yesterdaye's colloquie I promised a discourse of the present estate of thinges befallen this our land, nether will I goe from my word. Then, that I orderlie proceede in this busines, let us straine a noate higher and drawe from the fountaine, that it may appeare what it is that maketh a commonwealth happie. I say then, that state seemeth to me most blessed in which religion and civill pollycy florissh: and of these tow the former to have the precedency, as having a reference to divine, the latter to humaine and worldlie matters. That[11] directeth to a spirituall and heavenly end, the salvation of

---

[10] '*vidit, vel potius diligenter advertit*'

[11] i.e., religion

the soule; but politicall administration tendeth to this, that men live in peace, and be secured from their enemyes. So far then is the advancement of religion to be preferred before the good of the bodie, as the soule is more excellent than the bodie – which who so acknowledgeth not is rather of a brutish then humane nature. Againe, the feare of God wanting, which onely dependeth upon religion, their can be no politicall administration – men being not so easily restrayned by bandes ether of nature or lawe, as by a reverence of the almighty power and feare of His punishment (the print whereof yet remayneth in man's though corrupted nature). A prince therefore that liveth without the feare of God and care of religion turneth all topsie-turvie, and bringeth an irrecoverable ruine to the commonwealth.

Hos. Doe you understand this of what religion soever, or of that true and sincere religion onely which[12] we professe?

Poly. They which maintayne the Romish religion, or any other differing from ours, want much of that that should make them worthy the governing a well-framed commonwealth. Notwithstanding, civill obedience may not be denyed them, having once possessed the soveraignty, though they embrace not the true religion nor be perswaded of a more sincere worship of God than that to which they have been accustomed. I say therefore that such princes as be touched with any the least feare of God are not onely to be endured, but prayed for, untill God enlighten their heartes with better knowledg. For the prophet Jeremie enjoyneth the people of God to pray for the Kinge of Babilon and the welfayer of his kingedome, being a stranger to the true worship of God. But we are not now to dispute what incommodities proceed from a prince that is of a corrupt religion, but onely of the good that accompanieth the connexion of realmes mayntaining one and the true divine worship, that we may drawe this to an hypothesis of the union of the kingedomes of England and Scotland under one prince in one religion: the force of which conjunction is such (to pass by all civil commodities hence flowing, whereof we will entreat hereafter) that none of sound judgement and upright affections but will be moved, by this onely argument of religion, to

[12] Added later

approve this connexion of the realmes, the strongest band to tie
and knitt men's mindes together.

Hos. Great I confess is the band of religion; but what proffitt
hereby is gathered that may not as well be reaped if these tow
kingedomes stood still devided, so they professed the same
religion they now doe?

Poly. Very much.[13] For the distraction of religion commonly
followeth the separation of kingdomes, and contrarywise the
uniting of them doth confirme it, and make it more defensible
against all assaults of the adversary. An example we have in
God's people, the Israelites. So long as they remayned under the
rule of David and Salomon, true religion triumphed: but when
for Salomon's defection and suffering idolatrie God was growen
angrie with this united kingedome, sodenlie was their a revolt
from the posterity of Salomon, and a new empire of ten tribes
established – which was the cause of many calamities, and of an
alteration in religion. For Jeroboam, king of those ten tribes,
fearing if the people did ascend yearelie up to Jerusalem (the
onelie place dedicated to sacrifice and divine worship) by that
meanes the kingdome might be againe reduced into one entire
bodie, found out a new kinde of idolatrous service, and set up
two calves, in Dan and Bethel, invented new rites and holidays,
thinking this way to hold the people in subjection. But this sinn,
continued by the after succeding kinges, brought an utter ruine
and destruction to that kingedome. Nether fell it out better with
the realme of Judah in the raigne of Manasses and other idolatrous
princes who imitating the Israelites in their sinfull worship were
led captives into Babilon, and made a member of that empire.
But to come home to domesticall examples more moving and
perswasive, as fresh in memorie: but what was the reason of the
not uniting of these our nations in the raigne of Edward the Sixt
King of England, by mariage, so much of the English desired,
between the young mayden Queen of Scotland and Edward,
England's soveraigne? Was not dissent in religion the mayne
and onely barr thereof?[14] The Earle of Arraine, Protector of

[13] '*Multam certe*'. The ensuing passage approximates very closely to Russell. See below,
p. 108
[14] '*Ipsa fere sola religionis dissensio*'. Again, Russell makes the same point at length

Scotland, and the greater part of the nobility agreed to the mariage, yet kept not promise, disswaded by the Cardinal of St Andrew and clergie of the papall faction – who being the Pope's client, a stout champion of the popish religion and a cruell persequutor of the zealous professors, was for that reason a bitter enemye to the English nation and a disturber of the mariadge. Which breach was the roote of much evill bloodshed, slaughter and of the desastrous overthrow of the Scots at the river of Eske near Musleborow. One the other side after a peace made fiftie yeares since, what hath continued love and friendship inviolable betwixt these tow kingdomes which seldome before hapned? Did not I pray you the conformity in religion worke a correspondency in their myndes, and knit them in an unseparable bande of interchanged and reciprocal amity? How much more firme then and stable shall that peace be, and of what consequence by a consolidation of the realmes, when it, even then in a disunion of the members being uncertayne, and variable, and of small continuance brought forth such happie fruites as we then enjoyed?

Hosp. I know well that unity in religion is a great motive to concord, but the adversaryes say that in many pointes of religion the English and Scottish agree not.

Poly. It is a wicked slaunder. They agree in doctrine, and their difference in some matters of discipline empeacheth not so their religion but that their may be a sweet harmony in their kingedomes and unity in their churches. For where the fundamentall doctrine is (as the worship of one God, a true invocation of Christe's name, an assurance of salvation by Him onely, the right administration of the sacraments, baptisme and the supper of the Lord) although in matters and discipline their be not found in all an equality and like perfection, to such an assemblie the faithfull never douted to joyne themselves. Such a church was that of Corinth, which Paule acknowlegeth to be a true church although many vices and corruptions in manners and discipline had crept into it. Therefore for these wants the fellowship of the church is not to be forsaken. Nay, it is a dangerous opinion to hold that to be no church at all, which is not absolutelie pure and unspotted; with which erroneous poyson are many factious and turbulent spirits in England infected, who, renting themselves from the church, have hatched up a peculiar sect under the title of Puritanisme. Yet must I tell you this, that by some seditious fellowes and haters of true religion that name is very injuriouslie imposed upon many worthy, reverent and learned men, cleare from all such poison. We know that the heresy of the καθαροί[15] or Novatians is very ancient but whereof many in our age are wrongfully accused. Nether say I this that any man should please himself in error and imperfection, but rather that they ayme at purity and perfection, and square out their doctrine, discipline and all other matters whatsoever by the levell of God's written word. And as St Paule warneth the Philippians,[16] if all have not the same mynde with them that are perfect, yet let us be of one judgement and direct ourselves by the same rule, and pray to God to reveale to us what as yet is wanting, and by other already obtayned. But I will not dwell upon this argument. You I hope are of the same judgment with me.

Hos. I know that men are not endewed with angelicall perfection, but therefore is not the communion and fellowship of the faithfull to be reiected, amongst whom the true worship of God in the principall groundes of religion doth florish, nor they to be despised that notwithstanding the imperfections in discipline and manners ioyne themselves to their society in the unity of the church. For Heb. 10 the Apostell imputeth unto them as a heinous crime that, led with a praeposterous aemulation, abandon the church under a seeming of sincerity. Nay, he chargeth rather that we exhort one another to endevour by all meanes, that the church be not distracted but that we draw on one another, and bring home such as goe astray – which duty stretcheth itselfe even to aliens, much more to those whom God coupled with us and are accounted bretheren.

Iren. Lovely is the name of bretheren among the godlie, and pleasant the harmonie of peace; but the union of myndes dependeth cheiflie upon religion and true godliness, the ground of which is the sincere worship of God, and without it no perfect

---

[15] i.e., Cathars
[16] Philippians 3:15-16

peace of conscience, no true concord and fraternity – which I hope shall remayne firme and fast to all the inhabitants of Britaine living under the obedience of one kinge, a most worthy and principall instrument of this peace, seconded by the sage counsell of the nobility of both realmes, and a reciprocat assent of the ecclesiasticall state, against which I trust all the plots and devises of the Romish prelacy shall never prevaile.

Poly. Your zeale is worthy commendation,[17] and unless (which God forbid) the sinnes of the people hinder it, I hope the same that you desire.

Hos. It is well sayed, 'unless the sinnes of the people hinder it'. For although now for the most part idolatry be suppressed, and the true worship of God restored to both nations, yet their remayneth in the hearts of many an inward corruption and an idol that everyone maketh his God, ingraffed selfe-love,[18] and a contempt of the divine majestie, who resisteth the proud and giveth grace to the humble. This vice raigneth principally in England, and other no petie crimes that provoke God's judgments against both peoples: a proofe whereof is that raging pestilence that lately devoured so many thousand English, then which a sharper and more violent many yeares before they had not felt. And therefore I dout not to say, that this plague so furiouslie massacring was sent, as for many other heinous sinnes, so especially for the same for which in the time of Kinge David it swept away God's one people, in three dayes space having consumed no less than 70,000. I meane a vayne boasting in their multitude and number, and a proud lifting up of themselves above other nations.[19] For although it proceeded from David, led by wicked ambition to number them, yet was not the people guiltles: and albeit he layeth the whole fault upon himself and as it were absolveth the people, yet therein he speaketh only comparatively, for that he, being their head and shepheard, should have had more wisedome than his sheepe. Againe, we read of David's repentance, but not of the people's. Now in the Law it was provided (Exod. 30):[20] whensoever, even by God's

---

[17] '*Nae tu quidem, Irenaee, pie sentis*'
[18] In Greek in the original printed text
[19] i.e., Scotland   [20] Exodus 30:11-12

commaundement, the people was to be nombred, everyone was
to offer to God a shekell for the ransom of his life, that their
might be no plague amongst them. But they then made no such
oblation. Nether was Joab ignorant thereof when he sayed to
David, 'Why should my Lord doe this? Why should he cause
Israell to sinne?'[21] As if he had sayed, by numbering the
Israelites they are made liable to a plague, unless their be a
redemption. Now Christ is the redemption for our sinnes, if by
repentance we be reconciled to Him. For by this example we
understand what the fruites of sinne are and what befalleth the
wicked, unless they endevour by true repentance to appease and
turne away God's wrath from them. I affirme then, seeing the
pestilence is that common calamity which is immediately sent of
God upon His people for their transgressions, that it cannot be
removed without an unfained turning to God, which yett I
cannot finde in the Englishe nation. And therefore I dout it will
not so cease unless, abating their high and proud spirits, they
turne to God (that whippeth them with this rod of pestilence)
by true and serious humiliation.

Iren. This indeed is much to be feared, and God earnestlie to be
entreated to remove so mighty a lett, and confirme the hearts of
both nations in a true obedience, that they be not by their evill
lives a farther scandall to the gospell they professe. And let those
men be a mirror unto them, that for the contempt of God's
worship from the heigth of felicity had fallen unto the lowest
step of calamity. Which if they beware, their is no quaestion but
all things will fall out to the good of both kingdomes.
Otherwise, as sayeth the psalmist, 'What availeth it to carie the
face of religion, when a bad life staineth the profession?'.[22] But
let us return to intreat of union in a sincere religion, to which if
our lives be answerable, the state of the British Isles shal be most
heavenly blessed, under the protection of one kinge.

Hos. But marke, I pray you, what our adversaries the champions
of the papall superstition say against this union of religion, and
what they mutter [they] dare not speak plainly and openly, to
wit: that their is a great number of men under this our prince's

---

[21] II Samuel 24:3
[22] '*quid prodest veram profiteri religionem, si scelerata vita professio ipsa profanetur*'

dominion, in England cheifly and Ireland, who stoutly stand to
the Romish religion wherein they have been nourced and
noozeled together with their ancestors.[23] To whom, if liberty
of conscience were given, and free use of their ancient ceremonies, they protest all loyaltie and subjection – which now
cannot be so compleat, being debarred as they conceat the true
worship of God, and the king himself of a different religion and
likelie to set forth proclamations thorowgh out all his kingdomes for the observation thereof, whereupon banishment or
worse shall happily befall them.

Poly. Controversies in religion are no pettie matters: and such
are to be held enemyes of the state who stand against the religion
confirmed among the Brittons. For besides that[24] on it dependeth the salvation of our soules, how easilie is the civill
society of men dissolved, when once the bond of religion is
broken? But in this three things are to be considered: (1) first
what is true, what false worship: (2) what the state of that
commonwealth is, in which quaestion is made of religion: (3) a
view or examination of the commodities and discommodities
that grow in a commonwealth, upon the difference of religion.
For the first, I hold it not materiall to dispute which religion is
the true, it being by others so learnedly and largely handled.
This in generall let us mayntaine, that that religion is most
sincere which agreeth best with the holy scriptures, by the
English and Scottish nations onely professed and observed.
Which if any wil be so contentious as to drawe into quaestion let
him frame his plea out of the limits of these kingdomes. Not
that we distrust our owne cause, knowing it to be powerfull
against all gaynesayers, but that it is unreasonable to make
theirof a controversie, which so many lawes so long time hath
confirmed and ratified.

Hos. May not then other potentats also under the same colour
establish their religion so, that none different from theirs be
admitted within their territories?

---

[23] 'qui Pontificiam Religionem a suis majoribus multis retro annis, aut, saeculis observatem,
mordicus adhuc retinent, nec ab ea divelli queunt'
[24] 'besides that' added later in the same hand

[*Poly*].[25] They may, so they build upon the same foundation, that the sincere truth of God's word, the pure preaching thereof and a right administration of the sacraments may take place. Otherwise no praescription of lawes, custom or time ought to prevaile against God, and His truth. For the Turke might so foyst in his Mahometisme, if equall and like praerogative were given to every religion. But bicause we are not now to dispute the state and religion of other kingedomes, let us drawe this to an hypothesis of the realme of Britaine. I hold it then not lawfull for those that be subiect to the government of England and Scotland to profess any other religion than that which is publikely used and by law authorised. Of which nature is the pontificiall papall religion, which if it be not contrary to ours by parliament established, yet is it divers from it, yea in the manner of worship often opposit. For although the Papists profess with us one Christ, yet doe they deny him the office of an onely mediator and advocat to God the Father. They exhibit an idol of bread in his stead to be adored, they admit the worship of images as did the ancient heathen, and many more things ordayne they contrary to the true divine worship, defacing and defiling it with the ordinances and pollutions of men. Concerning the second point, which is a consideration of the state of that commonwealth where the matter of religion is quaestioned, particularly to speak of Britayne I mayntaine that the Romish religion is by no right or law here to be tolerated or admitted. For the true religion there professed hath taken deep roote and was many yeares since by edict commaunded; contrarily the papisticall for heresy condemned, and banished together with her fautors and fosters,[26] that at no hand they should excercise and practise it. For light expelleth darkness, and the bright shine of God's word driveth away all the cloudie conceats of man's braine. And if we will call to witnes God's sacred writ, it proveth the Israelites were forbidden all worship except that which God Himself praescribed and by His law confirmed; the

---

[25] Omitted from the manuscript; present in the printed text
[26] The word 'fosters', used in the sense of 'fosterers', is not completely legible. The printed text reads '*assertoribus et professoribus*', meaning literally 'declarers and teachers'. 'Fautors and fosters' bear the connotations of 'abettors and promoters'

cheif scope whereof is, that the people execute those praecepts and judgements which God hath commaunded, not adding to nor detracting any thing from it; and if any false prophet or seducer should drawe them from the true divine worship, were he brother, soone, wife or freind, they should slay him, their ey should not pitty him. If any say those lawes were given to the Jewes, and to be referred to the idolatry of the Gentiles, not to the ceremonies or other rites of the Christians that adore one God in the persons of the Trinity, I answer that as well Christians as Jewes are forbidden idolatry, and whatsoever els thwarteth the true worsip of God – nay much more, the gospell and knowledg of God now shining brighter. And we finde also that Christian emperors decreed lawes against idolatry and adoration contrary to God's word, as Constantin, and his soones Gratian, Theodosius and other,[27] as the ecclesiasticall history mentioneth, prohibiting under great penalties that none did sacrifice, worship images, erect statues or practise suchlike superstition. These good and godlie princes acknowledged themselves to be appointed by God Himself the keepers and guardians of the first and second table. If the Papists insist that they worship not the gods of the Gentiles, but in their images the true God, and saynts departed this life, herein they are no more to be excused then the Jewes that set up a golden calfe in the desert in Moses' dayes, whom God so severely punished as appeareth in the Book of Exod. Cap. 32.[28] For that people was not so blockish to think that the image of calfe was the true God, when they sayed, 'These are thy gods, O Israel, which brought the out of Egypt'; but they did make a shew of worshiping the true God, and did onely erect the image for a moniment of their redemtion, which the Romanists in those vulgar verses now pretend:

> Hoc Deus est quod image docet, sed non Deus ipsa,
> Hanc recolas, sed mente colas quod cernis in ipsa –
> 'The image here presented to thine ey,
> Be not deceaved, is no deity;
> This reverence with cap and bowed kne,
> In it let only God adored be'.

[27] Again, see Russell, below, p.109   [28] Exodus 32:19-35

But we must marke what the psalmist pronounceth of this praeposterous worship: 'They made', sayeth he,[29] 'a calfe in Horeb, and bowed before a graven image, turning their glory (that is the God of Israell, their glory) into the likeness of an oxe that eateth grass' – wherein he blameth their senseles brutishnes, that under the forme of an oxe would have God praesented. Manifest is this by Aaron's words[30] to the people, when he built an altar before the calfe and proclaymed 'Tomorrow shal be a festivall to Jehova'; whereby it is evident that in the calfe they worshipped the true God. The same is to be thought of the idoll calves set up by Jeroboam, for in this he professeth an imitation of Aaron. 'Behold', sayeth he,[31] 'thy gods, O Israell, that brought the out of Egypt'; insinuating hereby that he would have them worship the true God, but yet of whom those tow calves should beare a resemblance. Therefore these shifts of the Papists serve for nought, when in their idols they protest to worship the true God, Christ or any saint.

Now remayneth the third thing to be considered, concerning the discommodities which probably falle upon a well-reformed commonwealth by diversity of religion, which we will easily make good by the scriptures.

Let Salomon be cheif of this rank, as first restorer of false and idol worship after the erecting of that state into a monarchy – and for it was not onely sharply rebuked of God, but his kingdome rent from his posterity by God's just judgement, and the greatest part, even ten tribes, given from them. Likewise if we call to minde the examples of all times and ages, we shall finde that the God of Israel was ever offended with them that brought in, or tolerated in their government any idolatrous worship, after that the Israelites were brought into the land which God gave them to possess. For so soone as they enjoyed peace they fell to idolatry, and felt the heavy hand of God upon them so often as they declined. Many examples thereof are recorded in the Book of the Judges. Many times did God deliver them into the handes of their enemies, from whose yoak they were not freed

[29] *Ibid.*, verse 5
[30] *Ibid.*, verse 4
[31] I Kings 12:28

till, acknowledging their sinne, they put one a better minde. So, in the dayes of their kinges, for idolatrie they were often afflicted with calamities, untill at length for the false worship devised by Jeroboam in the ten tribes, and entertayned by the succeding kings and people, they were led into miserable captivity, never recovering their former state. After them the kingdom of Judah felt the same rod, undergoing 70 yeares captivity with the Babilonians, and a remnant onely returned into their countrey, deprived of kingedome and kingly state. And now to descend to the times of Christianity, we cannot without teares remember the fatall success of the Greek churches after they submitted themselves to the slavery of the Romish bishop, and imbraced his heresie in the adoration of the bread and worshipping of images, which now lie ruined and desolate under the most slavish bondage of the Turk. For what other cause can be conceaved, why God should suffer those persistent enemies to Him and His truth so to rage and run over not Hungary alone, but many other partes of Christiandom,[32] and to fill them with fire, blood and slaughter? These and many the like remonstrances sufficientlie prove the many miseries that befall those kingdomes which admitt and permitt worship dissonant from true religion to be hatched and fostred in their bosome.

Hosp. But what will you say of the realme and commonweale of Fraunce, where the contrary religions be tolerated by the king now raigning, with good effects of peace and tranquillity?

Poly. The kingdome of Fraunce and state thereof is no prece-dent: for in it the greatest part of the people for many ages past receaved, and still profess the papall religion, and although their be many which in doctrine joyne with us, yet that generally hath taken so fast hold that easily it cannot be pulled away and abandoned. Wherefore in such a state the old religion is to be suffered, untill God be pleased to give the meanes for an universall reformation. But in England and Scotland, where the religion we now professe is by law approved and confirmed, ought no other to receave a toleration or admission. And I hope so gracious a soveraigne (if our quiet by unquiet and restles

[32] '*Ungariam et alias Christianorum terras*'

spirits be not disturbed) will in no sort indure it: for the admirable favour of God, from his infancie extended toward him in the profession of the religion he now maintayneth, will not suffer him ether to fall or swarve from it, but will preserve both the inward peace of conscience, and the outward of civill pollicie which both nations enioye under his government sith God the author and the prince the defender of His true and undouted religion ar thus far paralel that with him it standeth and falleth. But it shall stand; God is of might to confirme both it and him.

Iren. Peace indeed, peace under one king, one law, one religion and fayth shal be the true happines of Brittaine, which God of His infinit goodnes continue to both realmes, and grant that King James may raigne many and many times happie dayes.

Poly. He hath for imitation the precedents of famous kinges among the Israelites that would not suffer any corruption in their dayes to creepe into the church. Of David, a man according to God's owne heart, that protesteth he will not take into his mouth the names of false gods or usurpe any sacrifice not agreeing with the praescript word of God. Of Asa, who put his grandmother Maacha from being queene, bicause she set up a detestable idol in the grove, which this good king cut downe and burnt by the river Kedron. He farther decreed that whosoever sought not after Jehovah the God of Israel should be put to death – were he smal or great, man or woman, that we think it not strange to have idolatrie punished by death. Of Josaphat, who with great zeale and wisedome ordered the state ecclesiasticall and civill. But Ezechias especially is a worthy mirror for all princes to behold their dutie toward God and His church: who not onely reformed religion, and pulled downe the hie places left standing by his praedecessors, but brake in peices the brazen serpent, which Moses by God's commaundement set up in the wilderness, and called it Nechuschtan, a peice of brass (2.RE.c.18).[33] And lastly King Josias (2.Paral. Cap 34),[34] who being invested into his throne at the age of eight yeares, at that time sought after the God of his father David, and in his twelth yeare purged the land of all hie places, groves,

[33] i.e., II Kings 18:4   [34] i.e., II Chronicles 34:1-7

graven images and monuments of superstition, and contracted a new covenant between God and His people. Yea, so great was the zeale of this godlie king that he extended and spread the reformation of religion, abolishing idolatry amongst the desolat and captived people of the ten tribes. I let passe the Christian and godlie emperors (partlie before remembred) to whom God gave a happie raigne for establishing and preserving His religion pure from error, and repressing the enterprises of hereticks, whose worthy deedes the ancient ecclesiasticall history sets downe at large.

Iren. Goe one, Polyhistor, proceed in your discourse, and perfect it.

Poly. What farther is to be spoken having discoursed, according to the time, of the combination of our realmes with the band of religion; unlesse happilie we turne the current of our speach to civill union, and the commodities that by it both kingdomes are likely to enjoye?

Iren. This order likes me well; for to these tow heads, religion and pollicy, may be reduced whatsoever can be sayed of the gaine arising from the connexion of the kingdomes.

Hos. This course pleaseth me also.

Poly. To intreat then of civill union. The first fruit springing out of this roote, as to me seemeth, is the enlarging of the empire: that is, a compacting of all the Brittish isles and reducing them within the circle of one diadem, whereby the renown and safety of the inhabitants and free denisons is encreased, the enemie's feare augmented, and his pride abated. For whom should the Britons dread (if God be favorable) being made one entire bodie undevided, of whom and their soveraigne may that worthy sentence of Salomon be usurped, 'In the multitude of people is the king's honour and [*blank*]'.[35] For as those countreyes easilie fall into the handes of their enemies where their is a small number to withstand the invaders, and the skirts of the empire ether hardlie defended or much impayred, so princes are cheiflie to provide for the encrease and augmentation of their subjects – I say not by crueltie and tyranny, but by iust and lawfull acquisition, and by carying an even and gentle hand over them.

[35] [but without people a prince is ruined]: Proverbs 14:28

Hos. Truely we strangers do wonder that these two nations of one and the same iland, surrounded by the Ocean, have mayntayned so deadlie and sharp war each against other so long a season. But proceed in your commenced discourse.

[*Poly*].³⁶ In the second place, consider with me the force and strength this association receaveth, the mindes and hearts of the inhabitants being knitt together. How strong a defence and bulwark it is against all the attempts and delignements of the forrain adversary, how soveraigne remedie against the plague of intestine sedition and rebellion, both to prevent and repell it, for that no traitor of what strength or force soever, within the iland or neighboring places, is able to endure the least impression of the imperiall conjoyned forces. So that the savadg wildnes of the Irish, and the barbarous fierceness of other ilanders shall easily be tamed: and they not dare to lift up a lance in hostill manner (that hetherto have been the authors of so many massacres, rapes, picories and what-not outrages) when they cannot find releif and starting holes, one in the other's countrey, being united and made one. Farther consider what honor, what joye, and triumphing shal be of all degrees, to behold the prince's court, frequented and beautified by the nobilitie and learned men of both nations, with lovely aemulation striving and aspiring to the service of God and their soveraigne – that so their may be an happie increase of learning, loyalty and religion, rewards aequallie distributed to the worthy and vertuos, and due punishment inflicted upon the troblers of the state, and an even course of justice held with the liberty and security of all men. And that it may be lawfull for the farthest dweller without impeachment, without pledg or pass, freelie to travell and traffique thorowgh so ample a dominion, enjoying the same language and lawes, and he that inhabiteth the utmost borders of the Orcades wheresoever in any coast of the kingdom is notwithstanding in his owne countrey, at his home, even as he that dwelleth in London; and marchants pass with their marchandize freed from many and divers sorts of toll and impost. By these, and other the like, who seeth not how honorable, how necessarie and commodious is the incorpora-

³⁶ Omitted in the manuscript; present in the printed text

 ting of these tow kingdomes into one? Farther, if we will weigh
the fruites of peace hence growing against the devastations and
slaughters of the warrs continued so many ages, who is so voyde
of sence and affection, so unnaturall to his countrey, as to desire
the maintenance of wars rather than peace betwixt tow such
neighbors or rather brothers? [*This is*] the cheif good and of
greatest consequence that can befall our commonwealth, next
the true and sincere establishment of religion. For as by God's
holy worship in which men voluntarily submitt themselves to
the yoak of obedience to one Almighty, Divine Power, the
inward peace of soule and conscience and the true blessedness
following it, both in this world and that to come is gayned: so is
their a temporall felicity enjoyed by the outward peace and
association of the citizens of one kingdome, the secondary good
of man's life. The full feeling whereof if a man cannot
apprehend, he may easilie by the contrary discerne it by
considering the evills that warrs and homebread dissentions do
beget, as the continuall vexation and distraction of the minde,
neglect and misprision of godliness; disobedience of lawes;
brutish rather then humane hatred, and felness; the desire of
reveng unbeseeming a Christian; dailie and dreadfull inroades,
and incursions of enemies; breaking up and sacking of homes;
raizing and fireing of cities, townes and hamlets; trampling
downe and wasting of graine in the fields; expence of vittailes,
loss of munition, captivities, imprisonment, bondage, rape
and effusion of blood without compassion; overthrowing of
churches, sacriledg; and to conclude, an exposing of all things
to the fury, lust, and insolency of the conquerors – wherin are
so many kindes of calamities and so divers faces of misery as
hell itselfe cannot invent a thing more hellish and divelish then
war. Oppositely, if a man will take an account of the fruites of
peace, and lay them upon an heap, he shall finde a large and
fruitfull soyle, and a rich harvest. But I, studying brevity by
these already gleaned, leave the rest to be gathered by[37] men of
more leasure and better experience.

[*Iren.*][38] The comendacions of peace are richlie set forth by

---

[37] 'be gathered by' inserted later in the same hand
[38] Omitted in the manuscript; present in the printed text

many: which being generally to be liked and loved, much more dearly is it to be embraced of neighbour nations and inhabitants of one iland. For what can be more welcome then a friend, what more profitable then a good neighbour? According to the saying of Hesiod?[39]

πῆμα κακὸς γείτων, ὅσσον τ᾽ ἀγαθὸς μέγ᾽ ὄνειαρ
'An evill neighbor evill much doth bring,
But from the good fayre fruites and pleasant spring'.

Mischeif therefore betide them that envie the concord, and consent of these nations: but far great[er] curse befall them that sowe the seeds of discord, and studie the dissolution of this peace.

Hos. But many are the matters by divers men opposed. As before that the English receaved this worthy and renowned prince[40] for their soveraigne lord, they urged against the incompetency of his person and consequentlie against the conjunction of the kingedomes.

Polyh. Such thinges I have also heard; but they were the calumnies of malevolent spirits, breathing onelie poison rather than proofes of regard and esteeme. And now it is a quaestion moved out of jealousy against a prince elected both by God and men, both by iust title and eminent vertues, and alreadie setled in his throne emperiall – against whom all the drifts and devises of malignant enemies are vaine and frivolous. But to stop the mouthes of these barking and bawling currs: who are they, a God's name, that envie Brittaine's happines? If forreiners, the fewell of their fire is the feare that possesseth them, for the greatnes and augmentation of the Britons. [*For*] whom this one word shall suffice; it gauleth and nippeth them to the heart that God's providence hath so wrought by this union for our weale, that maugre the malice and might of all enemies, we are made potent and strong to withstand all unjust and forrein violence. If homeborn, and inhabitants English and Scottish, or other here

[39] Hesiod, *Works and Days*, line 346
[40] '*sed varia sunt quae a variis hominibus ante assumptum ab Anglis in Principem serenissimum IACOBUM Regem*'. The 'incompetency' argument was of course pressed primarily by R. Parsons, alias Doleman, in *Conference Touching Succession in the Crowne* (1594)

dwelling, of what degree or condicion soever – let them understand the neglect they have of the common profitt and quiet, and that it is their owne gaine, immunitie, and impunity, that leadeth or rather misledeth them to the subversion of the weale publik, so much as in them lyeth. For they feare, lest the kingdomes reduced into one monarchy, the licentiousnes of rebelling and spurning against[41] good lawes be taken from them. For their are in both realmes of men of unquiet and restles spirits, headstrong and stuborne, not induring their necks should plie under the yoak of obedience, and therefore hunt after opportunities of discord, mutinie and murther. Of these men their be 4 sortes that distast this consociation (I speak not now of forreiners) and seek the disturbance and disquiet thereof. The cheif and principall are the patrons of the Popish doctrine with their followers, who are to be esteemed the most dangerous and pestilent enemies, bicause their plea is framed against God's true worship, whence cometh the salvation of men's soules; which band (of all other the strongest for the tying together of men's affections) being broken,[42] civill society is soone dissolved. But to them and their objections sufficient answer is alreadie given.

The second sort that desire this distraction of the parts are those that seek their own benefitt onelie, and they of divers affections. Some to prey and pill more licentiouslie, inhabiting and residing between the skirts of the Scottish and English pale[43] – theeves, I say, and assassinats, stealing and driving away whole heards of cattell, a late and ordinary traffique and trade without controll, or feare of punishment, inured and bred from their cradle in this marchandise, assayling quiet and peaceable men by night and stripping them both of their cattle and other goods. These know that nothing can be so oppositely praejudiciall to their designes as a confirmed and ratified unity betwixt England and Scotland: and not having learned, nor enduring labour and husbandrie (although their ground be rich and fitt for seed) they abhor all lawes made for the establishment of quiet and concord,

---

[41] 'against' is a later insertion in the same hand
[42] 'being broken' is a later insertion in the same hand
[43] ' limites antiquos inter Anglos et Scotos incolebant'

and obey them for fashion and upon constraint. In their
number let us account the wild and savadg Irish of the English
dominion, and of the Scottish ilands the Hebridiani, or
Æbudiani, who for the most part are enemies also to tillage, and
weare out their dayes in hunting and idleness after the maner of
beasts. These dout lest the English and Scottish once formed into
one bodie, that they by force shal be made subject to the lawes,
when as before for every light and trifling matter, as you would
say for the wagging of a straw, they were readie to flie out and to
ayde one another in their wicked defections. And if happely by
any sleight or stratagem they were hemmed in or empaled, the
Irish embarqued themselves for the Scotish iles, and these
Hebridiani with their complices had a foorth into Ireland –
which was no small troble and chardg to both nations. Which
disease and distemper may now soone be cured, the whole state
of Albion being reduced to the empire of one soveraigne, their
being no place of refuge for the rebell, amd the stubbornes of the
seditions easily tamed, the power of the prince being doubled.

The third sort that scandalise this union are the fierce and
insolent governours and pettie princes possessing large territories in the places most remote and abandoned of justice.
These tyrannise over their tenants, and others that are not of
power to withstand them: stripping them of their goods and
cattle, wresting from them their possessions and many other
wayes afflicting them, nor will be brought to any conformity
but with an high and strong hand. For if they be called to the seat
of justice upon their outrages, they so pester and throng the
places of judgment with their clients, followers and friends that
many times they prove terrible even to the judges themselves, so
as seldome justice can be had against them – especially in
Scotland, unless the king resume the cause and punish the
outrage as an offence against his crowne and dignity.[44] So that
the author of many villanies and murthers, being of power and
quality, for the most part escaped unpunished. This one reason,
if the many that are and might be alleadged were wanting, were

---

[44] '*si non Rex ipse suae propriae actionis foret persequutor*'. Again, this paragraph identifies
the same domestic opponents of union as Russell. See below, pp.117-18

of force to draw us to an union, that the unbridled insolencie of such laweles companions might be repressed.

Further the reason of these gainsayers is not good, by which they seeme to prove the expediencie of retayning these two bodies devided; namely the amplenes of the limits, and the diversitie of the dialect and manners of the people. For we have alreadie cleared this point, that for this very reason a conjunction is to be embraced, to bring this pluralitie to a singularity or unity. For the kingdomes being firmelie knit together, and one government setled, in tract of time it is to be hoped that all the inhabitants of this empire wil be fashioned to the same manners, lawes and language. For I finde by proofe that, by the litle commerce the English have had with the Scot (albeit many discoreds and jarrs have interrupted it) their tounge is now growen familiar and naturall, not onelie to the chief parts of Scotland but even to the Orchades and the iles of Zetland or Thule, the utmost bounds of the Scottish dominion.

Hos. This is very true; for being on a time in Zetland, driven thether by tempest, I heard the ministers preach in the English tounge, well understood by the whole auditory as a language familiar unto them.

Poly. This then is no disproffit but a singular commoditie, that we all of one countrey and nation, be also of one minde, manners and language. And what els I pray you, if example may move us, hath spread the use of the Latin tounge over all Europe but that they, being subdued and brought under the power of the Romains, learned their language and fashions? Which fell out happily for them. Againe, the accidents in the division of the Romaine Empire are worthy remembrance. For when they erected one empire in the East, and another in the West, they were soon divided in language – the East usurping the Greek, the West the Latin tounge. Which distraction caused the ruine and almost utter subversion of both empires. For that of the East, invaded by the Turkish armie, is kept under their tiranny: the Western, forced by the Goths, Vandalls and other barbarous people, did not onelie loose the greatest part of their soveraignty, but also the purity of the Latin tounge. You therefore that by long use and travell have attayned the experience of many things, may well perceave how weak and foolish these men's discourse is that seeke to overthrow by such feeble arguments the union of the kingdomes.

Hosp. But they add farther that this alteration is like to bring danger to both states.

Poly. Union of the kingdomes is not any alteration of the commonwealth, but an ampliation or enlarging, and a change onely of the persons of two in one.

Hos. But, say they, their will be a mutation of the lawes, which being varied and altered the state also of the commonwealth is changed.

Poly. This is not to be feared, for the lawes of England and Scotland are almost the same in substance; and if any small differences arise, a parliament of each kingdome being summoned, they wil be by sage counsel easily reconcyled. Or the ancient customes may be retayned, regard being had of the place and other circumstances, without any generall alteration in the commonwealth: for many nations under the Romaine Empire, using different lawes and customes, persevered in peace and obedience.

Hosp. Heare yet farther what an evill inconvenience they frame of their supposed conjecture. It is not to be hoped that their can be a perpetuall peace betwixt these two nations who so many yeares have mayntained so bloodie and cruell wars and were at such deadlie foode;[45] for if once they call to minde their ancient hatred, they will hardlie be retayned in one commonwealth.

Poly. To this I answer: they weigh not aright the meanes which the high God hath offered to this most renowned iland, which never had the happines since the first peopleing thereof to be reduced to the lawfull empire of one monarch, and the inhabitants by one generall and ancient name to be called Britons. Which thing no doute wil be of great force to excite and stirr up men's mindes to the embracing of a mutuall freindship and brotherlie concord. Againe, I would have these enemies to peace consider the cheif cause of such continuall jarrs and commotions in these kingdomes. Truelie I dout not to averr that man's sinne, and especially ignorance in the true worship of

---

[45] i.e., feud

God, usurpation of idolatry and false religion and other wickedness heaped upon this were motives of so long continued discord. But now the unity of a more sincere religion and the hereditary succession of a prince to both realmes by God's great mercie offered us, is of that vertue that all old rancor and sparks of hatred by it are quenched by which they were set on fire and devided to their mutuall destruction. For what other cause can be imagined that the kingedome of the Israelites in peace and happinesse intirely possessed by Salomon after him was distracted and made two? The Scriptures do not wrap it up in silence, but recorde it to the memories of all posterity.[46] I Reg. 11[47]: 'God was angrie with Salomon, for that his heart was turned from the God of Israell, which twise appeared to him and forbad him the following after strange gods. But he hearkened not unto that which Jehova commaunded him. Therefore He sayed to Salomon, "Bicause thou hast not kept my covenant and the ordinances I gave the, I will rent the kingdom from the, and give it to one of thy servants"'. Therefore for this sinne of Salomon, namely for the bringing in of idolatry, were the ten tribes given to Jeroboam. Now if God beheld the same causes in the inhabitants of this land, I say, an idolatrous and praeposterous worship, with other enormous sinnes, why may we not assume that the wrath of God kindled against us hath devided us into two, and many times into many kingedomes, idolatry being the occasion? Why, God doth not onely transfer kingdomes from nation to nation, but often layeth them wast, and suffereth by blood and slaughter, one to devoure, and consume another. Whereof alas the princes of Christiandom at this day are too feeling and lively examples: who for admitting and obstinately retayning the idol worship of the papists are at deadly warrs one against another, and made a derision and prey to the barbarous Turks, sworne enemies to our Christian fayth. And for the Britons, I dout whether religion, as it was delivered by the Apostles simple and free from superstition, was ever till of late planted amongst them. For of the English, as may be gathered by history, Beda was the

---

[46] '*Id certe sacre literae non tacent. Sic enim scribitur*'
[47] The quote is from I Kings 11:9-11

first to whom credit may be given concerning the propagation of Christian religion and increase thereof – a grave and learned author doutles, and in regard of the time wherein he lived not very superstitious. For what before him is delivered of the meanes, rites and ceremonies of the first planting it there, is ether uncertayne or fabulous; and out of Beda his own writings may be gathered that in his dayes many things were mixed with true religion, litle agreeing with the purity of the apostolical and primitive church planted by Christ. And such seedes of sincere fayth as were sowen by the holy and orthodox Father were not suffered to take any deepe roote, thorowgh the raging impiety of the faithles Saxons, untill by Gregorie the Great, Bishop of Rome, Augustine and Melitus were sent into England to instruct that nation addicted much to paganisme; but they came accompanied with many superstitions, as the erecting of monasteries for idle persons, of forcing single life upon the clergie, of erecting images in churches to be worshiped, with such other lik chafe. But more in continuance of time (when error grew up little by little under the tyranny of the Pope) was true doctrine corrupted. Amongst the Scots and Picts, although Christian religion is sayed to be brought in not many yeares after Christ's passion, yet can their nothing be found in ancient records worthy rehersall concerning the purity of doctrine. For albeit by the perswasion of Donwaldus and other Scottish princes the people were brought to embrace Christianity, yet was the effect of small worth, the customes and rites of sacrifising to divells being still by them stiflie mayntayned. So that it is cleare by the chronicles of these nations, that religion from the first planting was more or less tainted and stayned with the corruptions of superstition and false worship, till of late yeares. Although God was pleased now and than to enlighten the heartes of some in this time of darkness with the sunshine of his truth, and to open their mouthes to the profession of it, as then Wickleif and others, that the sincerity of the gospell might not utterlie be defaced. No marvell then if God for such impieties armed these nations with mallice and hatred one against another to their mutuall destruction, untill that now the goodness of God hath given unto us the purity of religion, and that wrought such a conformity of manners and mindes that all precedent mallice and discord being buried in the grave of oblivion, both nations may in a lovelie and perpetuall peace make one commonwealth if our sinnes hinder it not.

Hos. This, 'if our sinnes hinder it not', is a great exception.

Poly. I confesse it. But at this time my purpose is to answer onely their objections who (for that they distast this union) propound false and impertinent matter for the overthrow thereof. But let me here what farther you can object.

Hos. I have heard divers things alleadged by divers men, but bicause they seeme slight and of no worth I pass them over. Yet this will I add which I have receaved from many, that it ill becommeth the valarous and conquering nation of the English to stoope to the government of an inferior power, but rather that the Scots submit themselves to them, as often they have done by the testimonies of their owne chronicles.

Poly. It is too clear that this objection proceedeth from a pestilent minde voyde of all reason. For (to let that passe which out of season and to noe purpose they insert, of the subjection of the Scots) the contrary will rather be proved. For the stronger ever draweth to itself the weaker; and the rule of law is, that the accessarie ever followeth the nature of the principall. Therefore their is an addition of the Scottish as of the lesse to the English kingdome, the mightier, and so they to beare the English yoake and become subject to their lawes being once incorporated. Which the renowned and wise prince, Henry the 7th King of England, grandfather to this our soveraigne, did forsee — answering them that feared the union of the kingdomes by the mariadge of Margaret of worthy memorie his eldest daughter to James the 4th Kinge of Scots, as Polyd[*ore*] Virg[*il*] witnesseth in the 26 lib. of his historie.[48] 'That', sayeth the kinge, 'which I now doe, if it happen that the posterity of Margaret succeed by hereditary right to both the kingdomes can be no praejudice to England, seeing that it (being the more honorable part of the iland) would draw Scotland unto it, as Normandy or Neustria, Aquitaine and other provinces were before ioyned to the

[48] This incident, recounted by Polydore Vergil, is favoured particularly by Scots writers about the union. See, for example, Russell, below, p.102

English empire.' Which better may be sayed of Scotland, that hath nether ocean not other sea to divide it from the continent of England, so that it is almost against nature to have them dissevered.

Agayne, if any damage arise by this incorporation it will fall more likely upon them then upon the English: who are in hasard for the most part to be deprived of the presence of their kinge, it being problable he will choose his seat of residence and dwelling in the best and most fertile part of the kingedome, and so at London rather then Edenborowgh.

Hos. Farther they dout, that the king will rather respect his owne nation than the English, and will bestow greater favours on them.

Poly. Whence, I pray you, doe they gather that?

Hos. Bicause he was their borne and bred.

Poly. What then? Was he not brought into the world and fostered in the same iland of Brittaine, the common countrey to both nations? Doth he not fetch his title from the princelie stock of the English as well as from the Scottish, whose father was both borne and brought up in England? I spare to speake of his magnanimous and princely disposition, a proof whereof he gave living amongst the Scots before he injoyed the English scepter. Was their any of that nation, either noble or of inferior degree, having any matter of sute or busines, whom he did not as lovinglie and bountifully gratifie, as any Scot if not more? And will he not now, being the sole and whole heire of Britaine by vertue of the united blood royall, shew himself indifferent to all the Brittons? Especially when their shal be a commixtion of the commonwealth and blood of both nations, that a Scot in time will not be knowen from an Englishman. This jealosie then of putting difference betwene his subjects is voyded and to be held for the surmise of men hating and envying their countrey and countrey's weale.

Iren. Nay, I suppose that that which the English in vayne heretofore by so many yeares warr and such horrible effusion of blood have attempted, namelie to bring the Scots to their subjection, is now gayned without blood, that all controversies ended, the Scots may rest and live under the shadow and protection of the

English and an immortall peace betwixt both confirmed. Which is ever accomponied and fellowed with God's favour, whose spirit is the spirit of peace. Where therefore that[49] may be had with the preservation of the truth, I hold them brutish and savage that nether love nor desire it: and if any of the Scots seek to practise against it, let him loose the reputation and credit of a sage and prudent man, seeth God hath so honoured them that a kinge born of their princely race ruleth all the Brittish ilandes even to the utmost Tule. Now what is your conceat, Hospes, of the English nation?

Hos. Rather what judge you?[50]

Iren. I wonder if any well-affected to their commonwealth rejoyce not in the behalf of their nation, that that now at length hath hapned which by letters and ambassadges not many yeares since they wooed and seriouslie sought after – which not obtayned (the praelats and ecclesiasticall state unadvisedlie gaynesaying) was the cause of that dismall day in which many thousand of the Scots nere Muselborow covered the earth with their slaughtered carcasses. Nay the English victors became new wooers and suters to the Scotts, as is to be seen in that large '*Exhortatorie and commonitorie Epistle*'[51] which Edward Duke of Somerset, Protector of the Kinge and Realme with other of the Councell, sent to the nobility and commonalty of Scotland in the yeare 1548 – whereof not onelie the English cronicles but Jhon Sleidan, a German, in his commentaries maketh mention. Which are very pregnant and forceble to set out the commodities arising of this union, and to stop the mouthes of all, especially English, that traduce this conjunction. In those letters, it is declared by what meanes warrs cease, and kingdomes are brought to a harmonie and agreement: victory and mariage. But now to us hath God affoorded a third, that a prince without war or force, lineally descended from the ancient kinglie stock of the English, as the lawfull and undouted heire hath taken the

---

[49] i.e., peace
[50] The question mark is omitted in the manuscript but not in the printed text
[51] The Epistle may be found with other English propaganda of the period in *The Complaynt of Scotland*, ed. J. A. Murray (London, Early English Text Society, 1872). The Epistle is a favourite source for Scots writers on the union. See Russell, below, pp.120-1

possession of the whole land. It is further exemplified in those
letters, that to all men grounded in the knowledg of antiquities
it is a wonder how a nation of one countrey and language should
so long so mortally disagree, and therefore greatly to be wished
that the kingdomes might by some honorable meanes be united
and under the government of one. Which as it now hath hapned
by the hereditary right of succession, so hath God given us a
farther and more forcible meanes of love and concord, not
union onelie of the region but also of religion. Which may be an
assured pledg of immortall freindship, contracted I say between
the English and Scottish by God's especiall providence, strengthened by so many lawfull and godlie meanes, not gayned by
force and violence, and therefore ought to be the more sacred,
firme and lovelie. For victory obtayned by hasard of war, by
which the conqueror draweth the kingdom of the conquered to
his owne, is unconstant, the conquered by all means striving and
aspiring to libertie – as may by domesticall examples easily be
proved, if we mark what hath many times passed betwixt the
English and Scottish. How often did they invade the Scots and
how surely did they hold themselves conquerors after the victory
obtayned, yet they were againe repelled and beaten out of the
Scottish bounds, so that even unto our dayes they have enjoyed
their ancient liberties. I let pass many reasons which that letter
conteyneth, which if then, now much more doe, they binde and
tie the English that they nether enterprise nor speak against this
begun union. But farther inducements are yet conteyned in those
letters. 'We are hemmed in on every side by the ocean as with a
most strong wall or trench; so that if we were at peace and unity
amongst ourselves nothing might seeme to be wanting to perfect
happines and we might establish a perfect monarchie', with
much more to the same purpose. Now for that in the same
letters the English purge themselves of affecting dominion over
the Scot by matrimonie, which they then sought.[52] For they call
God to witness that it was the purpose of their noble prince to
conjoyne those nations, and that the English should communicate their kingdome with the Scot and all assume the ancient

[52] The following sentences are rendered in the printed original as a Latin quotation from
the Epistle. The translator has altered this

name of Britons. Farther that he had no intent to abrogate the ancient lawes of the Scots, for both England and Fraunce and the provinces of Caesar are severally governed by divers lawes; and that they which were disturbers of this peace draw the people into these feares not having regard to the safety of Scotland, but respect their owne proffit and advantage. Thus far went they then; which if now the English would call to minde and approve by their deedes their mindes' consent, the feare which possesseth the hearts of many Scottish would be soone voyded, and they assured that the English seek not to have the Scots in thrall and subjection, but with them to live in brotherlie concord and mutuall amity. For the English exceed the Scot both in number and power, and as I sayd before the inferior yeildeth to the superior, not contraryly. They then offered to the Scot the communion of England, how much more ought they[53] now injoy lik law and liberty, Scotland being communicated to them by a king common to both. Whereas then they refused not to impose upon both nations the ancient name of Britons, why should they now refuse it being offered them by the Scot? That which they add (for feare of the Divine Majesty) all good men of both kingdomes I am sure applaude it. They onelie despise and contemme it that oppose themselves to this union.[54] We neede not therefore fight against the adversaries of this combination with other weapons then are put into our handes by the English, and which the Protector of the land and the Counsellors then used. What think you now, Hospes?

Hos. Verely you are like to beat them with their owne weapons that contradict this union, which I think ether few or men of no great quality will doe. For God, by whom kinges raigne, I hope will not suffer, that the right in this kinge obtayned by His meanes be violated by the enemies of the common weale; and I now hold myself fully satisfied, nether would I have so long dwelt in the recitall of these cavills had not the peevishness of some moved me thereto whose mouthes it is meet should be stopped.

[53] i.e., the Scots

[54] 'Et quod de numinis divini metu addunt, cuius vocem et verbum contemnunt qui se huic opponunt coniunctioni'

Poly. Now, then. Seeing sufficient is sayed to that which is opposed by these janglers, and that we farther have declared the apparent commodities that flow from the union of these kingdomes, it is time to put a period to our discourse. Yet if you, Hospes, have anything to demaund farther of me or would here me dispute of the state of commonwealths, you have goode leave to speak your mind.

Hos. The night draweth on and will not suffer us to enter upon any new matter ether concerning the maintenance of this union or of enacting lawes necessary for the same. We will therefore put it off till a fitter occassion present itself. And seeing we are all now agreed and of one minde, I pray that mischeif befall them that at any time ether wish or procure the distraction of this union.

Iren. God save and bless King James.

[*Poly*].[55] Long live he, and happily.

Finis.

APPENDIX I

'Candidis Lectoribus'

This is found in the printed Latin text (STC 20103) as an introduction to the tract proper. It is omitted from the manuscript translation.

* * *

Quum de Unione regnorum Angliae et Scotiae passim nunc incidat sermo, sintque comitia utriusque regni in hunc finem (ut praesumitur) quamprimum celebranda, omnium bonorum virorum pacisque utriusque regni amatorum interesse puto, ut hanc Unionem quoadlicet, promoveant: Inter quos ego, quamvis non magni nominis, tamen pro virili pacis regnorum amator, manum plumae admovi, ut ea quae mihi viderentur, non tantum nostratibus hominibus, sed et exteris (qui haud dubie hac de re etiam curiosius inquirent) de regnorum horum, Unionis utilitate patefacerent. Proptereaque latino potius sermone, quam nostro vulgari (quod aliis relinquo) hoc argumen-

---

[55] Omitted in the manuscript; present in the printed text

tum utcunque tractandum assumpsi: idque in gratiam reipublicae utriusque regni Regisque, cui secundum Deum omnia
debeo. Quodsi qui alii melioris iudicii et acuminis in hoc
themate tractando dexterius incumbant, non equidem invideo,
sed melioribus ingeniis lubenter cedo. Hoc tantum a vobis peto,
ne meos hos qualescunque labores sinistre interpretemini.

APPENDIX II

'*Unionis Britanniae Elogium*' and '*Ad Omnes Brittannicarum Insularum Habitatores*'
    The Elegy and Poem of Address are found in the printed
    Latin text after the tract itself. They are however omitted
    from the manuscript translation.

* * *

'*Unionis Britanniae Elogium*'
Uniones semper omnes
  Rariores ante gemmas
Orbis et primarias
Delicias, precii culmen tenebant.
  Talium porro Unionum
Praedicant prisci feracem
Plurimum Britanniam:
Verum ibi Margaritas nasci minores.
  Sed sub Eoorepertis
Sole, candor, magnitudo,
Pondus, Orbis, laevitas,
Praecipuum dederunt dotes, honorem,
  Orbis at magni Unionum
Nuper unam praeminentem
Protulit Britannia:
Gloria cuius opes obfuscat omnes.
  Hanc enim mundi coaequant
Totius non Margaritae,
Vasta quae vel India,
Vel Tylos, aut Arabum corradit aequor.
  Unio nec illa quondam

Prodigo luxu, valentem
Centies sestertium,
Quam Cleopatra liquans caena voravit.
Unio si forte quaeris
Quae sit ista solatanti
Quam tulit Britannia,
Nominis aequivocum reclude sensum:
Uniones ut Latinus
Nuncupat sermo lapillos,
Quos marinae plurimum
Progenerant tumidae fervore conchae:
Vox ita illa nota vulgo
Dissidentium reductam
Denotat concordiam
Quum bene res hominum, vel corda quadrant.
Talos unio Britannis
Numinis summi favore
Nuper atqui nascitur
Omnibus Imperio iunctis sub uno,
Antea nunquam quod, ex quo
Primus occupasse Brutus
Fertur advena Insulam,
Contigit innumeris priscis ab annis.
Huius Unionis estque
Tanta virtus, haec feroces
Et domari nescios
Fortibus Angligenis Scotos adunit
Utque ferri frustra Magnes
Attrahit, sic utriusque
Corda gentis allicit
Iure pari dominans utrisque Princeps:
Uniones hinc et ortae
Plurimae beent Britannos:
Unitas ut mentium
Relligione pia, qua nulla maior.
Unus ut Deus colatur,
Omniumque Ecclesiarum
Christus, unicum caput:

Floreat una fides, erroris expers.
Deinde nomen hoc Britanni
Fiat ut commune cunctis
Utriusque patriae,
Ceu veteri soliti ritu vocari.
Una lex, Rex unus, una
Lingua, pacis et perennis,
Sitque morum ut unitas,
Mutuus arctet amor ut que unus omnes.
Tot supervehant beatos
Uniones ut Britannos
Hos regens foeliciter
Rex IACOBUS ovet, vivat, triumphet.

*   *   *

'Ad Omnes Britannicarum Insularum Habitatores'
O VOS foelici iamdudum sorte beandos,
Si bona noveritis praesentia vestra, Britanni.
Nam pater omnipotens, celsi regnator olympi
Quum genus humanum varias immisit in oras,
Et sua cuique dedit discreta habitacula genti,
Vos penitus toto divisos orbe, refusis
Fluctibus Oceani, quasi fortibus undique cinxit
Aggeribus, fecitque novo succedure mundo:
Et colere inspersas ventosa per aequora terras.
Frugum magna parens et fertilis ubere tellus
Interea est: mitis mira et clementia coeli,
Temperat excessus brumae vicis atque caloris,
Et pecorum omnigenis gratissima pascua turmis
Suppeditant laeto viridantes gramine campi.
Vos auri quoque et argenti, generisque metalli
Cuiusvis venis dives Natura beavit.
Addo tot egregias urbes, magnique laboris
Moenia, tot turres, surgentiaque ardua templa
Quid memorem riguos latices, quid stagna lacusque.
Fluminaque erectos subterlabentia muros?
Quid nemora et sylvas, saltus et lustra ferarum

Quid mare piscosum, quod et omnia littora lambit,
Caetera diffundit pleno et quae copia cornu?
Singula quae longo nequeo comprendere versu,
Vos genus acre virum, genus acre potentibus armis
Haec genuit vos terra parens: totumque per orbem
Nominis enituit vestri celeberrima fame.
Paulatim sed crevit honos: nam saepe priores
Mutavit dominos haec dicta Britannia maior
Insula, summo vere novi veteresque colonos.
Britones indigenas Australi fertur in ora
Nam primos habuisse lares. Quos deinde secuti
Pieti (gens antiqua) Caledoniique Britanni,
Arctoos versus regna extendere triones
Saxones at patria Germani, Britones armis
Devictos, meliore solo pepulere, coactos
Angustam in sedem, vetus est cui Cambria nomen
Et Scoti (quos Roma Caledonios vocat) omne
Delevere genus Pictorum, nomen et ipsum.
Ex quo praeteritis revoluto tempore saeclis
Iam duo sceptra diu rexere Britannides omnes
Quaecumque Oceani prostant e gurgite terras:
Anglorum hoc, aliud Scotorum nomine regni.
Anglorum sceptris accessit Hybernia, Scotis
Hybrides, oppositae trans et freta Pictica Dumae
Orchades et Zetae: quas inter et ultima Thule est.
Sed ferus interea Mars et Bellona subinde
Cognatos populos, eadem quos Insula nutrit
Movit in alternam ferro concurrere caedem:
Hinc Anglorum acies, Scotorum hinc agmina, satis
Heu nimis infestis, Angli protendere regnum
Dum studuere, suos defendere Scotia fines:
Scilicet, id Superum voluit Rex, ex utriusque
Peccatis populi iustam succensus in iram:
Dum meritas nunc his poenas, nunc irrogat illis.
At causas cupiens tandem removere malorum
Tantorum pater ille hominum miserator, amica
Iamdudum socians regna haec in pace ligavit,
Iure pari Regem populis dum praesicit unum.

Addidit huicque bono sincerae lumen et usum
Relligionis, in hac populum dum format utrumque
Quo nexu nihil est animos quod fortius arctet
Finitimis ne unquam belli nova semina surgant,
O vos foelici nunc ergo sorte futuri,
Si bona noveritis properantia vestra, Britanni.
Unio namque duos populos modo nectet in unum:
Unio non auro preciove parabilis ullo
Omnibus aut gemmis, (quibus est etiam unio nomen)
Sola benigna Dei sed quae donatio summi est.
Haec bene succedens si quidem unio (sineque vestra
Peccata obstiterint) preciosas multiplices res
Advehet unitas, Deus unus, Rex erit unus
Relligio, lex una, fides una, unaque lingua,
Una Britannorum veteri sub nomini erit gens
Unaque erit fratrum perpes concordia iunctis
Viribus, infensus quos non terrebit Iberus,
Aut Europaeis quicunque a finibus hostes,
Quantumvis magno minitantes agmine bella.
Papa stupor mundi cum semiviro comitatu
Arma fremat: stimulent mentiti nomen Iesu,
Hostis Iberus atrox imbelles alterat Iudos,
Et fera Turcarum rabies vicina fatiget
Regna, Deum timeant, hunc relligione sequantur
Sincera, nullo laedentur ab hoste Britanni,
Formidanda malis set et omnibus arma movebunt
Ergo hilares agitote Britannica regna veloras
Quicunque incolitis, magnas agnoscite dotes
Quas vehet innumeras divina hac Unio: vestrum
Ne quis eam temere violet, solvire laboret:
Alterius specie vel relligionis, iniquo
Vel libertatis praetextu, spe vel inani
Mutandi imperii, quovis aliove colore.
Nam si Scotus erit nemo hanc impune lacesset.
Tessera stasque Anglis, pereat male qui mala regnis
Cogitat unitis. Aliorum vosque Britanni,
Despicite invidiam, dum commoda vectra videtis
Principe sub tali, cuius depromere laudes

Digne nunc nequeo: nequeo quia dicere paucis,
Rebus hic Albinis, post tot fera bella, quietem,
Tandem et foelicem potis est imponere finem.

Finis

SITH GOD HATH MADE AL UNDER ONE,
LET ALBIONE NOW AL-BE-ONE.

A TREATISE ABOUT THE UNION
OF ENGLAND AND SCOTLAND

'A Treatise about the Union of England and Scotland,
to King James the Ist'[1]

. . .[2] and therefore some Roman writters doe call such kingdoms
provincias regias. We finde the kings of Portugall to have
followed the like forme in their conquests in the East Indies of
Malaca, Calecut, Cambar, Canoar and other kingdoms there
whereof they reteine homage, oath of fidelitie, and tribut,
without any further alteration of their estats. The kingdoms of
Poleland, Hungarie, Boheme, as also Dennemarke and Sweden
hath been oftentimes confused in the person of one prince
by election: Poleland and Hungarie in the person of Loys,
King of Hungaire by birth and of Poleland by election:
Poleland and Sweden in Sigismunde now reigning: Boheme,
Hungarie and Austrish in Ferdinande, late Emperour: Dennemarke and Sweden in the persons of Margarette, daughter to
Waldemar, Christierne the 1 and Jhon the 1. We might allegge
many mo examples of kingdoms in this maner confused, if it
were needfull; whereby it should be evident this forme of union
to be no wayes sure nor durable, for commonly it endureth no
longer then the lifetime of the prince elected, or whilst any
occasion of rebellion be offered to the prince vanquished.

The second forme whereby the sovreignites ar confused in
the person of one prince and tyed to his offspring is more

[1] This is the description of the treatise at the front of the manuscript volume in Trinity
College, Cambridge (R5.15). The actual title is missing, as is the beginning of the
treatise

[2] The missing fragment is certainly small, probably one folio. We are told later that the
tract begins with this discussion of types of union, and this opening text deals with the
first type, as the next paragraph indicates

frequent in monarches acquired by mariage or succession: for when any sovereigne prince is maried to the heire of any other sovereigne estate, the two sovereignities ar confused, and the right thereof acquired to their posteritie: oftentimes without any further annexation of the one with the other, or union of the realmes. So was the kingdoms of Castille and Leon in Spaine confused by the mariage of Sanctius, first King of Castille, unto Sanctia, only sister and heire to Veremunde, King of Leon, and enioyed by their posteritie until Alphonse the VII, who dissolved them to his soonnes: and therefter was againe united in Alphonse the IX by his mariage with Berengaria, only sister to Henry King of Castille, and Ferdinand the III, their soonne, inherited both the kingdoms. So Castille and Arragone were[3] joyned by the mariage of Ferdinande, surnamed Catholike, King of Arragone, to Isabella heire of Castille. So High Burgundie and Flanders were[4] united with Austrish by the mariage of Maximilian therefter Emperour to Marie, only daughter to Charles, last Ducke of Burgundie and Earle of Flanders. So were Austrish, Burgundie and Flanders joyned with Spain, by the mariage of Philippe the I to Jeane[4a], daughter to Ferdinande and Isabella of Spaine. So was Norrowa[5] and Dennemarke united at the mariage of Aquine, King of Norrowa, with Margarette only daughter to Valdemar, King of Dennemarke: as likewise the kingdoms of France and Navarre by the mariage of Philippe the IV, surnamed Le Bel, King of France, to Jeane only daughter to Henry surnamed the Grosse, King of Navarre. The like union hath been of kingdoms confused by succession: as in Spaine of Arragone and Navarre in the persons of Ferdinande the I; and in France of the kingdoms of Paris, Soissons, Orleans and Mets or Austrasie first in Clotare the I, then in Clotare the II, then in Childerike the II; and of the kingdoms of Noyon and Soissons in Charles the Great. Which forme of union, having no stronger bond then the pleasour and will of the prince, must neede[6] to be subiect to often dissolutions. So were[7] Castille and Leon dissolved by Alphonse the

---

[3] Corrected from original 'was'
[4a] For 'Jeane' read 'Joanna'
[6] Corrected from original 'behoveth'
[4] Corrected from original 'was'
[5] i.e., 'Norway'
[7] Corrected from original 'was'

VII: Castille, Arragone and Navarre by Sanctius the III: Castille, Leon and Galeca[8] by Ferdinande the III: and in France the kingdoms of Paris, Orleans, Soissons and Austrasie by Clovis the I, then by Clotare the I, then by Dagobert the I: the kingdoms of Noyon and Soissons by Pepin: of France, Austrasie and Baviers by Loys Le Bonnare: of France and Navarre by Philippe the V. Which frequent dissolutions caused both in Spaine and France many horrible and tragicall parricides, cruell battels and miserable desolations of those kingdoms, as may appeare by the recorde of their histories. Therefore for eschewing such inconveniences and establishing a solide and durable peace in the kingdoms by this waye united, it hath been thoght necessare to annexe such sovereignites the one with the other to remain inseparably joyned as the patrimonie of one crowne, tyed to the race of the prince in whois person they were first confused, or any other lawfull possessour of either; and when the sovereignites ar this way annexed, the realmes or bodys of estate falleth almost ever to be joyned either by subiection or incorporation.

The third forme of union of kingdoms may be by annexation of the sovereignites and subiection of the one estate to the other; which hath been most frequently used in the monarches or estats conquered or aquired by legacie and testament of the sovereigne prince deceassing. As touching conquests, the conquerours have ever been accustomed to annexe the vanquished contryes to their empire by redacting them under subiection and servitude: abolishing their ancient laws, magistrats and forme of government, and imposing to them new laws, imposts, tribute, magistrats, garrisons and such forme of governement as pleaseth them best. By this waye the Assyrians, Medians, Persians and Parthes enlarged their empire throughout all Asie and Ægipt, transferred the subdued nations in satrapias – such as was ordoned by Darius, oncle to Cyrus the first, to the number of 360, and in everie one of them a governour called Satrapa, and above those thrie principall, whereof Daniel the prophette was one (as recordeth Joseph). So Alexander the Great united his conquests of Asia and Ægipte to

[8] i.e., 'Galicia'

the Macedonian Empire: and the Romans to their empire the whole nations redacted by them under forme of provinces, which they conformed to the Roman laws and forme of government and ruled them by Roman magistrats, as consuls, proconsuls, praetores, propraetores, praesidents, questors and garrisons placed in the strong townes and fortresses of everie province. Such I saye was their maner of uniting nations not only subdued by force of armes in France, Germanie, Spaine, Grece, Asie, Africke and other partes, but also of such as were left to them by the later will of the sovereigne princes thereof: as was Pergame by Attalus, Bithinia by Nicomedos, Cappadocia by Archelaus, the Alpes by Coctius, the Ponte by Polamon. The Turke, the Sophy of Perse, the Great Ducke of Moscovia and other princes of signoriall monarchies in this oure age hath followed the Romans in that point. For the Turke governeth his conquest provinces called Beglerbegats and those devided in Sangialks by his Bassas Begi Cadi, and others such magistrats conforme to the Turkish laws and customes. The Kings of Spaine and Portugall have united after this maner many of their conquests in America and the East Indies. So Henry the II King of England annexed Irland to the crowne of England: Sigismunde the II the duckdome of Livonie to Poleland: Clemens the VI Pope Avignon boght⁹ from Jeane the I Queen of Naples to the patrimony of the Roman church. This forme of union, as it is contracted by force and violence, so is it entertened by violence, subiect to frequent rebellions and at lenth dissolved by violence; and therefore is not fit for such free royall monarches that are not by armes constrained to a forced union, but by the succession of one lawfull prince ar moved to contract a mutuall and naturall mixture of their estats, for the constitution of one true budy under one head.

The fourth forme of union is when the confused sovereignites ar annexed and the realmes incorporated: that is, drawn to an uniformitie or mutuall participation of those differences which was [sic] propre to either of them, whilst they were yeet severed – such as in name, language, laws, customes, habilites or freedoms both of naturalization and estate or participat sovereign-

⁹ i.e., 'boght Avignon'

itie. If then severall estats be drawen to an uniformitie or equall mixture of all these points they ar perfectly incorporated. Such was the union of the Romans with the Sabins, Cininenses, Crustamini and Antemnates, who for the ravishing of their virgins entered in warres against the Romans: but by the intercession of their daughters (as reporteth Livius) '*Non modo pacem sed civitatem unam ex duabus faciunt, regnum consociant, imperium omne conferunt Romam*'[10] 'Not only make they peace, but als of two cities one, they joyne their kingdoms: they draw the whole empire to Rome'. Neither did they by this waye (during the enfancie of their empire) incorporat to their estate such only nighbour contryes and people as did lye neere to the town of Rome: but also, their empire encreassing, farre distant cities and nations, by placing in a certaine portion of the contrey conquered their colonies. For so were they accustomed to spoille the vanquished nation of a certaine part of their lands, wherein they placed, for favoring and enjoying thereof, certaine number of citizens sent from Rome, by whois mixture and incorporating with the subdued people, the whole body so mingled became a member of the Roman Empire, whereto was communicated all the freedoms and habilites of the Romane people, such as was of mutuall mariage, of burgeship, of vote in the assemblies of the people, of enjoying honours and offices within Rome: and thereby was broght to an uniformitie of laws and forme of Roman governement. Such was the incorporation of the most part of all the cities and people of Italie with the Roman estate: as of the Latins, Sutrium, Setina, Nipe, Aritini, Tarracina, Lucorna, Alba, Ariminum, Beneventum, Placentia and many others within Italie: as likewise after the enlarging of their empire, without Italie, of Sicile, Carthage, Lyon, Narbon, Vienne in France, and others mentioned in the Roman historie. By the which incorporation of so many cities and peoples the Roman estate reaped two cheiff commodities: the one by unloding[11] their citie of a great number of poore and idill citizens, who at home like to naughtie humours

[10] Livy, Bk. I, cap. 13, sec. 4. For '*modo pacem*' read '*pacem modo*'
[11] Underlined, probably for correction, in later ink: 'disburdening' written above in the same ink

in a replet body, served for nothing but to disquiet and disease the body of the estate: the other in so enlarging and fortifeing their empire by such a sure and honorable a maner. Whereof the vanquished nation receiving honour, benefit and contentement, all occasion and affection of rebellion was cutt off. And certainly we shall find none or few Roman colonies stirred up against the Romans or dismembred by uprors.[12] But although this maner of incorporation be perfect, sure and commodious for both the estats so united, yeet it is not aggreable or meete for all estats. For there be many realmes and monarchies, whereof the sovereignites being confused or annexed, the bodys of the commonwealths wold not, yea might not well[13] suffer any either mixture or alteration of their ancient laws and customes, or of their privileges of estate and libertie of parleament, consell and officiers of estate, without a great hurt to the commonwealth and discontentement of the whole people – who otherwise may be induced to an uniformitie of name, language and habilites or freedoms of a naturall subiect. Which is a fashon of incorporation thought imperfecter, yeet fitter for the union of free monarchies then the other. Therefore the Romans, perceiving some people vanquished by them to be such zelatours of their owen laws, privileges and forme of governement, that the smallest innovation thereof caused often rebellions; they used towards those nations this imperfecter forme of incorporation, permitting to them free libertie of their owen forme of governement, laws and magistrats, and imperting to them the habilites and freedoms of the Roman citie – whereby they might contract mariage with the Romans, be bourgesses of Rome, and participat offices and dignites within Rome. For the which cause they were called *municipes*, and their contryes *municipia*: such as were Tusculanii, Volci, Norinici, Acerranes, Attelani and others ancient people of Italie who were by this waye of union distinguished from the provinces. Albeit the benefit of naturalization called *Ius Civitatis* was also granted to sundrie cities and provinces, and at lenth maid so common, that as recordeth

---

[12] Underlined in later ink
[13] Corrected from original 'goodly'

Aurelius Victor,[14] in Aurelius Antoninus the Emperour's dayes, *'data sit cunctis promiscue civitas Romana'* – denization was granted indifferently to all men and nations. But this Roman naturalization comprehended not the remanent freedoms of the Roman citizen, such as were *Iura matrimonii, suffragii et honorum*; but only benefited the naturalized person so farre that being accused of his liff or honour, he might reclame from the judgment of any provinciall magistrate to the Roman people or Emperour – which we finde to have been practized in the person of the Apostle St Paul. The use of this forme of partiall incorporation hath been more common in Europe since the decay of the Romane Empire, in so farre that in the union of many estats, expresse reservation hath been maid of their privileges, ancient laws and forme of judicatorie.[15] So the contrye of Dauphiné in France was left in legacie to Philippe de Vallois King of France by Humbert, Dauphin or sovereigne prince thereof, under condition that in all times cumming the Kings of France eldest soone should enjoy the contrey of Dauphiné and be stilled Dauphin: and that the people should retene without any innovation such freedoms, privileges and laws, which they enjoyed under the said Humbert. Brittannie acquired to Charles the VIII and Loys the XII kings of France by the mariage of Anna Duchesse thereof: and the Erldome of Tholose with the contrey of Languedock acquired also to the house of France by the mariage of Alphonse Erle of Poitiers, brother to King Loys the IX, with Jeane only daughter to Raymonde Erle of Tholose, were[16] both united to the crowne of France, with the foresaid reservations. Yea, in the union of Tholose it was expressly aggreed that the right thereof being devolved to the Kings of France, no governour should be appointed there but such as were princes of the blood royall: that no imposts nor tolles might be raissed there without advise and consent of the parleament or estats of the contrey: that they should reteine without any innovation their ancient privileges of estate, laws and forme of judicatorie according to the common written

[14] Aurelius Victor, *De Caesaribus Historia*, cap. 21
[15] Underlined in later ink
[16] Corrected from original 'was'

Roman law: that the stranger or foreiner indwellar and habituated[17] in the contrey of Languedocke specially in the towne of Tholose should be exempted from the law called in France *Droict d'aubeine*,[18] being denized by his only residence making and indwelling there without any other benefit or letters of naturalization received of the king or sovereigne prince – which whole conditions they enjoy to this day. The like reservations hath been maid and granted to Aragon at the union thereof with Castille by the mariage of Ferdinande and Isabelle: to Catalonnia at the union of it with Aragon by the mariage of Raymunde, Erle thereof with Urraca, only daughter of Raymire King of Aragon: to Lituanie, annexed to the kingdom of Poleland by the election of Jagello called Vladislaus the IV, Ducke of Lituanie, to be King of Poleland. Christierne the I, King of Dennemarke, having annexed to the crowne of Denmarke the Duckdoms of Holsace and Slevish[19] boght from Otto Erle of Shouembourg for the soume of 41,500 Rhemish crownes, granted to the estats thereof a speciall reservation of their laws and privileges of estate, and that he should undertake no warres without the advise and consent of the estats of both the provinces: that he should yeerly cause an assemblie of the[20] cleargie and nobilitie of both the provinces, where their controverses might be decided, with many other conditions no wayes tolerable in a kingdome cumming by succession. Borussia was with the like reservations annexed to the kingdome of Poleland under Casimire the I. Such and so many were[21] the reservations and conditions in the union of the realmes of Sweden and Dennemarke by the election of King Jhon in the yeere of God 1483, and of Portugall with the remanent kingdoms of Spaine, now lately by the succession of Philippe the II King of Spaine, that there appeareth no union to have been made of the estats or realmes either of Sweden and Dennemarke or of Portugall and Spaine, but only a confusion of the

---

[17] Underlined in later ink
[18] The law governing inheritance of land by aliens. See the discussion in Sir George Mackenzie's 'Discourse Concerning the Three Unions between Scotland and England' (1670) in National Library of Scotland, Advocates MS 31.7.7
[19] i.e., 'Holstein' and 'Schleswig'
[20] 'the' added later   [21] Altered from 'was'

sovereignites of Sweden and Dennemarke in the person [*of*] King Jhon without any further: and of Portugall and Spaine in the person of Philippe together with the right of succession thereof established to his posteritie. Wherin there can be no great assurance of continuance – leaving nighbour people of so disaggreing affections, in such difference of estate and disjunction of commonwealth, which can breed nothing ells but discontentment and enterteine their accustomed grudges until occasion serve of their disunion by rebellion of the one. So Sweden was disjoyned againe from Dennemarke under Christierne the II, King of Dennemarke, upon the occasion of the allegged breake and not keipping of their privileges and conditions of union accorded to them by his father King Jhon and ratified by himself.

This farre then touching the different formes of joyning severall kingdoms. Lett us now go to the hypothese of application of this our discourse to the union of those two kingdoms of England and Scotland, that we may enquire which of those formes be fittest to joyne those mightie and warrlike nations, by such an indissoluble knot of equall union that neither age nor violence may hereafter dissolve the same. For the better clearing whereof, it shall be needfull to digresse a litle upon the necessitie and commodities thereof. I may justly afferme, that God and nature inviteth, necessitie enforceth and evident commoditie doe draw ws thereto: for since God and nature (as sayeth the Philosopher) doe nothing in vaine, they seame to have placed two so mightie, free and bellicous nations, of such equall power conformitie of maners, humours and language in one so great and plaintifull iland, and to have enclosed and environed them with so strong and naturall a wall of the ocean sea, to the ende that by their mutuall union and incorporation a solide and perpetuall peace may bread wealth at home. The feare of our unified forces deterre the forcine ennemie from invasion, and the ground and fondation of a great, potent and durable monarche be laide in this iland. And therefore hath God suffered so many different peoples, of the Pights, Romans, Brittons and Dannes, who by times[22] have employed their forces

---

[22] 'by times' underlined

to domine in[23] this iland, to be utterly overthrown by the
English and Scottish nations: that at lenth after so long a divorce
and so much bloodsheed, nature, mutuall love, and willing
consent might effectuat the union of those nations, which no
force could ever have wrought. So also hath nature maid the
right and just title of both the kingdoms now to be devolved by
lawfull succession and discent of blood in the person of one
prince, so cutt of all jalosies of division and impediments of our
wished union: and hath blisshed us both with the happy and
wise governement of such a prince, who being equally charged
by God with both the diadems, is a father to both the people,
owing to both one dewtie, and willing to embrace both with
one affection – to the effect that in him and by him the periode
of our divorce and division may be atcheived and the Judiniall
union of both the realmes peaceably established to the full
quietnesse of the whole iland, contentement of all his Majestie's
good and naturall subjects of both the realmes, comfort and
securitie of the posteritie, terrour of the foreine ennimie and
happy encreasse of the monarche of this iland. Wherin we
may perceive how God by His singular providence, hath now
of His infinit mercy bestowed upon these two nations that
heappe of worthy blissings which was prophesied by Ezechiel[24]
to the devided kingdoms of Israel and Juda after their captivitie.
'I will (saieth the Lord) make them one people in the land and
one king shall be king of them all, and they shal be no more two
peoples, neither be devided any more hence fourth in two kingdoms'. Whereby the prophette as he foresheweth mistikly the
perfect and happy estate of the Christian church under Christ,
wherin both Jew and Gentill ar unified and drawen (as Christ
himself affermeth) unto one sheipfold, and one sheipherd: so
doeth he literally signifie that the fullnesse and perfection of all
temporall blissings which might be vouchsaffed by God upon
his people after their division, do consist in the union of their
civil estate under the obedience of one just and lawfull prince.

[23] 'domine in' underlined in later ink
[24] Ezekiel 37:22. This chapter was a favourite source of reference on the union. Besides
being used by tract writers, it provided Cecil with a possible inscription for the 'Unite'
coinage of 1604. See P.R.O., S.P. Dom. 14/10A/21

Now as God and nature by those evident demonstrations appeareth to induce and leade ws to the perfecting of this union, so the great and manyfold inconveniences, dangers and miseries wherwith this island (during the divisions of many kingdoms therein) hath ever been travelled, and which God willing shal be eshewed in all times cumming by this union, maketh the same the more forceable. What I pray yow is oure histories, but a recorde of perpetuall hostilitie between the devided nations of this iland: of infinite bloodsheed, seditions, rebellions, voleries, oppressions, unnaturall parricides, contempt of laws, justice and magistrats, and of other tragicall events, caused by the ambitious humours and mistrusting jalosies of the devided kingdoms in this iland. Whereof have had too much experience the Brittons and Pights to their utter wrake, the Saxons to the ruine of their monarchie, the English and Scotish to both their great losses and perilling of their estats. Neither hath such divisions procured those only miseries at home amongst the devided nations, but also hath ever geven occasion to foreine invasions. For by the perpetuall discords of the Brittons, Scotish and Pights, the Romans maid there conquest in the iland. '*Nec aliud*' (sayeth Tacitus, speaking of Brittanie) '*adversus validissimas gentes pro nobis utilius quam quod in commune non consulunt ita dum singuli pugnant universi vincantur*'![25] 'Neither is there anything more profitable for us against so mightie nations, then that they ar not united in consell and force. So whilst they warre everie one alone, they ar all overthrowen'. How miserable was the estate of England during the division of the seven kingdoms of the Saxons, and how by their perpetuall ennimitie the Dannes made[26] the waye to the occupying of their monarchie, it is evident enough by recorde of the histories. Lett us likewise call to memorie what great losses and calamities both the nations English and Scotish during their divisions hath suffered by their mutuall warres: and how often the Scotish have been moved to stay and diverte the English conquests abroad by their untimely incursions on England. Now then if for avoyding of such inconveniences and miseries both the nations, weried of mutuall hostilitie, hath been

[25] Tacitus, *Agricola*, 12. For '*vincantur*' read '*vincuntur*'
[26] Corrected from original 'freede'

enforced to enterteine peace by a mutuall confederacie these fourtie yeeres bygonne,[27] how much more should they be moved thereby to apprehende this occasion of perpetuall union – so often attempted by armes and soght by mariage, and now occasioned by the just and lawfull succession of his Majestie to both the crownes. As concerning the commodities which may be reped and enjoyed by this union of the two nations, they are so sensible that I thinke there be no man or good and naturall subject of either nation who hath not alreaddie had some sense and prouve thereof, by his Majestie's peaceable promotion to the crowne of England. Peace not expected is universally satled at home and abroad, and hopped to be perpetuall by this union: justice now duely administrated: publike robberies quenshed: libertie of mutuall trafficke entertened. Such idle and naughtie sprits who, assured of their retreate and recepte in the one or other nation, breathed nothing ells then oppression of their neighbours and rebellion against their prince, ar now keipe under due obedience. The foreiner is affraied of the encreasse of his Majestie's power, redowting more the force of oure union then hopping for continuance of oure amitie. And in a word, we may expect thereby the continuing of an assured peace, the mother and fontane of all worldly felicitie: '*Cuius*' (as sayeth Cicero) '*nomen dulce est; res vero ipsa cum iucunda, cum salutaris*'[28] 'Whereof the name is swette and the thing itself pleasant and holsome'. Wherewith it hath pleased God so to accompagnie his Majestie's entrie in England, that now by an assured peace abroad with all foreine nighbours they enjoy more then a wished libertie of free trafficke with all nations – which before they wold have boght with the danger of their liffs, and might not atteine thereto but by the employment of neutrall foreiners, neither that without perill and disturbance. But becaus there be some self-lovers in both the nations who valueth nothing more then their owen partialities, and, transported with malicious curiositie, searcheth a knot in a bulrush, grounding their discontentments and misliking of oure union upon certaine imagined difficultes, I think it shall be necessarie

---

[27] Underlined in later ink

[28] The actual line reads '*nomen pacis dulce est et ipsa res salutaris*', *Philippics* II, 113

to cleare the concerted objections of such bluddie brains[29] -- that the unlearned and weaker judgements may discover their insufficiencie and dispise their malice. First:[30] where it is feared that the union of the two estats cannot be perfected without alteration or deminishing of the fundamentall laws, liberties and grounds of governement in both the contryes: to the great lysion of both the estats and preiudice of the nobilitie and others, who enjoyeth the privileges of estate. This feare may be easely quenshed if they will consider rightly the imperfecter forme of incorporation of estats and kingdoms set doune by ws before, and which we shall show to be most convenient and apte for the joyning of those kingdoms – since the union may consist in the annexation of the two sovereignities and aequall communication of the habilities and freedoms of denization only, each realme reserving still their severall laws, forme of judicatorie and privileges of estate. Which forme we show to have been used by the Romans *in municipiis*, and, since the decay of the Roman Empire, in France, Spaine and other partes of Europe. So there is no necessitie to endanger any of the estats by innovation of their fondamentall laws or privileges: neither were it expedient that so should be, for such causes as we shall deduce more largely hereafter.

Nixt[31] there be of the English nation some so passioned with this self-love that they are not ashamed[32] to cover their private drifts and ill-affected myndes towards the present estate under the pretence of ane inequalitie of oure wealth: fearing to be diminished of their wealth by the Scottish alledged poovertie, and shortned of their benefits and employments by our multitude and advancement at court. It appeareth well that such giddie heads,[33] thought too much curious, have never called to memorie the dangerous dowtfulnesse of their former estate, nor entered in consideration of the manifold miseries and utter wrake eshewed. The great benefits obteined, and heappe of blissings now procured to them by the confusion of the two

---

[29] 'bluddie brains' underlined in later ink   [30] Marginal note: '1'
[31] Marginal note: '2'   [32] Underlined in later ink
[33] 'giddie heads' underlined in later ink

sovereignities in his Majestie's person and their peaceable
coniunction with Scotland. Was not their condition such during
the time of their late deceased Queene that they, laboring by
prevention of dangers and foreine invasions to enjoy ane
outwarde peace, were forced to spend their treassours upon
foreiners, consume the wealth and able men of their land to
repaire their losses abroad: underly at home many heavie
charges of extraordinarie taxes and subsidies: and travelled with
the oppen hostilitie or envious misliking of all their nighbour
nations. [They] was no lesse afraied of the future alteration of
their sovereigne then wearied of their dowtfull and diseased
state – like to a shippe overthrowen by a great storme of
weather, flotting betwene lyff and utter wrake. And if after the
death of their late sovereigne they had not so willingly acknow-
leged his Majestie's undowted right and so peaceably embraced the same, having recourse thereto as to the only phisike
of their diseassed commonwealth, how calamitous and miserable should their condition have been? Should not the home-
borne pretenders have rent asunder the body of their estate by
devided factions and civill warres? Should not his Majestie by
their ingratitude and contempt moved to a just persute of his
righteous title have been enforced to have used against them all
maner of hostilitie? Should not Irland then by an universall
rebellion have been dismembered from their crowne? Was not
Spaine breathing that occasion of their utter overthrow, and
abyding by their civil dissensions an easie entrie to their ruine?
Was not France waitting to have plaide a part of that tragidie?
And in a word: what should England have been but the stage of
all the tragidies of Europe for many yeeres, a praye to foreiners
and an unrecoverable wrake to itselfe? By which means then
have they escaped those calamities, and procured their safety?
By what phisike is the weaknesse of their former estate
convaleshed to a dowble strenth? From whence cummeth their
present prosperitie, and enjoying so securly both outward and
inward peace? If after God from his Majestie, and their
peaceable joyning with us.[34] Since we ar the instruments of their

---

[34] The phraseology is obscure, but the meaning clear – that these benefits came from
God's providence in uniting England and Scotland

peace and enriching, and by us they have received so many great
benefits, shall they not be ashamed to thinke us unworthie to be
parttakers of their wealth? Should they be suffered to bind up
his Majestie's hands from rewarding such of his owen native
subiects as have justly deserved or hencefourth may deserve it by
their honest and faithfull service? Could any indifferent judgment voide of envious self-love value them with ingratitude?
Well I know none of those self-lovers wold be contented with
such a valuation of their good deservings. Now whilst the
Scotish favorers are so enriched or advanced to honours, shall
the wealth of England be diminished thereby or the contrie of
Scotland bettered? No: for as their yeeres and services, so their
welth[35] and riches ar employed and spent in England – like to
the great rivers which floweth from the ocean and returneth
thereto. Neither is the number or wealth of such rewarded
persons that retire them home to Scotland so great that thereby
either our surmised povertie may be solaged, or their abundance
sensibly empared.[36] But perhapps they think that the free
entercourse of trafficke will be advantageous to us and pre-
iudiciall to them, either by the diminishing of his Majestie's
foreine customs, or by lake of commodities in Scotland for
enterteining the mutuall trafficke and enterchange.[37] As to the
emparing of the customs, it is his Majestie's only interest, who if
any losse thereof should be susteined by oure union, wold easely
dispense therewith for a greatter well to both the realmes. But no
loss thereof is to be feared: for by the encreasse of oure trading
and more frequent entercourse of commerce his Majestie's
ordinary customs should be much augmented in both the
realmes: both the commonwealths also more plaintifully enriched: the private mislikes of times past fully satled: and the
mutuall band of our amitie more and more festened. Neither is
oure contrye so emptie of commodities for enterchange, as they
wold give to understand. For concerning the necessares for
man's lyff, no contrye is better furnished. Our land is replenished with cornes of all sortes, with infinit kinds of foulles,

---

[35] Corrected from original 'moyens'
[36] Marginal note: '3'
[37] The author is precisely correct: see Spelman, below, pp.175-80

abondance of grasse, cattell and other bestiall; but with such
store of shippe that besyde oure ouen uses the northerne shires of
England are[38] yeerly helped therwith. We have such plentie of
fishess in all partes of oure seas specially towards the northerne
and westerne ilands, that the same wold suffice to susteine all the
people of the whole iland, thought there were no other
commodities therein: for the inhabitants of all oure nighbour
contryes, as France, Flanders, Holland, Zeland and a great part
of Germanie lyeing neere the coasts, resorteth either with a
greate number vessells dayly to fishe upon oure coasts, and buy
such as we have alreddie caught – by transporting whereof into
Spaine, Italie and other nations lyeing upon the Levant seas they
make great gains. Many English traffikers have experience of
this commoditie, and other nations do make no small accompt
thereof. Besyde the abondance of wolles, skinnes, hydes, linn-
ing, colle, salt and other common things, there is in divers partes
of our land riche myndes [i.e., mines] of gold, sylver, lead and
azure in Cliddesdale: of sylver, iron and lead in Argyll and
Loghquhaber.[39] Yea, there is no part of Scotland so barren or
improfitable, but it produceth either iron, tinne, lead or some
other kind of metalle – as may be easilie prouved throughout all
the westerne and northerne ilands adiacent thereto. So that if
oure people were industrious, skilfull and powerfull to dealle
therewith, they might matche any nighbour nation in wealth.
Such then is the commodities of our fishings, mynes of gold,
sylver, tinne, brasse, copper, iron, lead, azure and store of
bestiall,[40] that if by oure union the Englishmen were licencied
to trade freely therewith, I am assured the gains which they
might and wold make thereof should by many degrees sur-
monte any profit or advancement the Scotish might have or
hoppe for in England. And though we laked those commodities,
yeet should not there wealth, but reither ours be empared: for
the frequent trading of our marchands thither, having nothing to
enterchange but money, and resorting of our nobles, gentlemen
and others for their adois[41] towards court wold sucke up still no

---

[38] Corrected from original 'was'   [39] Lochaber
[40] Underlined in later ink   [41] Underlined in later ink

small part of our wealth. Now[42] the feare that their employments and benefits shall be hindered by the number of the
Scotish promoved to honours and offices must procede either
of ane envious jalousie, or of a plaine mistrust of his Majestie's
wisdome and discretion: as if he respected the nation and birth
of those whom he advanceth, beyond their vertues and good
deservings or well of the commonwealth. Hath not all his
actions since his entrance in England geven a sufficient prouve of
his aequitie, like favor and magnificence in rewarding such of
both the nations who have deserved of him by their loyall and
vertuous behaviour? After which assurance may there remane
any suspicion of his partialitie? Or since (as sayeth Plinius)[43]
'*omnium beneficiorum, que merentibus tribuuntur, non ad ipsos
gaudium magis quam ad similes redundat*' – 'the pleasour of the
benefits bestowed upon such as deserveth them redundeth no
more to the receivours then to those of the like deserving' –
should any man of good qualities and honest deserving of either
the nations feare to take advancement at the hands of such a
prince, who never hathe left vertue unrewarded nor vice
unpunished, who hathe ever tendered the well of his loyall
subjects more then his ouen profit, and hath been accustomed to
esteme lesse of the reward then of the deserver? Therefore
becaus (as sayeth the same Plinius)[44] '*princeps cum in uno
probavit amare se scire, vacat culpa, si alios minus amat*' – 'the prince
showing in love that he can love vertue, is without blame if he
beare less favour to others' – none should feare to lake
promotion by his maiestie, but such who have just occasion to
dispaire of their owen good deservings; or, being ill affected
towards the present state of the commonwealth, findeth no
fishing for them but in troubled watters, and wold cover the
malitious drifts of their private affections with the darknesse of a
confused governement.

But now to returne to our union. Sith God, Nature, necessitie
and commoditie appeareth to concurre at this time to the
furtherance of oure individuall embracement, and the hearts of

---

[42] Marginal note: '4'
[43] Marginal note: '*In Panegirico ad Trajanum*': *Panegyricus* 62
[44] Marginal note: 'ibid': *Panegyricus* 87

both the people seameth to be well disposed thereto, lett us now enquire which may be the forme thereof most commodious for both the nations and whereof the one and the other may receive contentement. Otherwise it is not lyking[45] to be of long continuance: for (as saide Plautius,[46] Consul of Rome in oppen Senat when they were advising of the maner and conditions of peace to be granted to the Privernates) it is certane '*neminem populum diutius ea conditione esse posse, cuius eum peniteat*' – 'that no people may long continue in that state wherewith they are discontented'. And therefore the Embassadour of the Privernates, being demanded by the Romans if they might be assured of a durable peace with them pardoning their rebellion, he answered no less wisly then freely '*si bonam dederitis et fidam et perpetuam: si malam, haud diuturnam*'[47] – 'if you give a good peace, it will be both trustie and perpetuall: if an evil, of no long continuance'. I have deduced at lenth before the different formes and fashons of uniting severall kingdoms both concerning the sovereignites and bodys of estate. Where I distinguished the confusion of the sovereignites in the person of one prince by succession and tyeing thereof to the lawfull discent of his race, from the annexation of one crowne with the other. Then sith it hath pleased God to confuse by lawfull succession the titles and rights of both the crownes of England and Scotland in his Majestie's person, and consequently tyed them to the lawfull discent of his race, either in the right or collaterall line, it wold seeme expedient, yea necessare, that by the advise and consent of the estats and parlements of both the nations the two crownes should be so annexed that they may remane in all times cumming individually joyned and affected to his Majestie's race – without any division amongst divers persons, either of his Majestie's owen ofspring or of distinct races pretending severall rights to either of those kingdoms. For unlesse this as an inviolable and fundamentall law be established in both the

---

[45] i.e., likely; underlined in later ink
[46] Marginal note: 'Livius lib. 8'. Livy, Bk. VIII, cap. 21, sec. 6. The actual quotation is: '*an credi posse ullum populum aut hominem denique in ea condicione cuius eum paeniteat diutius quam necesse sit mansurum?*'
[47] Livy, Bk. VIII, cap. 21, secs. 4-5

realmes, it may be lawfulle to the prince, righteous possessour
of both, for the time to devide them againe, at his pleasour:
either by testament amongst his soonnes, as did Alphonse the
VII Castille and Leon, Sanctius the III Castille, Aragon and
Navarre, Clovis the I in France the kingdoms of Paris, Orleans,
Soissons and Austrasie, and others which I remarked before:
or by geving any of them in dowrie with a daughter, as
now lately Philippe the II, King of Spaine hath geven Flanders
and Burgundie with his daughter Isabelle to Albert, Archduck
of Austrish. Yea, the prince leaving at his deceasse many
soonnes, they might willingly devide the kingdoms unannexed
by way of partage, whereof we have many examples in the two
first races of the crowne of France: wherein the often divisions
and reunions of the kingdoms of Paris, Orleans, Soissons,
Austrasie, Arles and Noyon made France during the two first
races of Merovie and Pepin the stage of infinit tragicall parricides, unnaturall attempts, firie factions, cruelle and perpetuall
warres betwene the father and his children, and amongst
brether themselfs – and travelled it continually with tempests of
seditions untill, at the changing of the line of Pepin and
usurpation of Hugh Capet, the law of annexation was sett
doune and ordeined to be kept in all times thereafter. Where by
the occasion of such disorders then being cutt away, the crowne
of France, wherein then was united the most part of all those
foresaide partiall kingdoms, remaneth undevided to this day,
and peaceably enjoyed by Hugh Capet his race. After this
maner was the dukdome of Lituanie joyned to the kingdome
of Poleland, and so resteth to this day annexed, thought the
two sovereignites were confused by election only, as we have
remarked in the owen place. By the lake of this annexation the
kingdome of Navarre, being once confused with the kingdome
of France as said is, was therefter separated therefro and
transferred to the Erle of Orleans, then to the Kings of Aragon,
then to the Erles of Foix, ever by mariage.

The two sovereignites being thus annexed so remane indissolubly with his Majestie's progenie and branches thereof. The
nixt consideration must be how to joyne the bodys of the
realmes. We have distinguished two sortes of uniting the bodys

of severall commonwealths: the one by subjection, the other by
incorporation. As to the subjecting of the one of those kingdomes to the other, their equalitie of power and love of naturall
libertie will not suffer it: no raison wold persuade it: nor no
conquest have enforced the one to receive law of the other. But
by the speciall providence of God, both ar devolved by lineall
succession in the person of one prince, native of the one but
naturall to both. Neither might either of those nations endure
servitude or slaverie, for avoyding whereof they have spent so
much blood and have ever chosen reither to losse their lyffs, then
their libertie – and for the which those two nations have warred
these many hundereth yeeres. Verely it is true that Plautius[48]
sayeth in favors of the Privernates: '*ibi pacem esse fidam, ubi
voluntarii pacati sunt: neque eo loco ubi servitutem esse velint fidem
sperandam esse*' – 'there to be a trustie peace where they ar
willingly peacified: neither to hoppe for faith, where servitude
is willed'. And therefore he concludeth, '*eos demum qui nihil
praeterquam de libertate cogitent dignos esse qui Romani fiant*'[49] –
'those who breatheth nothing but libertie to be worthie to be
citizens of Rome'. So must I justly afferme of two such free
nations '*unum populum unam Rempub[licam] fieri aequam esse*':
that it is reassonable 'that one people and one commonwealth be
made of both'. Resteth then the incorporation: which I defined
to be in uniformitie or equal communication of one name,
language, laws, relligion and habilites of two sortes of estate, and
naturalization in one common societie. Surely it were to be
wished there might be such a perfect incorporation of both the
estats in all those points, as was contracted betwene the Romans
and Sabins, Ciminenses, Crustamini and Antemnates – which
was easie to them, being then of so small a number as might
easely[50] inhabite one towne or citie, and the Romans having as
yeet established no certane forme of governement or laws. But
the like union is not appearandly possible to be effectuated by
those two so mightie and populous nations, which scarsly this so
great and large an iland may contene: none of them being either

[48] Marginal note: 'apud Livium lib. 8'. Livy, Bk. VIII, cap. 21, sec. 7
[49] *Ibid.*, sec. 9
[50] Corrected from original 'goodly'

willing or able to suffer such a great and hastie alteration of their different laws and customs, or any derogation or diminution of their severall privileges of estate without danger of sedition and miscontentment of the whole body of the estate, interessed by such innovations. And certanly in maters of policie, there is nothing more dangerous to entreat, more difficele to effectuat, more incertane of the issue, nor more fit to engender miscontentement, cheiffly in free and royall monarchies, then the innovation of their ancient laws, customes and forme of judicatorie[51] – or any change, which may import prejudice to their privileges of estate and libertie of parleament. Many princes for the attempt of such innovations have been cut of extraordanarly by their owen subiects. Agis King of Lacedemon, willing to restablish the ancient laws and civil discipline instituted by Lycurgus (which then by the tolerance and oversight of the magistrats were broght in non-use and dissuetude), after he had caused burne all his citizens' obligations and bonds of private debtes, wold have renewed the aequall partition of the lands according to the olde forme set doune by Lycurgus. But by this his souddane innovation he occasioned such a firie sedition in the commonwealth, whereby not only was he disappointed of his attempt but also lossed his liff with all his associats, and wraked the commonwealth. Neither was there any other cause of the often rebellions and seditions moved in England by the commons after the conquest of William the Conquerour, wherewith he and certane of his successors were much travelled, then the abrogation of St Edward's olde constitutions and establishing by force the Norman laws. Therefore August, knowing the danger of such alterations, in his speach to the Senat[52] adviseth them to keippe inviolably the laws once satled, neither to change any of them: becaus such as remane ever unaltered thought worse ar more profitable to the commonwealth then others induced by innovation thought better. So that, albeit the iniquitie of the ancient laws be evident, and appeare to be pernicious to the present estate of the commonwealth, yeet better it is to suffer them by time to go in

---

[51] Underlined in later ink
[52] Marginal note: 'apud dionem. lib. 52'

non-use and oblivion then by any souddaine innovation to abrogate the same. As did the Romans with certane their laws of the Twelve Tables, to the effect that the abrogation of some should not cause a contempt of the reste. For commonly the people is more easiely continued under the obedience and reverence of the laws wherewith they have been long time accustomed, then drawen to the embracement and observation of any new constitution, how profitable soever it be. Yeet were it expedient for the greater perfection of oure union that such laws and customes as were ordeined on each part, one directly against another, during the time of our division which may cause any let or hinderance of oure mutuall trafficke or entertene the memorie of our former grudges were now abrogated.[53]
Upon consideration of these raissons, at the union of Dauphinée, Languedocke and Litle Britaine to France, of Aragon and Leon to Castille in Spaine, of Lituanie to Poleland, the reservation of those things were specially conditioned and aggreed upon: and yeet inviolably keeped and enjoyed by them, as we have remarked heretofore. The kingdoms of Portugall and Naples, and Duckdome of Milan hath obtened of the kings of Spaine at their confusion with the crowne of Spaine so many great immunities and liberties both of estate and otherwise that there appeareth no incorporation or annexation thereof to have been maid with the realme of Castille. But as where there is no mixture of estate, there can be no long continuance of amitie and mutuall love: so for the perfecting of the union of annexed kingdoms, there is no necessitie to altere or change the laws, customes or privileges of estate, whereof the kingdoms have been in possesion by many ages. It may suffice to drawe them to an uniformitie of the other heades and points of incorporation. As it shall be easie in the union of those two kingdoms, for there is none or small difference in our language, humours and maners: so that by mutuall conversation and resort in a few yeeres, they may be drawen to a full uniformitie. But that most special point of this incorporation consisteth in the mutuall communication of the habilites and freedoms of denization or

[53] Abolition of 'hostile laws' was a part of the royal union programme: 1 & 2 Jas. I, c. 2

naturall subject, remarked in the first part of this discours: in such sorte that the Scotish be no stranger in England, nor the English in Scotland, but that whosoever be native borne of this iland and naturall subject to his Majestie may, according to the qualitie of his condition of birth or state be maid able to enjoy office, honor or benefice at the pleasour of his prince, and be parttaker of the common freedoms and privileges of naturaliz-ation in either of the kingdoms where he shall make residence: and that the mutuall commerce and entercourse of trafficke be enterteined amongst them, not as strangers but as naturall subjects of one lawfull sovereigne prince, members of one commonwealth and breathers of the common aire of one native soille. Which forme of incorporation, as it is sufficient, fittest and most expedient for the present state of both the kingdoms, so, being entertened with a mutuall love, a mingeling of the nobilitie of both the nations by reciproque mariages, and a due administration of justice without partialitie and corruption universally throughout all his Majeste's dominions, extinguish-ing the memorie and name of Bordours by drawing the people thereof on each side to a peaceable civilitie and labouring of their lands, may by progresse of time deface and burie all memorie of our former divisions, purge such distempered and contrarie humours or affections as have been engendered by so long a disjunction, make the knot of this our embracement indissoluble, and strenthen the loins of the monarchie of this iland – in such sorte that it, florishing by inward peace and wealth, may become encreassing in power more and more terrible to the foreine ennemie.

There is no dowt but the imposition of one name to both the nations, such as should be thoght meetest, by renewing the ancient appellation either of Albion or of Great Brittanie to the whole iland, and of Albanis or Brittons to both the people, might carrie much impression of amitie and be no small band to knit together the two peoples the faster. Yeet sith there have been certaine objections[54] (of greater curiositie then impor-tance) moved against this point, I think it shall be necessarie for

---

[54] The rest of the tract is grounded upon the reasons produced by the English House of Commons against the change in name. See *CJ*, i, 188

clearing thereof to answere to everie obiection severally after the same forme as they have been proponded. They ar reduced to foure severall heads or kinds: Mater of generalitie or common reason: Mater of estate inward, or mater of law: Mater of estate foreine, or mater of entercourse: and Mater of honor or reputation.

The first, grounded upon common reason, that neither of the nations ar forced to this innovation by any urgent necessitie, nor may be moved thereto by any evident utilitie or advancement to a better condition, is of small force: for thought this change of the name be not a mater of so great necessitie that without it the union might not be perfected, yeet should oure union reteine no small advancement and fastnesse thereby. For if in private societies and clannes the enjoying of one common name is a sufficient band of their friendship and mutuall leage both offensive and defensive, shall it not wourke the like effect in the union of two nighbour nations, of such conformitie of humours, maners and language? There was nothing more forceble for the union and leaging of the Atheniens, Lacedemoniens, Thebans, Boeotiens, Macedoniens and other Graeciens in their defense against Xerxes, then the common name and soille of Graecia.[55] What moved the Atheniens, Lacedemoniens and other Graecians to take upon them the mantenance of the Ioniens rebelling against Darius, but the respect of their common name of Graecians? For which cause also the Ioniens was [sic] persuaded by Themistocles to make defection from Xerxes at the battle of Salamine, which was a great occasion of that notable victorie obtened there by the Graecians against Xerxes. The leaged cities of Peloponesus under the common name and societie of Achaeans was so strenthened in their confederacies, and become so powerfull thereby, that they dowted not to aspire to the empire of whole Graecia, and was a great stay to the Roman conquest there. No man can deny but the common name of Quirites, geven to the whole people of both the nations Roman and Sabinien, carried much for the joyning of their hearts in a perfect amitie. Was not the Helvetian name common to the whole thretten cantons a great cause, and now is a speciall knott of their leages and

---

[55] A favourite argument. See Craig, *De Unione*, 395

confederaces, thought devided in religion? If the Ducke of Somerset, governour of England in the minoritie of King Edward the Sixt, and consell of England had not forseyne an evident utilitie to both the nations by the imposition of ane common name, should they have offered in their letter direct[56] to the nobilitie and estats of Scotland for the better uniting of the two nations by the mariage of their young king with Marie their only heire and Queene of Scotland to renew the ancient name of Brittanie to the whole iland – hopping thereby to induce both the nations to a mutuall love and tendernesse, and to extinguish the memorie if oure former jalosies, forgetting oure different names as propre markes of oure division, and continuall amulations? Shall this so profitable a change then so freely offered be now refused, when the cause and occasion is bettered to embrace the same?

Nixt, where they object that they find no president of the like change either at home or abroad. I give them there were none. Should they therefore stay to procure the well of both the nations – as if reason had no place, where experience laketh, or if the rule of governement should be squarred reither by examples then wisdome? Sith reason and wisdome hath decreed the renovation of the ancient name to be so profitable for festening the knot of oure union, thought there were no president thereof, yeet should it be embraced. And yeet there laketh no examples abroad of the change. The Romans and Sabins with others their associats, at the aggreement of their incorporation, appointed by their common consent that the whole people of all the nations incorporated should be called by the common name of Quirites, to the effect that by forgetting of their severall names, their former grudges might be extinguished. But perhapps this president is too ancient. We have in later memorie the common and ancient name of Spaine, renewed to the kingdoms first of Castille and Leon united by succession of bloud in Ferdinande the Thrid, soone to Alphonse the Nynt, King of Leon, and Berengaria heire of Castille: nixt to Arragon, joyned to those by the mariage of Ferdinande, King of Arragon with Isabelle, heire of Castille and Leon. And althought we find no speciall

---

[56] An example even more favoured by Scots writers. See Pont, above, p.29 and Russell, below, p.120

appointment or constitution to have been maid at the uniting of
those kingdoms, for renewing of the common name of Spaine,
yeet we may observe that since the union of Castille and Leon,
in the person of Ferdinande the Thrid, and of Arragon with
them in Ferdinande and Isabelle, their kings never to have used
in their stilles the particular titles of those kingdoms, but the
common name of Spaine.[57] And so they have ever been stilled
by foreiners, and the peoples of those contryes called by the
common name of Spainards, so that use and custome hath
wroght this change to them, without any confusion or harme to
their estats. Why then should we make any difficultie to
establish that by a law, which they have obtened by use and
custome – or fear that it should import no commoditie to us,
which experience have maid so profitable and acceptable to
them?

The thrie obiections of the second kind ar founded upon
estate inward or mater of law: where first it is objected that the
alteration of the name doth inevitably and infallably draw on an
erection of a new kingdome or estat, and dissolution and
extinguishing of the old – and that no explanation, limitation or
reservation can cleare or avoide that inconvenient but it will
be full of repugnancie, and ambiguitie, and subiect to much
varietie and danger of construction. In the first part of this
objection appeareth the objectors to sett downe the extinguishing of one kingdome and erection of a new, as a generall and
necessare consequent of the alteration of the name thereof,
which contineth a manifest and manifold errour. For if we shall
consider more neerowly the falling out of those changes both of
estate and name, we shall find the innovation of the name
whersoever it is altered by conquest, to ensue upon the change
of the kingdome or estate. For the conquerours of any land,
having first established their estate and new conquests or
monarches in the subdued contreys, thereafter to continue the
memorie of these victories, have commonly been accustomed
to impose thereto a new appellation framed after their owen or
their people's name. So Gallia was called France after the

---

[57] Certain English writers were adamant that the 'Kings of Spain' *did* retain the
particular titles. See Savile, below, Chapters 12-13

conquest thereof maid by the Frenshmen under Pharamond. So Insubria was called Longobardie, after the establishing of the monarchie of the Longobards therein; and, to pass over other infinit examples abroad, received not this iland the denomination from Albion, after his conquest maid thereof, and nixt from Brutus after it was subdued by him, and last of England, by a speciall edict and constitution of Egbert King of the West Saxons, after he had brought under his subjection the remanent kingdoms of the Saxons and Angles with Wales and Cornuale, and so established one monarchie of the all? Neither is the alteration of the name a necessare consequent of a new conquest or change of estate: for we may reade of many estats changed and contryes new conquered by the Assiriens, Persians, Macedoniens, Parthiens, Romans and other conquerours' nations without any alteration or innovation of their ancient name. Now if by the erection of a new kingdome we shall understand the change of any estate which before was no kingdome into a royall monarchie, we shall find many both new erected kingdoms which have suffered no alteration of their ancient name – as Boheme, Hungarie, Dennemarke, Poleland, Portugall and others – as also many estats to have changed their name without any such erection of a new kingdome, being royal monarches als well before as after their name altered. But if by the erection of a new kingdome and extinguishing of the old be meaned the new conquest of any kingdome by a foreine force, or usurpation of the sovereignitie and crowne thereof by a new race of princes, then as there hath been many new conquests in England, by the Dannes and Normans, in Spaine and Italie by the Goths and Vandals, and many usurpations in France by Pepin and Hugh Capet and in other kingdoms maid without any change of their names: so we shall find sometime their names innovated without any new conquest or usurpation. So Spaine, being called before Iberia, altered the name and was called Spania or Hispania from Pan or Hispan, nepuew to Hercules, without any erection of it in a new kingdome – for it was a kingdome long before. Neither did Hispan conquere or usurpe it, but succeded therein to his father Hispalis, soone to Hercules. Portugall likwise was first named Lusitania, from the solemnizing of Bacchus' feasts at the river of Anas rynning through the middest of that contrey, by Lusus, soonne to Bacchus, and Lysas his compagnone, whence it was indifferently called Lusitania or Lysitania. And nixt it obteined the name of Portugall, from the arrivel of the Galles at Portus, a citie in Galecia, with the Erle of Loraine – who by mariage of Taresia, naturall daughter to Alphonse the First, King of Castille, received that part of Galecia in dowrie without any either erection or usurpation of a new kingdome or estate. And althought the alteration of the name should inferre a new conquest or usurpation by a new race of princes, yeet this new conquest or usurpation can no wayes be called a new erected kingdome. For then should England have been erected in a new kingdome so often as it hath been conquered by Albion, Brutus, the Saxons, Dannes and Normans: and the monarchie of France, so often newly erected as the sovereignitie thereof hath been usurped by the divers races of Pepin and Hugh Capet: and the Roman Empire so often extinguished and renewed as it was acquired and possessed by Emperours of different races and nations – as be Traian a Spainarde, Caracalla a Galle, Heliogabile a Sirien, Philippe an Arabe, Totila a Gothe, Constantine a Brittane and such others. Then should we also recone the age and enduring of estats and kingdoms, not by their continuing under one forme of governement (as reason were) but by the antiquitie of the race of the princes and governours thereof, which ar manifest errours in civil philosophie. Attour[58] the name of Great Brittanie is no new name but old and much renowned amongst the ancient Grecians and Latins for the common denomination of the whole iland. Yea, the whole ilands of this Westerne ocean, now so happily reduced under his maieste's monarchie, was [sic] stilled *Brittaniae* or *Britannicae Insulae* – so that the renewing thereof can cause no innovation of the estate, nor draw on any such extinguishing or erection of a new kingdome. Therefore there is no neede of any exprimation, limitation or reservation to cleare or awoide that inconvenient which is not to ensue.

The second obiection grounded upon mater of law, contineth

---

[58] i.e., 'Moreover' or 'Besides'

an enumeration of certane speciall confusions, incongruities and mischieffs, that it is alleaged will fall out presently by the innovation of the name: in the summoning of parleaments and the recital of acts of parleament: in the seales of the kingdome: in the great offices of the kingdome:[59] in the laws, customes, liberties and privileges of the kingdome: in the residence and halding of such courts as follow the king's person: in the severall and reciproque oathes of allegiance, homage and obedience made and renewed from time to time by the subjects, and of maintenance and justice due by his Majestie at his coronation – all which acts, instruments and formes of pollicie and governement, with a multitude of other formes of records, writts, pleadings and instruments of a meaner nature runne now in the name of England, and upon the change would be drawn into incertaintie and question. No: for since some of those points ar nothing ells then necessare circumstances of the habilites and privileges of estate and forme of judicatorie – which, our union established after the imperfecter forme of incorporation as saide is, shall receive no alteration – no more shall those their circumstances be anywayes drawen in question by imposing a common name to both the nations. For each realme retening their owen parleaments, offices of estate, laws, customes and forme of judicatorie, as they may notwithstanding of our union in maner heretofore set downe, they shall also retene their owen severall formes in summoning of parleaments and recitals of acts of parleament, in the function of the great offices of the king-domes, of laws, customes, libertes and privileges of estate, whereto the renewing of the common name can impert no prejudice – no more than the common name of France prejudgeth any wayes the different formes of the privileges and habilities of estate, laws, customes and forme of judicatorie reserved to the contryes of Languedock, Dauphinee and Litle Brittanie, or the common name of Spaine hath caused any confusion of such liberties and formes in the united kingdomes of Castille, Arragon, Leon, Catalanie and Valence. As concerning the other thrie heads (of the seals of the kingdomes: of the residence and halding of such courts as follow the king's

[59] This clause was inserted later, in the same hand

person: and of the reciproque oathes to be made at the prince's coronation), as they ar prerogatives tyed to the sovereignitie, so must they be reserved or altered at the prince's pleasour. Yea, since the seals beare the impression of the prince's armes, as propre markes of his authoritie, they must be enlarged by the encreasse of his monarchie, and addition of any new sovereignitie, that the seals may represent the kingdoms confused and annexed in the person of one prince. Neither should this carrie any confusion or incongruitie but reither a more certaine argument of oure union, the seals bearing the inscription of our common name and impression of the united armes, as the enseignes of oure union. And certanly it is to be mervelled, what should have moved our objectors so to travelle to eshew the reformation of the seals – which ar alreddie altered,[60] as likwise the stamp of the new coine by his Majeste's authoritie and advice of his consell. Now what is their feare, that such courts as follow the king's person by the generalitie in name may be held in Scotland, but a confession of their will and desyre to borne and tye his Majeste's and successors' residence perpetually within England – and to berive them of their free resorting to what part of their dominions they shall think good to benefit with their presence? And albeit such courts should be held in Scotland, what inconvenient wold ensue thereupon more then when the kings of England resorted to their dominions in France? Should the parties resorting to the courts be prejudged or damnified by the place? as if such currant and ambolatorie courts either were tyed to the territorie of England, and not to the person of the prince, whereever he maketh residence: or that the prince might not dispense with the place where they might be held. Yea, they aught to accompt it no small commoditie for the greater assurance of our union, that by the generalitie in name this their jalosie of halding such courts or of the prince's sometimes resorting and residence in Scotland were taken away. As concerning the mutuall oathes due at the prince's coronation, I

---

[60] For an excellent example of the seal, bearing the arms of England, Ireland and Scotland on the Reverse, those of Cadwallader (last king of the Britons) and Edward the Confessor (last undisputed king of the English) on the Obverse, see B.L., Egerton Charter 370.

cannot understand what confusion or inconvenience may fall out therein by the common name; for sith it is necessare that as the sovereignties of both the kingdomes, by their confusion in the person of one prince ar now one, so the coronation (which in substance is nothing ells but the sacring and anoynting of the sovereigne prince) be also one for both. Shall it not be more expedient that the prince's voluntarie oathe of maintenance and administration of justice, made at his anoynting, and the oathes of his nobilitie there present of their alleagence, homage and obedience be made at one time under one common and generall name, then at severall times under severall names? For althought the Christian princes, knowing how God caused anoynte by his heigh priests and prophettes the kings of Israell in singulare token of his protexion, and of their privilege of honor and preheminence over the people, have followed the like example and added thereto in the solemnitie of their coronation certane ceremonies of greater majestie than necessitie (with a princely promisse to discharge honorably and truly those points of dewtie which the law of God and nature requireth of them, [and] hath also been accustomed to receive the alleagance and homage of their subjects by the oathes of the cleargie and nobilitie, and generall applause of the people there present); yeet since the whole substance of this action consisteth only in the prince's sacring and anoynting, and that ther is no necessitie to conveine his whole subjects thereto, who by his lawfull succession ar naturally obliged to him in their alleagance and obedience, there can ensue no inconvenient, howsoever or wheresoever either it shall please the prince, or necessitie for the time shall enforce his coronation to be solemnized. And as he is one prince to all his subjects, so may he reteine one anoynting and one crowne for all his dominions – as likewise such of the cleargie, nobilitie and others present for the time may represente the due submission and homage of the whole subjects.

The thrid obiection of this kind proponeth a possibilitie of the alteration (so they stille it) of the crowne of England to the line of Scotland, in case his Majeste's line should determine: supposing it to be a new erected kingdome by the change of the name (which we have shewen to be an errour) and that it must go in the nature of purchase to the nixt heire of his Majestie's father side. By the which their too curious or reither malitious forecast they wold appeare to provide beyond probabilitie, and diffide of God's providence – who hath blisshed his Majestie with many livelike children and a goodly appearance of a plentifull succession.

And althought it should please God to suffer his Majestie's right line by progresse of time to be determined, yeet I must answere to their objection that which Marttine, King of Arragon, laking children, voted in favors of Ferdinande then tutor of Castille (his sister soone) whilst the question of his succession was debatted in consell: 'Sicut intercisa' (those ar his words reported by Mariana)[61] 'fontis vena atque alio dirivata, rivi priores omnes, quibus antea deducebatur exarestunt, neque aqua recurrit in canalem pristinum, nisi irrigatis completisque omnibus posterioribus aut rivis aut areis : Ita progenies eris quo ni servet a successione contigit dimoveri, excludatur necesse est in perpetuum neque adeat hereditatem nisi sublata alterius successoris progenie: Nam cum res sint in iure et mancipio ultimi possessoris, non autem superiorum quorum ius est in alios transfusum ; ut quisque ei maxime coniunctus erit, ita optimo iure nitetur sibique ius succedendi vendicabit'. 'Like as a veine of a fontaine being cutt of and drawen from the former streames, the old channels where it did runne before drieth up. Neither returneth the watter therto agane untill the new channels and ponds whereto it is drawen be filled. So is it necessare that his progenie who is once removed and put bake from the succession, be perpetually secluded therefro; for since the title and right is now established in the person of the latest possessor, and no wayes apperteneth to his predicessoris, whose right is transferred to others (as any shall be neerest of bloud to him) so shall his title be best, and shall justly attaine the right of succession' – for the which reason the succession of the crowne of Arragon was adiudged to the same Ferdinande. And by what right doeth his Majestie now justly succeid to the crowne of England, but as neerest of bloud to the late deceassed Queene, last lawfull possessor thereof, proceding fromg [sic] King Henry the VII as the latest stock of this race; so that sith the other collaterals of the further discent of this race are

[61] Marginal note: 'Lib. 19, cap 20. Hist. Hisp.'

now secluded by his Majestie's succession, so the title of the crowne can never returne to them so long as any of his Highnesse' race either lineall or collaterall endureth. Therefore when so should fall out that the crowne of England were drawen to the line of Scotland, this wold be no alienation thereof from the just pretender but a lawfull continuing thereof in his Majestie's stemme and race whometo it wold justly appertene. Neither should the generallitie or commontie in name be the cause hereof, as is alleged, but the right of the crowne now established in his Majeste's person, and by him acquired to his whole race. Which law have place not only in new purchased (as is meaned in the objection) but also in old possessed kingdomes cumming by succession and propinquitie of bloud.

The obiections of the thrid nature, touching estate foreine and mater of entercourse, ar of none or small importance. Whereof the first shall draw no inconvenient; for if oure union take effect by the mutuall communication of all habilities and freedoms of naturalization (as it must do if any union be) were it not very reasonable that the leages, treateses and forreine freedoms of trade and trafficke, now peculiar to either, be made then common to both the peoples, thought their name were not one? Or should they have any freedome of foreine trade and trafficke which we should not enjoy, by whom they have been made able to traffick freely with foreiners? And since amongst confederat nations, leages and bands contracted by either with foreiners ar mad common to the whole confederats, when they please to accept thereof, how much more should peoples united under one lawfull sovereigne prince enjoy the like benefit? Neither shall the one empare the profit or surety of the other; but the strenth and wealth of both shall encreasse thereby, and the leaged foreiner, assured of both, shall be more willing to entreat and enterteine societie with both, and shall be more affraied to breake to both then to the one. Attour the King's Majestie, when it shall please him to renew such leages and treatesses with foreiners, may of his owen power and authoritie comprehend therein all his naturall subjects without any just occasion of offence to any person – yea, under severall names. So that the renewing thereof under a common and generall name shall not only not make those contracts and freedoms subject to any quarrell and cavillation, but reither make them the more assured and profitable to all his Majeste's subjects.

The second obiection to this nature, concerning the king's precedencie of place and honor before other Christian kings, is grounded upon an erroneous principle: for as we have declared heretofore, the imposition or renewing of a common name shall no wayes extinguish the antiquitie of his royall monarchie, which should be reconed from the first fondation of the monarchie and uninterrupted continuance thereof, and not from the innovation of the name or alteration of the race of the sovereigne prince. Neither maketh the union of two ancient kingdoms on new, but one more powerfull: otherwise the kingdoms of France and Spaine[62] should have been often renewed, since the first institution of their monarchie: France by the often reunion of the kingdoms of Paris, Orleans, Soissons and Austrasie, Spaine by the often reunion of the kingdoms of Castille, Arragon, Navarre, Leon, Valence and Portugall.

The thrid obiection is that the glorie and good acceptation of the English name and nation will be in foreine parts obscured. I wish it were such as they do esteme of it, then should they not feare that it might be obscured. Neither can the speciall names, glorie and heroicall facts and vertues of either the nations be either extinguished or darkened so long as the memorie of man may be continued by histories: and the generall name shall serve as a perpetuall marke and argument of the peaceable union of two so ancient, mightie and warlike nations, the like whereof have not fallen out in many ages before.

The last sorte of those obiections concerneth certane points of honor and reputation, wherein they think themselfs interessed – but so frivolous that they merite not to be respected in a mater of such weight. Is their name more deir to them then ours to us, or the names of England and Scotland more famous then it of Great Brittanie? Or should they preferr their name, which have been so often altered at the pleasour of their conquerours, to the furtherance of our perpetuall amitie and union? The

----

[62] 'and Spaine' inserted later in the same hand

Romans and Sabins were not this waye enchanted with the love of their severall names, or such superstitious worshippers thereof (thought very jalous of their honor) that they wold have preferred them to the peace and wellfare of their common-wealth. Now if any man disinherite his owen daughters, he doeth it not so much to continue his name then to keipe his housse and estate in the owen integritie, which otherwise wold be dismembered and rent in parcelles by the mariages of his daughters; and if he should respect the only continuing of his name, it were no reason that the commonwealth and encrease of a great monarchie were guided by the example of a private man's pleasure.

Now in vaine feare thay[63] that the contracted name of Albion, or Great Brittanie will bring in oblivion the names of England and Scotland: so long as the memorie of the two nations may be remembered by the historie, no more then the names of Athens, Lacedemon, Thebe and others renowned commonwealths of Grecia, by the common name of Grycia. And albeit they were buried in oblivion, yeet should we lose nothing but the markes of our former jalosies, and entisments of renewing the memorie thereof.

As to the degree of prioritie acclamed in the stille, it carrieth more ambition then reason; for the kingdom of Scotland is no lesse ancient, and much more free of foreine conquests then England. And since his Majestie having by himself, and his noble ancestours, possessed Scotland these two thowsand yeeres ago, hath now of late acquired the crowne of England by succession, England wold appeare to be accessorie to Scotland, and so to deserve the second place only in his Majestie's stille. Therefore thought it have pleased his Majestie to gratifie them at his entree there with this shaddow of honor, and the Scotish have been so modest as to yeeld to them such ceremonies – yeet should they not value it so much, that it may breade any stay or let to the perfection of our union.

Last, where it is thoght that the change of the name will be harsh in the populare opinion and unpleasing to the contrey. Albeit it may appeare so in the beginning, in the eares of some

[63] i.e., 'thay feare'

ill-affected myndes, yeet time and use shall make it pleasing and acceptable; and whither it be found expedient to renew the common name of Albion or of Great Brittanie, the memorie of the antiquitie of either name shall carrie the owen recommendation of honor, with a representation of the greatnesse of this monarchie, whereby it may become more familiar and plausible to the people.

Thus farre then have I endevored myself to cleare this mater of the causes, necessitie, forme and letts of the union of those kingdoms: wishing such an happy issue and effectuating thereof as may serve for a full contentment to his Majestie, a firme and long continuance with ane honorable encreasse of this monarchie to his Majestie's progenie, and a further heapping of those blissings which it hath pleased God of His infinit mercy to bestow upon both the nations in his Majeste's person.   AMEN.

A TREATISE OF THE HAPPIE AND BLISSED UNIOUN

by JOHN RUSSELL

A TREATISE OF THE HAPPIE AND BLISSED UNIOUN
betuixt the tua ancienne realmes of Scotland and Ingland,[1] eftir thair lang trubles, thairby establisching perpetuall peace to the posteriteis of baith the nationes, presentlie undir the gratious monarchie and impyir of our dread soverane, King James the Sixt of Scotland, First of Ingland, France and Ireland.

The contentis of this treatise:
First, thair is sett doun ane disputatioun of the negative pairt of this unioun, meantienit be the refractaris thairto, with the argumentis adducit be thame for confirmatioun thairof.
In the secound place, ane disputatioun of the affirmative pairt, with the argumentis lykuyis competent thairto.
The thrid pairt conteines the decisioun of the questioun, embracing the affirmative, reiecting the negative, with ane refutatioun of the argumentis proponit for confirmatioun of the said negative.
Ferdlie, certane articles ar proponit, contiening the forme and securitie of the unioun, as be gude reassoun it sould proceid.[2]

TO HIS GRATIOUS SOVERANE, THE KING
HIS MAIST EXCELLENT MAJESTIE

It will pleis your Majestie, the mater of this unioun intendit, betuixt the tua imperiall crounes of Scotland and Ingland,

[1] London MS: 'Great Britane'. This suggests that the London MS was submitted after James's proclamation of October 1604 changing the royal style
[2] London MS then follows on : 'Last, the description of the office of ane Christiane Prince, in the administration of his Imperiall crounes'

being daylie in all mennis mouthes, all your Majesteis gude
subiectis alreddy making congratulatioun for the happie concord of Great Britanie, now undir the obedience of ane king, yit
the principall subiect consisting in ane generall notioun, not
explicat (*tanquam in idaea Platonis*). This being ane uorthie
purpose, requyring ane politik disputatioun, offering ane spatious feild, bot easie to be effectuat, to your Majesteis honor and
contentment, following the counsall and determinatioun of
your Majesteis maist noble antecessoris, alreddy declairit herein
(as heireftir sal be deducit) quhilk your Majestie will evir have
in reverence. I have thairfoir presumit in baldnes, for that dew
affectioun I have to your Majesteis service, (albeit unuorthie and
not miet for sic ane grave subject, requyring the judgement and
opinioun of the maist learnit), to assay the handling of this
questioun, now putt in contraversie amangis your Hienes' subjectis: qhidder giff this unioun be necessar and profitable, to the
gude and florisching estait of baith the nationes or not? I will not
proceid be any langsome discourss, bot trussing up the mater sall
daill thairin be compendious narratioun, *non in hypothesi sed in
thesi*, concluding in end with ane trew resolutioun. This being
the subject, to qhome sould this uark be sua properlie dedicat as
to your Heines, having sua painefullie and cairfully utterit all
princelie doing, tending to the gude accomplischment thairof.
Bot as it is ane uorthie and uaichtie subject, sua uald it be uyselie
considerit, having mekle mair *in recessu quam in fronte*. Heirfoir,
sir, in humilitie, I will crave your Majesteis patrocinie in this my
labour, to vindicat me from all thais that be indirect dailing
uald misconstruct my honest meaning. As I have that honor to
be your Majesteis maist humble subject, borne in this your
Grace's native soill of Scotland, I think nane ueill-affectit can
iustlie find fault with me, that as I from my hairt, and all gude
men uald uiss this purpose (tending as appeiris to the weill of
baith the nationes) to proceid. On the wther pairt it may be but
ony prejudice to the ancienne estait, lauis and liberteis of this
your Hienes' first and auldest impyir, ather in religioun or
justice – quhilk I may assure myselff is your Majesteis awin
resolutioun. Trew it is, your Majestie most niedis love all your
gude subjectis, bot be gude ressone the first pairt of your
affectioun sould inclyne touardis ws, your Majesteis first and

auldest subjectis. Lett that glorie euir remaine uith ws and our posteriteis, howsoevir we be presentlie destitute of your Majesteis presence (quhilk we hoip your Grace will remeid). Yit that your Majesteis nativitie ues heir! Out of this heaven your Majestie ressavit your first sicht. In this soill your Grace sett your first footstep; qha can doubt bot this naturallie man bind your Heines to ws – notwithstanding the accessioun of ane greater kingdome, be richt and discent of your Majesteis maist noble blood? Lett it be to your Majesteis great advancement bot nauyis to our preiudice. And seing your Majestie is common prince to baith the nationes, Ingland man not acclame your Majestie as peculiar, and sua to become foryetfull of ws: being evir reddy to have bestouit our lyfes in meantinance of your Majesteis richt giff this last successioun, with uniforme consent, had not bein peciablie establischit. In end, lett nevir that uorthie speach of the poett be out of your Grace's maist noble mynd: ' *nescio qua natale solum dulcedine, cunctos afficit: immemores nec sinit esse sui* '.[3] Heir I will subsist, praying God to grant to your Majestie lang and happie governement, in the administratioun of all your imperiall crounes: to be rather superiour, nor equall, to the lait raigne of gude Quene Elizabeth of blissed memorie, to incress your Majestie in uisdome, knawledge and trew godlienes, to give your Majestie victorie againes all that uald attempt againes your sacred persoun; to accomplisch the uark alreddy begune in your Majestie, for restoring of the treuth, banising out of your Heines' realmes of all tyranie, haeresi and Romisch idolatrie, uith lang lyfe and hapie success in all your Majesteis adois.

Your Majesteis maist humble and affectionat subiect,

Jo. Russell.

Ane treatise of the happie and blissed unioun, betuixt the tua ancienne realmes of Scotland and Ingland, eftir thair long trubles, thairby establisching perpetuall peace to the posteriteis of baith the natiounes, presentlie undir the gratious monarchie and impyir of our dread soverane King James the Sixt of Scotland, First of Ingland, France and Ireland.

[3] Ovid, *Ex Ponto*, I, 3.35

Amangis the great and infinit benifittis bestouit heirtofoir be the providence of the eternall God upon the ile of Britanie, this last uithout question (as maist heich and singular) is uorthie to be recommendit to all posteriteis: that in the fulnes of tyme, tua natiounes, lyand in ane continent, althocht not far different in religioun, language, maneris, constitutioun of bodies, yit thir many ages bypast contineuing in ane hatrent irreconciliable, greatumlie afflictit be civill and intestine uearis, tending to na les than the perpetuall overthraw, desolatioun and subversioun of baith the kingdomes, mair blood spent in thair querrellis than evir be the Romanes in all their conquestis, at last ar brocht undir the prosperous monarchie and happie obedience of ane soverane monarch, our sacred and royall king send down from Heaven with ane triumphant majestie, bringand uith him peace, joy and tranquillitie to this ile forevir. The lyik blissing ues nevir hard nor sein in the heill universe. As it is thairfoir of great valour, sua aucht it not onely to be glaidlie embracit bot chearfully meantienit and confirmit: the saidis natiounes, not onely unitit in thair continent, bot in ane maist gratious and soverane lord and king, bearing reull and dominioun over thame, sua that thair restis na farder bot the cheiff unioun betuixt the inhabitantis to be unitit in heartis and myndis forevir, uith ane mutuall affectioun of all gude offices, to the perpetuall comfort of thame and thair posteriteis.

The ancienne poettis[4] of auld, as is also mentionat in the prophecie of Daniell, setting doun the periode of the uarld, maid calculatioun of four ages, resembling the monarcheis of the Babylonianes, Persianes, Gracianes and Romanes – the first of gold, the secound of sylver, the thrid of brass, the fourt of iron. Qhairby it hes bein aluyis estiemit that we, qha ar fallin in the last age, ar fallen in the decadence of the uarld; yit it may be justlie said to the inhabitantis of this ile, that we ar establischit in ane goldin age, all the properteis thairof cleirly schyning amangis ws.

Ane godlie prince reuling, qhais verteu, valour, royall qualiteis, qhais religioun, godlienes and unspeakable gudnes na

---

[4] Marginal note: 'Ovid. lib. metamorth [sic]. Daniel c. 2; v. 37'. For Ovid's 'Metamorphoses' see the translation by R. Humphries (London, 1957), pp.5-7

toung is hable sufficientlie to espres, the haill oratoris Greik and
Latine (Cicero, Demosthenes, Aeschines, althocht conjoynit in
ane bodie) could not be of sufficient skill to recommend the
samyn to the posteritie. Qhais praiss is aeternall, sealit up in the
heavenis, schyning abroad in all the corneris of the earth, the
rair pearle of Europe, first learnit prince in the uarld, patrone
and Maecenas to all learnit, verteuous and gude men, the lyik
qhairof hes not bein sein thir many ages bypast, not inferior to
Julius Caesar or Alexander the Great, yea the best that evir ues of
the Romane Impyir, or that evir reulit thir many yeiris bypast
over people or natioun: qhom God preserve with lang and
happie dayes, and prosperous success in all his adois. In his
persoun hes not onely cariit ane happie governement, in sic sort
that his praiss cannot be sufficientlie soundit, bot thairuith ritch
treasour to baith the natiounes of all sort of blissings – trew
religioun, justice, peace, ritches, force, joy, tranquillitie outward and inward. Na natioun enjoyis the lyik benifit, nor yit is
lyklie to enjoy heireftir.[5]

The ancienne chronographeris hes observit that about the
yeir of God 180 Britanie ues the first place of the uarld quhilk
publictlie ressavit the faith of Christ (to the great honor of this
ile): for Lucius, the first[6] King of Great Britanie, predicessor and
foreronner to his Majestie, in thais dayes deposit the preistis of
the gentillis, and substitut in thair places bischopis and Christiane pastoris. He banischit gentilisme out of his contrey, quhilk
happinit not in any pairt unto the tyme of Constantine the
Great. Tertulliane and Origene qha lievit about this same tyme
testifeis that the countreyis of Britanie, being inaccessible for the
Romanes, uar subject to Chryst, the bischopis of this ile uar at
the Counsall of Nice. The said Lucius become sua zealous to the
propagatioun of the treuth, and great enemie to idolatrie, and
uorschip of creatures of visible formes, that of ane king, (as the
historie makis mentioun) he become ane preacher: and in the
persecutioun of the Christianes undir Diocletiane and Maxen-

---

[5] London MS: 'And sua it cannot be justlie denyit, bot that this ile enjoyis the first
blissing, quhilk is ane gude and godlie prince reuling over his people. In lyik maner the
ile itselff enjoyes ane maist soverane blissing, seing'
[6] Marginal note: 'Plat. in vit. Thelesph' [sic]

tius, maid this kingdome as ane refuge to the afflictit Christianes
– as it has bein thir fourtie yeiris bygane in this age, to the lait
afflictit Christianes of all our nichtbour countreyis. The same
favor of God[7] touardis this ile contineuit in the second periode
of Christianisme, quhilk begane uith the maist happie impyir of
Constantius Chlorus, qha tuik to his uyfe Helene, borne in this
ile, of qhome heireftir we sall mak mentioun. He decessit at
York eftir he had instituted Constantine the Great his son,
quhilk wes na small grace of God pourit wpon this ile – for as
undir Lucius, Britanie ues the first pairt that banischit pagane
idolatrie. In lyk maner God raysit up of the same ile Constantine
the Great, qha expellit the same Romane idolatrie furth of all
the uther provinces of the habitable uarld.

Will any gude subject in this haill ile putt questioun, bot the
aeternall God hes raysit his Majestie in this age to be the vive
image of Lucius and Constantine, and to be successor to his
predecessoris and contreymen, to banisch paganisme and idolatrie furth of this impyir, thairby richteouslie to posses his auin
professit tytle to be Protector and Defender of the Faith. I say
farder: as God be the mariage of King Henry the Sevint uith
Quene Elizabeth his uyfe maid the unioun of the houses of York
and Lancaster, and richt sua be the mariage of King James the
Fourt with Quene Margaret eldest dochter to the said King
Henry the Sevint, and be the lineall discent of his Majesteis
blood furth of that mariage, hes maid the happie conjunctioun
of thir tua imperiall crounes of Scotland and Ingland, prosperouslie succieding uithin the space of ane hundreth yeiris.
Certanelie giff we be gude subjectis, fearing God, sall we not
hoip the same God sall imploy his Majestie to the unitie of the
Christiane and universall kirk, and to abolisch idolatrie forevir,
quhilk in ane maner hes suellowit up and devorit the trew kirk.
Without doubt, lett the enemies conspyir as they pleis, thair is na
questioun.

May not all men consider and cleirlie sie that his Majestie is
heichlie belovit of God, qha not onely hes indeuit him uith sic
royall qualiteis, specially of Christiane religioun, bot hes had ane
speciall protectioun of his persoun fra his nativitie, preserving

---

[7] Marginal note: 'Euseb. in vita. Constantin'

him againes all his enemeis and now establisching him peciablie in his auin richt and sceptor of Ingland, in the auin tyme, with ane universall congratulatioun of his haill people, sua that to his richt, the uniforme consent, sentence and sueit harmonie of his people dois concure. He is sett doun in his auin chair uithout armis or blood. Qha could evir have luikit for this, speciallie amangis people standing sua lang at intestine uearis? Qha dois reid in the annallis of uther natiounes, evir the lyik to have come to pas? Many kingis and princes baith in this age and heirtofoir hes been authorisit uith sufficient richt and title to thair impyir, and yit lang stayit and debarrit thairfra. Certanelie thair is nathing doun in this be chance, fortune, or humaine pouer and counsall, bot immediatlie be the great providence of God: using that happie and blissed Quene Elizabeth of uorthie memorie (qha hes bein ane uorthie mother to his Heines) to be the instrument to mak this mater sua suietlie to end – qha ues evir accompaniet uith ane great felicitie in all hir adois, for God drew hir first fra ane prison to ane kingdome, maid hir to raigne fourty and fyve yeiris, and to have discoverit in hir favoris above twenty machinatiounes intendit againes hir persoun and estait, to lieve threscoir and ten yeiris, and in hir last gasp to utter sic uisdome, sua profitablie and effectuallie persuading hir subjectis to acknauledge and embrace his Majestie, qhom scho knew to be the laufull and undoubtit air of Ingland, France and Ireland, be richt of consanguinitie and laufull successioun. Sould evir this depairt out of his Grace's mynd? The Lord mak his Majestie thankfull for his great benefittis, and for this honor, to the quhilk he is sua heichlie advancit, the greater qhairof na mortall man could evir have cravit.[8] This may prove sufficientlie that the ile of Britanie is fallin undir ane golden age.

This being the present estait of thir tua realmes, I think thair is nane of the induellaris thairof, of qhatsumevir estait, qualitie or conditioun, publict or privat, noble or popular, ecclesiastique or temporall, fearing God, loving his prince and native soill, tendering his auin standing, uielfair or posteritie, bot as of deutie he aucht to give thankis and infinit praise to his God. For this sua excellent and unexspectat benifit, resolvit in hairt and

---

[8] 'Sould evir this depairt . . . evir have cravit' deleted in London MS

mynd to be thankfull thairfor: sua, on the uther pairt, sould be cairfull to sie this happie unioun and conjunctioun of tua sua lang different kingdomes, perpetuallie establischit, now alreddy unitit in ane bodie and imperiall croune, to be farder knitt uith all bandis requisit – conformity of religioun, sympathie of myndis, conjunctioun in blood and mariage, mutuall in traffique, commerce and negotiatioun. And being so inteirlie joynit togidder, we neid not to feir any forrane force, bot be the contrair sal be great terror to our enemies, and sall utter daylie mutuall gude offices to the uiell of baith the natiounes, peace meantienit, and not habill to be disturbit be any that uald pretend in the contrair.

Notuithstanding qhairof, it fallis furth of this as of all gude thingis. Thair ues nevir anything sua trew, sua perfyit, sua sinceir, sua gude, of qhatsumevir great valour or consequence, bot be the variable dispositioun of the sprittis of men may be drauin in contraversie. Some ar not eschamit to contravert upon principles, and to dispute againes the principles of all sciences, againes that notable axiome, ' Contra negantem principia non est disputandum'. Wtheris (as atheists, Jeuis, Turkis, papistis, infidelis, Mahumetanes) ar not eschamit to dispute againes God himselff, the Auld and New Testament, and againes the principles of religioun and nature – and in ane uord, thair ues nevir any gude uark, sua uiell interprysit, bot oftentymes it is disturbit be the oppositioun of evill disposit persones, cariit auay ather uith hiech malice or foolisch ignorance (the tua great enemies of treuth and veritie). Quhilk also appeiris in this notable uark of the unioun, painefully sett doun be his Majestie. Qhairin as all gude men uiell affectit uald uiss from thair hairtis the same to be effectuat, thair ceasis not utheris be curiositie to move questioun, entir in dispute, not sua mekle for tryell of the treuth as cariit auay with their auin opiniones.

I doe not deny bot this unioun is ane uaichtie subject, craving ane great forsicht and deliberatioun, disputable wpon baith syidis, als uiell the negative as affirmative pairt thairof, besyidis the cautellis and provisiones, quhilkis man be annexit in caice the affirmative prevaill, quhilk man not be in the handis of the common sort, bot committit to men of greatest learning, experience and knauledge, best aquentit with the lauis, policie and effairis not onely of the saidis tua natiounes, bot with the estait and unioun of forrane countreyis. As also it is certane, giff any man uald inlarge his pen, this mater offeris ane spatious and ample field of disputation; yit being uiell considerit, and be ane gude methode redactit to ane schort overture and abrigement, satisfieing all uiell affectit, (as in sic ane publict earand, to stand to the posteritie, all craves uith ressoun to be satisfiet) all that apperteinis to the handling of this questioun (reservand the opinioun of the mair learnit) is reduceable to thre principall and substantiall poyntis, undir the quhilkis the particularis lurking thairin may be easiely espyit.

Thir thre questiounes, according to the doctrine of the phylosophes and logicianes, ar *'An sit, Quid sit, et Quale sit'*. First, qhidder it is expedient for the gude and florisching estait of baith the realmes, any sic unioun sould be, or not? For thais that ar refractaris to this unioun contendis and will dispute the negative pairt, that it is nather necessar nor profitable; and at the first schaw, their assertioun cariis ane great appierance, takand the ground thairof out of Plato.[9] *'Omnis mutatio in repub[lica] est perniciosa, etiam si aliquando de malo in bonum'*. They will affirme uith ane learnit urytar Bodine,[10] in his buik *De Repub[lica]*: *'Reipub[licae] faciem, leges antiquas, instituta, uno et eodem tempore, mutare perniciosum est'*. They will not lykuyis foryet Machiavel,[11] in his buik *De Principe*: *'de novo principatu, qui vel armis vel virtute acquiritur et quemadmodum civitates vel principatus regi debeant, qui suis legibus virtute et libertate vivebant'* – quhilk in verray died is ane axiome authorisit be the common opinioun of the historianes and best politiques. They will contend that new acquisitiounes of kingdomes, ather be richt of blood, succession, armes or vertew (housoevir they magnifie the acquyrer) man aluyis be but prejudice of the ancienne estait, and integritie of the first impyir, and inhabitantis thairof: wtheruyis in end will not faill to breid ane great alteratioun of the tua kingdomes

[9] Marginal note: 'Plato. lib. 7. de legibus'. 'All change in a state is pernicious, even if being from worse to better'
[10] Marginal note: 'Bod. lib. 4 de repub. c. 4.' See J. Bodin, *The Six Books of a Commonweale*, trans. R. Knolles (London, 1606)
[11] Marginal note: 'Machi. lib. de principe. c. 5'

unitit. This uith many utheris uil be alledgit for the pairt of the said negative, and at the first apprehensioun appieris to carie gude ressoun.[12] The nixt questioun is *'Quid sit?'* For giff the affirmative pairt prevaill, then it uil be demandit qhat sal be the forme, maner and nature thairof. The last questioun is 'Quale sit'? Qhat sal be the provisiounes and conditiounes annexit, baith tuiching the prince and people, sua that out of thir particularis, the contraversie dois arise: some fearing heich alteratioun in the estait (qha wtheruyis uald yeild), wtheris at the first forsieng the commoditeis of this unioun, quhilk be gude ressoun cannot be uiell denyit, and yit many questiones will aryse, specially anent the perpetuitie of this unioun. Thir particularis ar not to be ressonit heir, bot remittit to the conference betuixt the commissionaris[13] of baith the natiounes (giff it pleis God this actioun sal be endit), for that uald occupie ane great volumne. Lett thairfoir this unioun be uyselie considerit, that it may tend to the gude publict of baith the natiounes, qhairin this evir man be comprehendit, that it sall proceid, but prejudice of ather of thair richtis, breach or alteratioun thairof in any sort. The said unioun to be mutuall and reciproque, not the translatioun of the estait of ane kingdome in ane uther, not of Scotland as subalterne to Ingland, quhilk is not unioun bot ane plaine discord, the ane to be principall, the uther accessor, the ane to command, the uther to obey – thairby ancienne Scotland to loss hir beautie for evir! God forbid! Bettir that we of this age had nevir bein borne, than to sie that miserie in our tyme, thairby to amit that libertie quhilk our predicessoris have sua lang enjoyit. Lett it thairfoir be ane trew and hairtlie unioun of hairtes and myndis, quhilk is the end of all trubles and calamiteis bypast, qhensoevir any trew unioun is intendit.

The best handling and prosecuting of this mater sal be first to declair qhat is meanit be unioun, and the trew nature thairof, nixt to sett doun the negative pairt of this unioun uith the argumentis summarlie to prove the same, thaireftir the affirma-

---

[12] 'This with many utheris . . . carie gude ressoun' deleted in London MS
[13] 'Betuixt the commissionaris' replaced in London MS by 'determinatioun of the parliament', again suggesting a submission date after 1604

tive uith the rassounes properlie belangand thairto, last the
decisioun of baith, qhat sal be the constant veritie, embracing
the ane, rejecting the uther, with ane refutatioun of the haill
objectiounes adducit for confirmatioun of that pairt quhilk sal
be rejectit, togidder uith ane generall overture of the cautiones,
conditiounes and provisiounes of the said unioun.

The reull of the dialecticianes man be fellouit, quhilk is, that
qhen anything is put in contraversie, the first point of knauledge
of the treuth beginnis at the trew definitioun of that quhilk is
contravertit. I will thairfoir declair qhat is meanit be the uord
unioun. The uord unioun is derivat from the Latin phrase *unio,
consensus, concordia*: the lyik in Frensch *union, unité*, in the
Italiane *unionè, concordia*. Plinius in the 35th chapter of his nynt
buik sayis '*dos omnis unionis est in candore, ut duo amplius non
reperiantur indiscreti*'.[14] It is sometyme personall, sometyme reall,
wtheruyis mixt: lykuyis sometyme naturall, sometyme artificiall. Ane personall unioun is the conjunctioun of persounes:
the prince and people mutuallie, the husband and the uyfe in
mariage, uith utheris of the lyik nature, Christiane people unitit
in thair head and saviour Jesus Chryst, that great and hypostaticall[15] unioun of the tua natures of divinitie and humanitie in the
persoun of Chryist. Ane reall unioun is qhen tua thingis lyand in
ane continent ar unitit naturally, and this is baith reall and
naturall having na interjectioun. Ane mixt unioun is qhen
besyidis the unioun of persounes, that also is unitit quhilk
sometymes ues in contraversie. Ane artificiall unioun, qhen
thingis wtheruyis be nature cannot be unitit, being far distant
and different, yit ar unitit, sic as the unioun of landis, lordschipis,
baronies, realmes and kingdomes. Bot the principall unioun of
all, quhilk is the fontaine, is the unioun personall, the concord
and harmonie of hairtis and myndis – giff it be ane trew unioun,
and not affectat hypocrisie: the pretext of freindschip, and yit
ane particular monopolie, begynning at ane comedie and
ending in ane tragedie, as the traffiquin merchant begynnis at
the uord societie, but qhen it comes '*ad pronomina possessiva*

[14] Pliny, *Natural History*, Bk. IX, section 112
[15] from hypostasis, the one person of Christ in which the divine and human natures are joined

meum, tuum, suum' fallis furth in ane heich contentioun. I think na gude man uill lyik uiell of sic ane pretendid unioun.

All thais qha ar opposit to this unioun contendis that it is nather necessar nor expedient, for the uiell of baith the natiounes it sould proceid in any sort – and heir I begyne to dispute the said negative, uith the reassones thairof, to infer this conclusioun: albeit thair be syndrie argumentis usit, yit thair ar thre chieff and principall.[16] The uord unioun (say they) cariing in it ane great schaw, covertlie implicattis ane great prejudice, except the conditioun be uyselie sett doun at the first. For it cannot be uiell doun uithout alteratioun of that quhilk is unitit, and ancienne estait thairof. In end, in place of unioun, [*it*] sall infer the subversioun of the auld impyir: sometyme frie befoir the unitie, thaireftir be occasioun of the said unioun reducit to ane bondage and servitude, quhilk all gude men uill abhore – seing their is nathing mair pretious to the nature of man than to vindicat and acclame his ancienne libertie, ather in religioun or policie. The nixt argument, albeit coincident with the former, is that it is verray difficill to unit different kingdomes; housoevir landis may be erectit in ane lordschip, syndrie villages unitit in ane citie, syndrie cities in ane province, dyverss provinces in ane monarchie, bot not dyverse monarchies anyuyis different ather in religioun or policie, having different lauis and judicator, in ane soverane monarchie, and sua to bring that quhilk ues different of auld in ane present conformity uithout some dangerous alteratioun, the doing quairof uill occupie ane lang space, and many ages. Quhilk movit Machiavel[17] (ane man not religious, bot be experience verray politique), reassoning of kingdomes als uiell hereditare as mixt impyirs; in his buik *De Principe* [*he*] sayis that auld impyirs, '*regna avita et paterna*', ar far mair easelie keipit, meantienit and defendit than new aquisitiounes, the satling qhairof and perfyit establisching uill occupie ane lang space. Of thir groundis they ressoun that it is bettir to every kingdome to consist and remaine in the auin integrity, housoevir ony uther impyir sall accied thairto, than to translait the estait of the ane impyir in the uther, housoevir they be baith

---

[16] 'and heir I begyne . . . chieff and principall' deleted in London MS
[17] Marginal note: 'Mach. de prince. c. 2'

redactit under the obedience of ane monarch, ather be armes, vertew, valour, electioun or successioun of blood, and that this pretendit unioun is pleasant in the first schaw yit intrinsecally cariing uithin it many hid and lurking materis: in end being discoverit nathing ells bot ane feinyit and pretendit unioun.[18] The thrid argument is of greatest force. To qhat effect sould unioun be maid, except it may be sein to be perpetuall? Wtheruyis it uill evir be subject to ane breach, seing of the common law 'nemo cogitur invitus manere in societate'. And uithout some greater licht, it cannot be forsein to be perpetuall. And heir they ressoun fra the example of our nichtbour countrey of France. In our dayes, the haill race of the house of Valloys is extinct, and the kingdome translatit in ane uther. The last race of Ingland hes failyeit, and the impyir thairof gratiouslie establischit in his Hienes' persoun. Qhat say they? Giff God plies (as the Lord of His great mercy forbid), seing that all men ar earthlie, subject to the calling of the Creator to rendir that lyfe at His pleasour quhilk ues inspyrit, that his Majestie uith his haill offspring sall inlaik, to the great desolatioun of this ile: will it not then fellow, notwithstanding baith the countreyis ar now unitit and establischit in his Hienes' persoun, the saidis natiounes uill returne to thair auin estair – mair horrible uearis to be than daylie lookit for than evir of befoir. In end, they uill fall furth in ane heich exclamation, this unioun (est tanquam idaea Platonica) fluctuating in all men's myndis, daylie in all men's mouthes, yit few knauis or undirstandis the end and event thairof.[19] It is ane great loss alreddy [to] Scotland, to be destitut of the presence of thair naturall king and his appierand air – Ingland to enjoy all, qhairas we sould be pertakeris of thair felicity, now at last to mak ws ane pendicle of thair kingdome. God forbid! This mekle for the pairt of the refractaris to this unioun, defending the negative pairt thairof.

For probatioun of the first argument, sett doun for confirmatioun of this negative, they ressoun in this maner. Ather be this unioun intendit it is meanit that the saidis tua nationes, and ather of thame, sall remaine eftir the unioun in their ancienne

---

[18] 'and that this pretendit . . . ane feinyit and pretendit unioun' deleted in London MS
[19] 'uill fall furth . . . end and event thairof' deleted in London MS

estait and integritie, qhairin they ar and hes bein thir many yeiris bypast: or to ressave alteratioun in religioun or policie, in haill or in pairt, quhilkis ar the pillaris of ane commonuiell. Giff it be grantit that the ancienne estait sal be meantienit (as be gude ressoun it sould be) than appierandlie na unioun is requisit, bot rather ane mutuall league, contract and reciproque band for thame and thair posteriteis sal be mair expedient, for meantinance of amitie and freindschip betuixt dyverss impyiris, for imperting at all tymes requysit of all gude offices tending to the advancing of the florising estait of baith the natiounes, in sic competent forme as may be aggriet. In ane uord: ather this unioun is meanit for the gude publict of baith the realmes, or ells to advance the ane, prejudge the uther, quhilk can nather be unitie nor conformitie, the ane principall, the uther accessor, quhilk is not reall bot verball unioun. Giff it be maid to the uiell of baith, the securitie forsaid is sufficient. Giff it sall hurt the ane, and magnifie the uther, sic pretendit unioun is uorthelie to be rejectit, as being sua different from peax and concord, to be heireftir the perpetuall mother of discord. And last, giff the unioun of the saidis natiounes sall import ony alteratioun in religioun or policie, it cannot be without great prejudice. For as to religioun (praysit be God) thair is na reformit kirk in Europe injoyis the puritie of the evangell in greater sinceritie than Scotland. It uar to the great advantage of Ingland the lyik uar thair. I doe not deny bot in the policie ecclesiastique many thingis ar desyrit, sua giff that fundatioun be uiell sett doun, it niedis na alteratioun. The same argument is repeatit for the policie. Giff Scotland alreddy has als gude lauis, and judicator, as the nichtbour countrey (as I think na man acquentit uith baith bot[20] uill easelie grant) thair niedis na change bot fra the bettir to the uorss. And in conclusioun, giff it be meanit that the lauis, liberties, policie, judicator or religioun of ather of the saidis natiounes sal be imparit, than the meantineris of the said negative uil be furnist uith ane michtie and forceable argument, proponit in this maner.[21]

---

[20] The omission of this word in the London MS gives this clause an unintended meaning
[21] 'And in conclusioun . . . in this maner' deleted in London MS

Thair is nane aquentit uith the historie of baith the natiounes bot uill at first confes, Scotland is ane verray ancienne kingdome – mair ancienne nor Ingland, nevir conquest as yit be any forraine force, hes gevin repulss to Ingland and overthrauin utheris thair enemies, Pechtis, Danis, Northuegianes. Richt sua housoevir it be the north pairt of the ile of Britanie, Ingland mair pleasant in uealth and ritchis lyand at the south, yit in my judgement thair is na countrey in Europe, the inhabitantis thairof having contentit hairtis, fearing God, reducit to ane policie, verteuouslie employit, fellouing the example of uther politique natiounes, hes greater blissingis be sea and land, being uiell usit, and qha may bettir lieve uithin thameselffis uithout the aide and support of any forrane countrey, than Scotland presentlie possessis.

The countrey itselff is ane mixt countrey, abundant in all thingis necessar for lyfe: in cornes, cattell, feuall, mettallis of all sortis, great commoditie be sea and land, in fisching surpassing utheris: the soill maist peciable, uanting nathing necessar, uithout prodigall superfluitie to the honest estait of civill men: the people easielie governit, the naturall of the best sort uiell inclynit, of thair spirit and ingyne indeuit uith gude qualiteis, sua mony as hes ather gevin thameselffis to embrace liberall sciences trainit wp in the professioun of letteris, policie or martiall estait, uithout ostentatioun not inferior to any subjectis of mair renounit kingdomes, uiell estiemit in all pairtis, qhair they have gevin testimonie of thair valour. This natioun enjoyis verray notable and ancienne priviledges, richtis and immunities, grantit to thame and thair predicessoris, nobles, prelattis, barrones, burrouis, persones publict and privat, for thair valour, vertew and service doun to his Hienes and his predicessoris in peace and uear. Sall all this be lost in ane day, and be our auin voluntar consent? Sall ane frie kingdome possessing sua ancienne liberteis become ane slave, furth of libertie in bondage and servitude – and that of thair auin proper uill, uncompellit or coactit, to the heich honor of Ingland, perpetuall desolatioun of Scotland (now destitut of the suiet fruitioun of his Hienes' presence, as orphalines uithout father or mother, in qhais handis our daylie lamentis and complaintis may be pourit)? Sall

Scotland now eftir sua mony ages ressave schame, and amit hir
ancienne beautie? The Lord forbid. Qhen the refractaris to this unioun drauis nearer, they
reassoun politicallie in this maner. Is thair any man of naturall
senss, or evir acquentit uith the estait politique of any natioun,
that uill deny this axiome: the mutatioun, change and alteratioun of ane kingdome, ather in religioun or policie or baith,
and of the ancienne estait, lauis, statutis and auld constitutiounes
thairof, uiell establischit and lang observit, undir the pretext and
unioun of the uther kingdome, howsoevir conquest, be armes,
vertew or richt of blood, importis nathing ells bot the totall
subversioun and distructioun of the auld impyir? I say mair, the
smallest change and alteratioun of the lauis and ancienne estait
cariis na les than the exterminioun of that commonuiell quhilk is
alterit.

The probatioun heirof is evident. Giffand that Scotland uar
nat sua uiell establischit as Ingland, ather in religioun, lauis or
policie (quhilk is flatlie denyit, and the contrair propositioun
maist trew) and that the estait thairof inclynit to ane fall,
craving alteratioun, I reasson in this forme. Is it not bettir to
have ane republique (albeit evill governit) to stand, than to have
nane at all? Is it not bettir to sustein ane seik and languising
patient uith moderat foode, than to send for the physitiane,
presentlie to apply medicine to ane incurable seiknes, and sua to
cutt off lyfe? The medicines thameselffis usis not to apply
extreme and desperat remedies bot to desperat diseases.[22] Bot
trew it is that the meanest alteratioun of the estait, ather in
religioun or policie, importis the subversioun of the impyir.
Thairfoir they commit great error, that estiemis lauis taine fra
dyvers kingdomes to be uiell applyit to ane republique governit
be ane dyvers and contrarie forme.

Plato, in his sevint buik De Legibus,[23] estiemis giff the estait
publict be drauin in contraversie, thair is nathing mair nocive
than alteratioun of lauis and statutis – quhilk is of sic treuth 'quod
lex etiam iniqua quae sua vetustate nititur, antiquari non debet, ut
nova lex feratur'. Ane auld law is of sic authoritie, that uithout

---

[22] This sentence is deleted in the London MS
[23] Marginal note: 'Plato, lib. 7. de. leg.; Bod. ut supra c. 4 lib. 4'

ane magistrat it may defend itselff. Thair can be na sic profit
exspectit be ane new law (albeit be the progess of lang tyme) as
the present inconvenient imbrocht thairby. Quhilk is not onely
the opinioun of Plato, bot of the haill politiques: that it is ane
dangerous mater to schaik the fundatioun of ane kingdome,
standing lang undir the obedience of ane law.

   This be ane familiar example may be easielie demonstrat. Giff
the auner of ane heich building uald imaginat to himselff that he
micht repair the substructioun and fundament thairof, the
principall not being impairit, uald it not be comptit ane mater
ridiculous – seing it will ather import the distructioun of the haill
aedifice, or at liest the concussioun thairof, quhilk sall import
greater inconvenient to the standing of the aedifice than the new
mater could bring profit. Bot sua it is. Ane auld kingdome or
citie may be comparit to ane auld hous, the fundatioun qhairof
aucht not to be schakin. Thairfoir this discipline is maist miet
for conservatioun of kingdomes, that the auldest monarchie is
best and uorthiest of recommendatioun, that hes stand langest
uithout alteratioun of the estait and lauis thairof.

   For this cause be the auld law of the Athaenianes, inviolablie
observit in thair republique, quhilk lykuyis ues observit in the
popular governement of the Romanes undir Publius Philo the
dictator. It ues not laufull for ony man to present ane request to
the people uithout advyse of the Senat, undir the paine of laese-
majestie.

   The republique of the Venetianes, ane auld and uyiss seig-
neurie hes kiepit the same inviolablie; and being ane Senat, it is
not laufull to deall with the Senat for alteratioun of thair estait,
quhilk hes maid thame sua lang to florisch uealthielie, and I may
justlie say thair is not ane bettir governit republique in Europe.

   Bot thair ues ane mair severe decrie sett doun amangis the
people of Locrianes (as Demosthenes makis mentioun): that
every citizen that ues desyrous to bring ane new law sould come
and declair it publictlie befoir the people, uith ane halter about
his neck – to the end that giff his new law ues not thocht miet to
be ressavit, and verray profitable for the commonuiell, he micht
be presentlie stranglit as ane uorthie reuard for his raschnes.

   Aristotle doeth affirme that in everie societie, uiell ordaynit and instituted be lauis, great cair is to be had that na pairt of the law, althocht nevir sua litle, be diminischit or alterit, yea greatest cair to be had of that quhilk is doun be litle and litle: for giff resistance be not maid in the beginning, it fallis furth of the commonuiell as in the diseasit body of man, qhairin giff spiedie remeid be not usit in the begynning thairof it increaseth by litle and litle, and that quhilk micht have bein easielie curit is maid incurable. Nevir usis men (as Paulus Aemilius the Romaine Consul doeth affirme) to alter and change the estait of ane commonuiell, be making thair first entres uith some notorious resisting to the auld lauis: for seing the lauis ar the suir fundatioun of every civill societie, giff that faill it most niedis fall furth that the haill politicall building man come to ruine.

In consideratioun qhairof Bias affirmit the estait of that commonuiell to be happiest, qhairin the inhabitantis thairof fear the law as ane severe tyrane, and eftir the law be anes establischit, be the opinioun of Isiodorus: 'We must not judge of the law, bot according to the law'. And the best policie, according to the sentence of Chilon, ane of the uyse men of Graecia, is qhair the people harkenis mair to the lauis nor to the oratoris. This ues the caus that movit Pausanias the Lacaedemoniane to mak this answer, qhen it ues demandit qhairfoir it ues not laufull in thair countrie to alter thair ancienne liberties and lauis. The ressoun ues (said he) becaus lauis ar maistressis over men, not men over the lauis.

Ane uorthie and uyse sentence, or rather ane divine oracle maist uorthie to be fellouit be all men occupieing the place of judicator, to be daylie put in practise, acknauledging thameself-fis not to be maisteris of the lauis, bot servandis and ministeris thairof, and that the lauis ar appoyntit to be maistressis over thame – not to be thrauin and misconstructit according to thair phantasie. For thair can be nathing mair contrair to trew judgement than to iudge *ex arbitrio, non ex lege*, sua that the best historianes and politiques estiemis this nathing ells bot ane manifest corruptioun of justice, to subversioun of the realme and subjectis thairof. And takand occasioun to speak for restraint thairof, [*he*] condemnis expreslie all factiounes in judgement tending to privat monopolies – and searching out

the principall remeid, concludis that princes sould mak chose of
the learnit and best affectit of all gude qualiteis, to be sett doun in
the place of judgement, not that the offices of judges sal be
vendible, quhilk is nathing ells bot to make the judgement
mercenar: bot that the samyn sal be grantit to persounes for
thair valour and uorthienes, seing the tua pillaris to uphald ane
commonuiell is religioun and justice. The essential point qhairof
is this, that the law sall evir command the judge as minister
thairof, not to the contrair that the judge sall presume to
violat or break the law.

I cannot of deuty foryet that notable confessioun utterit be
the tua gude Imperoris of Rome, Theodosius and Valen-
tinianus:[24] '*digna vox est maiestate principis regnantis, legibus
alligatum se profiteri, adeo de authoritate juris pendet nostra auth-
oritas, et re vera maius imperio est submittere legibus principatum. Et
oraculo praesentis edicti prohibemus aliis, quod nobis licere non
patimur*'. Giff it then be trew, as it is expreslie confessit in the said
law, that the hiech throne of the prince is sett doun undir the
law, to be only governit thairby, may inferior judges or
magistrattis break the samyn, cariit away be partialitie, malice
or ignorance, quhilk cannot be justice bot injustice, according to
the decisioun of the common law. '*Praetor in iure dicendo, etiam
cum iniuriam facit, ius dicere videtur, sed non dicit*[25] *relatione scilicet
facta non ad id, quod ita praetor facit, sed quod praetorem facere
convenit*'. I cannot lykuyis foryet ane discourss maid be ane
jurisconsult Neapolitane, Alexander ab Alexandro.[26] '*Quid
censerit Hieronimus Porcarius, de iniquo iudice, quibusque modis
litigantes eludit: odio, gratia, prece, et amore*' with many utheris
enumerat in the said discourss.[27]

I nied not to insist farder in narratioun of the antiquities, and
constant abyding at auld lauis. Moyses ues the first lawmaker

---

[24] Marginal note: '1. digna. vox. c. de. leg.'

[25] 'sed non dicit' is a marginal addition

[26] 'in his buik *Genialium Dierum*' added in the London MS. Marginal note: 'Alex. ab.
Alex. lib. 5. c. 14'

[27] Insertion in London MS: 'And this may sufficientlie prove that as the ancient estait of
kingdomes sould not be alterit be ony new novation [sic], on the wther pairt the law
sould command the magistrat, and not the magistrat to have puer to break the law in any
sort'

amang the Hibreuis, Mercurius Trismegistus amangis the
Ægyptianes, Phoronaeus the King of the Graecianes, Solon of
the Athenianes, Licurgus of the Lacaedemonianes, Anacharsis of
the Schythianes, Numa Pompilius of the Romaines. Ten
notable men [were] chosin be the Senat and people of Rome for
the lauis of the Tuelff Tables: Pharamond amangis the Frensch-
men, the greatest pairt of the lauis of Germanie establischit by
Charles the Great, Imperour and King of France: the haill bodie
of the common law, that notable uark sett doun be the
Imperour Justiniane to the great comfort of all Europe. To
conclude, all natiounes and regiounes have dyverss lauis and
lawmakeris, according to the conditioun, circumstance of tyme,
place and countrey: sua that it is maist miet that every natioun
sall enjoy and fellow thair auin lauis, liberteis and constitutiounes. Bot certaine it is, *'quod novis malis nova quaerenda sunt
remedia'*[28] sic as in punischment of malefactoris, in the incress of
thair paine for thair new and extraordinar urangis: the lyik in
inbringing of merchandice, victuallis and cornes for the gude
publict, and sic uther ciuill lauis and constitutiounes quhilkis
have bein maid according to the circumstance of tymes and
places.[29] They ar aluyis in the pouer of the prince to be changit
and alterit, as occasioun servis; the ressoun of all this is that
uorthie assertioun, *' Salus populi suprema lex esto'*. Themistocles
appointit the toun of Athenis to be fortifiet uith strong uallis, yit
Theramenes did appoint the contrair, that they sould be cassin
doun – wtheruyis the Lacaedemonianes had prevailit, as the
historie makis mentioun. This ues onely doun for the uiell of the
people, and it is grantit that in all sic occasiounes alteratioun may
be maid in ane moment; bot this man be evir observit, that the
principall and ancienne fundamentis of the republique nevir
ressave any concussioun, speciallie sic as ar callit the lauis ratiefiet
and approvin in every monarchie, as it uar annexed to the
croune, and qhairupon every publict governement is first
groundit. This aucht nauyis to be infringit or changit. Sic as the
Law Salik in France, sett doun be Pharimond, thir lauis ar

---

[28] Marginal note: 'Plut. in. Agid' (i.e., 'Life of Agis')
[29] London MS reads: 'civill lawes and constitutiones, ordinances, edictis and customes,
quhilkis have bein maid and ressavit, according to the conditioun and circumstances'

annexit to the croune, and can nauyis be abrogat be the prince, bot his successoris may annull that quhilk he dois in preiudice of thame.

Solon tuik the people of Athenis suorne solemnatlie (as Plutarche[30] makis mentioun) that they sould suffer thair lauis to stand immutable for the space of ane hundreth yeiris at leist. This ues purposelie doun becaus they knew they uar not to lieve above that space. Licurgus [*was*] of that same opinioun, bettir to be undir ane evill law standing lang in continuance, than to abrogat the same in ane moment.[31]

The Venetianes, qha durst interpryis nathing againes thair chieff duik, callit Augustinus Barbarinus, during his lyfetyme, qhais pouer wtheruyis ues not portable be the citizenis; yit liest any contumelie sould be doun to the agit prince, and thairby to truble the estait of the republique, he ues sparit during his lyfetyme, bot eftir his deces lauis ues sett doun to the prince's future to keip ane bettir governement.

The example of Charles the Fyift of France (callit the Uyse) may be ane sufficient testimonie for confirmatioun of this purpose; qha in his young age (his father being captive) attiening to the administratioun of the kingdome, be evill counsall, having be ane law taine the governement fra the auld magistrattis, quhilk maid na litle truble in the realme. He repentit verray sair, and in the court of parliament haldin at Paris the xviii day of Maii 1359 (qhairof Bodine[32] makis mentioun in his fourt chapter of his fourt buik, *De Republica*) be his expres senatusconsult, acknauledging his former error, reducit the said first ordinaunce, finding that pretendit alteratioun to have cariit uith it ane heich commotioun and concussioun of the chief fundamentis of the said commonuiell.

The Senat and people of the toun of Basilaea in the countrey of Helvetia, ane of the chief cantones of the Sueises, now professing the Christiane reformit religioun, housoevir they maid desertioun from the Paip, yit uald not at the first put away

---

[30] Marginal note: 'Plutarch in Solone' (i.e., 'Life of Solon'). See c. 25

[31] 'for in this the physitianes and nature itselff aucht to be imitat, qha in curing of diseases dois nathing violentlie bot be great lasure' inserted in London MS

[32] Marginal note: 'Bod. ut. supra. c. 4 lib. 4'

thair munkis and moniall sisteris, bot sufferit thame to enjoy thair accustomit forme and libertie, estieming it maist meit sua to doe than to mak any present commotioun: thinking at last it sould come to pas (as it did indied) that in ane schort space thair colledgis be the death of thair companies sould be extinguischit. Lyik as it fell furth, that the Chartusianes leaving thair colledge ane only idle man ues left on lyfe, and sua be progres of tyme all succiedit uiell uithout alteratioun or mutatioun of thair estait.

Of this deductioun it is evident how perilous and dangerous it is to mak ony alteratioun or mutatioun in auld kingdomes standing lang in thair auin integritie: quhilk is sufficientlie provin and authorisit be the gude examples, testimonies and histories of all natiounes. Qhairupon thais qha ar refractaris to this unioun groundis thair chief and principall argument, and thinkis giff thair sal be ony change or alteratioun maid in ather of the realmes, bot speciallie in Scotland, ather in religioun, lauis or policie, in haill or in pairt, it can import na les than the subversioun of the kingdome: and giff na change be meanit, than this unioun is not necessar, bot lett every kingdome remaine in the auin estait, and ane reciproque band of thair amitie to be sett doun is thocht maist miet for the purpose. Sua that the manifest treuth of the said negative propositioun may easielie appeir be the argumentis forsaidis, and may be confirmit uith many uther argumentis and probationes, bot the few befoir rehersit is sufficient in this place.[33]

Of the common law the pairtis and memberis of the principall divisioun of the law ar *Ius naturale, gentium et civile*. [34] The law of nature is universall, bot that quhilk is civill is particular to everie particular natioun, people or citie. Bot uithout any farder ampliatioun this mekle sal be sufficient for probatioun of the first argument, proponit for confirmatioun of the said negative. And the same testimonies and examples ar usit for probatioun of the secound argument, proponit to induce the said negative. To uitt, that it is verray hard to unit auld and ancienne kingdomes different many thousand yeiris in estait, lauis, judicator and policie, standing sua lang in gude caice,

[33] 'Sua that the . . . in this place' deleted in London MS
[34] This sentence and much of the remainder of the paragraph deleted in the London MS

uithout any unioun. Quhilk, being made, uald aither import the subversioun of baith, at the leist ane of them.

Finallie it is plainelie affirmit be all gude men that his Majestie aucht to be uiell forsein in this unioun, seing it is alreddy sein in Ingland, that under the vaill of his royall presence thair that natioun affectis to have all in thair handis, and huntis eftir all offices, not suffering sua far in thame lyis that any of the gude subjectis of Scotland sall ressave any preferment (the gude of this land daylie imbrocht thair), craving nathing ells bot the alteratioun of this estait, and sua to mak Scotland ane pendicle of thair realme. Quhilk cannot stand with his Hienes' honor, and repugnis to the sentence, uill and determinatioun of the ancienne and uorthie kingis of Ingland: declaring thair earnestnes to have us establischit in ane perpetuall societie, not in disparitie and disconformitie bot in ane similitude, to be ane bodie, to ressave ane common name, to be callit at all tymes heireftir Britanes.[35] And this is the determinatioun sett doun be King Eduard the Sixt, repeatit be Eduard, Duik of Sommersait: and that it sould lykuyis procied uithout alteratioun of the estait, lauis and constitutiounes thairof. Takand the example not onely fra France (housoevir now erectit in ane soverane monarchie), yit composit of many dutches and seigneuries, bot also takand the lyik example fra the haill kingdomes of the Romane Impyir; for albeit the Imperor be stylit King of the Romaines, Germanie, Sicile, Jerusalem, Ungarie, Bohemia, Dalmatia, Croatia, Archduke of Austria, Duik of Burgundie, all thir natiounes ar unitit to the Impyir with many utheris, yit nane of the saidis natiounes ressaves alteratioun in thair estait, lauis, liberteis and priviledgis. The lyik in the dutchie of Milane, the kingdome of Neapolis, the republique of Genua in Italie, the kingdome of Portugall: quhilkis albeit they be now undir the obedience of the King of Hispaine; yit thair estait, in the integritie of thair lauis and policie is aluyis preservit. I have bein the mair large upon this point, becaus the chieff ground qhairin the disputatioun of this question consistis, standis in this conclusioun: be qhat meanis this unioun may procied, the estait

[35] Marginal note: 'Sleidane. comment. lib. 20. pag. 621': J. Sleidan, *Commentaries* (London, 1560)

not alterit. Thair be also many that estiemis, giff Ingland gett thair full intentioun of all thingis, to their advantage and to our prejudice, his Majesteis maist royall persoun cannot be bot in great hasert, as the uofull experience of the barbarous and unnaturall conspiracie practisit againes his Hienes' persoun schortlie eftir his Majesteis entres in Ingland can bier sufficient record – to the perpetuall schame and infamie of the authoris thairof, his Majestie in his native soill being aluyis in securitie. I cannot gudlie pretermit the unthankfulnes of Ingland, qha having ressavit na small blissing be thair lait alteratioun, decorit now be the schyning face of sua uorthie ane prince, yit ar become ingrait, uilipending and lichtlie regarding this thair nichtbour countrey, the inhabitantis thairof being als uorthie in all respectis as they ar. It is to the great honor and uiell of Ingland that evir they enjoyit sic ane royall prince, bot to our great loss. Qhat miserie Ingland sustienit befoir his Hienes' entres thair is over uiell knauin, qhat peace and joy they have presentlie they thameselffis can bier uitnes. As to the lettir pairt of the said negative, qhat sal be the estait of the saidis kingdomes in caice the said unioun proceid, the consideratioun thairof is referrit to the last pairt of this treatise, qhairin the conditiounes and provisiounes of the said unioun sal be sett doun. Bot befoir I putt ane end to the negative pairt, I uill draw this haill first disputatioun sustienit be the meantineris thairof [36] in ane schort epilogue. This unioun (say they) cannot be uithout some alteratioun of thir tua kingdomes, at the liest ane of thame, bot speciallie Scotland; for we cannot as yit sie ony experience of gude imbrocht to this natioun be the alteratioun: bot be the contrair the uther nichtbour countrey daylie florising, enjoying his Majesteis presence thair. Yea, it is farder suspectit it cannot be hairtlie eftir sua lang trubles, far les is it lyklie to be perpetuall, seing it tendis to magnifie the ane, prejudge the uther, Ingland to joyis all, Scotland in effect nathing. Qhat sall I say to make ws ane pendicle of thair kingdome, and sua to loss our ancienne glorie, liberteis and priviledgis, quhilk uithout questioun will fall furth giff euir ue sall happin to be imparit ather in religioun

[36] The long passage beginning 'Their be also many that estiemis' and ending here is deleted in the London MS

or policie, lauis and constitutiounes of this realme – thairby to
mak ane suddaine mutatioun of ane kingdome in ane uther, in
ane moment, bruiking friedome of befoir and now redactit in
bondage. Quhilk uil be na unioun bot ane plaine discord, seing
the nature of all unioun importis paritie and conformitie. And
to conclude, we may say (*ut ait Cassius ille*) '*Cui bono*'? Giff
Ingland gett this unioun effectuat it is to thair great profit
forevir, seing thairby they uill obtein that quhilk they have
socht lang be armes, and could nevir attein thairto. Lett it
thairfoir be in plaine paritie and conformitie, uithout alteratioun
of our estait undir ane soverane monarchie and obedience.[37]
The last argument is of greatest consequence, adducit be the
meantieneris of the said negative tuiching the perpetuitie of this
unioun. Gevand (say they) this unioun now proceid, thairby
baith the ancienne kingdomes erectit in ane soverane monarchie; yit it cannot be forsein to be perpetuall, for albeit the haill
ile sal be erectit in the kingdome of Great Britanie, and that the
inhabitantis sall tak upon thame the common name of Britanes,
that can stand na longer in the auin integritie than the kingdomes remaine uith his Majestie and his royall race – quhilk giff
it sall inlaik (as God forbid) will in effect dissolve the unioun,
seing ather of the kingdomes will returne to thair auin naturall
prince and obedience. The solutioun and direct ansuer to this
argument is referrit to the auin place, qhen as the dicisioun of
this questioun sal be sett doun.

> The secound pairt of this treatise, tuiching the af-
> firmative, with the argumentis adducit for confirma-
> tioun thairof.

Now it restis be gude methode according to the ordour sett
doun heirtofoir that the wther pairt quhilk is the affirmative of
this unioun sal be entreatit with the reassones thairof. Thais qha
uissis this unioun to be establischit estiemes all utheris[38] opposit

---

[37] The remaining lines of this section do not appear in the London MS

[38] The opening lines of this section to this point are replaced by the following in the
London MS: 'Howsoevir the former disputatioun wald appeir to be sett doun wpon
probable argumentatis, and groundit wpon gude conclusiones, yit being weill
considerit, can import na stay to this blissed unioun. And without questioun, all the gude
subjectis of this ile richteouslie estiemis qhatsumevir persones'

thairto, not onely enemies to baith the nationes, perpetuall standing and florisching thairof, in uealth and peace in all ages to come: bot to dispute againes the principles of nature and humaine societie. For giff they be contradictoris to this unioun, not uithstanding the infinit profit and commoditie imbrocht thairby it is nathing ells bot to put in questioun the gude unioun of mony persones, husband, uyfe, bairnes, lord and servand in ane famille, mony citizenis in ane citie, dyverss tounes in ane province, many provinces in ane monarchie, sindrie monarcheis in ane heich and soverane monarchie, for the bettir knitting, meantiening and preserving thairof. In conclusioun, to beir professit hostilitie to the increass of the policie of kingdomes to be manifest evertaris of the fundatioun, groundis and principles of all gude governement. And to prove the same the ressoun in this maner.

Giff it be of veritie, as it cannot be denyit according to the doctrine of Aristotle and rest of the politiques, that ane familie (quhilk is the beginning of societie) is maid be the unioun of husband, uyfe, bairnes, lord and maister, with the servand, the ane to command, the uther to obey, qhairby the oeconomie is constitut: the florising citie be the unioun of many gude citizenis, unitit in ane bodie in hairtis and myndis be gude lauis and constitutiounes – be occasioun qhairof tounes florisch, merchantis becomes ritch, the tread doeth increase, and the people of all sortis injoy thair libertie. In lyk maner the province is maid wp be the unioun of dyvers tounes and villages, the monarchie erectit furth of the unioun of dyvers provinces, dutches and seigneuries. Qha can justlie deny bot the unioun of tua ancienne kingdomes (albeit nevir sua ancienne) constitutis ane hiech and soverane monarchie, tending to the perpetuall comfort and felicitie thairof, and redounding not sua mekle to the commoditie of the chief monarch as to the haill subjectis and inhabitantis of the kingdomes unitit? Wes it not to the unspeakable joy and comfort of Ingland that the tua ancienne houses of York and Lancaster, eftir lang and bloodie uearis at last ues unitit in ane kingdome – the kingdome of Uayles be accessioun lykuyis unitit thairto, and thairby ane heich and soverane monarchie constitut? Wes not the expulsioun of the

Romaines, Pechtis, the overthraw of the Danis and North-uegianes, the unioun of the haill iles, to the great comfort of Scotland, thairby ane ancienne kingdome constitut? Sall it not be to the perpetuall blissing and felicitie of thir tua natiounes, lyand in ane continent, not far different in religioun and language, to be unitit forevir, and baith the kingdomes erectit in ane soverane monarchie: to the effect thair byroun trubles micht be putt in perpetuall oblivioun, and justice, policie, peace and ritches all to florisch at anes in this ile? Thair is na gude subject in ather of the kingdomes, fearing God, loving his prince and native soill, tendering the uiell of himselff and his posteritie (except he be out of his richt senss) but uill at first uillinglie aggrie thairto. Thir ar the groundis and assertioun of thais qha susteinis the affirmative pairt of this questioun.[39]

That notable saying of the famous poet is verray remarquable, 'et penitus toto divisos orbe Britannos';[40] qhairof it felloues, giff the ile of Britanie be devydit from all utheris, sould it not import ane perfyit unioun amangis ourselffis? Salomon in his proverbis sayis verray uyselie that the honor of ane king is in the multitude of his people, 'et in defectu populi principis contritio'.[41] It hes bein mekle mervealit, how it could be possible that tua natiounes lyand in ane continent, environit uith ane sea, sould have contineuit sua lang at intestine uearis, qhairof great inconvenientis hes enseuit to baith the countreyis. And it ues evir thocht it sould be best for thame baith they sould be unit be mariage, quhilk hes bein maist earnestlie affectit be Ingland, be dyvers expostulatiouns, albeit thair be now ane mair soverane remeid brocht to pas be the providence of God, in the laufull successioun of his Majestie to baith the kingdomes (quhilk is mair sure), seing be this unioun all seditiones baith intestine and outuard will ceass. The bordorer and Hieland man (althocht in the fardest iles) dar not exercise his uontit roberie, and the seditious sprit and unquyet man ar now reducit undir the obedience of law and justice. Treulie that uorthie narratioun

---

[39] 'in ather of . . . this questioun' replaced in London MS by 'will not willinglie yield to sic ane manifest veritie, quhilk niedis na farder probatioun bot the werray licht of nature and the present commoditeis to be imbrocht thairby'
[40] See Virgil, *Ecloga*, Bk.I, line 66
[41] Proverbs 14:28. The proverb is used by Pont, above, p.17

maid be King Henry the Sevint of Ingland sould be recommendit to all posteriteis (qhairof Polidore Virgil[42] in the
historie of the Inglisch natioun, in his 26th buik makis
mentioun) utterit be him, qhen as that uorthie princes Quene
Margaret of Scotland, his dochter, ues gevin in mariage to
wmqhill King James the Ferd of uorthie memorie, forsieing
uiell[43] that quhilk now is comit to pas: that giff evir the
posteritie of the said Quene Margaret, be heritable richt and
discent of blood sould succied to baith the realmes, it sould be to
the great uiell of Ingland, seing in end it sould bring the unioun
of baith the natiounes. And he gave the example of Aquitane
and Normandie, and utheris provinces adiectit to Ingland, bot
mair gudelie he thoch sould be estiemit of Scotland, the haill ile
being compassit uith ane sea, and sua sould be againes nature to
seperat thame. Yea, [he] declarit farder that giff ony in-
commoditie sould appier of the said unioun, it uald rather fall on
Scotland than Ingland, as the historie makis mentioun. Quhilk
his Majestie uill remember, seing uithout questioun it will come
sua to pas, except it be remeidit in the begynning. For, as he
concludit, Scotland uald be destitut of the fruitioun and
presence of the common prince, and that he uald tak his
habitatioun in the maist fertill soill, quhilk to our regrait we
now fiell. And giff this be not mendit (as I doubt not it sall)
certainelie this kingdome will fall furth in ane aristocratie, far
different fra ane monarchie, and this will nevir induce ane perfyit
unioun. Bot the remied hierof standis in his Majesteis handis,
quhilk uithout doubt his Majestie uill forsie in tyme. Wtheruyis
his Grace in end will loss the heartis of his people heir.[44]

I will desyir the gude reader of this unioun to address himselff
to that notable epistole and discourse send be Eduard Duik of
Sommersait, Protector of Ingland, be the aduyse of the nobles
and counsall of Ingland, to the nobles and counsall of Scotland,

[42] Marginal note: 'Polydor. Virgil. lib. hist. 26'. See Pont, above, p.27
[43] 'uorthie memorie, forsieing uiell' replaced in London MS by 'Scotland, of blissed
memorie, be the quhilk mariage and lineall discent thairof, this happie conjunctioun is
made. Said he, weill forseing'
[44] 'And giff this . . . his people heir' replaced in London MS by 'and yit hoipis for
remeid thairof. Wtherwyis thair can be na perfyit unioun bot rather daylie occasion of
discord, giff ane portioun of the ile sall draw the commoditie of the haill'

in the yeir of God 1548: sett doun at lenth[45] be Johne Sleidane[46] in the tuenty buik of his 'Commentaris': contiening baith the offeris maid be Ingland to Scotland, and the forme, maner and ordour thairof. To wit, to be in paritie in all respectis, not that the gude of the ane kingdome sould be imbrocht to the uther, without reciprocatioun: the ane natioun to florisch, the uther undir pretext of ane unioun to decay: the prince to be aluyis thair, and resident in that soill, and to foryett his auld subjectis heir. I will nevir believe his Majestie wil be of that resolution, seing it uald not onely be againes that naturall affectioun quhilk his Majestie sould beir towardis ws his people, bot againes the determinatioun concludit of auld be Ingland, againes the quhilk nane of that natioun can evir be hard to oppone.

It uar ane great oversicht to foryett that uorthie speach utterit be his Heines upon the 9th of March last bypast,[47] in the parliament hous of Ingland, qha in this earand sould be to ws all 'testis omni exceptione maior'. Giff twenty thousand men be ane stronge armie, is not the double thairof, forty thousand, ane double strong armie? Giff ane barrone enritch himselff uith als mony landis as he had befoir, is he not the double greater? Is not this ane great benifit baith to himselff, his haill familie, freindis and servandis? Sall it not be to the perpetuall peace and gude of Ingland, that Scotland be unitit thairto? Trew it is that realme is ane verray ritch and florising natioun, estieming thair pouer and force verray great, suallowing to far in thair pryid and ψιλαυτία, disestiming uther renounit kingdomes, speciallie this thair ancienne and nichtbour countrey of Scotland, calling ws pure and miserable, uttering verray irreverent speaches againes this estait. Bot with thair favour, I will speak the treuth. Giff the bak dure of Scotland had bein maid patent to thair enemies, speciallie thais of Hispaine, I think it sould not have bein uiell with thame. Lett thame think of ws qhat they pleis! We sall ansuer in modestie with the tua uorthie Romanes, Curius and Camillus, we prayis God for our estait, and will say uith

[45] 'sett doun at lenth' replaced in the London MS by 'eftir the feild of Mussilbruth, qhen as the mariage wes desyrit to be endit betuixt Eduard the Sixt and Quene Marie of Scotland, qhairof mentioun is maid'

[46] Marginal note: 'Sleidane. Comment. lib. 20. pag. 621'

[47] The date is 1604 in the London MS, again implying a later subscription

Horace[48] '*hunc et incomptis Curium capillis, utilem bello tulit et Camillum: saeva paupertas et avitus apto cum lare fundus*'. We ar content of our estait, and possessis als gude moyen for lyfe in all respectis as they doe, yit nevir resolvit to fellow thame in great ostentatioun. As for our valour, they knaw ue have bein aluyis scraching uith thame. Giff our people, in thair martiall effairis, had bein reducit in gude obedience (lett any man peruse the historeis of baith the nationes) they could not surpass us in any sort. Bot seing this mater tendis to ane unioun, lett all byroun trubles be condemnit in perpetuall abolitioun, and qhenevir it sal be concludit it uill tend mair to thair profit then ouris. Giff ather of thir kingdomes ues habill to meantien thair estait of befoir, is thair not farder to be luikit now be all men, giff they be perfytelie unitit? It is to our great loss, bot to the hiech honor of Ingland, that they presentlie enjoy our naturall prince. He is mair deir to ws, bettir lovit of ws, then evir be thame. We man aluyis seik our naturall prince qhair he is. Ingland sould not think he is come to be aluyis resident thair, and sua to foryett this his Hienes' auin soill. God give thame thankfull hairtis for that blissing quhilk they have ressavit, and to yeild to his Majestie the dew obedience of gude subjectis.

The meantineris of this affirmative propositioun of the unioun estiemis that it sould nauyis be drauin in contraversie, nor niedis any probatioun[49] for confirmatioun thairof. Qha will demand of Euclides ane uarrand of this propositioun and axiome, '*totum est maius sua parte, si ab aequalibus aequalia demas, quae restant erunt aequalia*'. Will any man be sua foolisch that he will crave ane probatioun of this axiome? This war to putt ane torch befoir the sone to give licht, quhilk uald be comtit verray ridiculous. Qha dar putt questioun, giff thair be ane aeternall God, Creator of all thingis, Lord over Heaven and Earth, qhais heich pouer and providence is ingraftit and expressit, visiblie sein in all His creaturis? Will any of upricht judgement crave ane mair soverane probatioun? Is thair any farder to be said to the atheist, bot at the first to convict him be

---

[48] Marginal note: 'Hor. lib. 1. Carm. ode. 12' (lines 41-44)

[49] 'He is mair deir . . . niedis any probatioun' replaced in London MS by 'Qhy then sall this gude purpose be drauin in questioun, or any probatioun cravit'

the principles of nature confessit be himselff; quhilk being confessit, man lykuyis bind him, that he seis ane visible uarld, the great uark of the haill universe uith the creaturis induelling thairin, and sua incontinent man yeild and be stupefact. For thir creaturis uill leid him directlie to the Creator, seing thingis creatit cannot creat thameselffis. The detestable Jew sal be lykuyis convincit be his auin principles. I suppone he uald deny the New Testament, yit he dar not deny the Auld Testament, quhilk is confessit and approvin be him, and be that same probatioun sal be also convict of his incredulitie. The Papistis not onely in thair haereseis uil be convict be the expres uord of God, bot thair king the Paip may be convincit be his auin cannon law, as heireftir sal be deducit. Sould any mair soverane probatioun be cravit, all sic materis cariing in thameselffis infallible equitie? They crave na uther probatioun.[50]

Menenius Agrippa, as Livius[51] in his historie makis mentioun, hes bein of that opinioun that materis cariing ane present veritie sould not be provin; and becaus the earand quhilk he had in hand ues maist trew, he adducit onely ane similitude in place of probatioun, be ane familiar example to move the popular estait of the Romaines, makand secessioun fra the nobles (callit 'patricii et optimates') to be drauin in mutuall harmonie and reconciliatioun amangis thameselffis for the uiell of thair impyir, quhilk is the end of this subject. He said in ane parable, that thair fell furth ane great contraversie amangis the haill memberis of the body of man (quhilk in itselff is ane microcosme) cariing ane perfyit unioun. The fiett and leggis maid questioun that they upheld the body, the handis that uar daylie trublit and employit in meantinance of the bellie, the head that it ues evir in cair and paine in nurisching of the body, finallie the haill memberis refusing thair ordinar and naturall exercise, and thairby not meantining the unioun of the bodie inclynit to ane distructioun. Evin sua, concludit he, sall fall furth of the estait of this kingdome, to the great distructioun thairof, giff ye amangis

[50] 'They crave na uther probatioun' replaced in the London MS by 'Heirof it is inferrit, to crave any probatioun of the commoditie of this unioun is to contravert againes ane manifest treuth'
[51] Marginal note: 'Tit. Livius. lib. 2. dec. 1'

yourselffis be not of perfyit unioun and hairtlie myndis; seing it is the blissing of all blissingis amangis people or natiounes, the restraint of seditiones and trubles, expres meantinance of peace and tranquillitie, '*concordia parvae res crescunt discordia magnae dilabuntur*'. Unioun is lyik ane bunche or schaiff of arrouis; tak ather of thame sindrie, be litle and litle the haill may be easielie broken, kiep thame togidder '*et sic vis nescia vinci*'. All this mater tendis to the perfyting of this unioun, cariing uith it sic ane infallible veritie that it niedis na probatioun.

I uill remember ane rehersall of ane uorthie urytar, makand mentioun of Ptolomey King of Ægipt, qha having callit to banquet sevin embassadoris of the best and maist florising commonuealthis in his tyme, to ressoun anent thair governementis: that it micht have being knauin qha had the best policie, with the best lauis and customes. The dispute being lang with many ressounes adducit, Ptolomey desyrit to be instructit be thame in the best and rarest pointis necessar for preservatioun of ane estait publict, and for this caus requestit every ane of thame to propone thrie of thais customes and lauis quhilkis war maist perfyit in thair commonuealth. The embassador of the Romaines begane and said 'In our impyir we have the temples in great respect and reverence, we ar verray obedient to our governoris, we punisch wicked men and evill lieveris severelie'. Thir uar the thre pointis for the Romaines. The Chartegeniane embassador said, 'In the commonuiell of Chartage, the nobles nevir ceasis from feachting, the common people and artificeris labouring, the phylosophes teaching'. The Schythiane said, 'In our commonuiell, justice is exactlie kiepit, merchandise exercisit with treuth, all men accomptis thameselffis equall'. The Rhodiane [*said*], 'At Rhodis auld men ar honest, young men schamefast, and women solitar and of few uordis'. The Atheniane said, 'In our commonuiell ritch men ar not sufferit to be devydid in factiounes, the poor men to be idle, nor yit the governoris to be ignorant'. The Lacaedemoniane said, 'In Sparta invy reagneth not, all ar equall, and gudes common, na stouth committit for all persones doe labour'. The embassador of the Sicyonianes said, 'In our commonuiell voyages ar not permittit, that they sould not bring hame ane new fassone at

thair returne, physitianes ar not sufferit liest they doe skaith to
the bodies of men, nor oratoris to tak upon thame the defences
of causes and suittis'.

Of thir premises it is ressonit in this forme, according to this
now intendit unioun. Giff all thir gude customes, be unioun,
uar precieslie kiepit and imbrocht in any estait and soverane
monarchie (as be this unioun, be God's grace it will fall furth)
sall it not tend to the heich increass and gudnes thairof, and cutt
off causes of seditioun, produce ane michtie and florisching
governement forevir in this ile? Giff we sall treulie speak uith
Horace in the begynning of his satyris, the fontaine and
uallspring of all vyces, and the story of unioun of people and
kingdomes, is nathing ells bot the discontentment of mortall
men, nevir man contentit with his auin estait. Qhat vyce is not
groundit upon the insatiable desyir of having, as may appier in
all thame qha ar not content of thair estait, nor appoint ane end
in that they have, bot place it aluyis in that quhilk they uald
have. Then it fellowes that this unioun, being sua agrieable to
nature, to the incress of the policie of baith the kingdomes, to
the glorie of God and the uielfair of the inhabitantis thairof, it is
ane superfluous mater to crave the probatioun of the commoditeis of sua evident and necessar coniunctioun.

Bot to convince the refractaris to this unioun, in thair malice,
the necessitie with the profit thairof sal be demonstrat, uith ane
manifest demonstratioun; and to kiep gude ordour, it sal be
provin it tendis to the meantinance baith of religioun and
justice. And incidentlie I uill mak ane apologie for the puritie of
the Christiane religioun, againes the Anti-Christiane.[52]

The tua fundamentis of kingdomes ar religioun and justice,
religioun touardis God, justice to the people. Than of necessitie
it felloues, unioun in religioun and justice is the trew and perfyit
unioun of kingdomes – the finall end of the ane the uiell of the
saull, quhilk is the straitest band qhairby people or natioun can
be bunde, the uther resolving at all tymes for the uiell of the
people, that they may enjoy peace and tranquillitie.[53] *Ergo a*
contrario sensu, distractioun in religioun and policie is the

---

[52] This paragraph does not appear in the London MS
[53] 'the finall end . . . peace and tranquillitie' deleted in the London MS

distractioun of kingdomes, quhilk na man of judgement uill deny. Giff thir tua pillaris of thir tua kingdomes may be uiell establischit to the comfort of this ile, can thair rest any farder? For certaine it is, nane uil be opposit to this unioun bot thais qha ather craves distractioun in religioun, or utheruyis desyiris not to be reducit be justice in obedience.

The people[54] of God in the kingdome of Israell, sua lang as the unioun of that kingdome remanit undir David and Salamon, the harmonie of religioun in the auin sinceritie lykuyis florischit. Bot sua sone as Salamon maid defectioun fra trew godlienes be invectioun of idolatrie (quhilk movit Godis great uraith againes that people) the gude unioun of the kingdome ues disturbit, defectioun maid fra the posteritie of Salamon, and ane new kingdome erectit of the ten trybis, quhilk brocht to baith the kingdomes great calamiteis and thairby mutatioun ues maid of the religioun. For Jeroboam, King of the Ten Tribes, fearing the people undir him for the caus of religioun sould pas to Jerusalem (qhair the trew uorschip ues constitut), to the effect the unioun of the saidis kingdomes sould not be redintegrat, he fand out ane new forme of idolatrie be erectioun of tua goldin calves in Dan and Bethell, to be uorschipit for the trew God. For the quhilk great sine committit be Israell, and contineuit be the ungodlie kingis succieding thaireftir, and fatall ruine and distructioun fell upon that kingdome.

The kingdome of Juda undir Manasses, and utheris imitatoris of the kingdome of Israell in thair evill-doing become idolateris, quhilk ues the onely caus of the ruine of thair republique. And thaireftir it come be accessioun to the Babylonianes.

The kirkis of Graecia hes laitlie felt thair auin infelicitie, qha having submittit thameselffis to the Paip of Rome, embracing his erroris and haeresies of the adoratioun of bread and uorschipping of images, hes now gottin thair auin recompence, meserablie redactit undir the slaverie and bondage of the Turkis – making thair daylie incursiones in Ungarie, and uther Christiane kingdomes to the great desolatioun thairof. The

---

[54] Prefaced in the London MS with the following: 'That religion bringeth with it the happie unioun and concord of kingdomes, and preservit thame in thair auin integritie, is prouin be the word of God. For . . .'

great sine of idolatrie, as direct contrair to the trew uorschip of God, hes evir bein straitlie prohibit in the Scripture; and giff any uald alledge that prohibitioun to have bein gevin to the Jewis for restraint of the idolatrie of the Gentillis, and not of the Christianes, the direct contrair is maist trew. Yea, it is mair forbidden to Christianes, speciallie qhen as the licht of the evangell dois cleirlie schyne. Quhilk[55] movit godlie and Christiane Imperoris sic as Constantine and his sonis Gratianus and Theodosius, as the ecclesiasticall historie makis mentioun, to sett doun verray strait lauis againes idolatrie and all sort of uorschip. In respect qhairof his Majestie as he loves his auin standing sall doe uiell to be uar of Papistis and meantineris of idolatrie, not suffering tua religiounes to be professit in this ile – quhilk, giff it be permittit, uill not faill in end to infer the distractioun of the kingdomes.[56]

Be gude ressoun[57] I should remember ane maist recent and notable example of the stay of this now intendit unioun, betuixt thir tua realmes, onely be distractioun in religioun: yit to his Hienes' great glorie reservit (be the providence of God) to be effectuat in his Grace's pouer and monarchie. Thair is nane acquentit uith the historie of baith the nationes bot he knauis perfyitlie how heichlie this unioun hes bein affectit be Ingland, be frequent expostulatiouns speciallie in this last age. First, be that famous and renounit prince King Henry the Aucht of Ingland, in that conference quhilk should have bein kiepit at York uith umqhill King James the Fyift his sister sone. At quhilk tyme ane godlie resolutioun ues taine for the uiell of baith the natiounes, to have thair byroun trubles pacifiet. The particular conditiounes niedis not to be rehersit, the uorthienes of his Hienes' guids[ir] sua uiell knauin and dierlie conjoynit in blood to the said uorthie King of Ingland.

The same unioun [ues] prosecut of new be Eduard the Sixt of

---

[55] 'The great sine . . . Quhilk' replaced by 'This' in London MS
[56] 'and all sort . . . distractioun of the kingdomes' replaced in London MS by 'Heirof it fellouis (kieping the first ground) that unioun in religioun is unioun of kingdomes, distractioun in religioun distractioun in kingdomes – quhilk may be mair particularly testifiet be the historie of thir tua nationes, as sal be heireftir deducit'
[57] The London MS omits most of the long following section on Papistry, etc. Instead, it includes a section on union as the bringer of happiness to nations. See Appendix 1.

Ingland, qhen as mariage sould have bein accomplischit betuixt him and umqhill Marie Quene of Scotland, his Grace's derrest mother.[58] Quhilk mariage, being not onely earnestlie cravit, as the historie makis mentioun, bot concludit and agriet to have bein effectuat be consent of the Erll of Arrane, Lord Hamiltoun, Protector and governor of this kingdome for the tyme, and of the haill nobles and people of Scotland (pledgis appointit to have bein gevin for effectuatioun thairof); yit verray unhonest-lie [ues] stayit and schamefully brokin be the indirect dailing of David Betoun Cardinall of Scotland, and cleargie of this realme – onely cariit auay by the diversitie of religioun, meantinance of the Paip his factioun and supremacie. Sua that nathing ues the loss of the effectuatioun of this unioun, at that instant, be occasioun of the said mariage (giff it hed fellouit) bot distrac-tioun in religioun – quhilk is now brocht to end be the royall discent of his Hienes, out of the lang race of his noble predicessoris.

Heirupon enseuit the battell of Mussilbruch, the slauchter of many gude subjectis in this land, in the moneth of September 1547. Yit thair is heir ane thing maist speciall and uorthie to be remarquit: that notuithstanding the breaking of the contract of mariage, the former suit ues reneuit be the conductoris of the Inglisch armie befoir the battall ues sett or the tua nationes enterit in conflict. [This ues] be thair maist Christiane lettir direct to the governour of Scotland, admonisching him and the estaitis that they, being Christianes, sould not be the occasioun of the effusioun of Christiane blood: desyring the said contract of mariage to be reneuit and kiepit yit as of befoir – quhilk, being doun, they sould presentlie reteir themeselffis bak in Ingland, and satisfie qhatsumevir damnage Scotland had susteinit be thair incomming. Quhilk lettir, being presentit to the governour to have bein communicat to the haill people, ues putt be him in the handis of the Archbischop of Sanctandrois, his brother, qha abstractit the same and uald nevir suffer it to be communicat to the people. Heirby this unioun [ues] not onely than impedit, bot be the impediment maid thairto, producing the occasioun of all

[58] The following section appears in the London MS below, p.119, after the sentence 'Thaireftir [it ues] repeatit be Eduard Duik of Sommersait, qhairof mentioun wes maid of befoir'

this miserie and of the said great battell. Can any gude or godlie man deny bot the occasioun of all this calamatie wes onely the distractioun in religioun? Lett all men think uith thameselffis qhat unitie of religioun at that tyme micht have purchest and procurit;[59] qhairas sensyne ue being unitit in religioun have kiepit peace continually thir fyftie yeiris bygane.[60] And qhairas it is alledgit ue agrie not in religioun, it is ane manifest calumnie, the contrair thairof being maist trew. For we agrie in all the groundis and substantiallis; as to the ceremonies and indifferent thingis, it is na mater of discord. Bot I pray God all the nationes in Europe uar als uiell unitit in religioun.

Qhat greater confirmatioun or testimonie is niedfull for probatioun of this propositioun – unioun in religioun is unioun in kingdomes, distractioun in religioun distractioun in king-domes? I say farder: qhat greater confirmatioun is requisit to prove the stay of this unioun, and suiet harmonie of all the nationes and florising kingdomes in Europe in thair harmonicall agriement amangis thameselffis for repressing and ouerthrauing the Paip of Rome, the Turkis, Infidellis and Mahumetanes, bot that uofull calamitie and experience quhilk Christiane king-domes hes felt thir many yeiris bygane in thair kingdomes, commonuealthis, kirkis and people, be the tirannie of that divilisch conspyrit enemie againes the kirk of God – the Paip of Rome and his felloueris, qha nevir ceasit nor daylie ceasis fra thair cruell machinationes againes all gude Christianes, and fra thair bloodie murthiris and massacres of many thousand persones, bearing professit hostilitie againes all Christiane princes? In ane uord, the onely efficient caus of all this truble is nathing ells bot the questioun and distractioun in Christiane religioun haldin at undir be the Papistis, falselie callit Catholiques.[61]

---

[59] 'Can any gude . . . purchest and procurit' replaced in London MS by 'Thir recent testimoneis bearis witness that the said unioun hes bein with great instance cravit be the lait Kingis of Ingland; and the occasioun of the stay thairof prociedit onely for the maist pairt [sic] be the cleargie of Scotland, be ressoun of thair distractioun in religioun, qhairupon great trubles enseuit'
[60] The London MS deletes everything from here to 'stay of this unioun' and adds 'To conclude this point, the onely'
[61] 'of many thousand . . . falselie callit Catholiques' replaced in London MS by 'and perpetuall perturbatiouns of monarcheis, realmes and kingdomes. All this proceids onely upon distractioun in religioun, invectioun of idolatrie in place of trew piety,

That horrible and bloodie massacre of Paris, to the perpetuall horror of thair conscience, can lykuyis beir uitnes heirof. Procieding onely for the caus of religioun, the blude of the martyris brunt at Rome and Hispaine, the infinit multitudes slaine in France, Germanie and Italie, and ellsqhair [hed] na uther efficient caus of thir trubles at all tymes bot the invectioun of the anti-Christiane religioun, meantinance of the Paip and his suprematie.

I have oftentymes mervealit that any (albeit not learnit, yit naturall) sould adhere to thair absurditeis, thair haill doctrine composit of all sortis of haeresies: transubstantioun, purgatorie, frie uill, justificatioun be uarkis, invocatioun of sanctis, adoratioun of ane piece of bread in place of the Creator: indulgencis, pardones, dispensationes, the supremacie of the Paip to be *Vicarius Christi* and head over kirk in Earth: with infinit paradoxes quhilkis naturall men uill abhore. Thair ar onely thre fundamentis qhairof the Papist kirk is constructit: first, thair pretendit antiquitie (albeit of the common law, *mala fidei possessor nunquam praescribit*); thair alledgit successioun, quhilk they esteime to be personall (albeit it be aluyis reall, and inhaerent to sincere religioun, trew preaching of the uord and administratioun of the Sacramentis); last, thair visibilitie and universalitie, quhilk they ar not hable to meantein. Thir erronious conceattis being taine away (as be gude ressoun they cannot be sustienit) all their pretendit religioun abusive callit 'catholique' consequentlie fallis. And thairfoir, returning to the first ground, unioun in religioun inferris the unioun of kingdomes, distractioun in religioun distractioun in kingdomes.

Bot now (to keip the methode sett doun of befoir) seing the forsaid propositioun is sufficientlie provin, that distractioun in religioun producis distractioun in kingdomes, remembering lykuyis that the questioun of trew religioun is heichlie contravertit in all Europe, I cannot of deuty pretermit to sett doun ane apologie for defence of the reformit religioun now sincerlie professit againes the pretendit catholique.

Qhat sould move the Papistis disdainefully to affirme that the

---

quhilk consequentlie hes importit and importis the distractioun of kingdomes'. This is the end of the transferred section of the London MS. The London MS then continues 'Now fellouis the offeris maid be Ingland to Scotland' (p.120, note 71)

Christiane religioun presentlie professit in the reformit kirkis in
Europe is ane new religioun, laitlie erectit (as they pretend) be
Martine Luther, Calvine, Zwinglius, Oecolampadius, Beza,
Bucere and mony utheris great personages, in the puritie of the
trew Christiane doctrine? Qhairas, the direct contrair is maist
trew, that the sincere religioun now professit is that verray
religioun quhilk sone eftir the death of Christ ues ressavit be the
Christianes, and first of all be his Majesteis predicessoris, Kingis
of Britanie, and people of thir realmes — qha have aluyis
contendit to expell paganisme and Romisch idolatrie furth
of this land, quhilk superstitioun is defylit uith the erroris and
fals uorschippis of the gentillis, Arrianes, Nestorianes and
Entichianes.

   Be gude ressoun it may be mair justlie said that the pretendit
catholique religioun, laitlie invectit, is new-patchit and pretexit
againes the clier licht of the evangell: ressaving the grouth
thairof be litle and litle, amassit be syndrie compositiones, as
may appear be Platina, and in the treatise callit *Fasciculus
Temporum*. The tyme, the grouth and increase of the mess, the
haill pairtis and pendicles thairof, iuth the authoris of the same,
may easielie appeir thairby. Bot it may be iustlie said to thame as
Chryst (qha is the treuth) ansuerit to the Phariseis and Doctoris
of the law, '*non sic fuit ab initio*'. Bot becaus this mater hes bein
treatit heirtofoir be mony learnit men I uill content me with thir
few uordis: that it ues ane verray proper comparison sett doun
be Theodoretus, ane Greik bischop, '*de curatione graecorum
affectionum*', betuixt the Romaine Impyre and thair lauis on the
ane pairt, the impyir of Jesus Chryst and his law ressavit
throchout the haill uarld on the uther pairt. He said that the
Romaines could nather move the Persianes and Parthianes of
the eist to be subject to thair lauis, far les the Cymbrianes, the
Daines and people of Great Britanie at the north: for (said he)
'Sanct Peter the fischer, Sanct Paull the tentmaker have maid the
Britanes subject to the lauis of Chryst, qha could nauyis obey the
Romane lauis'. This is the assertioun of Theodoret, ane Orthodox Father in the kirk, sua that this ile of Great Britanie hes ane
heich honor (besydis mony utheris) in the professing and
embracing of Christiane religioun. For the antiquitie dois

testifie that the Apostles preachit in this land: Metaphrastes, cited be the Cardinall Baronius, affirmis that Sanct Peter come heir. Joseph of Arimathie and Simon Zelotes come lykuyis – as the historie dois teach ws. Of this deductioun it is evident that this ile hes bein blissed fra the begynning in the professioun of trew religioun. And thairfoir lett na man call the trew religioun now embracit ane new religioun.

For confirmatioun qhairof I uill remember his Majestie of ane notable policie usit be Constantius Chlorus for tryell of his subjectis, qhairof Eusebius lykuyis makis mentioun.[62] He causit ane feinyit proclamatioun be maid, commanding all his subjectis to sacrifice to fals godis, and qhasoevir refusit sua to doe to depairt instantlie out of his armes and impyir. Certanelie this ues purposelie doun to knaw the qualiteis and conditiones of his people. Be this occasioun ane great number, to preserve thair uardlie estait, did sacrifice to the fals godis. Wtheris, qha uar trew Christianes, desyrit rather to loss all than to serve thame. Qhairupon the Imperor presentlie discoverit him, and dischargit all thais qha had uorschippit falss godis off his countrey, saying 'How can they be trew to the Imperor qha ar falss to God?' But as to the trew Christianes, qha left all that they had rather than to offend the trew God, he callit thame hame and sett thame about his persoun and estait – qhairof Eusebius makis mentioun.

Treulie, I uald not uyss his Majestie to mak ony counterfitt or simulat proclamatioun; bot his majestie will doe uiell to be successor to Constantius Chlorus, his auin predicessor in the electioun and chosing of his Hienes' subjectis – and that in his maist important effairis, nane be admittit bot sic as ar knauin to be uiell groundit in Chrystiane religioun. For ane modest woman aucht not onely to be chast bot to be frie from all suspitioun. Richt sua, all thais that ar employit in the effairis of Cristiane princes sould be frie from all suspitioun and indirect dayling, to the effect for thair particular commoditie they mak not his Majestie mislykit of his subjectis.

Lett the Papistis speak qhat they pleis, thair is nane acquentit with the ecclesiasticall historie bot uill cleirly prove that during

[62] Marginal note: 'Euseb. in. vita. Constan' (ca. 16)

the thre first periodis of Christianitie (qhairof ather conteins thre hundreth yeiris) the trew uorschipp of God quhilk hes bein plantit in this ile sen the tyme of the Apostles hes sua contineuit uith expres detestatioun of the Romisch idolatrie and abhominatioun of the gentillis, Arrianes and Nestorianes. And sua be gude ressoun they cannot give that style to our religioun, to call it new. Bot because learnit theologues in this age hes sufficientlie debaitit this purpose, I uill insist na farder thairin. Lett thame peruse Theodoretus, Justinus, Clemens Alexandrinus, as also Minutius Felix, Tertulliane, Origene and Arnobius, qha lievit in the thrid age of the first periode of Christianisme: qha testifys expreslie that the gentillis accusit the Christianes, for that they had nather temples, alteris, images, nor visibill and materiall sacrifices, and that they did hyid from sicht that quhilk they did uorschip.

It sal be best to convince the Paip in his erroris be his auin cannon law, and sua to give him ane uage of his auin tymmer. I am of that opinioun that the maist pairt of his erroris may be refutit be his auin law. Bot schortlie I uill recite ane few number. It is affirmit be the Paip in his sixt buik of the *Decretall Epistollis,* '*Papa non est homo*'. In the proeme of his buik of the *Clementines,* '*Papa nec est deus nec homo, ergo manifeste oppositus Christo, qui est et deus et homo*'. Heir I ressoun. '*Si neque in divinitate nec humanitate consistit, ergo vel angelus, vel bestia. Non angelus, ergo bestia; et per consequens, si bestia, Christi vicarius non est*'. In his extravagant, *De Verborum Significatione,* [*he says*] '*Papa non est purus homo, hoc enim facile credo, est etenim impurus ganeo*'. Qhat blasphemie cariis the uordis of Gelasius in the decreis of Gratiane: '*Romana sedes de omnibus iudicare debet, nulla de illa. Omnibus licet ad illam appellare, ab illa non licet absolutos in consiliis illa damnare potest, et damnatos absolvere*'. In his extravagant, *De Concessione Prebendae,* '*Nemo debet dicere domino papae cur hoc facis*'. The uordis of Anacletus ar thir: '*Deus est pater, quia condidit, ecclesia est mater, quia regeneravit. Hinc panormitanus in tractatu de consilio basiliensi. Ergo inquit, Si papa est filius ecclesiae, debet ecclesiae obedire. Eugenius et Paulus tertius in consilio tridentino noluit. Ego aliud ex his verbis colligo, est filius ecclesiae. Ergo non caput, est filius; ergo non sponsus, nisi se profiteri velit incestum*'. I have taine occasioun incidentlie in the disputatioun of this unioun of kingdomes to defend the trew Christiane religioun now professit againes the pretendit catholique.

I conclude that, presentlie and in all ages bypast, distractioun in religioun is distractioun in kingdomes: and the onely efficient caus of the haill trubles in Europe, thir mony yeiris bygane is the questioun in religioun: the constant platt of the pretendit catholiques, meantining ane earthlie synagoge composit of paganisme and Judaisme to be directlie opposit againes the heavenlie and spirituall kirk, the trew spous of Jesus Chryst. [*They are*] not eschamit to mentein ane implicit, not explicit faith (*credo ecclesiae*), to doubt in the last braith of any assurance of salvatioun (howsoevir Christianes be armit uith repentance for thair sines, perfyit resolutioun of the mercy of God, uith constant faith in the death of our Saviour Christ, yit nevir to be assured of gude estait). Qhy then sould not the benifit of this blissed unioun be concludit, to continew chearfully forevir? Qhat hes bein the truble of France this lang tyme bypast, bot the caus of religioun, and now tua religiones sufferit thairin – quhilk hes brocht the kingdome to na small miserie. I pray God that Papistis qha have thair eyis bent upon his Majestie, invying his gude estait, fearing his pouer and greatnes, sall nevir have pouer to doe his Majestie harme. The Lord preserve his noble persoun (to qhome all obedience and reverence is propir) from all his enemies. For the desyir of his Majesteis standing (to qhome besyidis the obedience of ane trew subject I am wtheruyis particularlie oblist) sall nevir depairt out of my mynd.

The nixt argument felloues, tuiching the unioun of kingdomes in policie. Will any man deny that the dilatatioun and incress of the boundis and dominiones of kingdomes tendis not to the advancement thairof?[63] Is it not to the great felicitie of this ile that haill Britanie is alreddy unitit in ane sceptor and jurisdictioun?[64] The bordorer theiff and traitour, the seditious

[63] The London MS omits or transfers the previous pages of this tract (from p.109, note 57), replacing it with the historical section at Appendix I. The two tracts now begin again to run in parallel.
[64] The London MS adds 'Qhat inhabitant hes not alreddy taistit of the gude procieding thairof? Qhat joy have we now by this sueit peace! Qhat sorrow and anguisch of mynd sustienit we of befoir, in daylie incursiones, expugnationes, captiviteis and exustiones!'

and uickit persoun [are] reducit to peace and obedience, having
na bak dure for his refuge – the lait execution of michtie and
strong malefactoris heir can bear uitnes. Is thair not ane great
difference betuixt the suiet peace now possessit be ws, and thais
great trubles quhilk ue have sustienit of befoir – in sic sort that
we neid not to be affrayit of any forraine countreyis, and na
occasioun lyklie to fall out amangis ourselffis? Qhat ioy have we
now baith in bodie and sprit! Qhat sorrow and anguisch of
befoir, in daylie incursiones, irreptiones, expugnationes and
captiviteis! Now certaine it is, that[65] reuard is to be exspectat be
gude men for thair vertew, as also punischment for malefactoris.
Qhat toung or pen is habill to declair the uorthienes of this
unioun? Without questioun thair uil be onely tua sortis of
persones, refractoris to this unioun: people forrane, of uther
nationes, on the ane pairt, wtheris of thir tua realmes amangis
ourselffis on the uther pairt. As for forraine persones, envy pre-
dominattis amangis thame. They cannot uiell digest our gude
estait and pouer, giff we uar treulie unitit, for they fear our
strenth (being now in ane bettir conditioun nor of befoir). Bot
uith thir men I uil be schort. *'Fremat Zoilus, et rumpantur Ilia
costro'*. Nature hes maid ws strong in ane continent,[66] ane king
and soverane monarchie; now unioun in religioun and policie,
with unitie in hairtis and myndis, sall mak ws double stronger,
freindis to our favorers, great terror to our enemies, the
inhabitantis daylie enioying peace, and increasing in uealth and
ritches. Qhat greater blissing than this can any man crave?

As to the persones refractaris uithin this ile, thair ar thre sortis.
First, Papistis, falselie callit catholiques, qha contendis ather for
subversioun of religioun or at the liest for peace (callit be thame)
of conscience. The second sort ar bordoreris, Hieland men,
deboschit idle men, seditious and unquyet sprittis qha thinkis it
nauyis for thair standing to be reducit undir law and obedience,
or that evir thir natiounes sal be in perfyit peace and unioun:
quhilk giff it uar perfytit uald bring sic ane coniunctioun in the

[65] 'Qhat joy . . . certaine it is, that' shortened in London MS to 'Bot, now'
[66] A frequent theme of all Unionist writers, arising in part from James's own speech to
the English Commons on 19 March 1604. See Tanner, *Constitutional Documents of the
Reign of James I*, p.26

auin tyme, be mariage, commixtioun of blood, ane name common to baith the nationes, *idem velle, idem nolle*, that the profit thairof cannot be espyit at the first. The thrid sort [*ar*] certane lordis and landit gentlemen of clannes, leaning overmekle to thair auin force, far fra the feitt [sic] of justice, usurping upon all men, estieming thameselffis kingis uithin thair auin boundis, bakkit uith great convocationes, comming to the tribunall place with boist, nauyis uilling to be censurit be justice.

I cannot believe thair is any in Ingland that uill oppone againes this unioun, for tua causes: first becaus they ar now to ressave but truble that quhilk they not onely lang affectit and expostulat, bot for the quhilk they have long contendit be armis, and yit could nevir prevaill: nixt, of the law the air or successor can nevir be hard to come againes the died of his predicessor, quhilk propositioun hes place alsuiell in publict as privat successiones. It is alreddy provin that Ingland has affectit this mater maist heichlie, and being many tymes cravit, is now brocht to pas by all mennis expectatioun, be the providence of God, be richt of his hienes' maist noble blood. It has bein na litle forsicht, in that uorthie prince[67] King Henry the Sevint, in the mariage of Quene Margaret, his dochter, qhen as the treatise ues thair qhat allyance sould be embracit. Some cariit auay with Hispaine, wtheris uith France, some uith Burgundie; yit he preferrit the allyance uith Scotland to all utheris, and at last declarit and resolvit (as is now come to pas) that giff evir it sould fall furth that of the ischew of that mariage any persoun sould succeid to the croune of Ingland, as it is now establischit in his Hienes' persoun, it sould redound to the profit of Ingland forevir, and uald in end produce the unioun of baith the nationes – and sua reservit be the providence of God to be now effectuat, in his Majesteis happie governement, to his Grace's heich honor and glorie forevir.

---

[67] The long passage, 'nixt, of the law . . . that uorthie prince' is replaced in the London MS by 'Nixt, they have not onely maid thair earnest suitt, bot thairwith sett doun thair particular offeris to Scotland, as sal be manifest be the deductioun eftirfellouing, testifiet be thair auin historie. And giff the saides conditiones war perfyitlie concludit as they war offerit (albeit mekle mair man be now exspectit be Scotland than of befoir) this gude unioun wil be accomplischit to the confort of the haill ile. The first project of this unioun in the last aige began with'

The same unioun [*ues*] repeatit of new be King Henry the Aucht, as ues declarit heirtofoir; qha, as he ues ane famous and victorious prince, for his great victoreis recoverit in France, in lyk maner perceaving King James the Fyift of Scotland to be ane uorthie prince, indeuit with many gude qualiteis, and in that respect affecting in his hairt the unioun of Scotland and Ingland – considering it uald import ane great blissing to baith the nationes, directit his embasadoris in Scotland, craving ane mieting and conference uith King James the Fyift (his sister sone) to have bein kiepit at York, for great materis tending to the uiell of baith the nationes – as the historie makis mentioun: of deliberat mynd (uther materis being aggriet) to give his dochter to him in mariage, and eftir his deces to mak him King of all Britanie. And to the effect King James the Fyift micht the bettir repose himselff upon this resolutioun, it ues offerit that he sould be presentlie pronuncit and declarit Duik of York and Leutennant of Ingland. Ane mater uorthie to have bein embracit, lyik as his Hienes' guids[*ir*] in hairt and mynd ues finallie resolvit to embrace the same. Wes not it ane great loss at that tyme to baith the nationes that this unioun sould not have bein endit – and onely seditiouslie stayit be the prelattis and cleargie of Scotland, repeating the captivitie of King James the First of Scotland deteinit in Ingland be the space of auchtein yeiris, [*and of*] the ancienne kingis, King Malcome and King William, drauin upon fair promises to Londoun be King Henry the Secound, to schaw ane countienance againes the King of France uith qhome they uar undir great freindschip. Bot this is evir the forme of evill-disposit persones, to remember upon auld querellis qhen any concord or unioun is intendit?

The last testimonie qhairof mentioun ues maid of befoir, is mair recent: of Eduard the Sixt, sone to King Henry the Aucht, maist earnestlie affecting this unioun be mariage uith his Hienes' darrest mother. Thaireftir [*it ues*] repeatit be Eduard Duik of Sommersait,[68] Protector of Ingland, in the yeir of God 1548 be

---

[68] 'qhairof mentioun wes maid of befoir' added in the London MS. In the London MS the sections on pp.110-11 now appear as an insertion. Russell's treatment of the Henrician and Edwardian proposals is typical of the Scots writers. See, for example, Pont, above, p.29

his lettir send to the nobles and counsall of Scotland, contiening the haill forme, maner and ordour how this unioun sould be establischit – of the quhilk Epistoll Johne Sleidane makis mentioun in the 20[*th*] buik of his 'Commentares'. And giff his Majestie will fellow the determinatioun proponit thairin be Ingland, I think it sould decyid the questioun: for it is aluyis best to convince ane contradictor be his auin armour, thir testimonies procieding onely fra thameselffis. Bot seing they have sett doun thair securitie of auld, I pray God that this natioun of Scotland be uiell forsein and circumspect in our securitie.

In[69] materis of unioun commonlie thair ar tua ordinar remeidis, specially of kingdomes. First be armes and victorie, quhilk is the end of all deidlie feidis and trubles. This concord be armes is not sure, for the ane pairtie uill evir be luiking for his best advantage. The uther, be mariage, is mair sure. Bot the third is maist sure – quhilk is, be the laufull successioun of the richteous air, our gratious soverane succieding to the richt of[70] thir tua imperiall crounes be the noble discent of his blood. This unioun [*is*] uanting nathing to the perpetuall uiell and felicitie of ane soverane monarchie, bot the hairtlie unioun and harmonie of the inhabitantis.

Bot now I man remember his Majestie of the offeris of Ingland to Scotland: that they[71] protestit befoir God that the effectuating and accomplisching of the said mariage betuixt Eduard the Sixt and his Majesteis derrest mother Marie Quene of Scotland wes nauyis to acquyir any dominioun or superioritie in Scotland, or the servitude of the inhabitantis thairof, bot that he ues resolvit in mynd to knit up sic ane sure necessitude betuixt thir tua nationes, quhilk sould nevir be infringit – making ane verray fair discourse. Quene Marie

---

[69] In the London MS this paragraph is moved down, appearing after the section on Somerset's epistle.

[70] 'richteous air . . . richt of' replaced in the London MS by 'laufull successor to baith, as is now in his Majesteis maist gracious persoun, succieding be the noble discent of his blood to baith'

[71] Marginal note: 'Sleidane ut supra. lib. 20. Comment'. In the London MS this paragraph follows the insertion from pp.110-11 and begins: 'Now fellouis the offeris maid be Ingland to Scotland in the epistole direct (as is befoir said) in the year of God 1548 eftir the feild of Mussilbruth – testifieing not only thair earnest affectioun to the said unioun, bot be qhat maner it sould be concludit. First, Ingland'

behovit to be mariit, ather uith some forraine alliance or ells
uithin hir auin natioun. To marie uithin hir auin countrey, it uar
to bass. Giff scho sould marie uith ane forrane alliance, could any
be sua propir as Ingland? The reassoun ues that mariage uald
import the pacificatioun of all trubles, and the quyetnes of the
haill ile. Bot giff scho sould happin to marie uith strangeris,
thairby to bring in forrane people to Scotland for thair
meantinance, it uald in end tend to thair subversioun – takand
the example fra the Saxones, qha being brocht in Ingland for
thair support maid thair conquest thair. Bot thair is farder, that
the lauis of Scotland sould nauyis be abrogat: seing that France
and Hispaine, the kingdomes of the Impyir housoevir unitit yit
bruikis thair auin lauis. And heir I pray his Majestie that as to his
perpetuall honor and glorie, this unioun is to be concludit in lyk
maner, uith his gude affectioun thairto:[72] [that] he be also indeuit
uith uisdome to be cairfull for the haill ile, in the quhilk cair that
he nevir foryett his naturall deutie to Scotland. Giff his Majestie
tendis to ane heich monarchie of the haill, he man not be aluyis
resident thair: for the Kingis of Hispaine and France doe not sua.
The soveraine monarch man not be aluyis resident in ane pairt
or citie of the monarchie. Wtheruyis, the rest of the kingdome
unitit, be progres of tyme, will fall furth in ane aristocratie. Lett
thairfoir his Majestie forsie the weill and standing of this his first
and auldest impyir – wtheruyis it wil be na unioun, bot ane
manifest discord. Bot be gude argumentis ane overture heireftir
sal be sett doun, how this mater sal be best satlit to the uiell of
baith the nationes.

Qha can deny bot harmonie and agriement tendis to the
preservatioun, meantinance and knitting of all civill companies?
Is not ane citie ane multitude of men, of dyvers qualiteis and
conditiones, yit lieving in unioun obedient to ane law and
magistrat – kieping ane harmonicall proportioun, ane touardis

[72] 'seing that France . . . gude affectioun thairto' is replaced in the London MS by 'bot
baith the countreys to be in paritie and conformitie in all respectis, as memberis of ane
bodie. Qhat farder testimoneis can any man crave, ather tuiching the necessitie of this
unioun, or anent the forme, maner and securitie thairof, then that quhilk wes concludit
of auld be England, bot specially in this last age'. In the London MS this is then followed
by the paragraph above, as per n. 69. The remaining part of the paragraph, to 'uiell of
baithe the nationes' is omitted in the London MS

ane uther, be dew analogie, althocht the memberis be of dyvers ordouris and estaitis, yit agreis in concord? The harmonie of musick consistis of unequall voces and soundis; yit be proportioun conspyiris altogidder to ane harmonie. Qhat is in the creatioun of the haill universe, in the office of the creaturis? Nathing ells bot harmonie, mony dyvers creaturis yit everyane auaiting upon thair auin functioun. The lyik in the elementis, in the mixtione of bodeis different amangis thameselffis, yit serving to the compositioun and constitutioun of the bodie. Sould not this be ane similitude serve for the conjunctioun of Scotland and Ingland? Thair uill na gude man doubt heirof. Ane Christiane uill not deny bot thair is onely ane God, ane baptisme, ane father of all qha is above all and in us all: qhy then sould it be denyit, that all that believe in Him sould not be of ane heart and mynd, ilk persoun referring thair graces and benifittis to the exercise of perfyit cheritie. Oh[73] how happie ane thing it is to sie mony gude people of dyvers kingdomes in unitie and conformity, governit undir the obedience of ane soverane monarch in trew religion and policie! For albeit they be dyvers memberis, yit they constitut onely ane bodie.

Six sindrie thingis ar requisit to ane happie and civill societie. First, trew and sincere religioun touardis God. Nixt, justice to the people. Thridlie, armes to be usit againes enemies. Ferdlie, ritches to meantein the estait publict and privat. Fyiftlie, the people to be aluyis verteuoslie employit. Last, gude faculteis and alimentis. To thir six, thair ar sic sortis of men ansuerable: the pastor for religioun, the magistrat for justice, the nobles, burgesses, artificeris and husbandmen to accomplisch the rest of the estait. The pastor sould not be ane dume doig bot, acknauledging him to be callit to ane heich charge, sould be about to discharge his functioun faithfullie, be teaching of gude doctrine and leading ane honest lyfe conforme thairto – not to sitt in the chair of pestilence, qhairof David makis mentioun, nor in thair pontificall seattis as the Scrybes and Phariseis, in the chair of Moyses: bot according to the doctrine of Sanct Paul, to be irreprovable, not frouard and angrie, or gevin to fylthie lucre, uith the remanent qualiteis enumerat be him. The

[73] 'Ane Christiane . . . perfyit cheritie. Oh' deleted in London MS

magistrat aucht to be endeuit uith four properteis: first, to tak
nathing injustlie fra ony persoun, nixt to give to ilk man his auin,
thridlie to prefer the gude publict to his auin particular, and last,
above all thingis to be diligent in his calling. Thir ar the four
essentiall pointis requisit in ane magistrat. As to the nobles,
artificeris, and utheris of the common sort, corresponding to the
remanent of the saidis six qualiteis, they man lykuyis attend
upon thair calling. And of tham dois aryse ane great harmonie,
unitie and conjunctioun, to the meantinance of ane familie,
citie, kingdome and monarchie – and in end, dyverss monarcheis unitit in ane soverane monarchie to the glory of God and
uiell of the people. Qhat sall I say? Conteines not the haill uarld
ane musicall unitie and harmonie, composit of mony dyvers
pairtis, yit in end resolving in ane unioun and concord? Giff
thairfoir this be trew, as it cannot be denyit, will any uiell-
disposit persoun be ane stay to this unioun and happie concord
of tua sua lang different and ancienne kingdomes?

The mater of this unioun, as I said of befoir, uorthelie offeris
to any man that uald inlarge his pen in the dispute of this
purpose ane verray spatious field. And for confirmatioun of the
affirmative pairt of this unioun, infinit argumentis and ressones
micht be adducit, seing it cariis uith it na small blissing. Bot for
schortnes I uill subsist, contenting myselff with the particular
deductioun befoir rehersit. To wit: that it sall import perpetuall
unioun of thir nationes, baith in religioun and policie, ane
ritch treasure to the inhabitantis, for thair florisching estait in
peace, uealth, joy and tranquillitie forevir. In ane uord, they sal
be strong amangis thameselffis, freindis to thair favorers, great
terror to thair enemies. Qhat kingdome in Europe is hable to
surpas thame, enjoying all the commoditeis of this ile? Providing aluyis, that be this unioun Ingland acclame na prerogative
above the realmes unitit. The lichtlie regaird and disestimatioun
of Ireland (being ane ancienne impyir) wes the occasioun of the
uearis meantienit be Ingland. It is now peciable, qhairas thir
mony yeiris bygane, the meantiening of the uearis exhaustit the
thesaure of Ingland. The devyse of the erectioun of the tent
penny in the Law Countreyis of Flanderis ues the onely caus and
occasioun of the defectioun of the estaitis of Flanderis from the

King of Hispaine. And thairfoir, as princes heichlie affectis thair kingdomes to be unitit and incorporat in ane soverane monarchie, they man nevir foryett the auld impyir and gude estait thairof. Of this deductioun it is evident [*that*] giff Scotland in the gude estait thairof sall not evir be in recommendatioun to his Majestie, this unioun sal be altogidder ineffectuall. Qhairas, be the contrair, being uiell and uyselie concludit, it sal be the greatest blissing that ony mortall prince or people could have cravit heir on Earth, by that celestiall beatitude quhilk is to be exspectat hiereftir. This sal be sufficient for the affirmative pairt of this unioun uith the ressones thairof – praying God it may be hairtlie in hairtis and myndis, to the glorie of God, perpetuall uiell and florisching estait of baith the nationes.[74]

The thrid pairt of this treatise conteinis the trew decisioun of the questioun, embracing the affirmative pairt of this unioun, rejecting the negative, with ane refutatioun of the haill argumentis adducit for probatioun of the said negative.

I have bein about to keip the methode sett doun in the beginning of this treatise, thairby to discharge the faitfull deutie of ane dialectitiane: quhilk is to reassoun probablelie, ather of the pairtis of the questioun, with the argumentis belangand thairto, and to pretermit nathing that may appeir substantiall – of deliberat mynd (sua far in me is) to satisfie ather of the contradictoris. Now it restis in this place to sie qhat sal be uith gude reassoun thocht to be best of this purpose, and quhilk of the parteis forsaidis meanteinis the best caus: seing the end of all disputatioun tendis *ut veritas eliciatur*.

Without questioun, the affirmative pairt of this unioun justlie sould prevaill, cariing with it manifest treuth and infallible equitie. In sic sort that thair is na gude man in ather of thir tua realmes bot he man esteime that it sall produce ane great[75]

---

[74] The preceding two paragraphs are replaced in the London MS by a single brief paragraph.
[75] 'and infallible equitie . . . produce ane great' replaced in London MS by 'baith in necessitie and commoditie, and importing ane perpetuall'

blissing to the haill ile. The negative thairfoir man be altogidder rejectit, uith the argumentis adducit for confirmatioun thairof, quhilkis in the auin place sal be refutit. Bot housoevir I inclyne to the affirmative, it is with this speciall limitatioun that it sall not import ony alteratioun of the kingdomes in haill or in pairt, in religioun, policie, lauis, liberteis and ancienne priviledgis, bot to tend to the gude of baith, prejudice of nane: to be ane hairtlie concord, suiet harmonie and reciproque band of amitie and freindschipp, with mutuall imperting of all gude offices, on ather syid, to the uiell of baith the nationes. And as it hes bein many tymes cravit be Ingland, now to be embracit and effectuat. In accomplisching qhairof, Ingland cannot be hard evir, to come againes thair auin offeris maid be thame of befoir to Scotland. And giff we sould all now become ane bodie and soverane monarchie, thair man be mekle mair yeildit to Scotland, yit nauyis to thair prejudice. Giff it sal be ane unioun, it man be hairtlie, it man be perpetuall. It man be in paritie and conformitie in all respectis, uith ane mutuall participatioun of benifittis and blissingis: not to be verball, bot reall: not to be the translatioun of ane kingdome in ane uther, reducit out of libertie in servitude, with alteratioun of lauis, constitutiones and policie and, as I said of befoir, to begyne with ane comedie and end uith ane tragedie. This uil be na unioun, bot discord: yea, albeit it uar amangis brether and persones nevir sua deirlie conjoynit in blood. Thairfoir the generall of the unioun of necessitie man be grantit, qhat sal be the particular it man be tryit be the conference. It is trew, the generallis cariis evir ane fair schaw, and uil be easielie grantit – bot qhen it comes to the particular, thair the questioun standis. In ane syllogisme the propositioun oftentymes uil be grantit, yit *communis fallacia* for the maist pairt is in the assumptioun. Albeit the particularis of particularis heir ar not to be explicat, yit necessar it is that ane generall veow, or rather ane perfyit platt of this unioun (as be gude ressoun it sould be concludit) be presentlie sett doun, to the effect every man may consider thairof, reservand aluyis any bettir resolutioun of all uiell affectit to this unioun.

As the mater in itselff is verray ueachtie, and the greatest subject that hes occurrit in Europe thir many yeiris bygane, sua on the uther pairt it uald be verray wyselie considerit, and that be ane speciall law and consitutioun to remaine uith the posteritie: and be expres Act of Parliament to be sett doun uith uniforme consent of baith the nationes, contiening in the first place be narratioun the caus thairof, nixt in the uordis dispositive of the said Act the forme and ordour thairof. I will thairfoir (according to my mein knauledge) in ane schort abrigement propone the principall and substantiall groundis heireftir to be enlargit, eftir the conference of the tua nationes.[76]

That the haill ile of Britanie, contiening thairin the tua ancienne kingdomes of Scotland and Ingland, uith the haill iles and pendicles thairof, sal be erectit be his Majestie uith uniforme consent of baith the nationes and estaitis in ane soverane and heich monarchie forevir, to be callit the Kingdome of Great Britanie. That the saidis nationes as ane bodie sall remaine in paritie and conformitie, reciprocallie, ather of thame mutuallie to utter all gude offices quhilkis may tend to thair advancement, without disparitie bot speciallie uithout alteratioun of any of the tua kingdomes ather in religioun or policie, lauis, judicator, priviledgis and immuniteis thairof.[77] That they sall tak upon thame ane common name, to be callit heireftir Britanes.[78] That the traffique and negotiatioun of merchandis sal be mutuall, ather of the tua nationes to injoy the priveledgis of the uther, and quhilk ues grantit of befoir to Scotland in the alliance uith France, the tyme of the mariage of wmqhill Quene Marie his Majesteis darrest mother uith the Daulphine of France. To be joynit as ane kingdome in blood and mariage, and that it sal be laufull to the inhabitantis of ather of thir tua realmes to duell

[76] The long preceding section beginning 'This uil be na unioun' is replaced in the London MS by: 'As to the particularis they wil be concludit be his Majestie with advyse of the estaites of baith the kingdomes. I will thairfoir sett doun ane generall overture. For seing this is the greatest subject that hes occurrit thir mony ages bypast, thairfoir it wald be weill establischit be ane perfyit law and constitutioun in parliament, contiening in the narratioun the causes and commoditeis thairof, and in the words dispositive the forme, nature and ordour of the said unioun, qhairof I will sett doun the cheiff and principall groundis'

[77] This sentence is replaced by 'The ancient names of Scotland and Ingland to be putt in perpetuall oblivioun, in semblable maner as wes the houses of York and Lancaster'

[78] 'for thame and thair posteriteis. The saides nationes to remaine in partie and conformitie, reciprocallie to stand without alteratioun of thair estait, to be mutuall in traffique, commerce and negotiatioun' inserted in London MS

peciablie in ather of thame at thair plesour, acquyir benifices, ecclesiasticall digniteis and offices, uithout imparitie, to uplift and ressave the fruittis and emolumentis thairof. To conqueis landis, lordschippis and seigneureis, gudes and geir movable and immovable in ather of the realmes at thair plesour, to be peciablie bruikit and possessit be thame and thair successoris in all tyme comming – being ather acquyrit be successioun, alienation, donatioun *inter vivos vel causa mortis.* And that airis and successoris sall laufullie succeid thairto uithout ony truble and impediment, as giff they uar naturallie borne uithin ather of the kingdomes – and this to be uith indemnitie, and uithout any finance thairfoir. Giff ather of thame hes to doe uith utheris in proces, to prosecute thair debaitis befoir thair auin ordinar judge, according to that common reull, *actor debet sequi forum rei.* And in conclusioun, to lieve in ane sueit harmonie forevir, fellouing now the gude determinatioun sett doun be King Eduard the Sixt and the offeris maid be Ingland to Scotland. This is ane schort abrigement of the principall groundis of this unioun, to be heireftir mair particularlie sett doun in the conference to be had befoir his Majestie – seing I dispute at this tyme not *in hypothesi, sed in thesi.* And yit, in the fourt place of this treatise, I uill sett doun be schort articles the forme of the securitie of this unioun, as be gude reassoun it sould be concludit.[79]

Now it restis in this place, as the negative propositioun is rejectit, to answer to the argumentis sett doun for proving thairof. The first argument is that alterationes and mutationes in republiques, kingdomes and commonueillis, albeit it uar fra evill to gude, ar pernicious: the concussioun of the fundamentis of ane auld commonuiell verray dangerous: the translatioun of ane estait in ane uther, not to be sufferit. The alteratioun of auld lauis and gude policie, verray convenient for the kingdome, is not to be permittit, seing it uald tak many ages to satle the auld impyir be introductioun of ane new law. Thir ar the first tua argumentis to the quhilkis I uill answer *unico contextu.*

I answer directlie to thir tua argumentis, and grantis the

<hr>

[79] This concluding passage at the end of the paragraph was much altered in the London MS

propositioun sett doun in ather of thame to be of veritie: to witt, that the alteratioun of kingdomes, realmes and monarcheis in thair lauis, estait and policie (albeit in the meanest pairt thairof) in ane moment can import nathing ells bot the subversioun of the auld impyir. And to this assertioun, I uillinglie agrie as maist trew. Bot giff this unioun may proceid and be effectuat to the great gude of baith the nationes, uithout alteratioun of ather of thair estaitis in religioun, justice and policie (quhilk I doubt not is meanit be his Heines, seing be gude reassoun it can be na utheruyis), than the pretendit fear of that alledgit alteratioun – quhilk is not to fellow – sould not be adducit, *tanquam argumenti medium*, to stay this unioun. Sua, the propositioun being grantit, the questioun uil be onely in the assumptioun, giff this unioun sall import any alteratioun of the kingdomes or not. And heir I will prove that the unioun sall proceid hairtlie, in sueit harmonie and concord, to constitut ane florising and soverane monarchie, and yit the publict estait of ather of the nationes nauyis alterit or imparit.

The first ground quhilk I sett doun is that unioun of the auin nature importis not alteratioun of thingis unitit, bot be the contrair it procuris the sueit harmonie of thingis unitit – as is evident in the visible fabrique of the haill universe. Thair ar four sortis of four syndrie and different creatures: the first of thais that consistis of thair auin simple essence, the second that hes baith essence and lyfe, the thrid that has essence, lyfe and senss, the last having lyfe, essence, senss and ressoun. The four elementis consistis onely in thair essence, uithout lyfe or sense. The plantis have baith essence and lyfe. The brutall beasts having baith lyfe, essence and sense, yit they tak thair vitall nuriture fra the plantis and elementis. The last and hiest creature is the race of man, prefectit to all the rest of the creatures, having in himselff lyfe, essence, senss and reassoun, to qhome the elementis, plantis and brutall creaturis dois daylie service, and he is prefectit as lord over thame. Heir is[80] ane michtie fabrique, heir ane creatioun of dyvers creatures: and yit in end resolving evir in ane perfyit unioun and sueit harmonie, with interposi-

---

[80] This sentence thus far appears in the London MS simply as 'And last man, prefectit to the haill, qhome the rest dois serve. Is nocht this. . .'

tioun of gude offices ilk ane to ane uther. Ane diversitie in the creatioun and creature, bot in conclusioun ane sueit unioun uithout alteratioun.

Of[81] thir premisses I reassoun in this maner. Qhy sall it be thocht, becaus thir tua kingdomes thir mony ages bypast hes remanit dyvers and syndrie monarcheis undir dyverss kingis, that thairfoir ather of thame, kieping thair auld and ancienne estait uithout alteratioun thairof, may not now be reducit to ane soverane monarchie, to keip the unioun – seing the varietie of creaturis and diversitie thairof (as said is) is not ane stay to unioun, bot rather producis the same? Qhy then? Will any man deny, qhatevir hes bein or is the estait of thir tua nationes, qhidder altogidder conforme or in some respect in disparitie ather in religioun, lauis or policie, bot out of thair verray varietie and disparitie may be reducit in unioun[82] be erectioun of ane soverane monarchie? For the nature of unioun, speciallie of kingdomes, is not to alter the nature of thingis unitit, bot to mak ane greater harmonie. Mair nor in the fabrique of the haill universe (kieping daylie ane perfyit unioun) ony alteratioun is maid of the creatures unitit thairto. Sua that they ar in ane great error that estiemis that this unioun cannot be concludit uithout alteratioun of the estait – qhair be the contrair, ather of the kingdomes sall remaine in thair auin integritie, uithout alteratioun in religioun or policie. For it is not to bring ane prejudice to the inhabitantis, bot ane great benifit in all respectis; and uithout questioun, it had bein ane great oversicht in his Majestie (this happie occasioun having sua uiell and prosperouslie fallin furth be the noble discent of his Majesteis blood) not to have bein about to prosecut this happie and blissed unioun.

This mater of the unioun uithout alteratioun of that quhilk is unitit is cleirlie provin in all civill societies be the deductioun befoir rehersit. The unioun of the familie is composit be the unioun of dyverss persouns, yit uithout alteratioun: the florisch-ing citie composit of mony gude citizenis of great disparitie and

---

[81] A passage beginning 'This unioun is not only trew in the elementis', transferred from p. 130, is inserted here in the London MS. See below, note 83.

[82] The remaining part of this paragraph and its successor as far as 'na unioun to be maid betuix Scotland and Ingland' do not appear in the London text

disconformitie, yit all lieving undir ane law be unioun and harmonie in the obedience of justice: the province in lyk maner. And richt sua monarcheis and kingdomes [are] erectit in heich honor, furth of many and different pairtis, yit kiepand analogie and proportioun. Qhy sould not this be fund out in the erectioun of this heich and soverane monarchie – that ane perfyit unioun sal be, and yit uithout alteratioun of the kingdomes united in haill or in pairt? It is ane great errour in any man to think that unioun cannot be uithout alteratioun of that quhilk is unitit. Sua that, for ane direct solutioun to the argumentis proponit be the meantineris of the said negative, I mak this ansuer: that alteratiounes in estaitis, republiques and kingdomes ar pernicious, the concussioun of the fundamentis of ane commonuiell uerray dangerous: the translatioun of ane estait in ane uther is not to be sufferit: the alteratioun of auld lauis and constitutiounes lang contineuing not to be permittit. Lett all this be grantit, bot I deny the consequence, *ergo* na unioun to be maid betuixt Scotland and Ingland. The reassoun is becaus the making thairof sall not import any alteratioun at all, bot sall tend to thair heich honor and profit – sua that all that sould be grantit to the adversaris sal be grantit, and yit can infer na stay to this purpose. And giff ather of the kingdomes ues in ane gude conditioun of befoir, they sal be in ane far bettir now: for any man may keip his auin and yit stand in freindschip uith his nichtbour. And this I repeat as ane generall ansuer maid to the haill argumentis proponit of befoir in the contrair.

Lett[83] any man entir in contemplatioun and consider the heaven, the sea, the Earth, the haill creatures sett doun to tak habitatioun on the Earth, the elementis, the planettis, the motioun of the heavenis, the sone gevand licht to the day, the moone to the nicht – governit onely be the great providence of God – man himselff, of sic ane notable structure of saull and bodie, keiping symmetrie, analogie and proportioun (*et in ipsa compage*), in end making ane microcosme. In all thir creaturis thair be varieties and motiones, and yet qhat gude ordour! Qhat sueit

---

[83] This section in the London MS begins, 'This unioun is not onely trew in the elementis but in the haill creatures, planettis . . .' and is promoted to appear after 'ane sueit unioun uithout alteratioun', p.129

degreis! Qhat gude distinctiones and subordinationes ar sein in
disparitie keiping proportioun in varietie great concord, in end
resolving in ane perfyit and absolute unioun – every ane of thir
creatures doing ane gude office to ane uther, and yit be this
unioun nane of thir creatures ressaving alteratioun. Giff then this
be the gude unioun of creatures (albeit in diversitie of natures),
and uithout alteratioun, qhy sould any be sua preposterous in his
opinioun as to think that unioun of thir tua kingdomes cannot
proceid uithout alteratioun, the direct contrair being mair nor
evident.

Bot yit I will adduce ane uther maist soverane probatioun. Is
thair any that dois not confes and acknauledge ane onely God,
to qhome we most cleave, qhome onely we most serve and
uorschip: qha is aeternall, omnipotent, incomprehensible, invisible ane in substance yit distinct in thre persones, be qhome we
confes and believe all thingis als uiell invisible as visible to be
maid? In this godhead, as thair is ane heavenlie trinitie, richt sua
thair is thairuith joynit ane happie and blissed Unitie, and the
same unitie sein in that great hypostaticall unioun of divinitie
and humanitie in the persoun of Chryst – uithout alteratioun or
mutatioun in ony sort. Heirof it felloues, returning to the first
ground, perfyit unioun may aluyis proceid uithout alteratioun
of thingis unitit.

Qhat is the caus that the forme of governement be monarchie, or regall power, be consent of the uorthiest phylosophes
and best politiques hes bein taine for the best and happiest
commonuiell? Qhairin the lauis of nature gyid ws, and thairfoir
[*it is*] justlie preferrit to aristocratie, albeit it be the pouer of the
best men, and to oligarchie (quhilk is the governement of ane
few noble or ritch men, rejecting the pouer of the basser and
meaner sort), ane kynd of corrupted commonuealth tending to
nathing bot thair auin privat and particular profit, uithout ony
cair of publict commoditie. As also monarchie be gude reassoun
is preferrit to timocratie, quhilk we may call the pouer of mean
or indifferent uealth. The ressoun of all this is: that qhidder we
luik to the litle uarld and microcosme of the bodie of man, and
over all the memberis thairof, qhairin thair is ane onely head, of
the quhilk the will, the motioun and the sense dois depend: or

qhidder we luik upon the great uarld, quhilk hes bot ane onely
soverane God: as also qhidder we cast our eyis upon heaven, we
sall sie bot ane sone, or luik upon thais creatures on Earth, we sie
they cannot abyid the reull of many amangis thame – I say, the
onely caus of all this is the perfectioun of unioun, according to
that notable speach of the poet Lucane, '*Omnisque potestas
impatiens consortis erit*'.[84] And uithout questioun, in ane civill
governement and policie multitude importis confusioun, and
for the maist pairt aluyis in distractioun amangis thameselffis. In
end, I conclude that not onely in monarchie, bot in all civill
societie, unioun cariis with it perfectioun, and the finall
resolutioun of all is unioun: and yit it is evir effectuat uithout
alteratioun of that quhilk is unitit.

Unioun and unitie is the beginning of all numberis, and caries
uith it ane perfyit gudnes. The commander of the haill uarld is
ane and infinit, fra qhais unitie all utheris diversiteis dois depend,
as in the quantiteis fra the point the lyne dependis, fra the superfice
the bodie, fra the numerall unitie *perfectum, imperfectum, cubicum,
quadratum*: and in end qhatevir is multiplyet thairupon arysing
upon the numberis, concludis in proportioun and harmonie.
This uith gude reassoun may satisfie all ueill disposit, for
solutioun of the first tua argumentis sett doun for confirmatioun
of the said negative. I have usit thir similitudes, to the effect
every man may undirstand that ane trew unioun may be maid
uithout alteratioun of the ancienne estait of the kingdomes.

I cannot gudelie foryet in the end of this disputatioun the
uordis of the prophet Ezechiell[85] in his 37[*th*] chapter, sett doun
in this forme: 'Moreover, thow sone of man, tak ane piece of
wood and wryit upon it, "to Juda and the people of Israell his
companiones". Tak also ane wther peice of wood, and uryit "to
Joseph the trie of Ephraim, and to all the hous of Israell his
companiones". Thow sall ioyne thame ane to ane uther in ane
trie. They sall be as ane in thy hand, and qhen children of thy
people sall speak to the, saying "Will thow not schaw us qhat
thow meanest of thais", thow sall ansuer and say, "This sayit the

---

[84] Lucan, *Pharsalia*, Bk. I, line 92
[85] Marginal note: 'Ezech. c. 37, v. 16'. The following quotation in fact covers Ezekiel
37:16-22

Lord God: 'Behold, I will tak the trie of Joseph, quhilk is in the hand of Ephraim, and the trybes of Israell his felloues, and will putt him evin with the trie of Juda, and mak thame one trie, and they sal be one in my hand'" – and the peices of wood qhairin thow uryitis sal be in thy hand and in thair sicht. And say unto thame, "This sayit the Lord God: 'Behold, I uill tak the children of God from amangis the heathen, quidder they be gone, and will gather thame on every syid, and bring thame in thair auin land: and I will mak ane people in the land wpon the montaines of Israell, and ane king sal be king to thame all. And they sal be na mair tua people, nather be devydit any mair hencefurth in tua kingdomes.'"'[86]

I cannot lykuyis of deutie foryett the uordis of the prophet David, in his 133 Psalme: 'Behold, how gude and how comelie ane thing it is, brethren to duell togidder. It is lyik to the pretious ointment upon the head that rane doun upon the baird, evin to Aarone's baird, quhilk went doun upon the borderis of his garment: and as the dew of Hermon that fallit upon the montaines of Zion, for thair the Lord appointit the blissing and lyfe forevir'.

Thair restis as yit ane solutioun to be maid to the last argument, meantienit be the refractaris to this unioun, that it cannot be forsein that it sal be perpetuall: seing giff it pleis God that his Majestie uith his haill race (as the Lord forbid) sall inlaik, housoevir ane soverane monarchie sal be now constitut, and baith the kingdomes establischit in his Hienes' persoun and princelie race, yit thaireftir ather of the kingdomes will returne to thair auld and ancienne estait: for of the common law, 'unio non est de natura, sed contra naturam, et res omnis facile revertitur ad suam naturam'. Treulie, I cannot deny bot this is ane uaichtie argument, and maist speciall to be considerit in the haill treatise of this unioun. In lyk maner, it is trew giff the principall monarch and his haill race be extinguischit, the undoubtit richt of successioun to thir kingdomes will appertein to the laufull air having richt thairto. And yit this uil be na stay of the unioun of

[86] 'All gude subjectis of this ile sould luik for the lyik blissing, having now one monarch to governe, and the conjunctioun of thir tua kingdomes under his scepter' added in the London MS

the kingdomes, for as nature hes unitit theme, lying togidder in ane continent, and now ane soverane monarch succieding to baith hes maid ane greater unioun, and last this unioun to be concludit sall unit the inhabitantis forevir, quhilk is the finall end of this purpose, qhatsoevir sal be the estait of this ile heireftir, the pretendit fear of the inlaik of his Majesteis race sould be na stay to this happie and blissed unioun. For housoevir thir tua kingdomes sal be gouernit, be ane monarch as it is now, or wtheruyis be dyvers kingis as of befoir, yit the hairtlie unioun of the haill ile sall stand. For it sal be than as now, and now as than, the kingdome of Great Británie, housoevir the north pairt thairof sall happin to have ane severall king, it sal be hairtlie amangis the inhabitantis for thame and thair posteriteis forevir, and sall import ane mutuall and reciprocall band in amitie and conformitie in maner as is sett doun of befoir. And uithout doubt it uill evir produce this benifit, that it sal be the personall unioun of the subjectis of baith the natiounes for restraint of all querrellis and seditiones, and sal be ane conjunct force agaynes all forraine enemies. In conclusioun: as Scotland of auld hes concludit thair perfyit alliance uith France, being tua countreyis not lying in ane continent, and governit be dyverss kingis, in lyk maner the lyik or bettir unioun is to be luikit for betuixt thir tua ancienne impyiris. Bot now it is to be exspectat be all the gude subjectis of this ile that God, as He hes peciablie establischit his Majesteis governement of the haill ile, right sua be multiplicatioun of blissings he sall continew his lang race to the uarldis end – sua that the kingis of this ile sal be *nati natorum et qui nascentur ab illis*. And this I use as ane direct ansuer to the perpetuitie of this unioun. Qhat farder is to be considerit heirin uil be ressonit in the conference, for thair is na questioun betuixt any people or natioun bot be ane ueill-provydit securitie may be easielie determinat.[87]

---

[87] This long passage is replaced in the London MS by the following: 'Thair restis onely the last pairt anent the perpetuitie of the unioun. Qhy sayis the adversares, "Sall it be concludit except it may be forsein to be perpetuall?" This is ane evill argument. Yea rather, qhy sall ane present blissing be neglectit upon the suspision of ane future event quhilk is not lyklie to fall furth. Trew it is that all kingdomes have thair auin tyme to ryis, to stand, and in the last period to fall. Princis also and thair race ar mortall, yit that sould be na stay to this blissed unioun. Reposing evir upon the providence of God, qha

The ferd pairt of this treatise, contiening be schort
articles, the principall headis, conditiounes and provisiounes of the unioun, to be considerit be his
Majestie and commissionaris of baith the nationes.[88]

1. First, that the generall of the said unioun be considerit, and
that it may be debaitit, giff any of the tua nationes wil be
refractar thairto.

2. Giff the affirmative pairt prevaill (as uithout questioun it
sould) than the secound disputatioun uil be anent the forme,
maner and ordour thairof, seing it uill consist of thre principall
pointis: the first tuiching the unioun of the tua kingdomes in ane
soverane monarchie, the nixt concerning the unioun of the
prince and people forevir, the last the unioun of the inhabitantis
and thair successoris amangis thameselffis, to the effect na
contraversie aryse in the estait publict heireftir.

3. As to the unioun of the tua kingdomes. be gude reassoun it
sould proceid be this ordour: that the tua nationes of Scotland
and Ingland, governit of auld be severall kingis and princes, sall
now be unitit and erectit in ane heich and soverane monarchie,
undir the obedience of his Majestie and successoris: to be callit
the kingdome of Great Britanie, the names of Scotland and
Ingland to be putt in oblivioun, in semblable maner as the
houses of York and Lancaster ar foryett eftir the unioun thairof
in ane kingdome.

4. As the saidis tua nationes ar to be unitit in ane heich and
soverane monarchie, it felloues that the inhabitantis thairof man
fellow the nature of the unioun, and thairfoir to ressave ane

---

hes peciablie establischit his Majestie in his richt, and hes gevin to his Hienes' royall
posteritie of great expectatioun. And sua it is to be hoipit be all men, that it sall ressave
propagatioun in his Hienes' laufull discent, and to be reulit *per natos, natorum et qui
nascentur ab illis.* And gevand that his royall race wald inlaik (as the Lord of His great
mercy forbid) yit the unioun of thir tua kingdomes in thair happie concord and
meantinance of peace within the haill ile amangis the subjectis will subsist. For albeit
they sall happin at any time heiraftir to be reulit be dyverse kingis, yit giff they be willing
to keip the unioun anes perfyitlie sett doun, thair hairtlie concord and sueit harmonie
will mak the samyn perpetuall'.

The London MS ends this section with a paragraph promoted from the very end of
the Edinburgh MS. See p.137

[88] The final part of the London MS is at Appendix 2

common name, to be callit na mair Scottis or Inglisch, bot Britanes for thame and their posteriteis.

5. That be this unioun thair sal be na alteratioun maid to ather of the kingdomes in thair publict estait, religioun or policie, lauis, judicator, priveledgis, liberteis and immuniteis in haill or in pairt.

6. That the same unioun sall proceid in paritie and conformitie, as the hairtlie unioun of tua ancienne kingdomes, for the bettir knitting, enlarging and preserving thairof in ane heich and soverane monarchie.

7. That the byroun trubles and querrellis of baith the nationes in thair estait publict sal be perpetuallie abolischit, and condemnit in oblivioun forevir.

8. That his Majestie in his princelie duelling, uith his noble court and royall tryne, mak his residence als ueill in Scotland as Ingland, and that be certane proportioun of tyme as sal be thocht maist expedient be his Majestie with aduyse of the estaitis: '*et ut rex apum in medio alveario se continet, ita princeps in meditullio suarum ditionum, sedem si fieri possit habeat, quo commodius adiis possit*'.

9. That his Hienes' patrimonie and revenew of Scotland sal be aluyis preservit to the meantinance of his Hienes' estait publict heir qhen his Majestie and his successoris sall mak thair residence in this countrey – seing the gude of the impyir sould be aluyis destinat to the auin use.

10. As ane ancienne kingdome in the gude estait sould not be alterit in any sort, and speciallie the fundamentall lauis, on the uther pairt qhatsumevir erroris be litle and litle hes bein imbrocht in ather of the kingdomes concerning religioun or justice be gude reassoun aucht to be repressit and reformit.

11. Concerning the people amangis thameselffis, that they leive togidder in sueit harmonie and concord, daylie imperting all gude offices the ane to the uther, uithout commemoratioun or exprobatioun of byroun trubles, uttering of irreverent speaches or qhatsomevir thing cariing indignitie on ather syid.

12. That gude ordour be taine for repressing of seditious and evill-disposit persones in the haill ile, and that idle persones be putt to vertew.

13. That the places of judgement and judicator sal be onely gevin to the maist uorthiest, for thair vertew, learning and gude qualiteis.

14. Anent the merchand estait: for incress of all gude traffique and negotiatioun in ather of the realmes, that sic sufficient ordour may be taine as may tend to the gude and florisching estait of baith the nationes. All extraordinar extorsiones, customes and exactiones, quhilkis daylie dois impovrisch the people, ar to be dischargit.

15. The last (quhilk sould have bein first in ordour) to be sett doun, for restraint of Papistis in baith the kingdomes, and nevir any contrair religioun to be sufferit uithin this ile. And this sall bring out ane florisching kingdome forevir. Lett thairfoir Britanie florisch now in the sicht of all utheris renounit kingdomes.

This questioun of the unioun being now sufficientlie ressonit, I pray God it may proceid uith uniforme consent of baith the nationes, to the glorie of God and uiell of the inhabitantis thairof. It is now ane great comfort, that qhairas the subjectis of this ile remanit of befoir in ane sea of discordes, dissentiones and civill uearis, againes the law of God and Christiane cheritie, now in the fulnes of tyme sal be perfytlie and hairtlie unitit forevir. I uill end this purpose uith Sanct Augustine, qha verray appositlie compairis the haill Trinitie to the thre pairts of the saull of man – vegitative, sensitive and intellective, distinguischit in dyvers functiones and operationes, yit all unitit in ane essence. And thairfoir it uar ane happie conditioun in the subjectis of the haill thre kingdomes, that being bund togidder, they micht represent the thre persones of the Trinitie in ane unioun and essence: and, be thair agriement in ane uill, undir ane monarch, they may be maid the trew image of the Heavenlie Unioun, to be all ane in Christ, as Chryst is ane uith his father.[89]

The Lord preserve the kingis maist excellent Majestie.

[89] 'I uill end this purpose . . . uith his Father'. This is the passage promoted in the London MS to end the third section

APPENDIX I

'Unioun of Kingdomes tendis to the Great Advancement of the Policie' (B. L., Royal MS 18.A.LXXVI, fos. 16-17).

This long section in the London manuscript replaces the even longer digression in the Edinburgh manuscript on distraction of religion as the chief cause of distraction in the kingdomes, and attacking Papistry. See pp.109-16.

The nixt argument is that the unioun of kingdomes tendis to the great advancement of the policie thairof. Christ our Saviour affirmit that everie kingdome devydit in itselff sal be desolat. David did rather chose ane plague amangis his subjectis than tumult or seditioun. Pythagoras willit that thre thingis could be removit – disease from the bodie, ignorance from the saull, and seditioun or discorde fra the kingdomes. Plato said that thair could be na greater evill imbrocht in any estait than divisioun, to mak tua of ane, and nathing bettir than that quhilk wes joynit and unitit togidder. Demades objectit to the Athenianes be way of reproche, that they nevir intreatit of unioun and concord, bot in mourning gounes eftir they had lost mony of thair kinsmen and freindes in battellis. Agesilaus, King of Lacaedemonia, bewailit qhen he saw the cruell and intestine weares betuixt the Athenianes and Lacaedemonianes, people of ane countrie. And althocht he had wonne ane great battell neir to Corinthus, to the great loss of his enemeis, yit not rejoicing bot rather lamenting, uttering thir wordis: 'O Graecia, how miserable ar thow to slay with handis sua mony of thy valient men, as wald have sufficit to putt att under [sic] all the barbarianes joynit togidder.

The Imperor Trajane, wryting to the Senatt of Rome, sett doun this schort lettir. 'I recommend to yow above all thingis freindschip and brotherlie love amangis yourselffis, becaus ye knaw civill weares ar mair noysome than weares againes strangeris. For giff kinsmen and nichtbours had nevir begune to hait ane another, Demetrius had nevir overthrouin Rhodis, nor Alexander Tyrus, nor Marcellus Syracusa, nor Scipio Numantium'; for the principall occasioun of the fall of the

Romaine Impyir wes thair civill and intestine trubles, not being unitit amangis thameselffis.

This is testifiet be the historeis of all nationes; for qhat wes the occasioun of the miserie of Italie in thir lait dayes bot the civill contentioun or rather furie of the Guelphis and Gibellines (of qhome the ane syid held with the Paip, the wther with the Imperor) – proceiding onely upon ane civill contentioun quhilk begane betuixt tua brether, Guellip and Gibellin. This kindlit all Italie as ane fyir, and qhenevir any tumult araise it wes devydit in Guelphis and Gibellines – qhairas that florising countrey, being in perfyit unioun, wald have bein fred of that miserie.

The lyik is testifiet in the divisioun of the houses of York and Lancaster, qha gave in thair armes the qhyit and reid roses. This begane qhen Henrie the Fourt, qha wes Duik of Lancaster and Erll of Darbie, usurped the kingdome upon Richard the Secound, qhome he causit to be slaine in prison eftir he had compellit [him] to resigne the croune of Ingland. This contentioun wes greatest in the raigne of King Henry the Sixt, qha, succieding to his father and grandfather, wes crounit at Paris King of Ingland and France. Thais factiones (as Philippus Comineus wrytes) indurit about 28 yeires; thair diet at syndrie battellis many persones of the blood royall, with the flour of the nobilitie of Ingland, besydes infinit numberis of the best and maist valient men of that natioun. The ancient policie of that kingdome decayit, justice contemnit, the ile impoverisit. In end the Erll of Ritchmond overcame King Ritchard, enjoyit the kingdome peciablie, and having mariet Elizabeth dochter to Eduard the Fourt (ather of thame being the onely aires of the famileis of York and Lancaster), be occasioun of that marriage the dissentioun ceasit in Ingland, and the reid and qhyit roses wes unitit in ane armes – as now (praysit be God), be the richt of his Majesteis blood and lineal discent furth of that mariage, the happie conjunctioun of thir tua ancienne realmes hes gratiouslie succiedit.

The greatest factiones that wes in France wes thais of Burgundie and Orleance, quhilk causit ane pernicious civill war, indure threscoir and ten yeiris. Ather of thir parteis brocht in Ingland for their support, qha thaireftir seasit thameselffis upon the croune – ane pietiefull sicht for France, to be sua miserablie distractit, all this procieding wpon the ambitioun of thir tua houses, seiking to obtein the governement under Charles the Sixt. Be the occasioun of the quhilk divisioun, Henry the Fyift of Ingland, taking to his wyff Katherine the youngest dochter of King Charles, wes putt in possessioun of Pareis be the Duik of Burgundie, and proclamit air and regent of France be consent of the estaites. And thaireftir the kingdome was restorit to Charles the Sevint.

The Kingdome of Hispaine in the divisioun thairof was greatumlie afflictit; for the Moires rane over it on the ane pairt, France and Ingland devorit it on the wther pairt – takand pairt at the first with the dissentiones quhilkis was in Castilie betwixt Don Pedro and Don Henrico, nixt the contentiones quhilkis araiss betuixt Castill and Portugall. Qhairas sensyne Hispaine, being unitit, hes extendit hir dominioun to Afrique, and into the new fund landis, hes borne armes in Ungarie and Germanie, commandit over the cheiff ilandes of the Mediterrane Sea, over Naples, Sicile, Milane and Flanderis. Qhair be the contrair Italie, having sometyme hir forces knitt togidder, obteinit the impyir of the warld, now being devydit in many seignories and potentates aggries hardlie togidder – and having sufferit many calamiteis, lyis oppin to the injureis of strangeris, qhairas in caice it war unitit micht be justlie callit the paradise of the warld. Sic is the nature of seditioun and divisioun, importing in end the destructioun of kingdomes – qhairas unioun importis daylie the florising estait, meantinance and preservatioun thairof.

Be the same caus of divisioun the power of Germanie is diminischit. The princis of Saxonia not lang since war bandit ane againes ane wther. Johne Frederick Philippe of Hesse, the Duik of Wittemberg, with many frie citeis rebellit againes the Impyir, the popular raiss againes the nobilitie to putt thameself-fis at libertie, the Anabaptistes possessit Muntster and maid ane botcher thair king and held out the seage for the space of tua yeires. Ungaria, quhilk valiantlie resistit the Turkis almaist be the space of tua hundreth yeires, at last war subdeued throw thair auin divisiouns – as Polonia is greatumlie threatnit be the Muscovite. Sua in Persia eftir the death of King Jacob, his tua sones strave for the governement of the countrie – but the Sophie Ismaell, comming upon thame in the meintyme with his new religioun, slew ane of thame in battell and compellit the wther to flie in Arabia.

Be thir notable recordis and historeis, it may be easilie sein and considerit that as ane building weill situat upon gude fundatiounis, and composit of substantious materiallis, well knitt and joynit in all the pairtes thairof, feares na assaltes bot resistis windes, stormes and violence, sua ane perfyit kingdome cannot easielie admit alteratioun sua lang as the memberis thairof continew unitit and joynit togidder wpon the fundatioun of thair auin lauis. Of this deductioun the propositioun sett doun befoir is sufficientlie provin, that unioun of kingdomes in police tendis to the great advancement thairof. And as divisioun and dissentioun is the efficient caus of destructioun, in lyk maner unioun produces the meantinance and conservatioun thairof.

APPENDIX II

'The Securitie of the Unioun, comprehendit in schort Articles, as be gude reassoun it sould be concludit' (B.L., Royal MS 18.A.LXXVI, fo. 22).

This section in the London manuscript replaced the 'ferd pairt' of the Edinburgh manuscript outlining the 'headis, conditiounes and provisiounes of the unioun'. It should be read in parallel with pp.135-7.

First that the tua ancient kingdomes of Scotland and Ingland, with the haill iles and pendicles adiacent thairto, sal be erectit in ane soverane monarchie to be callit the kingdome of Great Britanie for evir, the ancient names of Scotland and Ingland to be putt in oblivioun, as the houses of York and Lancaster wer of befoir eftir the unioun.

As the kingdomes sould be unitit and the ile to ressave ane common name, sua the inhabitantis aucht to ressave ane denominatioun, to be callit Britanes for thame and thair posteriteis.

The ile and the subjectis being sua unitit will infer ane blissed unioun betuixt the soverane monarch and his people; and for the bettir meantinance thairof, that his ordinar residence sall not aluyis be in ane pairt of the ile, for the advancement thairof, to the prejudice of the rest, bot devydit be certane proportioun of tyme.

That be this unioun thair sal be no alteratioun imbrocht to ather of the saides kingdomes in thair estait, ather in religioun or policie.

That the said unioun sal be in paritie and conformitie in all respectis, as the hairtlie unioun of tua frie kingdomes of auld, to constitut and unit ane soverane monarchie.

Concerning the people amangis thameselffis, that they lieve togidder in harmonie and concord, daylie imperting all gude offices ane to ane uther, without commemoratioun or exprobatioun of byroun trubles.

That they be mutuall in traffique and negotiatioun, injoying mutuall liberteis; in ather of the nationes ordour taine for advancement of the traffique, and to be frie of extraordinar impostis, customes and exactiones.

That werteuous men in all degreis sal be advancit, and offices gevin specially in justice to men of best qualiteis, for thair gude merit.

That it sal be laufull to the subjectis in ather of the kingdomes to enjoy and conqueis landis, honoris, offices, digniteis, benifices and to mak thair residence thairin at thair pleasour, with indemnitie and without finance.

In lyk maner that ordour be taine in baith the nationes for repressing of malefactoris, the poore and laborious employit to wertew, and quatsumevir corruption be progres of tyme hes enseuit ather in religioun or justice to be reformit.

The patrimonie and revenew of Scotland to be aluyis preservit to the meantinance of his Hienes' estait publict and resort heir, and ordour taine with the officiaris inbringaris thairof.

Last (quhilk sould be first) that nevir any contrair religioun sal be ather sufferit or admittit within thir tua kingdomes. This done, Britanie sall florisch to the glorie of God, in sicht of all wther renounit kingdomes.

A BREIF CONSIDERACION OF THE UNYON

by JOHN DODDRIDGE

Written in Anno Domini 1604

A BREIF CONSIDERACION OF THE UNYON OF TWOE
KINGEDOMES IN THE HANDES OF ONE KINGE

Wherin 3 things are to be considered:

First, the commodities that maie result of such unyon;

Secondlie, the discommodities that maie happen thereby;

Thirdly, a discourse or relacion of sundrie manners and formes of united kingdomes, whereby maie bee conceived which manner of them may serve as fittest.

[I] As touching the first, namelie a consideracion of the commodities arrising of suche unyon, theis motives, among many others maye be remembered.

1. People of severall nacions, of severall natures and condicions, brought upp under severall lawes, and yet subject to one king or monarche, are not without muche travail and providens held together in unytie or good agreement, except some equall bond or knott or unyon may be devised to combyne them.

Therefore such unyon is necessary, and the fruite thereof is tranquilitie, peace and future felicitie[1] of government, when bothe people shal bee equallie respected by the lawes, stand

---

[1] D and E read 'facility'

uppon equall termes in the favour of theire soveraigne, and enjoye equall immunyty and priviledges of the persons and possessions.

2. When the people of a kingedome which is more remote [shall be]² conjoyned in the bond of league, loialtie, and obediens with a people of a setled estate and condicion, of larger meanes, welthe, strengthe and power, there must of necessitie insue a greater civilitie and [a]³ better temperatur in the people so knitt and conjoyned together. Wherefore the domynyon of Wales unyted by the Statute of 27 Henry 8 unto the realme of England dothe yeld plentifull exampl[es]. Sithence which tyme of unyon thereof unto England the same hathe produced instead of contynuall rebellions and tummults, tranquilitie of state, civilitie of manners, better manurance [of]⁴ soile, more welthe and habilitie⁵ in the Welche then was found formourly in that nacion. For that they nowe are capable of the same ymmunytyes and stand in equall degree with the Englishe nacion, everie man beinge naturallie given (where nature by error and barbarousnes is not corrupted) to commytie, society and civilitie.

3. Malefactors and evill doers doe eschew the condigne punishement whiche their mysdemeanors have deserved [and] doe comonlie flie from one territory to another, where they think that the sworde of justice either cannot at all, or at least might not without some difficultie, pursue them, and hence it is that the confynes, frontiers, borders, and marches of kingdomes are most subject to incursions, spoiles, rapines, and other detestable outrages, the offendors flieinge from the one into the other, uppon the hope they have to eschewe the punishment.

All whiche are easily taken aweye by the unyting of bothe kingedomes into one, whereby the battable groundes⁶ are confined, partelie into the one and partly into the other

² Supplied by D
³ Ibid.
⁴ Ibid.
⁵ E reads 'abilitie'
⁶ See W. M. Mackenzie, 'The Debateable Land', Scottish Historical Review, xxx (1951), 109-25

kingedome,[7] and the borderinge people brought under the obedience of the lawe, which manyfestlie shewith itself when Kinge Edgar reduced the Heptarchye as seven severall kingedomes in this country into one monarchie, so that the myserable estate of this land, torne into sundrie empires, and so consequentlie beinge full of incommodities, was thereby in a short season exceedingly reduced. (The avoidinge of whiche enormyties, and to take awaie the like occasion of ympunytye of offenders) is recited in the preamble of the statute made in anno 27 Henry 8 to have bene the cause of unytinge Wales into England made by that statute.

4. If the lesser united kingedome have therein any commoditie worthe regard either in respecte of fertilitie of soile, commerce of traffique, riches of mynerall, or the like, the people of the greater domynyon will soe fasten theire footinge therein as that they wil bee never thence rooted oute or removed again, whiche is a benefit to the kingedom to which the unyon ys made. The consideracion whereof caused Kinge Edward 3, when he attempted the conquest of France and had proclaymed himself kinge thereof anno 14 regni sui, to provide by Acte of Parliament that the crowne of England should be ever[8] disjoined and be in him and his posteritie a distincte domynyon from the kingedome of France, fearing as it seemeth least soe in tyme the lesser (namely England) territory might be confounded in the greater, as to the diligent reader of the Acte of Parliament made anno 14 Edward 3 maie appeare.

[II] The difficulties and discommodities that might result of suche unyon.

1. Whereas betwene the kingedomes to bee unyted there is no equalitie or mutual retribucion, that is, where the people of the one kingedome in shewe cannot enjoye as much benefit and proffit by that unyon as the people of the other kingedome, there suche unyon cannot be made without sedicion, murmur, and discontentment of that nacion, which maie have the lesse evident proffitt or advantage thereby, for suche unyon maie

---

[7] D and E add the phrase 'and are in the heart of both'
[8] Supplied by E. A reads 'never'

drawe a greater number of the people united into the other kingedome then is convenyent, of whose multitude the people of that other kingedome wil bee ever jealous and maligne theire peculier favour, which suche people maie require[9] at the handes of their comon sovereigne.

2. By the unyon of kingedomes a totall alteracion of lawes of those nacions, or at the least of one of them, is introduced. But lawes were never in any kingedome totallie altered without great danger of the evercion of the whole state. And therefore it is well said by the interpretors of Aristotle that lawes are not to [be] changed but with these cautions and circumspeccions: 1. *Raro, ne incommodum*; 2. *In melius, ne periculum*; 3. *Prudenter et censim ne reipublicae naufragium ex innovacione sequatur.* Lawes are to be changed: 1. Seldome lest suche change prove to the disadvantage of the State; 2. For the better, lest it breede danger to the State; 3. Warilie, and by little and little, lest the shipwreck of the commonwelthe and the totall evercion of all be occasioned by such innovacion.[10]

3. Thirdly, there cann bee no perfect unyon of twoe kingedomes except there be established a meetinge of bothe states and, as it were, a comon parliament for bothe king-domes, for the generall causes which shall equallie concerne bothe people. Suche a parliament or assemblie have all the cantons or confederat states of the Helvetians and Swisors for theire generall causes, althoughe every estate perticulerlie have nevertheles his proper and peculiar parliament. [In constituting of which general parliament][11] and assembly of bothe nacions in any unyon to be made, great care and vigilancy is to bee used in appoyntinge what persons shal bee called together of those estates, least the one exceede the other in number of sufferage or voice, *et sic sepenumero maior pars vincat meliorem.*

4. Where an unyon of twoe kingedomes is made, there consequently dothe followe theis inconvenyences: the people of the one nacion, as they stand in the favour of theire prince, may procure unto themselves the greatest offices, the ecclesiasticall

---

[9] D and E read 'acquire'
[10] *Politics*, Bk. II, cap. 8: 16-25
[11] Supplied by D and E.

dignities, the possession of the fortes and military strengthes, bothe by lande and sea, of the other nacion, to the greate disadvantage of the state of that nacion whiche shal bee so surprized[12] if diligent care bee not had thereunto.

[III] The thirdde thinge proposed was the consideracion of the divers formes of unytinge of states and kingedomes, whereby maie be observed whiche shal bee the best and fittest to bee followed.

1. There are sundrie manners[13] of unytinge of kingedomes under the governement of one sovereigne. The first maie be called the unyon of freedome and denizacion. That is when the people of bothe kingedomes is made free of eche other nacion to enjoye equall liberties and immunytyes in bothe states and to be capable to purchace landes and beare office in eche other's domynyon without ympechement or regard of the want of naturalizacion or birthe. In this manner the Scottes were free in France by an edicte made by Henry the 3 and [likewise the French were free in Scotland][14] by a like Acte of Parliament made *octavo parliamento Mariae Reginae*, ca. 65, in the Scottish statutes, which was donne duringe the mariage of that Quene with the Daulphin of Fraunce. And this is not greatlie prejudiciall to be yelded unto by [the][15] parliaments of both nacions, for that the subjectes of eche nacion whiche hereafter shal bee borne, and havinge one king and soveraigne, wil bee suche even from theire birthe, and that by the lawe of nacions. And it is onelie a benevolence and grace unto those that were borne before bothe kingedomes discended into one hande, and suche a grace it is, as the kinge of those nacions maie conferre and bestowe by his regall power without assent of the states. For it is a prerogative royall incident and belonginge to everie kinge to naturalize and make denizen whom he shall think expedient by his chartre. And this manner of unyon is easiest to be assented unto, and a good grounde or[16] foundacion of suche further

---

[12] D and E read 'dealt withall' for 'surprized'
[13] Supplied by E. A reads 'manner'
[14] Supplied by E
[15] *Ibid.*   [16] *Ibid.* A reads 'of'

unytinge, which onely tracte of tyme hathe power to constitute, consolidate, and make perfect.

2. The second manner of unytinge of kingedomes or domynyons is the unyon of lawe and justice, when as besides the privilege of denizacion enjoyed equally by bothe people, bothe nacions are governed by the selfsame lawes. This kynd of unyon conquerors for the most parte doe pursue and followe, and so did the kinges of England conqueringe Callice, Gascoigne, and Gwisnes[17] in France and Barwick in Scotland, conjoyninge the same to the crowne of England, causing the Englishe lawes to bee there practized and putt in execucion. But where 2 kingedomes doe discend unto one monarch, ruled formourly by several constitucions and lawes, this manner of unyon is more difficulte to accomplishe, becaus no nacion willingelie dothe alter theire lawes, to the which they have bene [endured and under which they have been][18] borne and brought upp, as the provinces of Netherland maye well witnes, whiche soe many yeres have waged warre and endured sundrie assaultes of the King of Spayne for the mayntenance of the lawes and auncyent priviledges, and for the abandoninge of the In-quisicion, which was attempted to bee introduced amonge them. And therefore this kynd of unyon requireth tracte of tyme. *Ut leges mutentur in melius, idque sensim et pedetentem,*[19] *ne reipublicae naufragium ex innovacione sequatur.*

3. The thirdd kinde of unyon is the moost absolute unyon of kingedomes that maie bee, when not onelie the people enjoye like libertye of denizacion and are ruled by the selfsame lawes, but also the name of one of the kingedomes is abolished and surrownded in the other, or else a newe name devised for bothe, so there is made only one imperiall crowne of bothe. And this unyon was used by Kinge Alvred by bringinge the seven severall pettie kingedomes in this countrey nowe spoken of into one entier state, meltinge, as it were, all theire crownes into one, and intituling himself in sundrie of his chartres *Totius Britanniae Basilius* and in some other charters *Totius Angliae Monarcha.* This

---

[17] E reads 'Calais, Gascoign and Guynes'
[18] Supplied by E
[19] For 'pedetentem' read 'pedetemptim', i.e., gradually

manner of unyon some kinges have eschewed as [a][20] meanes to work the dymynucion of the stiles and titles. And therefore the Kinge of Spayn, havinge united the severall kingedomes of that countrey, did nevertheles in theire stiles preserve the memorie and titles of those domynyons, as kinge of Castile, Arragon, Leons, Catalonia, Malorque, Murcia, Granado, etc.

[IV] The meanes to accomplishe this unyon. Sith nothinge but tracte of tyme cann consolidate this kinde of unyon, lett us consider by what meanes in tyme the same may best be accomplished.

1. The first and principall meane is unyon of religion, and this is the undoubted unyon of hartes, when they doe agree in the profession of one faithe. For where ther is no unytye of religion, there can bee no hartie love. And therefore, althoughe the cantons of the Swisors, beinge of some difference in religion amongest themselves, are nevertheles combyned, yet that league is not grounded uppon hartie love, but hath his foundacion rather upon the feare of theire comon enemye, and is many tymes subject to sundrie and sinister opynions con- ceived eche of other. Who thereupon will attempt the unyon of 2 kingedomes must not [only] endevour to have theire religion in doctrine to be one, but also must introduce by little and little churche discipline in them bothe, and that discipline must alone bee imbraced of either whiche is farthest of from populer faction, moost obedient to thecclesiasticall and civill magistrat, and lest subject to mutabilitie and fantasticall oppynions.

2. The second principall meane is commytie in marriage, whereby is ingendered betwene the parties in present love and good likinge, and in future betwene their posterity a commix- ture of bloud, whereof sundrie alliances have theire ofspringe and originall, whose spreadinge afterwardes into many bran- ches doe drawe the knott of this unyon as close as the same maie bee knytt by an arme of fleshe, for soe is this communytie sometymes called. Of bothe theis spake the sonnes of Jacob and Shem[21] and Heymor his father, wherein althoughe the mean- inge of the said sonnes of Jacob was decceiptfull, yet their

---

[20] Supplied by E   [21] For 'Shem' read 'Shechem'. Gen. 34

persuacion was exceedinge effectuall. If you wil bee, as wee are, that every man child amonge you bee circumsised (there is unytie of religion required), then will wee give our daughters unto you, and wee will take your daughters unto us (there is the communytie of mariag offred) and will dwell with you and bee one people (there is unytie promised as the conclusion resultinge oute of the 2 formour proposicions by waye of a good induction). By this meane did the Conqueror of England, amonge many other[s], seek to settle and secure his conquest and wasshed oute the bloudie spottes of his sword in the bride cuppe of sundrie of his moost powerfull subjects. For the greatest wardes of the Englyshe bloud he married to the Norman nobilitie, from whom are descended our moost auncient and honorable famylies remayninge at this daie, and moreover did assume this as a prerogative roiall nowe worne oute of use, that if any person of great possessions of the Englyshe nacion had died havinge no masculine issue, but onlie daughters, and thelder of them married in theire father's lieftyme, the kinge bestowed the yongest daughter with all his father's possessions and patrymony in marriage where it pleased him. The wordes of which prerogative are thus conceived in the bookes of lawe:

> Si aliquis baro domini regis tenens de rege obiiset et non haberet heredem nisi filias et primogenitae filiae maritatae sunt in vita patris. Dominis rex daret post natam filiam quae reman[er]et in hereditate patris sui de qua obiiset servitus. Ita quod aliae filiae nihil recuperent versus post natam filiam in vita sua, et omnes reges habuerunt hanc dignitatem a conquestu.[22]

3. A third meane is the educacion of yonge noble personages, so that those of them which are borne in one kingdome maie bee brought up either in the universitie or at, or nere, the courte in the other kingedome wherin the kinge in person is resident, whereby although they bee by nature of the one nacion, they shal bee nevertheles, by nurture and institucion, of the other nacion, and soe participate of bothe.[23] Of this will result a

[22] Marginal note: 'Anno 3 H. 3. Fitzh. titulo prescripcion, partito 56'. See Anthony Fitzherbert, La Secounde Part du Graund Abridgement (London, 1577), fo. 102, no. 56. The scribe omitted one line in transcription
[23] Compare with Hume, 'Tractatus Secundus', which argues for the education of sons of Englishmen at Scottish universities as well

double commodyty to the king. For not onelie by this meanes
their educacion shal bee conformable to his highnes' good
likinge and theire acquayntance and famyliaryty growe stronge
towardes them with whom they have bene enbred from theire
youthe, but also they maye serve as secret hostages for theire
parents' fidelity under the pretence of theire more civill
educacion, and so maye bothe states rest by [*being*] soe much the
more secured to the king and his posteritie. This stratagem hath
bene often putt in practise to exceedinge good purpose in
sundrie seasons and is verie auncient, as may appeare by the
Babilonian monarches, who after theire conquest of Isralites
especiallie retayned the children of the nobilitie of that nacion
and brought them up at Babilon under the master of the kinge's
eunuches, that they should teache them the artes and tonge of
the Caldeans, so to wayne them from theire religion and make
them more assured to that state and soveraignetie.

4. A fourth meane is transplantacion, a practise also aun-
ciently used by sundrie nacions, for the like did the Babilonian
monarches when they transported the brides of Israell into
Babilon and into other the regions of the East, placinge theire
owne people in theire rowme, from whence discended those
Samaritanes that after enjoyed the best and greatest parte of the
promised Land. Whiche this pollicy also our Norman Conqueror was not unaquainted when he carried with him into
Normandie some of thenglishe nobilitie, whose fidelitie he
stood moost doubtfull of, and placed them there, which tended
to a double purpose, for by that meanes he ymploied them to
withstand the rebellion of the Normans, and also was free of all
feare of theire revolt in England.

[V] Certayne examples of unyted kingedomes moost famous of
the kingedomes of Europe.
    In Englande: The Principalitie of Wales to the crowne of
    England by the statute called Statut. Walliae 11 Edward 1 at
    Ruthland in Wales. Also Sta. 27 Henry 8 and 34 Henry 8.
    In Spayne: The kingedomes of Navarre and Arragon with
    that of Castile and of Spayne and Portugal.
    In France: The Duchie of Normandy and the Duchie of

Britaign to the crowne of France.

In Germany: The Netherlandes and unyted provinces of the howse of Austria.

As for other[24] unyons of kingedomes, they are either lesse famous or els amonge barbarous nacions, from whom no sound president cann be drawen and deduced. And therefore somewhat shal bee said of every of the formour in order, as they are proposed in what manner the same were made.

[1] Wales

The principalitie of Wales was auncientlie a dominion of itself, yet holden in fee of the Crowne of Englande and governed by a prince of the Welche nacion, for after the Britains (from whom the Welche challendge to discend) were invaded by the Saxons, and the remnant of them that escaped the invaders' sword were fledd into the mountaines of Cornewall and Wales for theire refuge, the Cornishemen were subdued afterwardes by King Athelston, and they constituted certaine principalities of theire owne, as the Principalitie of Northwales, Southwales, and Powisland, whiche territories afterwardes were reduced into one and governed by a prince of theire owne nacion untill King Edward I made a conquest of Wales in *anno regni sui* 11. Shortlie after which conquest, he held a parliament at Ruthland in Wales, where a statute was made for the unyon, called comonlie *Statutum Walliae*, and hathe theis wordes:

> *Divina Providentia que in sui disposicione non fallitur inter alia suae dispensacionis munera quibus nos et regnum nostrum Anglie decorari dignata est terram Walliae cum incolis suis prius nobis iure feudali[25] subiectam iam sui gratia in proprietatis nostrae dominium obstaculis quibuscumque cessantibus totaliter et cum integritate convertit et corone regni praedicti tanquam partem corporis eiusdem annexit et univit, etc.*[26]

And so proceedeth on, devidinge certaine partes of Northwales into shires, as Anglesey, Caernervon, Merionith, and Flinte,

---

[24] Supplied by B and C. A reads 'theise'
[25] Supplied by B and C
[26] 12 Edward I, preamble.

appointinge a Justice for theire regiment, and framing[27] writes
after the manner of the Englishe lawes for theire judiciall
proceedinges. And thereupon shortelie created Edward, surnamed of Carnervon (becaus he was borne there at Carnarvon
Castle), beinge his sonne and heire apparant of the Crowne,
Prynce of Wales.

Nevertheles Wales was not totallie governed by the lawes of
England [neither had the inhabitantes thereof any voice or place
in the parliamentes of Englande][28] untill anno 27 Henry 8 that
the rest of the domynon of Wales, not beinge formourlie shire
groundes, together with the Barons' Marches, were devided
into shires and officers appointed for the governement of the
same as justices itinerant, shiriefes, coroners, escheators, justices
of peace, and residinge councell appointed uppon the borders.
Afterwardes some defectes of this statut were amended in
anno 34 *dicti regis*, and so was that domynyon subdued wholie
to the lawes of England, and made parte of the bodie of this
realme, as by those statutes appeareth. And in this manner was
the unyon made of Wales unto England.

[2] The unyon of the kingedomes of Navarre and Arragon to
the kingdome of Castile.

Touchinge the unytinge of the kingdomes of Navarre and
Arragon to the kingedome of Castile, in what manner the same
was made, maie best appeare by certayne constituciones of the
lawes of those countries called *Taurinae Constituciones*,[29] wherein
to this purpose are inserted theis wordes:

> Licet regnum Navarrae, Arragonnae[30] fuerunt adiuncta coronae
> Castiliae non tamen submissum hoc factum, nec regno Castilio
> illa regna sunt submissa seu[31] pristino et solito robore re-
> manserunt et suas proprias leges retinuerunt et ipsorum legibus et
> consuetudinibus deficientibus jus civile et canonicum observant

[27] Supplied by B and C. A reads 'strange'
[28] Supplied by B and C
[29] The cortes of Toro promulgated the *Leyes de Toro* in 1505. A commentary on these laws, *Legum Taurinarum a Ferdinand et Joanna* (1588) by Salon de Paz, was referred to as *Taurinae Constitutiones*. See Lincoln's Inn Library, Maynard MS 83, item 10, fo. 10
[30] B and C read '*regna Navarrae et Arragoniae*'
[31] B and C read '*sed*'

legibus Castiliae pretermissis. Verum quamvis reges Castiliae Arragoniam et Navarram iure obtimo[32] *obtineant. Originarii tamen Arragoniae quoad Regni Castiliae beneficia sunt externi et alieniginae: originarii Navarrae naturales Castiliae quoad beneficia reputantur.*

Moreover, that the kingdome of Arragon, notwithstandinge suche unyon, enjoyed his auncient priviledges, lawes and customes, even untill our tyme, maie appeare by the cause of Anthony Perez. In the late kinge's daies of Spaine whiche Perez, havinge bene one of the Secretaries of State to the same kinge, fallinge into disgrace with his master, and beinge imprisoned in Castile, shifted himself thence, and beinge an Arragoniste by birthe, fledd into that territory [*and*] challendged the benefit of the lawes of that countrey different from those of Castile, from whence he had fledd; whiche thinge beinge denyed unto him, he then, remayninge a prisoner at Saragossae in Aragon, was an occasion that the said countrey made an insurreccion and were upp in armes for the maintenans of theire auncyent *fueros,*[33] customes, lawes and jurisdiccions.[34] In no other manner was the unyon of Navarre and Arragon to Castile.

[3] Portugale

Touchinge the unyon of the kingdomes of Spayne and Portugale, what articles were graunted to the Portugale by Kinge Phillippe, the 2, late King of Spayne, for preservacion[35] of the formour lawes, liberties, and jurisdiccions of Portugale appeareth by a late historie of Portugale wrytten in Spanishe by Anthony de Herrara and imprinted at Madrid anno 1591.[36] Whiche liberties by the same author in the third Booke of the said historie are comprehended in 25 severall articles shortlie collected as followeth:

    1. First, that the kinge should bee sworne accordinge to the auncient forme for the preservacion of the auncient lawes,

[32] B and C read '*optimo*'
[33] Supplied by B and C. A reads '*fucras*'
[34] For these events see G. Maranon, *Antonio Perez* (6th edn., Madrid, 1958)
[35] Supplied by B and C. A reads 'preferrment'
[36] Antonio de Herrera Tordesillas, *Cinco libros . . . de la historia del Portugal* (Madrid, 1591)

liberties, and priviledges of that kingedome graunted by the kinge's predecessors.

2. That there shold bee no parliament concerninge Portugale holden oute of that kingedome, and that no treatie of state touchinge that kingedome shuld bee dealt in oute of the same.

3. That when[37] the kinge should goe oute of that kingedome and make a viceroy, the same to be a Portugale, or of the bloud roiall, the sonne, brother, or kynnesman of the kinge.

4. That all offices of justice or concerninge the treasure shold bee executed by Portugales and by no stranger.

5. That all formour offices usuall, as well of the Court as of the kingedome, shuld stande and contynue, and bee exercised by Portugales.

6. That the same should bee understood also of all other offices, great and small, within the kingedome, and that the garrisons of souldiers usuall in places of defens of that kingedome should be Portugales.

7. That the traffiques and navigacions of India and Guinea, as well then discovered as after to bee discovered, appertaine to Portugale should not bee in other manner then was then and [had][38] bene formourlie used, and that the officers in those businesses[39] should bee Portugales and should accomplyshe theire navigacions and traffiques in Portugall shippes.

8. That all money coyned in Portugale shold bee stamped onelie with tharmes of Portugall without any other.

9. That all places, benefices, pencions, and offices ecclesiasticall within that realme shold bee conferred onelie upon Portugales.

10. That the kinge shold not enjoye the goodes of churches nor laye taxes or subsidies upon the same, and that no bulles shuld after bee obtayned to any suche purpose.

11. That the jurisdiccion or governement of any cittie,

---

[37] Supplied by B and C. A reads 'then'
[38] Supplied by B and C
[39] *Ibid.* A reads 'busines'

towne or place within the kingdome shuld not bee commytted but to a Portugale.

12. That the kinge preferre to all escheates whiche he[40] purposeth of newe to grant to Portugales well deservinge of the kinred of them, by whom suche escheates have happened, and yet not to exclude Spaniardes whiche then were in Portugale and had served the formour kinges.

13. That the state of the military orders of that Realme bee in no case altered.

14.[41] That when the kinge or his successors shall come into Portugall, they doe not take up lodginges for theire trayne after the manner of Castile, but after the auncient manner of Portugall.

15. That the King or his successors, beinge oute of the realme, shall take with him one person ecclesiasticall, a Treasouror, a Secretary, a Chancelor, and twoe judges Portugales, which shal be the Councell of Portugall, and also 2 clarkes of the chamber, and the kinge by them and with theire advise shall dispatch all matters of the kingdome of Portugall, and that in the language of Portugall.

17.[42] That all Corrigadoes[43] and others havinge chardge of justice shal bee and stand in the realme in the absence of the kinge, as hathe bene formourly used, and that the like bee used in all the offices of receyvors and Auditors of the Treasure.

18. That all matters touchinge justice and the Treasure shal bee fynally determyned within the realme of Portugall.

19. That the kinge and his successors shall keepe his chappell residinge in Lisbone, as the formour kinges have donne, except when the kinge in person, viceroy, or governor shal bee in any other place within the Realme, where then also the same Chapell maye bee.

20. That the kinge shall receave and advaunce unto offices

---

[40] Supplied by B and C
[41] B and C contain a clause, omitted in A, which reads 'That the gentlemen which have had tenante rightes of the kinge's possessions, having enjoyed the same twelve yeares, be not put out thereof, etc.'
[42] No. 16 is omitted
[43] B and C read 'Corigadors'

in Courte, Portugalles as well as Spanyardes equallie.

21. That the queene should admytte aboute hir person ladies and maides of honour as well Porteguesse as Spanische, and seek to advance them equallie.

22. That there shal bee free passage for bothe people in theire wares and marchandises in and throughe the borders and frontyers of eche kingedome without impedyment, taxes, or imposicions.

23. That there shal bee extended all favour possible for the bringinge of bread and corne oute of Spaine into Portugall.

24. That the kinge shall yerelie bestowe upon the Portugales by benevolence of 300,000 cruzadoes, to bee bestowed after this manner (videlt): [120,000][44] for the redempcion of Portugall captyves[45] to be distributed at the discrecion of the brethren of the Misericordia of Lisbon; and 150,000 to be laid oute and disposed in suche places necessary, as the Chamber of Lisbon should ordayne; and the 3000 remayninge for releif of the countrey, beinge visited with the plague (as then it was), the same to bee distributed by order of the Archebushop and Chamber of Lisbon.

25. That the provision of the Amayles[46] of the Indies and speciallie for the defence of the realme, chactisement of pirates, and the conservacion of the frontiers of Africa, the kinge shold take suche advise with the kingdome of Portugale as should bee thought fitt, althoughe it were with the helpe of his other states and muche expence of his roiall treasure.

For the love the Portugalles beare to the kinge, they desired amongest them his perpetuall residence. But whereas the governement of his other domynyons and estates wold not permitte the same, they desired he wold bee resident as longe as he might, and in his absence he wold appoint over them suche an one as wold tender them, esteeme them, and love them as his Majestie did.

---

[44] Supplied by B; omitted in A and C
[45] Supplied by B and C. A reads 'captaynes'
[46] B reads 'Armads'; C reads 'Armadors'

Those graces were graunted and published as saieth that Anthony in the towne of Tomar 20 May 1580 and after imprynted and caused to bee kepte amonge the recordes of the kingedome and of the Chamber of Lisbon for perpetuall memory.

[4] The unytinge of the Duchie of Normandy to the Crowne of France.

Kinge John of England was the lawfull inheritour of the duchie of Normandy, discended unto him from his auncestors, kinges of England and dukes of Normandy. But hee, beinge intangled with civill discord, and much vexed with the revolt of barons in England in that intestine warre which is commonly called the barons' warre,[47] the Kinge of France takinge that oportunyty, assaulted the duchie of Normandie and obtayned moost of the possessions thereof, partlie by [the][48] sword, partlie by the yeldinge of the Normans.[49] King Henry 3, his sonne, purposed to levie a great power and to passe into France, thereby to recover that whiche his father had lost. But after some expence to litle purpose, there was a conclusion of peace betwene the King of France and the said King Henry of England, whereby it was agreed that the King of France should hold the duchie of Normandie to him and his successors forever, except the Iles of Jersey and Gernsey and other Iles formourly beinge partes and belonginge unto the said duchie, paienge unto the said King of England thre hundred thousand livers of Tourne, and by this meanes becam the said duchie annexed to the Crowne of Fraunce.[50] And yet nevertheles the auncyent cutomes, lawes and privileges of the said duchie have ever remayned inviolate and were confirmed to the estates of the said duchie as well by King Lewys the 10 as by other the succeedinge kinges of that kingdome, as maie appeare by the coppies of the charters thereof published under the titall *La Chartre aux*

[47] Supplied by B and C. A reads 'warres'
[48] Supplied by B and C
[49] Marginal note: 'Mathew Parris in Histor. Magna in Rege King Johanne Anno 1203'. See *Matthei Parisiensis Chronica Majora*, ed. H. R. Luard (London, 1847), ii, 481-3
[50] Marginal note: 'Matthew Parrish, 45 Henry 3, Annoque Dom. 1261'

Normans, in that treatise intituled *Custumers de Pais du Normandi*, printed at Avranche in anno 1593.[51]

[5] The Unytinge of the Duchie of Brittaine to the Crowne of France.

Certayne Britaynes, beinge the auncient inhabitantes[52] of this land, passed into that parte of Gallia that then was called Armorica, and after of them Britania Minor, and there setled a certayne dominyon, first under the title of kingedome, and after under the name of dukedome. The dukes whereof were of the nomber of the peeres of the royalme of France, and some of them alyed to the English were also erles of Richemond here in England. This discent of the said duchie so remayned in the bloud of the said dukes by lyneall succession untill the tyme of King Henry 7. The same cam to the Ladie Anne, sole daughter and heire then left alive of the last duke, whose marriage beinge muche affected to Maximilian themperor, he was nevertheles prevented by the French king, who married the said ladie and thereby annexed the same to the crowne of France. Yet notwithstandinge, in a parliament holden by the states of that duchie, theire formour lawes, customes, and priviledges were ever preserved, as by the histories of that duchie collected oute of the best authors and the record of that countrey by a learned man of the same nacion not longe sithence imprinted maie appeare.

[6] The unyon of the lowe countreys of Germany in the howse of Austria.

The Netherlandes or provinces of Belgia come for the moost parte by the title of severall marriages to the howse of Burgundy. And afterwardes Mary, the sole daughter and heire of Charles the warrior, the last duke of Burgundy by hir marriage with Maximilian, the sonne of Friderik themperor, brought the title of those domynyons into the howse of Austria. Nevertheless the states of the said provinces used theire customes

---

[51] *Coustomes de Pais de Normandie, anciens ressors et enclaves d'iceluy* (Rouen, 1588). The edition referred to has not been traced

[52] Supplied by B and C. A reads 'Inhibantes'

and lawes and had theire convencions whiche formorlie they practized, without which convencions they challendge that no taxe, or imposicion cold be ymposed upon them or newe lawe promulged. And for the infringinge of those their liberties they tooke armes against the said Maximylian after the deathe of their said Lady Mary duringe the nonage[53] of hir sonne, Phillip the first. This Phillip the first, sonne of Maximilian and Mary, married Joane, sister to Phillip, kinge of Castile, who after- wardes was heire to hir brother of the kingedome, from whom it discended to Charles the 5, hir sonne by the said Phillip, whiche Charles was grandfather to the kinge of Spayne that nowe is. And this is the unyon of those lowe countreys to the howse of Austria for the preservacion of whose liberties (as the parte of the Estates alledged) there hathe bene in those tymes so muche Christian bloud spilt.

Finis

[53] Supplied by C. A reads 'marriage'

OF THE UNION
by Sir HENRY SPELMAN

Emanuell

[*Preface*]

Attempting so weyghty an argument as the uniting of twoe most puissant kingdomes England and Scotland, blame me not, though I stand in a mase, what preamble to use that might bothe fitt for a faire excuse to so bould an enterprise and for a semely headde to so mighty a boddy. But touching the first parte, since it is a cause of Comonwealth and thereby conccarneth every member and so me in particuler, I crave the benefit of an old pardon that giveth men leave to speak for themselves. And touching the other par[te], since I dare not take uppon me the person of an orator, I hold not myselfe tyedd to his strickt rules of methode. And therefore without other induction will come to the matter.

[*Introduction*]

In the uniting of England and Scotland it is first to be considered what manner of union is intended: whither to unite the kingdomes and royall dignityes under one tytle and Crowne or the people and subjectes only in conformity of lawes, manners and immunityes.

Touching the latter parte as more particularly concerning us the subjectes of England, it is to be considered what benefit or inconveniences may thereby come unto us.

The benefitt must be eyther to increase us in ritches or in strength – in riches eyther by communicating their comodityes with us or enducing us with their libertyes and freedomes, etc. As for ritches, what have they to enritche us withall? What marchandize of worthe? What freedomes, what libertyes to endow us with? The comodytyes of their cuntry, though they be many and good, as some sortes of clothe, woolle and corne, yet as they can spare any notable quantity[1] ar they not such as we neede but such as we ar already laden withall and desyr to vent into other places? For salt we are indeede beholden unto them, not that England is voyde of salt but insufficiently furnished of itself.[2] So likewise is it with Scotland touching corne, and therefore the corne, beanes and pease transported yearly out of our partes of England into Scotlande will ever be sufficient to retourne us their salt or any other commodyty whatsoever. As for their loughbourne heringes, which some of wantonnesse rather than otherwise desire, who knowes not that yf they bring us one last[3] barrell of them into our harbors, they fetch tin[4] for them off of our coaste.

If then the realme of Scotlande afforde us so smale store of marchandize and trafficque, how litle then shall it avalyle us to be invested with their freedomes and liberties? What profit shall our merchants have by being eased of their tolls, customes and tributes when they trade so little into these partes? The aptest ports for trade with Scotlande are those of Yarmouth, Lynn, Boston, Hull and northwarde, and these continually receive many vessels from Scotland. But yf you aske how many they send thither, they muste need answere you: very fewe, for in trafficque Scotland hath much neede of England but not England of Scotlande. As for cattell it is very true that Scotland aboundeth therwith and may helpe us sometymes and we them. To be made capiable of landes and possessions in Scotland wold litle avayle us unlesse we had as good meanes to atteyne unto them as they have to ours in Scotland.

[1] MS: 'quanty'
[2] Marginal note: 'Norff.'
[3] Interlineated without caret.
[4] Marginal note: 'silver, lead, mercury, iron copper, munster'. If 'ten' was intended, Spelman changes the ratio to five to one, below, p.171

But let us see what manner of union it is that must supporte this our greatnesse and felicity. Is it union of lawes, union of freedomes, union of inheritances? No, but union of our loves, of our strength, of our obedience and pollicy: of our loves, as brethren to cherish our mother; of our strength, as armes to defende the body; of our obedience and pollicy, as dutifull subjectes to execute whatsoever our king and common necessity shall impose uppon us, not to devide ourselves by factions and partialityes following Paule or Apollo,[5] nor to be enveighed with private respectes standing uppon poyntes of England and Scotlande, but with one assent to spend both our hartes and indevours for advancement of relygion and our countrye's honor. What els but in a worde as the late Lord Thesaurer[6] taughte us, *Cor unum via una.*

Touching the strength that the uniting of Scotlande bringeth unto Englande, who doth not see and confesse that we (yf any nation under the sonne) ar now invincyble, for yf England alone by the vertuouse hande of our predicessors hath in tymes passed invaded the most puisant kingdomes of Europe, beaten and captivated their kinges, disposed of their kingdomes and triumphantly carried the glory of armies from all other nations of that tyme, as indifferent writers do testifye, how much more puisant and dreadful must it of necessyty nowe be when the populous and mighty nation of the Scots, which hitherto impeded[7] our victoryes and honor, is now conjoyned and associate unto us? What hath always moved the French kinges so importunately to seeke the marriages, league and amity of Scotlande, but to have them as the Cananites were to the Isralites, pricks in our sides, always gawling and vexing us, and as hookes in our nose to pull us back and divert us from our attemptes against France? Is it most certayne that of all temporall felicities no greater could befall us then after so many calamit[ies], such cruel battals, such violent and implacable malice wherewith each

---

[5] For 'Apollo' read 'Apollos'. 1 Cor. 1:12, 3:5
[6] An illegible word is interlineated. 'Thesaurer' was restricted in general use to the Scottish Treasurer. Spelman may hve been referring to Alexander Elphinstone, who resigned as Treasurer in 1601
[7] Written in margin in a different hand; 'hindered' is crossed out

nation pursued [*the*] other for these 1000 yeares, and more now (in our dayes), to have them united in love and peace under one monarche and indifferent governour? The union of the twoe houses Yorke and Lancastre brought greate happinesse to this kingdome, but this union of our twoe kingdomes hath now accomplisshed the felicity of the whole isle. We have now no inlande enemy, no borderer, none to make roades, incursions or sudden attempts uppon us. Our enymyes must nowe come a far off and before us, for our frendes ar everywhere about and behind us. The sea hath taken us into her protection and sequestered our enemies and none can assayle us but with duble preparation and manifould danger. O (said Pericles) if we were an isle, we were invincible. And that did greate Alexander himselfe confesse when [*the*] sylle Isle of Tyrus cost him more tyme, more ly[ves], more bloode, more honor then the Cilician victory whereby he obteyned the empire of Asia. Therefore to conclude this pointe, the strength and felicity th[*at*] this union bringeth to England cannot be expressed.

To come then unto that other kind of union which tendeth to the incorporating of the very kingdomes themselves, let us see howe that will stande with the good or hurte of either kingdome.

[*Part I*]

This union will stande uppon twoe partes, one for uniting the crownes and imperiall dignities of both kingdomes under one tytle and monarchy, and the other for uniting the subjectes and commonwelths of bothe kingdomes into one conformity of lawes, priviledges and inheritances. To unite the crownes is no strange thinge, since many examples do warrant it. The kingdom of Algarania united to the crowne of Portuigell; Castile, Leone, Aragon, Granado and many more confounded in the title of Spaine. Our own country as touching the kingdomes of the Saxons gives us many examples. But no union cannot be without losing the name of one or both kingdomes. To retayne the one in our case and refuse the other would much offend the refused. That was it that so much greived the Albans when they and Rome were united bicause the fame and memory of their people was now drowned under the name[8] of Romans. In uniting of Wales unto Englande by the statutes of Edward 1 and Henry 8 the same course is observed, and no question about it, seing it was a smale principality, devided amongst diverse, and certayne of noe heade.

But as the kinges of France did ever entende the dukedomes of Normandy, Anjou, Aquitane and Britainge, though they were governed by their peculier princes, to be members of their crowne and conteyned under the vassalage and stile of France, and therefore never enlarged their stile when any of them by escheate or inheritance returned to the crowne, so the kinges of England, always concluding the kingdomes of Scotland and Wales (for Wales was sometyes a double kingdome) to be of the fee and homage of their crowne of England, and to be conteyned under that title, never altered nor augmented their stile, though Scotland and Wales cam often to theire handes. For all the Scottish wrighters[9] will confesse that many kings of England were possessed of Scotlande and disposed it at their pleasure. Yet none of them did thereupon alter their stile and assume the particuler name of King of Scotland. Edward the first, before the Conquest surnamed the elder, subdued the Scottes and Welchmen and in the yeare 921 was by both those nations chosen for their king and soverainge governor, yet was he stiled but King of England as before. Athelstane subdued Constantine King of Scotland and appointed him to rule under him, yet Athelstane's tytle was but *Rex Anglorum*. So likewise did Edred, brother of Athelstane, Cnute and Edward the Confessor. And though it playnly appeareth that Cnute was Lorde of 4 kingdoms, England, Scotland, Denmark and Norwaye, and this Buchanan himself confesseth, that Malcolumb King of Scottes was subject unto hime, yet we finde not Cnute to be otherwise stiled then *Rex Anglorum Danorum et Norwegiensium*, not nameing *Scotorum*, for that it was houlden to be included in *Anglorum*. Since the Conquest, Edward the 1, having uppon theise reasons taken into his handes the decydinge of the greate controversie touching the crowne of Scotland

---

[8] 'title' is interlineated above 'name'
[9] 'and Buchanan himself' is crossed out

amongst the competitors, and [*having*] brought King John Baliol, to serve as a pere of England in his parliament at Westminster, and where also he caused him to answere in person some matters of misgoverning his people, and having after all this 5 severall tymes subdued the Scottes and at length removed the king, taken the government wholy into his owne handes, and disposed the offices at his pleasure and was absolute proprietary of the kingdome, yet his stile was but *Rex Anglorum*. So when Edward 3 had entred the Realme of Scotland as confiscate unto him, and not only obteyned it by victory but also by resignation of Edward Baliol made at Roxburgh in Scotlande anno 1356 (anno reg. 30) where Edward 3 accepted the same, and thereuppon caused himselfe to be there crowned King of Scotland, not as supreame lorde but as the very proprietary of the kingdome, yet for all this he altered not his style as touching Scotland. But as sone as he entertayned his tytle of France (a kingdom out of his feu), he presently styled himselfe Kinge of England and France.

To come unto later tymes, when King Henry the 8 undertooke warres against his nephue King James the 5th of Scotland, in a declaration of the witnesse of his cause, he standeth uppon it that Scotland is parte of England,[10] and besides many of theise proofes alleadgeth the geographie of Antonius Sabellacus,[11] shewinge it to be so taken, and yf neede had bene might also alleadged diverse other authorityes to the same effect. For who doubteth that the inhabitantes of the lower parte of Scotland, which they calle Lawlandmen, to be discended of our auncestors the Inglesh Saxones as well as ourselves, and from them to have received the semblance of language which we and they doe now paticipate? Besides, it hathe ever bene an ordinary custome for kingdomes and nations to impose their name uppon other people annexed to them, as the Athenians uppon Attica, the Lacedemonians upon Laconia, the Thebans in Ægypt uppon the cuntry Thebaides. The Grekes (as Thucidides witnesseth) were at firste a smale people in Phthiotis (Achilles' cuntry), yet at

---

[10] See Edward Hall, *Hall's Chronicle* (London, 1809), pp.846-57

[11] Marcus Antonius Coccius Sabellicus (1436-1506). The reference to Sabellicus appears on p.851 of *Hall's Chronicle*

length they spredd their name on all Achaia and the rest of that greate region now called Grece.[12] So when the Frenchemen cam first out of Germany and sett downe in a parte of Galia, Celtica, they gave the name of France only to that parte, but ere longe this name dilated itselfe over Aquitane, and since to all of the greate kingdome nowe called France. So likwise the cyttye of Naples, growing to be the heade of a kingdome, hath within theise 600 yeares spread her name over all Campagnia, Apulia, Calabria and halfe of Italy, and in the yeare 1050 conteined the very kingdome of Scicile also. To leave forreine examples, the kingdome of Scotland hathe in some sorte swallowed upp the auncyent kingdome of the Pictes. And the name of Englande, conteyninge once no more in that appellation then Norffolke, Suffolke, Cambridgeshire and the Ile of Elye, by an edict of King Egbert's was imposed uppon the rest of the kingdomes of the Angles, that is, Northumberland and Mercia, and also uppon the kingdomes of the Uites and Saxons, and encreased at laste to the greatenesse it now obteyneth.

If any man doubt whether the dominions of Wales to be comprehended under the name of Englande, the statutes of 12 Edward 1 and 27 Henry 8 may sone resolve him, and yet those actes as touching the annexing it to England did but rather affirme and explane the boundes of the kingdom of England then enlarge it, for before this act of Edward the 1, his father King Henry the 3 held those cuntryes as parte of his crowne of England, and as proprietary thereof invested his sonne and heier apparant, the said Edward, with the tytle of prince thereof. In like manner also may be done as touching Scotlande yf so it please his Majestie to have them united. But in respect his Majestie himselfe is of that nation and that the nation is of such notable marke amongst the princes of Europe, and in histories mighty, in people florisshing, in honor bothe of cyvill and military vertue, very noble for antiquity, and to confesse the truthe as auncyent a kingdome in that name of Scotland as ours in this name of England, it is not therefore to be thoughte that in any union it shal be buried in the name of England (as Wales is), but rather that the comon name of Albion or Brytane should be

[12] Marginal note: Plin. lib. 5, c. 9; Thucid., lib. 1

taken for them bothe. And so much was offered by the Duke of Somerset unto the Scottes when as Lord Protector of England he sought the uniting of the twoe kingdomes in the mariage of King Edward the 6 with the Lady Mary then Queen of Scotland.

Let us then examyn what is conteined under the name of Brytane, for in truth the worde is diversely taken and to be explayned. The Auncyentes attributed the name of Brytane not only to this isle but also to Irelande and all other the neighboure islandes. But the Romans, not medling with Irelande, first called this whole isle by the name of Brytane, and after erecting a province, devided it into *Brytania prima* and *Britania secunda*, according to some *Maior* and *Minor*.[13] *Brytania prima*, which they comonly called *Britania* without any other addition, conteined the parte afterwardes called Anglia and *Brytania secunda* was Scotland, so that when they intended the whole islande they used the worde *Brytaniae* in the plurall number, as *Britanniarum vicarius*, *Britanniarum praesides*. But *Britania* in the singuler number comonly imparted no more than Anglia or England. And therefore, though later wrighters of our histories have often extended the worde *Britania* to the whole isle, alleadging diverse of our kinges to have reigned over all Britane, yet Buchanan and other Scottish authors, taking advantage of that Roman usage, will by no meanes have it otherwise understoode then of England only, illuding thereby the plaine intent and truth of diverse of our historyes. Therefore it shal be requisite (if it be his Majestie's plesure to unite them under the title of *Regnum Britanniae*) that it be likwise explained howe the worde *Britanniae* shal be taken, or els that according to the Roman phrase his stile be *Rex Britanniarum*, as the King of Spaine's uppon like occasion is *Hispaniarum et Judearum*.

And because it is not impertinent to the matter in hande I have here added the stile of one of the most potent kinges that ever reigned in the isle of Britane before his Majestie, I mean King Edgar the Saxon, victorious for armes and famouse for peace, of whence I find ii several stiles, and bothe do followe.

The firste is taken out of the foundacion of the cathedral church of Worcester in theise wordes:

[13] The phrase is interlineated without caret above the preceding line

Altitonantis Dei largiflua clementia qui est rex regum. *Ego,*
Aedgarus Anglorum Basileus omniumque regum insularum,
oceanique Britanniam circumiacentis cunctarumque nationum
quae infra eum includuntur Imperator et Dominus, gratias ago
ipsi deo omnipotenti regi iuro qui meum imperium sic ampliavit
et exaltavit super regnum patrum meorum: qui haec monarchiam
totius Angliae addepti sint a tempore Athelstani qui primus
regnum Anglorum et omnes nationes quae Britanniam incolunt
sibi armis subegit. Nullus tamen eorum ultra eius fines imperium
sunt dilatare aggressus est. Mihi autem concessit propitia
divinitas, cum Anglorum imperio, omnia regna insularum
oceani, cum suis ferocissimus regibus, usque Norwegiam Max-
imamque partem Hiberniae cum sua nobilissimus civitate Dub-
linia Anglorum regno subiugare. Quos etiam omnes meis
imperiis colla subdere (Dei favente gratia) coegi. Qua propter,
etc.[14]

The other is in the fundation of the cathedral church of Ely, viz.:
Omnipotentis Dei etc. Ipsius nuta et gratia suffultus. Ego
Aedgarus Basileus Dilectae Insulae Albionis, subditis nobis
sceptris Scottorum Cumbrorum ac Brytonum et omnium circum-
circa regionum quieta pace perfruens, etc.[15] *Octavo decimo mei*
terreni imperii anno etc anno incarnationis Domini 973.

> *Ego Aedgarus totius Albionis Basileus, hoc privilegium*
> *(tanta roboratum authoritate) crucis thaumate*
> *confi[r]mavi, etc.*[26]

In the first of theise twoe stiles, though Edgar sheweth himselfe
to be supreme Lorde of Scotland, yet he nameth not Scotland
particulerly. But in the seconde he tearmeth himself to be king
of this isle by that name that without all controversie was ever
understoode to comprehend Scotland as well as England, and in
the report Albion is much more certayne then Britannia, which

---

[14] Marginal note: 'die 964 regni sui 6'. See *Codex Diplomaticus Aevi Saxonici*, ed. J. M. Kemble (London, 1890), ii, 404 (no. 514); *Cartularium Saxonicum*, ed. W. de Gray Birch (London, 1893), iii, 377-8 (no. 1135)
[15] Birch, *Cartularium Saxonicum*, iii, 557 (no. 1266); Kemble, *Codex Diplomaticus*, iii, 56 (no. 563). The date of this excerpt is 970. The date that follows, 973, comes from the charter quoted below.
[16] Birch, *Cartularium Saxonicum*, iii, 613, 616 (no. 1297); Kemble, *Codex Diplomaticus*, iii, 99, 103 (no. 579)

besides the variety before alleadged includeth also the people of Britannie in France, somtyme called Aronovica.

I have stoode too longe uppon the name of the intended corporation, yet must I needes add this: that if the honorable name of England be buried in the resurrection of Albion or Britannia, we shall change the goulden beames of the sonne for a cloudy day, and drownde the glory of a nation triumphant through all the worlde to restore the memory of an obscure and barberouse people, of whome no mention almoste is made in any notable history author but is either to their owne disgrace or at least to grace the trophyes and victoryes of their conquerors the Romans, Pictes and Saxones.

Another thing to be considered in the union of these crownes is that the propagation of the royal posterity (which God graunt may ever continew) may notwithstanding faile and thereby England and Scotland againe be severed. How then shall the treasure, plate, juells, munition, shipping, ornamentes and utensiles of the kingdome be devyded, or to which of the successors shall they be adjudged. For as to my understanding, each realme may pretende like intereste to them, howsoever the poss[ess]ion of the one or the other may comende the case of the possessor. And this pointe in the marriag of King Phillip with Queen Mary was neither forgotten nor unprovided for.

[Part II]

But I dare not raise my thoughtes to theise highe misteryes of the Crowne, and therefore (retracting my fote) will speak of that which more particulerly concerneth the subject, whoe in this as in other things aymeth a[t] his profitt and demaundeth therefore what benefit should come unto h[im] by this concorporation. What welthe the Scottes have to enriche us with? What marchandize of worthe? What freedomes? What libertyes to endowe us with?

The comodityes of their cuntry, though they may be many and good, yet ar they not such as we seeke, but such as we sell: corne, cloth, woolle and such like. And to bring theise to England were to bringe wine to Burdeuxe, apples to Calabria.

And yet yf [we] needed them they could spare us no notable portion thereof. For as touching the lynning cloath and the yarne, they bring us to mak fustians on, though the quantity is not greate, and yet the flaxe (whereon for the moste parte it is made) g[rows] not amongst them but is brought, as I heare, out of the East cuntryes. And their woollen cloathes for the most parte be so meane and so course as we little respect them, and [they] themselves ar f[ree] to buy up our carses[17] (whereof some 2 or 3,000 pieces ar yearley laden for them out [of] London besides other places). As for our broadecloathes, they goe seldome to the price of them, but when they doe, they chuse rather to buye them of the Frenchman at the seconde hand then of us at the firste, for those that we sould to the Scottes were often decceiptefull, but those that we sende into France ar well sh[r]unke and lawefull, otherwise they must not come there. As for their corne it is ever so scarse by reason of the continuall want of their islandes and the north partes of the kingdome that they ar alwayes buyers rather than sellers of that commodity.

For salt I confesse wee ar beholden unto them, and they use to bring year[ely] into England some 16 or 20,000 salt fish taken at the Orchardes and some few herring. Their saltfish is neither good nor well handled and therefore unknowne to good housekepers; and their herringes ar rather desired for variety then want. For the herringes that they fetch in one yeare off of our coaste ar more worth then the herringes and fish they bring inn in fyve. And to be short it is thoughte (by good estimacion) that the corne alone carryed unto them out of Lynn porte [is] much more valuable then the commodityes yet brought from them into all partes of England.

If then the realme of Scotland afforde us no smale store of marchandize and trafficque, how little then shall it avayle us to be invested with theire freedomes and libertyes. What profitt shall our marchantes have by being eased of their tolls, customes and tributes, when they trade so little into those partes. The aptest portes for trade with Scotland ar those of Lynn, Yarmouth, Boston, Hull and northwarde, and theise continually receive many vessels from Scotland to carry away our English

---

[17] i.e., kersies, cheap woollens made mainly in Devon and Yorkshire

comodityes. But yf you aske how many they sende to fetch in Scottish they will answere none in effect. For in pointe of trafficque they have neede of oure wares, not we of theirs. To be made capiable of landes and possessions in Scotland would somewhat avayle us yf our meanes to obteyne them were as ready as the Scottes in England.

Since[18] then so little is like to come unto England by this kinde of union, let us se to whome and how it may be hurtfull. And that will fall out to be first unto the Kinge; secondly to all [*the*] kingdome in general; thirdely to Scotland itselfe in many particulers.

[1] To the Kinge, for that he shall not only lose the straunger's custome which the Scottes pay him in England and the English in Scotlande, being a matter of greate annuall value in respecte of the corne, beare, carsies, coles and other comodityes carried by them out of Englande, but also the taskes and subsidies of straungers which ar usually double as much as the Englishmen paieth and now by reason of the greate repaire of Scots into England will dayly encrease to a further comoditye. For though a greate number of them shall obteyne the favour (which many have already) to be made denizens, yet yf they be not as the lawers tearme it naturallized (which this union should effect), they must still paye all customes, taxes and subsidies and other dutyes as straungers by the statute of 22 Henry 8, c. 8, for their endenization doth only enable them to enjoy the lawes but not give theise exemptions. The kingdome of Moab was annexed to the kingdome of Israell and the kingdome of Edome to the kingdome of Juda, 2 Reges c. 3. Yet the Moabites were not free in Israel no more then the Edomites in Juda. Neither is it reason that the children of the kingdome and straungers should have like priviledges. And therefore the wisdom of auncient tymes exempted the children and layde the tributes and customes uppon strangers only, as appeareth by the discourse of our saviour Christ in the 17 of Mathue, concluding 'The children to be free'.[19]

---

[18] The manuscript has been rearranged in accordance with the author's symbolic instructions on fos. 8v and 9r.

[19] Matthew 17:25

But it may wounde his Majestie's customes in a deeper sorte, for yf the statuts made against Scotland be abolished (as heretofore hath bene offered by the Duke of Somerset and is now like to be required, for in reason many of them would be) so as England and it to all intents become one realme, then the Statute of Transportation also (as concerning the Scots) wil be repealed. And to carry corne, clothe, beare, malte, coales, etc. into Scotland shal be no more then to carry it to Newcastle or other partes within this realme wheare the King hath no custome. And then hath he not only loste the stranger's custome but the principall custome itselfe also which the English paid unto him, a matter amounting yearely in one porte (yf his Majestie be well delt withall) to £1,000.

His Majestie's customes ar the pretiouse stones in his crowne, synewes in the arme of his kingdome, and the only cheynes whereby aliens ar tyed unto him as well as his subjectes. Let it please his Majestie to comande his auditors and customen to make an estimate through England what the customes of corne, cloth, malt, beare, coales and other comodityes laded yearely for Scotland and by Scottes and the subsidies and taskes likely to growe unto him may amount unto.[20] And it may be he will then saye with King Richard the first, 'The crowne cannot spare them'. Besides I am suer his Majestie hath some fines, some benefitt for denizing the Scots by his lettres patents, which by this union will be loste and his meanes of favor towards them the lesse.

But it may be objected that theise immunityes of strangers custome and other English freedomes were heretofore voluntarily offered unto the Scottes by King Edward the 6 upon the union then in hande, and that therefore the reason to gratifie them is now as much, and the hurte to the Kinge as little, as it was then. I must answere that King Edward in that case delt like the wise marchant in the scripture: that to obteyne such a pearle of price as the relme of Scotland would have devested himselfe of many things that were very deare unto him, for he could not

[20] For an estimate of the customs and subsidies of tonnage and poundage, inwards and outwards, paid by Scottish merchants during the seven-year period 1597-1603 see PRO, S. P. Dom. 14/5/47

otherwise arrive his purpose then by composition and capitulation wherein the Queen and realme of Scotland must be satisfied. But now it hath pleased God to make us possessors of that which our auncesters not only with liberall offers but also with their boddyes and lives moste earnestly soughte and yet went without. And therefore no reason for them to condition with us being possessors, as yf we were yet but beating the bargane, or for us to bydd th[em] for our owne already as yf we were still to buye it at the marchante's hande.

But some perhaps will demande why I now tearme the Scottes aliens and str[angers]²¹ since before I have shewed them to have bene taken as members of England. Therein I spake of the ancyent claymes of our kinges of England according to our cronicles, but now I speake of our lawes according to the present tyme. For though it be true which our cronicles affirme in that point (which the Scottes will denye) yet the Scottes have long since departed from that alleageance and remayned wholy and only in the faithe of their peculier kinges. So that now the kinges of England and the lawes of this land have accepted them for aliens and strauugers as well as the Normans, Portouines and Frenchmen, which in the same manner exempted themselves from the alleageance of England.

[2] Touching the 2d point, which is the hurte of England in generall, England is already by our longe and happy peace (God continewe it) so overladen with multitudes of people as we wante meanes, and longe have done, to releive or employe the[reby] a greate number of them. This makes our townes to abounde with poore and our prisons with theves. Therefore in her Majestie's dayes much speach was of sending forth colonies. Sir Thomas Smithe led one into the north of Ireland anno 1572.²² Afterwards the Earle of Desmend's cuntry received another.²³ Others were ordeined to other places, but god wott they were so smale as England, still swelling with repleation, desiers some honorable meanes to disburden herselfe. And shall

---

²¹ Marginal note: 'freinds' in a different hand
²² For an account of this Irish venture see M. Dewar, *Sir Thomas Smith: A Tudor Intellectual in Office* (London, 1964), 156–70
²³ The plantation of Munster (1586), which comprised 210,000 acres

we then comitt that greate error against nature, to charge the stomach with new meates before the old be digested? Shall we give entertaynement to strangers before we have taken order for our brethren? Charity begins first with herselfe, and the Appostle telleth us that they ar worse then infidells that provide not for their owne family. The English ar our family; shall we then give awaye their breadde, which is their freedomes and libertyes, unto straungers? Mak the Scottes free of Englande, what will be the sequele? First, many of their nobles and principall gentlemen will strive to seate themselves as neare the Coorte as they cann. And good reason they shoulde, for who doth not desier the influence of the sonne. But our houses, our landes, our lyvinges shall by that meanes be boughte upp in all places. The citty and cuntry shal be replenisshed with Scottes. The Courte shall abounde with them not as passingers but as commorantes. And they having favour of the prince to begg and now capacitye by the lawe to take, shall not only obteyne leases and inheritances in all partes of England, but the offices of State and goverment also. And whereas the lawes of England do not permitt the alien nor the denizen himselfe to beare any office touching the peace of the lande (no not the meane office of a cunstable), now by this union with the Scots shall become capiable of the High Cunstableshipp of all England.

So likewise by the lawe of the lande as it now standeth the Scots as aliens ar not capiable of any benefices or ecclesiasticall lyvings without especial license from his Majestie.[24] And King Richard the 2, in whose days that lawe was made, commanded all his subjectes and other[s] by express wordes in that statute that they should absteyne from praying him for any such license to be given, promising also that himself would graunte none before his warres were ended. And shall we now at one push expose all the eccles[i]asticall lyvings of England unto the Scotttes and make their waye for atteyning them as ready as our owne. The pointe is well to be considered, for clergymen flowe in Scotland and benefices ebbe. This made them in her Majesties's time to seeke abroad, and many of them spedd well in England even whilst they yet were straungers and under

[24] Marginal note: St. 7 R.2 c.12; St. 3 R.2, c.3

grace. But now they shall come amongst us like brethren and cuntrymen, compelled by necessityes at home to seeke their fortunes abroade. And whither should they seeke but into England, where our churchmen be more then our benefices, yet our benefices more than in Scotland. Here they shall finde their cuntrymen and frendes greate in power as well as in multitude and by one meanes or other shall obteine their purpose. For we must note that the churchmen of Scotland ar for the most parte gentlemen of good houses (their yeomanry bringes not upp their sonns in learning so usually as ours in England) and therefore their meanes to prevayle by their aliance and kindred is much more potent then our[s] of England. When any of them ar thus placed, their nexte care will be to strengthin themselves with the neighbourhoode of some other of their kinsmen, frendes and cuntrymen, and so by little and little interlace the Scottes with the English in all places. For example, the north partes of England ar good cuntryes, but the ecclesiasticall livings thare so fewe (by reason of their greatness) that many of those cuntrymen have bene driven to seeke their preferment abroade, and falling by good happ into Norffolke, have not only placed themselves there but also called their frendes in so thick amongst us that at the day (yf it were well examined) a s[   ]²⁵ parte almost of our benefices reste in northern men's handes. But some will demaunde why wee should not endowe the Scottes in our benefices as well as our auncestors did the French and Italians in elden tymes. It is true that strangers in tymes paste have possessed a cheife parte of the benefices of England, yea, to more than treable the value of the crowne landes, but what inconveniences followed thereuppon I think fitter to suppresse then reporte, as hating to remember the presidentes of those irregular ages. Let this suffice, that experience, tyme and lawe sone threw them out, and yet learned men to supplie their places were not then so common as now they be. But there is yet another feare touching Scotland, that whilst we receive their flowers and hearbes so plentifully into our churches, we shall now and then shuffle in some of the[ir] weedes also. I meane those fiery spirited ministers that in the fury of

²⁵ The remainder of the word is blank

the[ir] zeale have not only perverted the stable goverment of that church but even wounded the very kingdome itselfe, of whose levynn Scotland shall ever give us warninge, I hope. Besides, as it falls out in the cuntry touching benefices, so shall we finde it in our universityes and principall scho[ols] touching places there; yea, the very wrighting offices and clarkeshipps in coortes of justice, whereby many good men's sonnes are provided for will in short tyme become usuall to the Scottes. Some colleges that by their particular lawes must shutt their gates against our brethren and ancient members the Welchemen muste nowe open them to receive Scots into their schollershipps and fellowshipps.

To come unto their marchantes, whose passage to Colchis for the goulden fleece shal be opened by this union, they shall nowe be mastis[26] of our commodityes to lade and unlade what them liste. The statutes of 5 and 35 Elizabeth, cap. 5 et 7, (made for maintenance of the navy) against lading in strangers' bottoms shall now (as touchinge the Scottes) be cancelled and repealed. Their shipps shall flye with sailes at sea whilste ours lye unrigged att the harbor. For who will hier an Englishman's shipp that may lade a Scottish a greate deale cheaper. For the Scotttes (as also the Easterlings), being traned upp with harder lyfe and diett, will performe a viage a 3d parte cheaper then the English, as our marchantes do knowe, and by that meanes (yf those statutes had not prevented it) would have drawne away much of our gaines.

Our corne hath bene heretofore plentifully carried into Scotland (10,000 quarters in a yeare out of one porte) upon the customes and dutyes then in use, which being released by this union, wyll be occasion [to] the Scottes to carry without measure. For their corne cuntry of Scotland is seldome or never able to feed both itselfe and the ilanders, which in effect is barren of corne but especially of wheate, rye, beanes and pease. And though this may rather be profitable then hurtefull to the corne partes of England, yet the care of the Comonwelth (that equally respecteth the whole boddy) muste also provide for the rest of the members.

[26] 'masters' probably was intended

Our woolles shall also be at the pleasure of the Scottes to buy them wheare they thinke good (not after Candlemas, as merchant strangers, when our owne turne is served) but as our clothiers of Norffolk and Suffolk at the clipping and cheapest hande. And thus our owne countrymen shall either want of their worke or be driven to pay more for their stuffe, for plenty of chapmen maketh scaresity of wares and rayseth the price in every market.

As for our beare, cloth, victualls and other comodityes, they shall take and lea[*ve*] them as the fynde the proffitt.

Their artificers also, whither should they resorte but to places of greatest concourse, there they shal be suer of the best price and most store of worke and of all the customers their cuntrymen can give them. Nowe what cometh into their purse shal be theire owne as cleare as the Englishman's. The differences of bonde and free, alien and home borne, are out at doores. The customes, taxes, subsidies to the kinge, to the cittyes and townes, to the wardens and officers ar all forgiven and must be forgotten. And this no doubt will much offend our artifficers, to have their wools and victuals thus engrossed by strangers, as the late attempted rebellion in Norwich against the Dutchmen fore-warneth us.[27]

It is also to be considered that none of all thiese sortes of Scottishmen that shall thus remove into England but there will hang about them greate numbers of their poore and idle people, seeking places of aboad and service amongst us, to the greate hurte of our owne poore and the encrease of idlenesse.

But at last to come unto Scotland itselfe.

[3] Touching Scotland: as the sunne, distending from the north partes of the world into the south, carrieth with him the spring and pleasure of the yeare, leaving winter and an uncomfortable season to succeede, so his Majestie, the great sonne of our Brytish orbe, having now removed his royall presence out of the northern kingdom into the south, and therewith brought the springe of a glory[*ous*] and florishing government amongst [*us*], it can hardly be avoyded but the winter of a desolate state

---

[27] The rebellion took place in 1570. See K. Hotblack, 'The Dutch and the Walloons at Norwich', *History*, vi, n.s. (1922), 237

will creepe uppon them. Yet have we this comforte, that as in the absence of the sunne[28] the starrs ar the lightes of the firna[me]nt, so in the absence of the kinge the nobles are the lightes and glory of the kingdom. But yf they also be drawne out of their cuntry, which this union thretneth, as is shewed before, must not the light of nit, leaving civility, pollicy and government, consequently also decaye through all the kingdome.

   Therefore as to my understanding it were very expedient for Scotland that her nobles and gent[ry] were mearly inhibited from seating themselves in England and compelled to keepe hospitaly at home, as in tyme past, for maintenance of their houses, townes and castles. For otherwise it cannot be eschewed but their country will retourne to rudenesse, and the government of the future, wanting so many of her principall members and ornamentes, declyne bothe in estimation and authoryty. Neither is it an easy matter to prevent this inconvenience, though much care be taken therein, for the uniting of one nation to another dothe so deminish the glory of that united, and that by little and little maketh it (being remote from the seate of the prince) to growe into barbarisme and obscurity. By this meanes, after the Asyrian kingdome's decline subject to the Persians, the Persians to the [Greekes], the Greekes to the Romans, every one of them declyned not only in glory and greatenesse but in letters, armes and cyvility also. So the Carthaginian dominions of a long tyme contended with Rome for the garlande, being conquered and added to Rome, becam at length to her barbarisms of no memory. Hath not Burgundy in some sort lost her fame since she was coopled to Spaine? And Portuigaly, a while since as gloriouse a kingdome as any of the rest, is it not nowe by that meanes turned to an obscure and servile people? Many examples might be alleged to this purpose, but it maye be alleadged that most of theise cuntrys were conjoyned by force and not by inheritance and that therefore the conquerors were compelled to pull them by all the meanes they coulde; I confesse it to be true. But yet they had runn togither a longe tyme in a lawfull succession (so as there

---

[28] Written vertically above 'the'

was now no cause of feare), yet they continued still in obscurity, never rising to any notable reputation. For the affaires of theire state were always acted with the prince in another cuntry, and as fast [as] any notable witt, any greate spirit, any excellent and rare men sprang up amongst them fitt to governe and adorne the comonwelth, such would not be buried at home in this work, but applyed themselves unto the courte, the theater of the State, be in the eye of the prince and receive employment according to their virtue, leaving theire cuntrye for the most parte to be governed by men of meane quality and estimacion. The way therefore to supporte the reputation of Scotland is to keepe their nobles at home as much as may be, to invest them with honors and eminency in that government that so they may become studiouse thereof to negociate as many greate affaires within the kingdome as may be convenient be drawne thither, and therein to use the solemynityes of State which lifteth upp the hartes of the people, and the frequent concourse of nobles and gentlemen which magnifies the government and confirmeth regalitye. So likewise in the commonwealth of the Church, in the universityes and schooles of learning their excellent men would be reteyned at home and not suffered to departe, for theise ar the goulden candlesticks in the spiritual government, the lightes of religion and vertue to the comonwelth. If they want living and preferment his Majestie no doubt will have care thereof.

Another thinge to be considered touching Scotland is whither this consolidation of the kingdomes may be brought to passe without changinge the lawes and auncyent usages of Scotland, and as it seameth to me that cannot bee done. For yf we differ in lawe we must differ in manners and goverment,[29] and yf our govermentes be severall our nations will still be severall. For what devideth all the nations of the worlde one from another but difference of lawes, manners and language? Touching their lawe (which is chiefly the civill) they ar liker to Fraunce then England, holding almost no conformitye with us and therefore the harder to be reduced unto us, and as for their manners and language, though in parte often resemble us, yet the greatest parte concurres with the naturall Irishe, embraceing their

---

[29] 'and goverment' are underlined, perhaps to indicate expunction

mariages and customes in that respect and the unfitter also to be united. But some will say a Parliament can do anything. I say it may quickly change the lawe but not the myndes of the people whom in this union we must seek to content. And therefore, though it be an ordinary thinge for them that enter by conquest to impose lawes at their pleasure, as the Normans uppon England, the English uppon Irelande and Wales, for when all is in their power what should lett them to doe what they liste, yet what danger it is for him that is in by lawfull succession to attempte such a matter the experience of all ages and the present case of the King of Spaine with the lowe cuntryes do well declare. In tymes past this is it that made our cuntrymen the Welchmen to rebell so often. And the fear of this one pointe above all others overthrew the mariage intended betwene King Edward the 6 and his Majestie's mother.[30] The Scottes were then so jeliouse hereof that they would not putt it in hazarde, though when the Lorde Protector in the worde of the kinge, in the honor of his own person and the resolution of the whole couinsall had assured them the contrary. I feare also that the Scottes at this instent ar so fearefull thereof as they chuse rather to lyve in old poverty[31] then to studdy new lawes.

   Besides it is no suddayne action to change lawes, but a worke of tyme and of many ages to be entred into with longe deliberation and to be preceded by steps and degrees with a speciall preservation of oportunity and other concurrantes. It is above 400 yeares since Henry 2 made a conquest of Irelande and began to plant English lawes amongst them, and yet how often even in theise ages have[32] many of them taken upp rebelliouse armes to restore their auncyent cuntry usages. Yet the lawes of England were never thruste uppon the Irish in grosse but infused into them by little and little, so that til the 18 yeare of Henry 7th the whole boddy of the statute lawes were not layde uppon them.[33]

[30] The interlineated words 'so vehemently to withstand' are not deleted with the rest of the passage, probably by accident
[31] Literally 'proverty' if strict rules regarding abbreviation and transcription be followed   [32] Followed by 'ho' (crossed out)
[33] The date should read 10 Henry 7. See *The Statutes at Large passed in the Parliaments held in Ireland, 1310-1761* (Dublin, 1765), i, 56-57 (c. 22)

It were good therefore in my conceipte before we enter to
deepe into this union that the Scottes and the English might
have vii yeares experience one of another in the state they nowe
stande, that the Scottes in meane tyme mighte consider of our
lawes and we of their fellowshipp, eache of us mutually of [the]
other's desy[re], for I thinke it not reason to bestowe our favours
and freedomes otherwise then wheare it is well deserved. And
this I learned of the Romans, whose goverment is a sacred
president to all florishinge kingdomes. For it was not their use to
bestowe their immunityes and privileges uppon every nation
annexed to their empire, no not uppon the cyttyes of Italy itselfe
that were under their nose, but as they deserved more or less at
their handes, so they invested them with more or lesse of their
prerogatives, making some of them colunies, some of them
municipals, as they tearmed them, some of them prefectures
whose condicion was hardest, some of them provinces, some of
them confederates, and by this meanes it cam to passe that the
Citty of Tharsus in Cilicia, many C miles from Rome, enjoyed
greater libertyes then Capua itselfe, that was harde by it.

Besides all this the union of England and Wales adviseth us
not to be hasty herein, for though Edward 1 was carefull to
bring it to passe with speede by the Statute of Walliae in the 12
yeare of his reinge, yet by that tyme King Henry the 4 came to
the crowne, experience had taught the English to repent it, and
therefore in the 2 yeare of his reinge they were glad to mak a
new lawe to revoke all libertyes that the Welchemen had in
England and to disable them for purchasing any landes or
ten[emen]tes there.[34] And when that lawe had bene examined
by 45 yeares continuance, it was still founde so profitable for
England that it was then ratified by the parliament 25 of Henry
6, ca. vii and remayned in force till the Act of grace in 27 of
Henry the 8, whereby Wales was then finally re-encorporated
into England. The like inconvenience did also then finde the
Irish, for in the 1 yeare of King Henry 5 they made a lawe
against them, also enforcing them to avoyde this realme and to
gett them home into their owne cuntrye, that the English
mighte be owners of England and the other cuntries mainteyned

---

[34] Marginal note: 'cap. 20'

by their naturall members, and I feare we shall one day be enforced to do the same by the Scottes, for theise actions of fomer ages ar like the counsell of oracles to posterityes. And we ar the happier in this greate affaire that we have the lighte of suche presidentes to direct us.

But to conclude. The freedomes that God giveth to nations by their birth is no lighte thinge, fo[r] though Paule came easely by that meanes to be a Romann, yet the cheife captin in the Actes paide deare for it. Let us not then with Esau make little accompte of so greate a blessing, nor let us with Glaucus give a golden armour for a brasen corpslet. Let us not, I say, exchange our ritch freedomes of England for those other of Scotland whereby so little commodity is like to redounde unto us. Nor let not the Scottes take unkindely at our handes, though we refuse with Naboth to sell our inheritance or with Abraham to forgoe our water pitte. This we will doe: we will joyne with them as neare as God shall give us grace in the syncere profession of his holy name, in faithefull obedience to our magnificent kinge, in the straighteste knottes of amity for defence of the whole ilelande. We will also give them the righte hand of fellowship in matters of services, as James and Cephas did to Paule and Barnabas.[35] We will make a covenant of peace with them as Israel did with Juda. Yea, we will sweare unto them an inviolable league, as Jonathan with David.[36] We will say unto them as Abraham said unto Lott: Let there be no st[r]ife betwene us.[37] Yet we will doe unto them as Abraham did unto Lott: adventure our lyves and our fortunes to revenge and rescues both them and their goodes against all the nations of the worlde. Yet after all this, let us say with Salomon, be loath to devyde the kingdome. And as Abraham (notwithstanding all the kindred and kindnesse betweene Lot and him) entreated Lot to departe from him, either to the righte hande or to the lefte, so let us also entreate them to rest contented with their owne cuntry. As for those eminent nobles and gentlemen whome the affaires of estate his Majestie's service hath or shall calle into the

[35] Marginal note: 'Gal. 2'
[36] Marginal note: '1 Sam. 18.3'
[37] Marginal note: 'Gen. 13.8'

kingdome, let us truly honor them with purple as those whom the king will have honored, and let us thinke their greate worthe and vertuouse blosomes to be ornamentes in the garland of the cuntrye. Yf any as Corab murmur against them, let him perish with Corab and his companion. Yf any would rydde them out of our coaste, as the hoggish Gorgesines our saviour, let them falle in the sea with their swyne. And to conclude this matter, as a fayre river (keping his channell) is a comfortable neighboure to a godly meddowe, so is the neighbourhoode of the Scots to the English.[38] And as the law hath gyven his Majestie a prerogative to admit such other amongste us as pleaseth him, so let us embrace all those plantes of his hande with a frendely and loving hart, knowing that as he that standeth on the topp of an hill discovereth more than they in the valley, so his Majestie's great wisdome from the heighte of his dignity, looking downe uppon us his humble subjectes of England, shall easly perceive what is expedient for us and will no doubt governe and moderate his hand to the glory of God and his owne renowne.

[38] The text here reads 'But yf' and then includes a long deleted passage on the following folio, which reads: 'the waters should rise upp so faste as by little and little they surrounde the grasse, the meddowe should then have smale cause to bragg of that mixture. And therefore it is good wisdome to look in tyme to the bankes and shures, leaste more water be lett in by one Parliment then can be well governed in many'

HISTORICALL COLLECTIONS
by Sir HENRY SAVILE

Historicall collections left to be considered of,
for the better perfecting of this intended union
between England and Scotland set down by way of
discourse in

Chapter 1

Of the kinds of unions and of their severall differences

Unions of states be of different natures; their differences
consist either in the matter of union or the forme. In respect of
the matter or pieces united there be three kinds of unions.

The first, where two subject states or seignories are united in
one. Of which kind likewise there is another division, for either
they are both under the subjection of one superior soveraign,
as in the uniting the earldoms of Darby and Lincoln with
Lancaster, before it came to the Crown, or they are under the
subjection of two distinct soveraign princes.

The second kind is when a state subject is united to a
soveraign, and that is of two sortes, for either a state subject may
be united to a foreign state soveraign, as the county of Anjou
was to the kingdom of England by the mariage of Geffrey
Plantagenet with Maud the Empress, and the dutchy of
Aquitane to England likewise by the mariage of Henry the
Second to Ellenor, or a state subject to his own state soveraign,
which for difference we will call consolidation.

Now for consolidation, it may either come by forfeiture and
way of attainder, as many of our dutchys, earldoms and
baronies are that way this day in the Crown; or by conquest, as

Normandy and Aquitane to the crown of France in King John of England's time and Henry the Sixth's, and as Wales is united to England, the princes whereof, as Matthew Paris saith, did homage and fealty to William the Conquerour as to their superiour lord;[1] or it cometh when a Duke, for example, or inferiour lord by extinguishment of a former line becomes soveraigne of the same, as the dutchy of Aquitane and kingdome of France were united in the person of Edward the Third, and the dutchy of York and kingdom of England in Edward the Fourth.

Of which kind of consolidation we have likewise great and fresh example in the dutchy of Britany united to the crown of France anno 149[1] in the person of Charles the 8th of France and Dame Anne, dutchess of Britany; and againe anno 1498 in the person of Lewis the 12th and the forenamed Dame Anne; and thirdly anno 1515 in the person of Francis, King of France, and Dame Claud, the elder daughter of Lewis the 12th by the same Dame Anne aforenamed.

Chapter 2

Of the county and dutchy of Britany, and how it hath allwayes bin a depender and an homager to Normandy, and Normandy to the Crown of France.

Now because this example is like of all others to be most pressed as being the most perfect and full (as hereafter shall be shewed) and in some men's opinions most resembling to ours, it will be necessary to clear one point, namely that Britany was not then, nor 600 years before a soveraign state, as I have heard some maintain, and the stories of Britany in magnifying themselves and their countrey doe sometimes seem to say, where they do but florish, and speak not precisely to the point.

For I say positively that Britany was antiently and from the very first foundation of Normandy, which was about anno 900, so far from being an absolute state as it was homager to him that was an homager himselfe to a superiour lord; I mean to the duke of Normandy, who was then and always homager to the king of

[1] See *Matthaei Parisiensis Chronica Majora*, ed. H. R. Luard (London, 1847), ii, 17

France. '*Pax*' (saith Walsingham) '*favente Christo stabilitur; Rollone jurante Regi Franciae fidelitatem, et Rege illi filiam cum terra praetitulata Normanniae donante, superadditur ad supplementa sumptuum tota Britania; jurantibus Rolloni super sacramenta principus illius terrae, Berengario et Alano*'.[2] Peace is made by the grace of Christ, Rollo (who was the first duke of Normandy) swearing fealty to the king of France and the king giving him in mariage his daughter, and with her the former title and territory of Normandy, and adding to supply the charge all Britany, the princes whereof, Berengarius and Alanus, took their oathes upon the sacrament to Rollo for the said lands.

And towards the latter ending of his daies, the same Rollo '*convocaris*' (saith the same author) '*totius Normaniae proceribus cum Alano et Berengario Brittonibus, Willielmum filium suum pulcherimae juventutis flore vernantem illis exponit, jubens ut eum sibi dominum eligerent militiaequae suae principem praeficerent. Meum est, inquit, mihi illum subrogare, vestrum est illi fidem servare*'.[3] Having called all the nobility of Normandy and Alanus and Berengarius the Brittons together, he presents his son William, being then in the fairest flower of his youth, unto them, commanding them in his stead to choose him for their lord and master, and to place him prince of their wars amongst them. For, my part it is, saith he, to establish him in my room after me and yours to obey and be faithfull unto him.

Malmesburiensis, writing the Conquerour's life, termes *Cenomaniam et Britaniam Normaniae appendices*, the appendances of Normandy.[4]

And Henry the 2d, having made Henry his eldest son king with himselfe, and Jeffery his third son duke of Britany, '*commonuit*' (saith the same Walsingham) '*Gualfridum Britaniae ducem ut cum fratre suo, rege Domino, suo ligeo fideliter staret etc.*',[5] advises Jeffery, duke of Britany, to stand faithfully to his brother his king and liege lord; and a reason why he termeth him his

[2] Marginal note: 'Hypod. Neustriae, p.6'; see Thomas Walsingham, *Ypodigma Neustriae*, ed. H. T. Ridley (London, 1876), 14
[3] *Ibid.*, 16
[4] Marginal note: 'Lib. 3'. See *Willelmi Malmesbriensis Monachi De Gestis Regum Anglorum Libri Quinque*, ed. W. Stubbs (London, 1887), ii, 294
[5] *Ypodigma Neustriae*, 107

liege lord he addeth, '*Rex pater nempe ante parum jusserat filio suo Regi, ut de ducatu Brittaniae, quem Gualfridus frater suus possidebat cum Constantia, filia Conani ducis unica, simul et haerede legitima, homagium ejus reciperet et ligientiam. Hoc enim vinculo debitae*[6] *subjectionis, de liberalitate Regum Franciae, Ducibus Normanorum ab antiquis temporibus Comites, sive duces Britanniae tenentur astricti. Quod ergo Pater pettiit, factum est Andegavis'.*[7] For the king, the father, a little before had willed the king, his son, that he should take homage and fealty of his brother Jeffery for the dutchy of Britany, which he obtained by mariage with Constance, the only daughter and lawfull heir of duke Conan. For by such a bond of duty and subjection were of antient times the earles or dukes of Britany (for both in this writer and in others 'tis indifferently called sometimes *Comitatus* and sometimes *Ducatus*) straightly tyed to the dukes of Normandy by the liberality and free donation of the kings of France. What therefore the father required was performed at Anjou.

And in the beginning of King John's time, '*Arthurus comes Britaniae* (son of the afore-named Jeffery) *patruo suo Regi Angliae*' (saith the same Walsingham) '*fecit homagium pro comitatu Britaniae, qui spectat ad feodum Ducatus Normaniae*'.[8] Arthur Earl of Britany did his homage to his unckle, king of England, for the earldom of Britany, which is feudary to the dutchy of Normandy.

The same is also certified by Pollider Virgil, l. 15: '*Arthurus beneficiarius Angliae Regis ob Britaniam in verba Johannis juravit*'.[9] Arthur, the bound liege man of the king of England, took his oath for Britany to King John. Towards the latter end of whose days, Normandy being conquered by the French, the dukes of Britany did their homage and fealty to the crown of France, to the which crown the dutchy of Normandy was by conquest then united; and so it continued even to the end, as appeareth by the story of Britany written by the Seigneur d'Argentir anno 1532: '*Le Roy Francois*' (saith he) '*bailla en advancement de*

[6] The correct words are supplied by B. A reads '*unico debito*', the words having been inserted above '*unicum debitum*'
[7] *Ypodigma Nuestriae*, 107
[8] *Ibid.*, 123
[9] *Polydori Vergilii Urbinatis Anglicae Historiae* (Basil, 1557), 265

succession au dauphin (who was afterward Henry the 2nd of France) *la jouissance du duché de Britagne, sans rien en retenir; fors seulement la foy et homage liege, laquelle le dit dauphin fit en personne es mains du Roy à Amiens'.*[10] King Francis gave to the Dolphin in augmentation of his succession the possession of the dutchy of Britany, reserving nothing thereof to himselfe, but only fealty and lawfull homage, the which the said Dolphin performed in person between the hands of the king at Amiens.

So clear it is that Britany was neither at the time of the union nor for 600 years before an absolute state. All this being said by way of digression, to satisfy perhaps some obstinate or ignorant persons, let us pass to the third kind of union.

Chapter 3

The third kind of union in matter and how it is divided into union by conquest, by blood and by marriage

The third kind of union in respect of the matter and peeces united is the union of two states absolute and soveraign, which cometh to pass ordinarily by one of these three means, answering in proportion to the three latter sorts of consolidation:

1. First, when two states absolute are united by conquest, as the kingdomes of England and Ireland in Henry the 2nd's time, so many states in Italy and so many kingdomes abroad to the Romans in antient times.

2. Secondly, when a prince absolute of one state by extinguishment of a former line cometh to be prince of another. In this sort Navar and France are united at this day in the person of Henry the Fourth, now king of France, and in this sort the great dutchy of Lithuania (which for ought I know to the contrary was alwaies and is an absolute state) was united to the kingdom of Poland, first under Yagello, great Duke of Lithuania and King of Poland about the year 1384, and so hath continued ever since without any notable interruption.

3. The third and most usuall means of this kind of union is by mariage. So Castile and Leon were united about anno 1217 in

[10] Bertrand d'Argentré, *L'Histoire de Bretaigne* (Paris, 1588), fo. 827v.

the person of Ferdinando, son to Beringuela, heir of Castile, and Alfonso, King of Leon;[11] and so of a fresh date was the kingdom of Aragon united to Castile and Leon in the persons of Ferdinando, King of Aragon, and Isabella, Queen of Castile and Leon about anno 1478. For the ending of this point it remaineth only to be considered unto which of all these kinds, and unto which subdivision thereof our union at present in hand doth appertain. For it is not so plain as some would make it. For the examination whereof, if I speak by words, it is by way of disputation.

Chapter 4

Under what kind of union it seems our union in hand doth fall, and how that Scotland hath of long time bin homager to England

By way of disputation it is alledged by some that this our union is within the compass of the second kind and under the third species of consolidation. For say they (to leave former examples such as in King Canutus' time, etc.) ' *Willelmus Rex Scotorum* ' (saith Walsingham) ' *in Normaniae pago Constantia homo regis Anglorum devenit de Scotia et de omnibus terris suis'.*[12] William, King of Scotland, became the man (or vassal) of the King of England in the town of Constance in Normandy for Scotland and all his other lands.

And not only to Henry the father was this homage done by the king of Scotland but to his son also, ' *fecit homagium Henrico, filio Regis, et fidelitatem, salva fide Patris sui'.* Likewise he did homage and fealty to Henry, the king's son, reserving the faith due to his father. And the same William King of Scots (saith the same Walsingham) ' *Cantuariae fecit homagium Regi Ricardo'*, did homage to King Richard at Canterbury,[13] And King John (saith the same author) ' *apud Lincolniam, in conspectu totius populi, Regis Scotorum suscepit homagium, qui super crucem Cantuariensis Archiepiscopi fidelitatem juravit eidem'*,[14] at Lincoln, in the presence of all the people, took the king of Scotland's

[11] Ferdinand III, King of Castile 1217-52 and King of Leon 1230-52

[12] Marginal note: 'Hypodag. Neustri p.43'. See *Ypodigma Neustriae*, 104. The original text of Walsingham reads ' *in Normannia, pago Constantiensi, apud Valonias'*

[13] *Ibid.*   [14] *Ibid.*, 123

homage, who sware unto him fealty upon the cross of the arch-bishop of Canterbury. I omit the homage done by Balioll to King Edward the first, because it was done as is pretended in faction between him and Bruce. Albeit I have heard it confessed by some that Balioll had the better title to the kingdome, the which I dare not affirm.

To these authorityes I know it is alledged by way of answer that these homages were for the earldomes of Cumberland and Huntington, given to the king of Scotland by King Stephen, which answer (besides that it is meerly frivolous and false, the plain words of Walsingham being *'devenit homo regis Anglorum de Scotia et de omnibus terris suis'*, he became the king of England's man for Scotland and for all his other lands) is most manifestly confuted by Mathew Paris, who in his history of the Conqueror before King Stephen perchance was born, *anno* 1072, saith that the king *'accepto regis Scotorum* (as not trusting his oath of fealty) *cum obsidibus homagio [ad] Angliam [remeavit]'*,[15] having taken the king of Scotland's homage. And in William Rufus' time *'Rex interea Scotorum Malcolmus'* (saith he) *'homagium Regi fecit Anglorum et fidelitatem juravit'*.[16] In the meantime Malcolm, King of Scotland, did his homage to the king of England and did swear to him fealty.

And in another place, *'David, Rex Scotorum, qui Imperatrici Matildae, filiae et haeredi Henrici primi, fidelitatem fecerat'*, David, King of Scots, who did his fealty to Maud the Empress, daughter and heir to Henry the First. At which very time, as by the story appeareth, viz. *anno* 1136, the king granted to King David Carlile and the county of Cumberland, but he would not do homage to the usurper of England, *'quia fidelitatem fecerat filiae Regis, Matildae'*, because he had done fealty to Maud, the daughter of King Henry. But his son, *'filius autem regis homo Regis Stephani effectus est, et dedit ei rex jure perpetuo Huntindoniam de se tenendam'*.[17] But the king's son became the man of King Stephen, and the king gave him Huntington, to be held rightfully of him forever. (Note that in this place his homage was before the king's donation.) I know the common Scottish

---

[15] *'ad'* and *'remeavit'* supplied by B. See *Chronica Majora*, i, 16-17
[16] *Ibid.*, ii, 30   [17] *Ibid.*, ii, 164. For *'tenendam'* read *'tenendum'*

exception is these writers were monks, but they were such monks as well enough knew the world, as whosoever shall look into their writings shall easily see. And with these monkish writers, the writings in the Tower, and the records of both kingdomes, if they be well looked into, do fully agree.

Or if all these allegations be not receivable, this union of ours in hand must be put in the third kind, and the last member of the subdivision. And so much of the diversity of unions in respect of the matter or peices united.

Chapter 5

Of temporary and perpetuall unions, and what are perfect and imperfect

In the form of unions two points are principally considerable:
1. First of their perpetuity or temporary natures, albeit the time be determinable by the Almighty alone;
2. Secondly of unions perfect and imperfect, as namely, what conditions are requisite in a perfect union and what part thereof this union in hand is capable of, a point of all others of the greatest consequence, and therefore requiring longer time to advise of.

Concerning the former points, I say that for the first kind of union before set down, and the first member of that subdivision, it were idle to say much. For by the courses of our laws, by acknowledging a fine, or suffering a recovery, that may be united to the world's end, inseparably, without an act subsequent to the contrary.

And as concerning the second member of the two mean seignories under the subjection of two severall soveraigns, if a man can be born but in one countrey, and a stranger be not inheritable (as with us), I say it is *causus impossibilis* and as such to be cast away.

For the second kind of union, and the first sort of that union, which is of a state subject united to a foreign prince, I say it cannot be in its own nature perpetuall. For it happening in a manner always by mariage, it can be united no longer then the issue of that mariage remains, which no mortall man can assure shall be perpetuall, albeit the two mariages ther expressed with Anjou and Aquitane have bin so fruitfull that we may safely say there are at this day in England and abroad, of one quality or other, above 5000 persons issued from them, so that, had not a conquest come in the way, which cuts of all titles, in probability it would have continued to the end of the world. But we speak here what they are in there own nature, not what they may be by accident.

Chapter 6

How unions by conquest and attainder are indeviseable, as also unions confirmed by Act of Parliament, which is stronger then upon mariage, as the dutchy of Britany was to France

Now resting still in the same kind of consolidation, it is there that unions by way of attainder or conquest are *de jure communi*, by the common law of nations, indivisibly annexed, the right of all heirs or of any third person in that case being foreclosed.

And for the other third member of that subdivision, albeit that in preciseness of justice, the two states united may have divers lines prejudiced,[18] although not by any act of their own, nor of their predecessors, yet in so much as they are but members of the great bodies wherunto they are annexed, and so subject to the disposition of the great court of parliament or of the assembly of states, which have a soveraign power in their hands to do justly injustice. For, under reformation, I am of opinion that by the authority of the parliament with us, or an assembly of states elsewhere, a state inferiour may be insepar-ably united to his superiour, of which opinion it seems, was the king and council of France in the time of King Francis the 1st, who made small reckoning of the union transacted between the maried parties, as they had indeed small reason to do. For Dame Claude, the older sister who maried King Francis, had a younger sister named René maried to the house of Ferrara, of which René the house of Guise is descended, who with her issue could not be excluded by ordinary course of law from the succession of the dutchy of Britany, the heires of Claude failing.

[18] Supplied by B. A reads 'times prejudices'

Of which Dame Claude there is no lineall heire, to my remembrance, left, but onely the Infanta Isabella Clara Eugenia.

Which point was the matter and subject of the last war between France and Spain in Britany, this present King Henry 4th of France being neither descended from Claude nor René, and so having no right in succession, but only by virtue of the union. Which change King Francis the First foreseeing might happen, and desiring in all events a perpetuall union and a perfect incorporation of the dutchy with the kingdom, making as he said small reckoning of the three unions covenanted before by the parties maried, caused it upon better advice to be passed by the estates of the kingdome and dutchy. *'Le conseil du roy'*, (saith Monsieur de Argentir in his history of Britany) *'qui vouloit obvier à ce que y pourroit advenir, fut d'advis pour la repos et seureté perpetuelle du pais, de tascher d'unir au royaume ce duché, et à faire une declaration, que d'oresenavant appartiendroit au fils ainé du Roy, c'estoit chose qui ne se pourroit passer sans decret d'estat; et pour ce fut le Roy Francois conseillé de faire un voiage en personne en Bretagne, pour faire traiter de cette affaire'*.[19] The king's councell, desiring to provide for all that might happen, determined for the quiet and perpetuall peace of the country to do his best to unite to the kingdom the same dutchy; and thereupon made a publick declaration that from thence forwards, the said dutchy should appertain and be a part of the appanage of the king's eldest son, the dolphin of France, which was a thing that could not be performed but by the decree of the assembly of states of that kingdome and dutchy; and therefore was King Francis advised to make a journey into Britany in his own person, there to negotiate and treat of this business and affaire.

Chapter 7

Whether a country conquered may by the conqueror be severed, and whether the right heir may by any means be put by

Now for the third kind: the first sort of unions of states absolute by conquest is *de jure* and in its own nature perpetuall, a

[19] Argentré, *Histoire de Bretaigne*, fo. 821. The quoted text deviates from the original source in a number of places

conquest cutting off all titles to the country conquered. A question hath bin made whether it may not again by a voluntary guift be disunited, whereof we have two greate examples that it hath bin.

The one of Alfonso, King of Aragon and Sicily, who having conquered the kingdome of Naples from René, Duke of Anjou, '*moriendo poi*', (saith Guiciardine) '*senza figliuoli legittimi, non fatta memoria di Giovanni suo fratello* (who was father to Ferdinand, husband to Isabel of Castile) *et successore ne' Regni di Sicilia et d'Aragona; lasciò per testamento il Regno di Napoli come acquistato da se (et però non appartenente alla Corona d'Aragona) à Ferdinando figliuolo suo naturale*'.[20] He dying then without children lawfully begotten, and making no memory of John his brother, who was father to Ferdinand the husband of Isabell of Castile and lawfull successor in the kingdomes of Italy and Aragon, did leave by his last will and testament the kingdome of Naples (as gotten and achieved by himselfe and therefore no way appertaining to the crown of Aragon) to Ferdinand, his bastard or natural son.

The second example is of *Alfonso il bravo*, Alfonso the gallant, King of Castile and Leon, who, having conquered Portugall from the Moores, gave it in mariage with his bastard daughter to Count Henry of Lorein, which first was held *con reconosciemento de vassallaje*, with an acknowledgement of servitude to the kingdome of Castile, which vassalage or servitude was afterwards by *Alfonso el Savio*, the wise, remitted.[21]

So that herein we have two great examples, one by testament and the other *per donationem inter vivos*, by gift in lifetime. But here a distinction is to be made that he that conquered may in person dispose of it away, in which case both these examples do fall. But for any of his successors who is by lineall and lawfull discent and not by his own purchase come to it, I hold absolutely, it cannot by any means justly be disunited or

[20] Franceso Guicciardini, *La Historia d'Italia*, ed. T. Porcacchi (Vinegia, 1583), fo. 7v. The quoted text has been corrected on the basis of B
[21] Estevan de Garibay y Camalloa, *Compendio Historial de las Chronicas y Universal Historia de Todos los Reynos de España* (Annverse, 1571), Bk. XI, c. 22; XIII, c. 7. The quoted phrases have been corrected on the basis of B

severed. As for a king of England now to alien or disunite the kingdome of Ireland from the kindome of England, I hold it not only inconvenient, but meerly unlawfull and *ipso juro nullum*, in very law nothing, if it should *in facto* be done. My reason is, if a king after many discents may give, alien or any way transport a kingdome conquered, then may all the princes in the world at this day give, alien or transport their kingdomes, which now they possess, all of them and perhaps all that ever were being first purchased by conquest. But to say that all princes in the world may do so is most absurd.

Chapter 8

That no act of the next heir, neither by himself nor others,
can prejudice his succession to the crown

And now for the more confirmation of the minor of the late recited syllogism and further declaration of the perpetuall or temporary nature in the second and last member of the third kind.

I say and positively affirm that no king in a monarchy that is by antient custome and the fundamentall laws of the realm meerly successive, either to the heires males or heires generall, can any way dispose of his kingdom in prejudice of the next heire in bloud according to the custome (I mean male or generall); no, not though the parties interested in the succesion should commit treason, or should surrender as much as in them lay their title or interest; or (for it is confessed) that an infant is not excluded, for he may have a protector; nor *furiosus*, a mad-man, nor *idiota*, and ideot, who may have their *curatores*, their guardians or keepers; nor a woman, where the law is for the heire generall.

Although I must confess that with us in England, albeit a woman hath bin sufficient to conveye the crown, as a pipe from one to another, yet was it never seen in England before Queen Mary that a woman was permitted (*propter infirmitatem sexens*, for the infirmity of her sex) to have the raines of the kingdom in her own hands. Example in Maud the Empress, who conveyed the right from Henry her father to Henry her son, and yet living many years in her son's time, never held the scepter in her own hands, nor was ever accounted by any in the rank of soveraign princes.

That treason cannot avoid a lawfull succession in blood, we have example in Lewis the 11th, who was in armes against Charles the 4th, and the whole house of Bourbon in a manner bare armes in the civil wars of France against the crown. And Henry the 7th of England stood accused of treason at his coming into England.

But whether an act of the estates or parliament may exclude the succession in blood is the greatest question; and for our parts here in England we have statutes that make it treason to deny it,[22] although never otherwise made, then only for fear or flattery of the present prince and afterwards never observed. For in the civill wars between the two houses of York and Lancaster how many statutes have bin made to the disinherison of the title of York and yet all vanished into smoak; the statute likewise of the 25th of Henry 8th in disinherison of Queen Mary, and confirmed by another, how were they, I pray, observed?[23] And lastly, that great act of the 35th Henry 8th, which gave authority to the king that after his own life he must dispose under his great seal or by his will of the kingdome,[24] did we not see it, I pray you, in these our latter days, to the greate and unspeakable joy of us all, most happily neglected, yea so far, as that the case then first falling which in that statute is put of the extinguishment of Henry the 8th's line, and a will also made (such as it was) to the disinherison of the Scottish line, the validity whereof was never so much as once considered upon by our councell and Lords, as being a matter that whether the will were a will or not a will skilled not at all, the act itself being a void act which should give strength to the will. Which point if it be true, as I take it to be most true, then doth it follow that in the second and third members of the third kind of union there can be no union perpetuall where the monarchy is meerly and antiently successive, but only in a case which never happeneth, which is if the one line should have no heirs left in the world. In which case and no

[22] 13 Eliz. I, c. 1
[23] 25 Henry VIII, c. 22; 28 Henry VIII, c. 7
[24] 35 Henry VIII, c. 1

other I take the establishment of a new to be in the states and parliament; and so consequently this union intended, if it be of the second kind, to be failable *in aeternum*, and of the third kind (which will be stiffly held) not possible to be perpetuall, when as of both lines there are so many who cannot be prejudiced either by their own act, or by the act of others.

Chapter 9

A form of union gathered out of Virgil

Of all unions both perfect and unperfect, especially of the third kind, the most inseparable mark and quality is conjunction under the obedience of one soveraign power, be it power in the hands of one or of many. For as with it, though otherwise lacking all other marks of conjunction, it is an union; so without it (having as many other conditions as you list to knit them together with) it is nor can be no more but a league.

So that we may desire an union of the third kind (which must be our principall butt) to be a conjunction of two or more states absolute in one head, this conjunction in the head, being simple in itselfe and of absolute necessity, may in the body admit many particular diversities, according as the union is more or less perfect.

Juno in Virgill, perceiving that by the inevitable course of state the Trojans were to conquer the Latines, intreated, notwithstanding of her husband Jupiter, as a poor comfort that at least the union might be made in honorable sort for her party:

1. *Ne vetus indigenas nomen mutare Latinos,*
2. *Neu Troas fieri jubeas Teucrosque vocari,*
3. *Aut vocem mutare viros, aut vertere vestem,*
4. *Sit Latium, sint Albani per secula Reges,*
5. *Sit Romana potens Itala virtute propago;*
6. *Occidit, occideritque sinas cum nomine Troja*

Change not the homebred antient Latines' name
Nor be they termed Troy-Teucers to their shame
Nor be the men transformed in clothes or tongue
Let Latium last and Alban kinges rule long
Let Rome be powerfull, vertuous in her race

And torn-down Troy let never more have place.
To which words Jupiter answereth in brief and agreeth:
7. *Sermonem Ausonii patrium moresque tenebunt*
8. *Utque est nomen erit; morem ritusque sacrorum*
9. *Adjiciam, faciamque omnes uno ore Latinos.*[25]
The Ausonian speech and manners I'll maintain
And change no name; laws divine and humane
Shall be to both alike in Latines name.

Chapter 10

Five principall points observed out of these verses in Virgil

Now out of these verses (albeit a poet, yet a wise man) we may gather five properties of an union:

1. The first, the community of name (verses 1st and 2nd), which as it seems was the greatest matter that stickes in a woman's stomack, though in substance the least trifle of a thousand.

2. The second is the community of language (verses 3d and 7th).

3. The third is community of apparell (verse 3d).

4. The fourth is the community of religion (*morem ritusque sacrorum*, verse 8th).

5. The fith and last is the community of laws and customes: for *patrios mores* (verse 8th) I take to contain both, there being no difference between them but written or not written, *conseutudo* (custome) being *lex non scripta* (an unwritten law), and *lex* (law) nothing else but *consuetudo scripta* (a written custome).

Of the which five points of the poet (not that I will peremptorily maintain the division, though it may be stretched far) I will indeavour to say somewhat, both in generall and in this our particular, and the first for the name. In the union of states, either the peices united do still retain their old separation of names, or else they do change their names. Of the first, infinite examples of all the three sorts of the third kind of union present

---

[25] *Aeneid*, Bk. XII, lines 823-8, 834-7. Savile omits the words '*commixti corpore tantum subident Teucri*' on lines 835-6, perhaps deliberately, since he does not discuss an incorporating union in this context

themselves unto us, as Lithuania and Polonia, France and Navar, England and Ireland, and in one selfesame continent, Castile and Aragon, and where not?

The second may be in two sorts, for either both the states united do take the one name and drown the other, or both the former names are extinguished and they take up by consent a third. So that we have herein three cases to be considered of:

1. First, where both the names are retained;
2. Secondly, when onely one;
3. Thirdly, when neither the one nor the other, but a third for them both is assumed. The last case is fittest for a peaceable union, the middle more proper for a violent, which kind of case is where one is retained and the other drowned, and this receiveth another division:

1. For either the party conquering imposeth his name upon both, which is the general way, and *de jure gentium*, by the law of nations, as it were;
2. Or else (which may seem strange and yet lacketh not examples) the name of the conquered party prevaileth. The Romans at their beginning, after their conquests incorporating the Cenonenses, Crustumiani and Autumnales into their city, extinguished all their names with the Sabines; the union of which estates to the Romans, coming partly by conquest and partly by composition, in respect of the name participated of both sortes. For the name of the Sabines being in them that were incorporated extinct, yet the whole body of both the one people and the other, *ut Sabinis aliquid daretur*, that the Sabines might have some contentment (saith Livy), *Quirites a Curibus* (a chief town in the Sabines' country) *appellati*, were called Quirites.[26]

Neither did the Romans after their beginning in many hundred years, conquering almost all the then known world, unite any to their names, untill in the latter age and declining times of the state, for a great favour, or as St Luke saith for a great sum of money, that grace was granted sometimes to whole countries and towns, sometimes to particular persons, to use the name of Romans.[27]

[26] Livy, Bk. I, c. 23
[27] Acts 22:28

Chapter 11

Of altering and keeping the antient name

As to the change of the name of Britania into Anglia, it was by a conquest, and a depopulating, not an uniting conquest, the Saxons not only killing such as bare armes against them in the feild, but extirpating and expelling all the British blood, even to the women and babes, and planting their own race in their room.

But as to that member of the division, where the conquered party carried away the name, and the conquerour's was extinct, we have the example of our poet in the Trojans, who conquered the Latines and in very good policy left their own names and assumed theirs. '*Aeneas*' (saith Livy) '*ut animos Aboriginum sibi conciliaret, ne sub eodem jure tantum, sed etiam nomine, omnes essent, Latinos utramque gentem appellavit. Nec deinde Aborigines Trojanis studio ac fide erga Regem Aeneam cessere: fretusque his animis coalescentium in dies magis duorum populorum, Aeneas, etc.*'[28] Aenas, that he might winne to himself the minds of the antient people and that they might not only be under one law but also obtain one name, called both the nations Latines. Neither were the antient people from that time any whit inferiour to the Trojans themselves in faith and diligence unto their king Aeneas: and the two nations having their minds daily more and more thus conjoined together, Aeneas, etc.

For it seems that Aeneas in his judgment thought the communication of name to be an increasor and strengthener of coalition and union, which perchance is a true proposition, either when the superiour state in reputation and forces, to honour the inferiour and bind them faster, taketh upon him and his people the inferiour name, or else imposeth his own, when by long continuance of time it will be taken for a favour and not a note of subjection, as it could be peradventure at the first beginning of this our union. Neither in this kind have we only examples out of poets and those *fabulosa tempora*, fabulous times, but even here at home how William the Conquerour (if it were

[28] Livy, Bk. I, c. 2. For '*tantum*' read '*solum*'

a conquest, for he pretended for his colour a certain donation from Edward the Confessor and published also a far-fecht title from Emma) of Normandy, subduing the English by armes, could not nor would not subdue the name. The posterity of him and his Normans, of whom thousands at this day are discended, never knew any other name but of English.

Chapter 12

Of assuming a third name for both

Of the third case (which now as I hear is the question with us), where both the former is extinct and a third name is assumed, I do hardly remember one example. Well I do call to mind and do find in history how the same question was debated in the councell of Spain when as Castile and Aragon, with their appendices, were united in Ferdinand and Isabell, but upon some reasons a new name was refuted. '*Los reys*' (saith Gavarra)[29] '*trataron en Consejo de la forma y orden de precedentia de los titulos reales que devian tomar y aunque muchos fueron de parecer, que se llamassen Reyes de España pues era suyo lo mas y mejor*'. The king treated in councill of the precedency of those royall titles, what were best to be assumed; wherein many were of opinion they should be called kings of Spain, whereupon followed, etc. Now the reason of the refusall, as the author reporteth, was *por non hazian alguno manera d'agravio a Los Reys de Navarra y Portugal*,[30] that there might be no case of discontentment given to the kings of Navar and Portugal, both which kingdomes were then in esse. It may now be well a question, when as both these kingdomes are united with Castile, why still that diversity of names doth remain in the Spanish king's stile, when no man at this day possesseth one foot of land from the Pyrendan hills to the ocean, which is the whole compass of antient Hispania. but he alone. And that he doth still bear them so distinctly in his stile, it is most certain, though by some ignorant or simple schollers that have seen now and then *Rex Hispaniarum* in the title of a

---

[29] For 'Gavarra' read 'Garibay'
[30] Garibay, *Compendio Historial*, Bk. XVIII, c. 14. The quoted text has been corrected on the basis of B

book I have heard the contrary affirmed. But his true stile in his authenticall writings, as in the treaty of Vervins[31] with the French and in the new treaty with us at Boulinge and at London,[32] I do assure myselfe to be as I say and no otherwise, and with that stile the last Phillip went into heaven, if he took that way, for I am sure the stile of his last will and testament is *Rey di Castiglia di Leon y Aragon*, King of Castile, of Leon and Aragon.

Of the not altering the stile into *Rex Hispaniarum* (the causes of refusing it in Ferdinand and Isabell's time being now taken away, as I said before, all antient Spain being in the present king's subjection) the true reasons and grounds were very considerable in this our purpose, if they could by my weak wit well be penetrated into, for conference I never had with any wise man of that nation. I hope Antonio Perrez will pardon me, an escaped secretary from that estate.

Chapter 13

The causes of the keeping of the several titles by the kings of Castile

To talk of the *Modernall Hispanos*,[33] and that they are now a settled nation, not easily induced to novelties without evident utility or urgent necessity, it were but idle, seeing their predecessors, who were as good Castilians as they, would have done it, and we do plainly see, by that which I have aforesaid, in the common course of justice with power they could and might have performed it. Seeing then I find not what in good sadness to say by way of merriment, I think it was negligence in Phillip the son, and conscience in Phillip the father. For the first, the custome of yong kings, who have not their minds most fixed where they should have it, upon their affaires and state business, will easily approve the allegation for probable at the least. Now for the father, the Spanish factions throughout Christendom do

---

[31] The peace of Vervins was concluded on 2 May 1598
[32] The Treaty of London, which was signed on 19 August 1604, was preceded by negotiations at Boulogne in June 1603. See *CSPVen 1603-1607*, 49, 161-3
[33] D reads 'the *sossiego Español*'

in their *Jactanza Spagnolla*,[34] their Spanish bragges, beautify his stile with *Philipus justus*, the just Phillip; and it might be he was somewhat conscientious in a kingly measure. Therefore knowing (as all the world sees, the wrong done to the deceased Duke of Parma) he had no right to Portugal and as little to Navar, which his [great grand]father[35] conquered craftily by treachery and perfidiousness, he felt himself rightly[36] excluded from that stile of *Rex Hispaniarum*, neer upon the same causes by the which Ferdinand and Isabell were in their times.

And that I may not seem altogether to speak without book, and upon no ground, I do find in the codicill annexed to King Phillip's will, a true copy whereof I have in my keeping, that the emperour his father, Charles the 5th, at the time of his death, finding himself to be *male fidei possessor*, an unconscionable possessor of that kingdom, left with his last will or testament, [a paper][37] or codicill annexed concerning Navar, after some preface in *hec verba: Para mayor securidad di nostra conciencia encargamos y mandamos al serenissimo Principe don Phillipe mi hijo y successor en todos nuestros Reynos y Sennorios, que haga mirar y con diligencia examinar y averriguar llanamente y sinceramente si de justicia y razon fare obligado a restituir el detto reyno ò in otra manera satisfacer ò recompensar a persona alcuna, y lo que ausi fuere hallado, determinado, y declarado por justicia si cumpla con effeto por manera que mi anima y consciencia sea descargado.*[38] For the great quieting of our conscience we do charge and command the most serene Prince don Phillip our son, successor in all our kingdomes and dominions, that he be carefull to provide and diligently to seek which way best he may do justice and give satisfaction therein, binding him to restore the said kingdome to the right heir and owner, or by some other contentfull way and meanes satisfy and recompence all persons whatsoever, which shall either in justice be thought any way interested or shall take themselves to be wronged by the said kingdom, that our mind and conscience

---

[34] B reads 'iattanza Spagnuola'
[35] Supplied by B, C, and D. A reads 'father'. The reference is to Ferdinand II of Aragon and Castile, who conquered Navarre in 1512
[36] C and D read 'he found himselfe excluded'
[37] Supplied by C and D
[38] The quoted text has been corrected on the basis of B

may thereof be discharged. Which charge and commandment King Phillip receiving from his father, and adding of his own thereunto another injustice by possessing himself of the Marquisat of Alexander di Caretto Final, near unto Genua,[39] a good marquis and true owner thereof, in the codicill annexed to his own will, bearing date 7 Martii anno 1594, putteth off both the one matter and the other (as a man having some feeling of conscience, though not too much) cleanlily and handsomely by a double post to his son the new King Phillip, who no doubt will strain himself therein to do nothing at all.[40] As we see, conscience for wronge done is allwaies greatest in the wrong doer. Example is Henry the 5th, who perceiving that his father at his death had a remorse of conscience for the wrong done to King Richard the 2nd, took up the crown (as the story saieth) from his father's bed's head and said that his conscience would well enough serve him to wear, and keep that which his father had gotten howsoever.

And to say the truth, if kings should be scrupulous and nice-conscienced, we might say of them all, or of most part of them, as Carneades said: ' *Si justitiam sequi velint ac suum cuique restituere quod majores ipsorum vi et armis occupaverunt ad casas et egestatem*[41] *revertantur necesse est*'.[42] If they will precisely follow justice and strictly restore to everyone what their predecessors have by force and conquest compassed and gotten, of necessity they must return back again to poverty and beggery (and so they may prove just fools for their labours).

Chapter 14

Of the profit or discommoditys in holding or altering the ancient stiles

Having now long laboured in this case and not found one example discending to our particular, first I say that I wish with all my heart his Majesty could be pleased the names of England

---

[39] For 'Genua' read 'Genova'

[40] For a discussion of this problem see Luis Cabrero de Cordoba, *Historia de Felipe Segundo* (Madrid, 1877), iv, 288-92

[41] The words '*casas*' and '*egestatem*' are supplied by B. A reads '*calas et necessitatem*'

[42] Marginal note of D: 'Tul. lib. 3. de repub:'. The text is a paraphrase of Cicero, *De Republica*, Bk. III, sec. 12

and Scotland might still continue, as they have long done and are, following the example of all Christian kings this day in the world, who all of them do think it neither vanity nor dishonour to bear the stile of many kingdomes no more then they doe the armes, the which to make quartered with a single stile is in my opinion a plain solecism; and to charge one field with rampant and regardant,[43] besides that in the likelyhood the one would eat up the other, four beasts are perchance too great a charge for one field; those being likewise in severall colours and positions, it lacketh example in heraldry; and in my knowledg I know not what is well to be done with the imbrodered border of the French flowerdeluces (given by Charles the Great to Achaius, King of Scots) for such a scutcheon.

The only reason that can truly be alledged for an union in name is for that it is conceived the antient enmity and heartburning between the two nations will by that meanes be the better and sooner qualified and quenched, when they shall communicate not only in the head, but in the name of the body.

To the which I adde also this of no less consequence, that the Scots, being incorporated into one name with us, will the more easily fall from the straight dependency which of long time they have had and do yet hold with France. And to say the truth, the French themselves will be thereby the more cold to imbrace them. Which dangerous dependency I say and positively affirm (things standing as they do and so like to induce) the kings of this land must by all means endeavor to break, unless they can be contented to nourish within their own bowells a party that will at all times be ready at the sollicitation of the French to set up an anti-king in Scotland or break out into open rebellion, which from a people of their humour in the absence of their king, who will not in likelyhood much dwell but in the sunny side of his kingdomes, it were simplicity not to fear, or in a manner not to presume of, if not [in][44] this, yet in the next age.

Neither is that prince to be held for wise that will, if he can otherwise, *hostem Telemacho parare*, prepare an enemy for his son

---

[43] The first of these heraldic terms refers to a lion standing on its hind legs, while the second refers to its looking backwards
[44] Supplied by B

Telemachus, as Ulisses saies in Seneca, and leave an everlasting thorn in his son's side.[45] But be it so, it may be wiseness will find other meanes to break this dependency.

Chapter 15

That it is neither impossible nor inconvenient to take up a third name

And for that we daily see old heartburnings are quickly changed into new kindnesses, the causes being once removed and the wood of ill will taken away from the fire, which by exemplary justice and severe government in the bordering parts (easily to be blown into a blaze) will no doubt be quickly effected. Although I persist in my former wish that the names might stand as they do, yet I confess myself unable to answer the late reasons to the contrary, for first, there was never more antipathy between English and Scotts then there was between Castillians and Portuguez, and yet there that union in name was never thought needfull to breed a new kindness, but they do at this day live kindly together without it. True it is that the Portuguez have no foreign dependency, which is here the knot, which for my part I leave for wiser men to undo. And therefore, secondly, I say that notwithstanding my former wish, I do find neither impossibility to drown both names of England and Scotland in a third, nor in my learning and capacity any great inconvenience. For proof whereof I alledg a late domesticall example of our own set down by Du Tyllet in his book of treaties between England and France.[46] The English, saith he, had the victory over the Scots, meaning by Mussleborough feild, '*ce non obstant tost apres appellerent les dits Escossois à la reunion de tout l'isle par le moyen et lieu[47] du dict mariage*', yet notwithstanding, a little while after, they called the said Scotts to the reuniting of the whole island by the meanes and occasion of the said mariage between King Edward the 6th and the late

---

[45] See Seneca, *Troades*, line 593. The exact words are '*bella Telemacho paras*'
[46] See Jehan du Tillet, *Receueil des Guerres et Traictez D'Entre Les Roys de France et D'Angleterre* (Paris, 1587), fo. 168v. The quoted text has been corrected on the basis of B
[47] '*lieu*' should read '*lien*' and hence should have been translated as 'bond'

Scottish Queen, '*offerans reprendre l'ancien nom de Bretagne, affin d'oster la jalousie de la domination d'une nation sur l'autre*', offering to resume the antient name of Brittany, the better to take away all jealousy from them by the difference which might breed between them by the divers denomination[48] of one nation over the other. And therefore to hold that which our state then thought to be convenient to be impossible, is impossible to be other then an obstinate folly and perverseness. And as to the multitude of inconveniences alledged by our common lawyers, I confess I know not their mysteries, but this I am sure of, that all or the most part that was alledged out of that art against a third name seemed to me rather trickes and sharpness of wit to overthrow that by wresting of law and wrangling which they had no liking should go forwards, then either sound or substantiall objections, the dissolving whereof I leave to men of the same profession and contrary opinion, for as the proverb is: No smith is so cunning to make a lock, but that another is as cunning to pick it.

Chapter 16

Which stile is seemlyest for the king to use

We will, putting the case that a third name is neither impossible nor absurd, consider now what name will be the best. Wherein if it must be done and be possible to be done, we need take no paines, having, the path beaten so lately before us by our forefathers for the name of Britany, and that name so well allowed by his Majesty and, as I hear, very well received in Scotland, and for the Welsh I dare be their sureties, for they by this meanes will have two prophecies (*prima specie* terrible) without shedding one drop of blood fulfilled. The one is that the Britons (for so the Welsh-men call themselves and so are indeed) shall by this be Lordes of London (Lord Mayors I meane) and there at their pleasure measure out the velvets and silkes, no man daring to controll them. The other, which is solemnly recorded by Henry Huntington in his history written about 400 yeares ago: '*Praedixit*', saith he, '*Anglis vir quidam Dei*

---

[48] For 'denomination' read 'domination'

quod non ea gens solum Normannorum, verum et Scotorum, quos vilissimos habebant (for they be the words of my author whom I may not falsify) *eis ad immeritam confusionem dominarentur'*.[49] A certain man of God fortold the English how that not only the Norman nation but also the Scotts, whom they esteem most basely of, should rule over them to their undeserved confusion.

Now for the word *Britania*, I find it in antient writers in two senses. Tacitus[50] and the Roman writers before him take it in opposition to *Hibernia*, Ireland, and so to contain the continent of this iland, England and Scotland only. But Ptolomeus (writing in Adrian's time, when the country was more fully discovered) in his *Geography* makes the two Britanies ilands, namely Albion and Ireland,[51] and so doth Eustathius in his commentary upon Dionysius Afer,[52] also a modern Gretian but a diligent observer of antiquity. And Dyonisius himself say[s][53] the great and little Britany severed, etc. And the same Ptolomy in his *Almagest* setteth down two Britanyes likewise, great Britany and litle Britany, which are not (as some ignorant men have thought) England and Scotland;[54] for in his time and divers ages after there was no division in this continent. But the continent of England and Scotland together is *Britania magna*, great Britany, answering to Albion in the geography, and Ireland *Britania parva*, answering to Hibernia, as by plain words and graduation there set down may appear. So that by this reckoning, we have choice of three stiles:

1. *Rex Britaniae, Franciae et Hiberniae* (taking Britany in the notion of Tacticus and the antientest);
2. *Rex Britaniarum* (*vel utriusque Britaniae*) *et Franciae*;
3. *Rex Britanicarum insularum et Franciae*.

---

[49] Marginal note: 'In procemio lib. sexti'. See Henry, Archdeacon of Huntingdon, *Historia Anglorum*, ed. T. Arnold (London, 1879), 173-4, for the exact text

[50] Marginal note: 'In Vita Agricola'. See c. 10

[51] See *Geography of Claudius Ptolemy*, ed. E. L. Stevenson (New York, 1932), 48-51 (Bk. II, c. 1-2)

[52] *Dionysii Alexandrini De Situ Orbis . . . cum Eustathii Thessalonicencis Archiepiscopi Commentariis* (Basil, 1556), 182

[53] Supplied by B. A, which includes both 'Afer' and 'Dionysius' in the subject of the sentence, reads 'say'. The punctuation has been changed to indicate Savile's original intention. A omits the Greek quotation

[54] *Almagest*, Bk. II, c. 6, nos. 19-25

Of all the which the last is in truth the largest, for it containeth also Wight, Man, Garnesy and Jersey, etc., but it is somewhat disgracefull for so great a prince to be stiled king of ilands in his first title, although it be true that the king of Spain hath also in his stile *Rey de las Islas del mare Oceano*, King of Ocean Iles, but it cometh after many great kingdomes. The second stile of both Britanys answereth very well in proportion to that of the Spanish stile *Reye de las duas Sicilias*, that is, King of the Iland of Sicily and Kingdom of Naples. '*Il Reame di Napoli*', (saith Guicciardine) '*nelle investiture et bolle della chiesa Romana, delle quale e feudo antichissimo e detto, il regno di Sicilia, di qua dal faro*', and the other consequently '*il regno di Sicilia di la dal faro*'.[55] The kingdom of Naples by the investiture and bull of the church of Rome, which is very antient, is called the kingdome of Sicily on this side the streight, and the other consequently Sicilia beyond the streight. For as our two Britanys are separated by the sea, so are his two Sicilys by the streight of Regium.

But perchance if the stile should be used, King of both Britanys, men's conceits would be carried into Britany in France, and therefore the first form I like the best of the three, *Rex Britaniae, Franciae et Hiberniae*, and *Rex*, not *Imperator*, which name the Spanish in their pride sometimes have usurped, and least of all *Monarcha*, which though in the nature of the word it be more (perhaps less) than *Rex*, yet because in the vulgar understanding the word *Monarcha* is drawn to the four great renowned monarchies, it would be imputed but a vanity in us, as I think, no other king before ever using it.

Chapter 17

Whether the title of King of Britany be an innovation or a renovation

Now whether this title, King of Britany, be a meer innovation or but a renovation, I have heard it in question, that is, whether ever there were a king of Britany *in rerum natura* or no. If we believe *Galfridus Monmouthensis*, Jeffery of Monmouth,

---

[55] Guicciardini, *La Historia d'Italia*, fo. 6v. The quoted text has been corrected on the basis of B

we have kings of Britany enough from Brutus to Cadwall-
lader,[56] but leaving him with his Welsh fables, it must be
confessed that at the Romans' coming into this iland (before
which time we have no true record) and many years after them
also we find *Rex Icenorum, Rex Brigantum,* etc., but nowhere to
my remembrance in Roman stories *Rex Britaniae.* Only Beda
calleth Lucius *Britannorum Rex,*[57] which how it is to be
understood, during the time of the Romans being here as they
were, I know not.

After the Romans' departure in Malmesburiensis I find
Voltigerne called *Rex Britaniae* and Guartimar his son; and
lastly Ambrosius is termed by him *Monarcha Regni Britonum,*
monarch of the British kingdomes.[58] After whom, the Saxons'
heptarchy coming in place, extinguished the name of the
kingdom of Britany, Neither at the reuniting of them again in
Egbert, Alfred and Athelstane, being otherwise great and
glorious kings, do I find the stile of Britany retained, until King
Edgar's time, who not by misprision incident to a simple
chronicler, but even in an instrument of his own making and
beyond all exception stileth himself *totius Albionis basileus,* king
of all Albion. *Totius* excludeth all cavills and agreeth plainly
with our *Rex Britaniae.* This instument is recorded by Malmesburiensis, and in like form I have seen an originall of the same
king's containing, as I remember, a donation of somewhat to
the Abby of Abbington.[59]

Chapter 18

Of the community of language

Let us now proceed to the second point, which is the community of language, the which no doubt is a great bond of union, but
where it is not before is not easily brought in, except in a
depopulating conquest, as into Britany by the conquest of

[56] See Geoffrey of Monmouth, *History of the Kings of Britain,* tr. L. Thorpe
(Harmondsworth., 1966), *passim*
[57] Beda, *Historia Ecclesiastica Gentis Anglorum,* i. 4
[58] *De Gestis Rerum Anglorum,* ed. Stubbs, i, 7
[59] *Ibid.,* 173-4

Saxons. And yet there is another example of a moderate conquest, of a perfect bringing in of a language, in my opinion to be marvelled at, I mean that of Alexander the Great and his successors into Asia and Ægypt, where he extinguished utterly the former languages of that country and planted generally the Greek, at least in all great townes, where it was afterwards their mother tongue; for before in Asia (excepting some maritime townes which were Greek colonys) it was not generally[60] spoken, and in Ægypt not at all. And he not only brought with him into Asia his own language but also the son of the Macedonian year and their reckoning of the months.

I must confess indeed that many of their great townes were built by Alexander and his successors and so perchance replenished with some Grecians. But what are thirty or fourty thousand, for he conveyed no more over with him and some daily wasted with the warres, to plant a new language, whereas William the Conquerour brought in with him many more Normans and yet could not conquer the language. True it is that the English were very desirous to learn the French, and none was else esteemed a gentleman if he spake not French, at least of Stratford of the Bow, if the French of Paris were to him unknown,[61] as it fareth in all conquests. The Britons, saith Tacitus, in Domitian's time desired not only to understand and speak the Roman tongue but to be eloquent in it.[62]

And as Alexander did in the East in his conquest, so generally all the west part of the world which was conquered by the Romans understood and spake ordinarily the Latin, as France, Spain and Affrick. The east part of the world, though conquered alike allso by them, prized their own at a higher rate and disdained to lay Latine upon Greek, as they thought a churle upon a gentleman.

Generally in all modern conquests there rather followeth corruption of language than change, as in Italy, France and Spain by the Goths and Vandalls. The Latin which they found there prevailing was diversely abbastarized, as we see.

[60] B, C, and D read 'naturally'
[61] The phrase 'at least . . . unknown' is omitted in B, C, and D
[62] *Agricola*, c. 21

In our present example we have by good fortune that band of community of language to strengthen our union, both nations using one and almost the same dialect, to wit the Saxon language. And the Scots and north people of England speak more incorruptly than the South, which by reason of the Conquest and greater commerce with foreign nations, is become more mingled and degenerate from the antient tongue, as will easily appear to him that shall compare the two dialects with the Germane, mother of them both.

Now if any man marvell how these two nations, derived from so divers rootes, the English from Germany and the Scots no doubt from Ireland and perchance originally from Spain, should fall into one language, I answer under correction (for I know I shall breach a paradox) that the body of both nations are Saxons, conquered on the one side by the Normans, which are the southern people, on the other side the northern people by the Scots out of Ireland with the ilands adjacent and the northwest part of Scotland. So that, as in England we do hold the antient gentry Normans and the mass of the common people Saxons, so do I beleive in Scotland the great houses, as conquerours, to have bin Scottish and the comminalty (at the least all the south side) were Saxons. My reason is, for that I find that as the Saxons exterminated the Britons and peopled with themselves all the now-England (Wales excepted), so did the same Saxon nation also and at the same time the greatest part of the now-Scotland, chasing into the highland and farthest part of the iland the Picts, which were then the antient inhabitants thereof, and so I think of our antient Britons, the now-Welsh.

It is cleer by Beda, a witness without all exception, and by all stories since, that of the Saxon heptarchy the kingdom of the North-humbers was subdivided into two great and mighty kingdomes, whereof the far greater both in strength and reputation was *Regnum Berniciorum*, which falleth (some skirts of Northumberland excepted) wholly within Scotland; so that making it but equall with *Regnum Deirorum*, which compasseth Cheshire, Lancashire, Yorkshire, Durham, Westmorland and Cumberland, to which it was much superiour, the most part of Scotland, as it is now, must needs fall within the compass of the

Bernicii, a people meerly Saxon. And this I take to be a more probable cause of the community of language than either the confining of the countrys, which worketh no more then a reciprocall understanding one of the other for civility sake, in the borders only, which is not always and everywhere so. For even in these daies I have heard that in the borders between England and Wales there are some towns where on the one side of the street they speak and understand but English, and on the other side Welsh only. Which proveth that vicinity and neighbourhood penetrateth in that kind not so far as into the midle of the country and to the king's court. Neither can the overrunning of Scotland by King Edward the 1st be the cause, who possessed it not long enough to alter the language, it being confessed on all sides that the antient language of the Scots was Irish, whereas we in almost 500 years being Lords of Ireland, and sending mony, colonys and armies thither, have not bin able to work this alteration of words in all this time, yea scarce in two or three words.

But be the beginning of the alteration as it may be, the language is common between us and so we have gained one step to our union.

Chapter 19

Of conformity in apparel

Conformity in apparrell as well as in language is of great force to unite men's minds, especially in the bas and domestick sort of people brought up at home, who mock at all that cannot speak as they speak, or do not wear as they wear. In which point there is no great odds between our two nations, the prophecy of Henry Huntingdon being verifyed in both: *Praedixit nihilominus varium adeo seculum creandum, ut varietas quae in vestibus hominum latebat et in actionibus patebat multimoda variatione vestium designaretur.*[63] He prophesyed notwithstanding that so variable an age should come, as the diversity and difference which lay hid in the garments of men and was apparent in their actions should be discerned by the manifold difference of their clothes and

---

[63] *Historia Anglorum*, ed. Arnold, 174. The quoted text is corrected on the basis of B

fashions. Notwithstanding all which constancy of us both, yet
the manner of apparelling in the main is all one, bewraying in
the generallity rather a German originall, which hath in time
prevailed over all, then an Irish.[64] For whereas the Germans do
and of antient time did the better sort of them use, as Tacitus
sayt, *veste stricta et singulos artus exprimente*, a close and a straight
garment to their body, and the Irish both now and antiently
veste fluitante, a loose garment, it is evident that the Scots, as well
as we, are Germans in the manner of their apparelling, rather
then Irish.[65]

Chapter 20

Of conformity in religion

But let us now come to that powerfull part of union which
among the antients who knew not God, or at least not rightly,
was of small estimation, but which is (and so ought to be) of
greatest account, I mean conformity in religion. The diversity
of opinions wherein, in my reading, I cannot find made any
impression at all in the minds of great statesmen or any
alteration at all in the government of their states, saving only in
the Jewish and Christian religions, the two only true religions
and which only touch the heart and leave a feeling and a deep
impression in the consciences of men.

Under the name of Christian religion I comprehend all
schisms and deviations, being not direct apostacys to Gentilism,
as well as the Orthodoxall faith; yea the Turkish itself is no other
but a bastard branch, out of from the stock of Christian religion,
composed of two main heresies, Judaism and Araism,[66] as
Sergius the father of it was.

Now that in the religion, or rather the superstition, of the
Gentiles there was far greater and more variety then in ours,
besides that books show [it][67] most plainly, we have a direct
testimony of Themistius, a pagan (for ought I find in his

[64] Supplied by B. A reads 'them and Irish'
[65] See Tacitus, *De Origine et Situ Germanorum*, c. 17. The quoted text is corrected on the
basis of B
[66] C reads 'Arrianisme'
[67] Supplied by B

writings), who affirmed in an oration before Valens the emperour, which I think is extant among his works, that the diversity and dissention of sects in the Christian religion was but small in respect of the multitude or confusion among the Greeks or Gentiles, for that amongst them there are about 300 different sects of religion.[68] Yet I never heard that ever any state among them made war upon another for religion sake, to reduce them to their faith, or to maintain their own; neither cared they, nor even strived in religion for the truth, which can be but one. But the precept of the politicks of those times was this only: each to serve God after the manner of his own country.[69] But true it is that if any sects make private conventicles tending to an universall corruption of good manners (whereof there is a notable example in Livy of the Bacchanalia in Rome), it was ever with them capitall, but as a matter of state, not matter of faith.[70]

Instead of this contention in religion I do find amongst the antients an ambition of theirs somewhat resembling this of ours. I mean that of the Athenians and Lacedemonians, who as we now fight one with another to plant our faith, or at least do make that our pretext, so did they also upon no other grounds but to plant in the allies and countries and towns subdued by them their manner of government (the Athenians a popular state and the Lacedemonians an oligarchy), as in Thucydides and other Greek stories it is to be seen.

If any shall demand, if the pagans were so careless of their religion, why did they so violently oppose ours, my answer must be that to bring in or perswade a new religion or new gods was allwaies in all states capitall, as Socrates found, though innocent thereof, their violent proceedings used against us having their ground rather perchance from us then from them.

But let us lay aside this, and the whole point, as a needless babling, their being in our particular, by God's merciful providence, between us a perfect uniformity in religion.

[68] Marginal note: 'Socrates in Hist. Eccles. lib. 4, c. 32.' See *The Ecclesiasticall Historie of Socrates Scholasticus* (London, 1577)
[69] Marginal note in B, C, and D: 'Plato, de Repub. et alii'. See Plato, *The Republic*, Bks. III-IV
[70] See Livy, Bk. XXXIX, c. 14-19

Chapter 21

Of conformity in laws and customes

Let us now come to the last and most important point of our union, conformity in our laws and customes. The characters of a perfect union so far as concerneth this 5th and last point I make to be three principally:

1. The first is to be governed by the same lawes.

2. The second is to enjoy the same liberties and priviledges.

3. The third and last is to sustain and undergo the same burdens.

If any require an example of my such opinion, I produce here at home Essex and Kent, sometimes two severall kingdomes; and in these days [they][71] yet do hold a very different custome in inheriting of land, so hard a thing it is to find a perfect union.

And if you urge me further whether ours in hand can possibly be such a one, my answer is I will set down in order what wise men have done in the like cases, so far as my books and my remembrance will serve me, for experience I have none at all in the matter, but do leave the judgment and choice to them that do sit at the helm.

In union of states upon conquests, which in rigour leaveth all at discretion, the Romans used perpetually one and the same temperate course, which was to send with instructions from the Senate a certain number of commissioners (ten commonly into a great country, and five into a less) of the principallest men of the state *ad ordinandam provinciam*, for the ordering of the province, with the advice and consent of the generall, by whose vertue and fortune the countries were conquered and obtain :d. So ten commissioners were sent to Publius Scipio into Affrick after the overthrow of Hannibal and the Carthaginian army; to Lucius Scipio into Asia after the defeat of Antiochus; and twice into Macedonia to Titus Quintus after the overthrow of Phillip; and lastly 10 to Aemilius Paulus after the conquest of the kingdome and five to Amitius into Illyricum.[72]

[71] Supplied by B
[72] Livy, Bks. XXXVII, c. 34: XXXIII, c. 24; XLV, c. 17; LI

The articles and capitulations of which treaties set down by Livy in the places quoted I ommit here to report (many of them being articles of a league, not of an union) and will content myself with some few of the Macedonian union upon the conquest:

1. *Ut suis legibus viverent, suos magistratus haberent;*

2. *In quatuor regiones describi Macedoniam suum quaeque regio consilium haberet, commune concilium gentis nullum esset;*

3. *[blank]*

4. *Sale invecto non uti;*

5. *Navalem materiam nec ipsos caedere, nec alios pati;*

6. *[blank]*

7. *Dimidium tributi quod regibus ferre soliti sunt populo Romano pendere.*[73]

1. That they should live under their own laws and enjoy their own magistrates;

2. Macedony to be divided into four provinces, every province to have a severall councell, and no general councell to be for them all in common;

3. That none of one region might marry or traffick with any of another;

4. To use no foreign inbrought salt;

5. Neither to fell any timber, nor suffer any matter for shipping to be taken either by themselves or others;

6. The impost upon wines to be taken away;

7. To pay the people of Rome half of that tribute which they used to pay to their kings aforetime.

Chapter 22

The articles of union between Lituania and Poland

But let us leave these examples, which besides that they were old, are of the union by conquest, and let us come to neerer times and like examples. My second example shall be of the union of the great dutchy of Lithuania to the kingdome of Poland. The articles between Jagello and Hedinges, the Queen, before the mariage ar in Cromerus these only:[74]

[73] *Ibid.*, Bk. XLV, c. 18, 29

[74] Marginal note of B: 'This union was meerlie by marriage and belongs to the third sorte of the three kindes of unions, not to the second sorte, as there I wrote'

1. *Jagellonem thesauros suos omnes et majorum suorum in Poloniam comportaturum.*

2. *Jagellionem Lithuaniam Poloniae adjuncturum, ut eodum deinceps cum ea imperio censeatur,* and after the mariage (which was solemnized anno 1386) *Lithuaniam omnem cum Samogetia et ea parte Russiae, quae in ditione ejus Jagellionis erat, Poloniae jure sempiterno adjunxit Jagello, et in unum corpus redegit jure jurando interposito.*

3. *Lituani et Russi duces ac proceres omnes in verba regis et reginae jurarunt, consignatisque diplomatis in fide et clientela ipsorum et regni Poloniae se cum dictionibus suis semper fore promiserunt; extantque in archivo regio ea diplomata* (which *diplomata,* if it had pleased Cromerus to have set down *as verbum,* word by word, or any other writer had done the same, they would be very well worth the diligent reading and perusing over, but I have seen no farther but Cromer.)[75]

1. Jagello should bring all his own and his ancestors' treasures into Polonia.

2. That Jagello should joyn and unite Lithuania to the kingdome of Polonia, that henceforth they might be esteemed both under one government; and after the mariage, which was solemnized anno 1386, Jagello did annex and joyn by an everlasting right all Lituania, Samogetia and that part of Russia which then was under his government, and by a solemn oath taken reduced them into one body.

3. Further that the Lithuanian and Russian dukes, with all the nobility, should swear allegiance to the King and Queen, the instruments being thus signed and sealed by them, by the which they did promise that themselves and all that were under them should ever remain under the faith of the kings, and obedience to the kingdome of Polonia. And these instruments remain amongst the records of the kingdome.

In the year 1412 (saith Cromerus) the same league was renewed between these two nations:

1. *Concessum nobilitatis proceribus Lithuanis (iis dumtaxat qui ritus Ecclesiae Romanae Catholicae servarent) iisdem ut insignibus, iisdem praerogativis, quibus Poloniae nobilitas uterentur, praeterquam*

[75] See Marcin Kromer, *De Origine et Rebus Gestis Polonorum* (Basil, 1568), 240-1

ut justu magni ducis arces conderent vias publicas reficierent, tributaque solita penderent.

2. *Senetus et magistratus more Polonorum haberent eosdem honoris et magistratus ne alienis ab Ecclesiae Romanae institutis moderentur.*

3. *Ducem, quando usus postulat, non nisi de sententia regis et amplissimi consilii Polonorum eligerent; vicissimique Poloni ut ne insciis et inconsultis Duce et Senatu Lituano Regem sibi crearent; consiliis communibus quoties opus esset ut ea Lublinae, vel Possonio, vel alias quo videretur mutuo consensu indicerentur.*

4. *Ordo ecclesiasticus ut eodem jure iisdemque praerogativis, quibus in Polonia uteretur.* Haec omnia proceres Lituani approbarunt et literarum monumentis consignarunt, saith my author, *anno* 1412, Jagello yet living.[76]

1. It is granted to the cheif Lituanian nobility (but to them only which are Catholick Romanes) that they shall enjoy the same titles and prerogatives which the nobility of Poland did bear and did use, and moveover that with the pleasure of the Duke they should build castles, amend the common highwaies, and pay the accustomed tributes.

2. That after the manner of Polonia they should have their councells and magistrates, and the same honours and offices, so they agreed with the rights of the Church of Rome.

3. That they should not chuse a duke whensoever need required but by the consent and allowance of the king and the most great councell of Poland; and likewise that Polonians should not create them a king without the assent and liking of the duke and councell of Lithuania; and whensoever need should be, to summon or call a general diet for both the nations, that the same should be held either at Lublin or Possonium, or elsewhere to the liking of both nations.

4. That they should use the same ecclesiasticall ceremonies, rites, and priviledges as was used in Poland. All the which the Lituanian lords did approve and put in writing under their hands and seals (saith my author) anno 1412, Jagello yet living.

Anno 1499 adjecta est antiquis pactis declaratio de electione regis et magni ducis; nempe ut neutri alteris non convocatis principem sibi

<hr>

[76] *Ibid.,* 277

eligerent et crearent.[77] In the year 1499 there was added to this antient agreement a declaration of the choosing of the king and the great duke, to wit, that neither nation should choose them a prince without the consent and approvement of both.

Anno 1501 the union between these two nations was renewed: the originall whereof (saith mine author) '*extat in archivo regio Cracoviensi, adhibita autem*' (saith he) '*in foedere moderatione quadam nonnullorum capitum*', is extant of record in the king's Exchequer at Cracovia, but with the moderation of certain articles in the same treaty. But this following seemeth to me the most straight union of all which was made between these two nations.

1. *Quod Polonus et Lituanus unus deinceps debet esse populus sub uno Rege.*

2. *Rex in Polonia creetur Lituanis etiam proceribus his locis in eo conventu suffragia ferentibus.*

3. *Concilium unum sit duobus populis.*

4. *Societas in fecundis juncta et adversis rebus.*

5. *Moneta par atque similis utrique populo.*

6. *Foedera antiqua serventur.*

7. *Magistratus, senatores, praefecti, nobilitas et alii quivis Lituani jurent in verba regis quoties a consiliariis Polonis praemoniti fuerint.*

8. *Jura et praerogativa utriusque populi simul et eodem contextu literarum a novis regibus confirmentur.*

9. *Caetera ut judicia utrobique more antiquo exerceantur.*

10. *Nulla utcunque occasio dirimendae conjunctionis captatetur.*[78]

1. That from henceforth the Polonians and Lithuanians shall be one people under one king.

2. That the king shall be chosen in Polonia by the voices and and assents of the nobility of Lituania, they being there assembled for that purpose together.

3. One councell shall be for both the nations.

4. A friendly society shall be between them as well in prosperity as adversity.

5. One manner of coine shall run currant between both the people.

[77] *Ibid.*, 436
[78] *Ibid.*, 439

6. All judgments and causes of law shall be kept and observed as in former times, and all treaties and leagues continued with foreign nations.

7. All magistrates, councellors, governours, noblemen and all other Lituanians whatsoever shall swear faith and obedience to the king, as often as they shall be by the Polonian councell summoned.

8. All rights and priviledges of both the nations, and also all letters patents whatsoever shall be confirmed, ratifyed and allowed by the new succeeding kings.

9. All judgments and pleas of right shall run and continue in their antient course, as they have bin used in both nations, and as they have bin accustomed in former times.

10. That no cause whatsoever shall be taken hold of which may in the least break this conjunction. And thus much I find concerning that union.

Chapter 23

The articles of union between Norwey and Sweden

My third example of union shall be that between Norway and Sweden about anno 1320 in the person of Magnus, King of Sweden, who united Norway (as Crantzius saith), lib. 6, by conquest from Ericus, King of Norway.[79] But in his story of Suecia, lib. 5, '*Magnus*' (saith the same author, either forgetting himself or being better instructed when he wrote the Norway story then when he wrote the Sweden) '*adjuvante virtute, favente fortuna, paterno Regno Norwegiae consociavit; quod unde factum sit, memoria nulla in annalibus extat, hoc quia factum sit non siletur*'.[80] Magnus by his own worth and by the favour of his fortune conjoyned Norway to his paternall kingdom; which how and when it was done, there is no mention made in the chronicles, but that it was done is manifest. But Norway and Sweden, united howsoever, were both conjoyned to the kingdome of Denmark in the person of Margaret, daughter and heir of

---

[79] Marginal note: 'lib. 6. Norv. p.418'. See Albertus Krantzius, *Chronica Regnorum Aquiloniarum Daniae, Suetiae, Norvagiae* (Frankfurt, 1575)
[80] Marginal note: 'Lib. 5 Sue. p.314

Waldemarus, King of Denmark, anno 1407. '*Et ex illo die*' (saith the same Crantzius) '*Dania et Norwegia pene semper mansere conjuncta, [Norwegia] nunquam discrepante, licet Suecia aliquoties se tentaverit sejungere, rediit tamen ad eam unionem, quam trium regnorum proceres, sentientes regnis profuturam, unanimi consensu servandam constituerunt*'.[81] And from that day (saith the same Crantzius) have they remained almost alwaies firmly conjoyned together, Norway never misliking, although Swedeland hath sometimes assayed a separation, yet hath returned back again in the same union, which the nobility of the three kingdomes thought proffitable with one consent to be observed by them all. And father of the articles of this union, if any were, I am not able to say.

Chapter 24

The articles of union between Aragon and Castile

My fourth example of union shall be that between Aragon and Castile in Ferdinand and Isabell. In which union, besides the disputation in councell concerning the name of Spain and a question, the generall name of Spain being refused, to change the marshalling and precedency of the particular kingdomes in the stile, I do find nothing. For articles of the union I think there never were any, saving one solemn plea set down by Gonsalvo de Ilescas in the 6th book of his *History Pontificall* between the king and queen, whether of them were the more rightfull heir of Castile and Leon. The cause of the doubt was (saith my author) '*por quitar dudas para en lo por venir si a caso Dios dispusiesse d'alguno dellos sin tener hijos*',[82] for to obtain quietness and peace in time to come, if God should so dispose of them, as to leave no sons between them. As indeed in part it happened, they leaving none between them but daughters.

This cause was solemnly argued in law before judges delegated for that purpose, and sentence went on the queen's

---

[81] Marginal note: 'Lib. 5 Sue. p.317'. For '*mansere*' read '*permansere*'. '*Norwegia*' supplied by B

[82] See Gonsalo de Illescas, *Historia Pontifical y Catholica* (Burgos, 1578), Bk. VI. fo. 127v. The quoted text is corrected on the basis of B

side, which sentence was so punctually executed that the cause happening, which they presumed might happen, of Isabell's death without issue male, which a little while after came to pass, Ferdinand was removed from the government of Castile, giving place to his daughter Joan and her husband, and went home to Aragon, where he marryed Garmanie de Foix, a young French lady of great birth, with great hope of issue male by her to inherite Aragon, had not the immoderate desire of issue male in this fair lady carried her so far as that by advise of her woman she gave her husband in a potion a mess of broth[83] to strengthen nature, which wrought his finall bane and destruction, and he settled the crown of Aragon upon Joan, upon whose heires it standeth at this day.

I think it allso not amiss to adde how in this union all gold was coyned with both their faces, all silver and brass mony with both their names, all seals graven with both their armes, and all charters and grants under both their names, Ilescas, lib. 4.[84]

Chapter 25

Articles of the marriage between Queen Mary and King Philip

No less carefull then Queen Isabell that no wrong should be done to her lawfull successors in favour of her husband was Queen Mary matching with Philip the Prince, afterward King of Spain, which shall be my fift example of union. Wherein I cannot but exceedingly commend the wisdome and circumspection of her councell and nobility, that making a match so honourable and with such advantages as that was, they were so carefull and precise in the point of succession as they allowed Philip not so much, the case happening, as tenancy by curtesy, nor any further interest then as a meer bedfellow to the queen, with a vain name of a king, without any power in patents, grants or any other publick act of sovereignty whatsoever, either to assent or deny, as by the statute Mariae, cap. 2 doth appear.

[83] 'A potion in a mess of broth' was probably intended
[84] B corrects 'lib. 4' to read 'libro quo ut supra'

Out of the which and the treaties inserted it is not amiss to set down these few points following:

1. The queen, notwithstanding that mariage, shall have the whole disposition of all benefices, offices, lands, revenues and fruits whatsoever within her realm and dominions. and they shall be all signed by her alone, which, so signed, shall be a warrant to all other seals.

2. That they shall be all and allwaies bestowed upon such as shall be her naturall born subjects and not otherwise.

3. That all matters of the said realm shall be treated and managed in the same tongue they were wont to be, and by the naturall born subjects of the said realms, for fear, as I think, of bringing in of Spanish laws, as we have of French,[85] or extinguishing the English tongue in time.

4. That all rights, laws, priviledges and customes whatsoever of the said realme shall be forever preserved and maintained intire.

5. That nothing be innovated in the state or right, either publick or private, or in the laws and customes of the said realms.

6. That the king shall admit into his service and Court English gentlemen and yeomen as his proper subjects.

7. That the king shall not promote, admit nor receive to any office, administration nor benefice any foreign-born.

8. That if Queen Mary dy without children, the king surviving, he shall not challenge any right at all in the said kingdome, but without any impediment or hinderance whatsoever shall permit the succession thereof to come to them to whom it shall belong and appertain by right and the lawes of the said realm.

9. That the king shall not carry nor suffer to be carried out of the realm the jewells, guns, ships, ordinance nor ammunition of war whatsoever for defence, but shall require and shall provide that the same may be allwaies ready in their strength and force for the defence of the realm.

[85] Savile follows Hayward in this statement regarding French law. Like Hayward, Savile was critical of common lawyers, and although he was not a civil lawyer, he was an honorary member of Doctors' Commons. See D. C. Squibb, *Doctors' Commons* (Oxford, 1977), 179

10. That the king shall not alien any of the appurtenances of the said realm, nor suffer any part of them to be usurped by others, but shall faithfully keep and cause to be kept by the naturall born of the same, and shall also preserve all and singular places of the realm, especially all forts and frontires of the same.[86]

Chapter 26

Articles upon the uniting of Britany to France

The treaties between France and Britany upon their uniting I will make my sixt example, which were in number three. The effect of the first between Charles the 8th and Dame Anne were: *Que la duchesse lors aagée d'environ 14 ans, avec l'advis de son conseil donneroit irrevocablement à 30me aage au Roy et ses successeurs Roys de France* (in case she should dy before him without heires of their bodies) *son Duché et tout le droit qu'elle avoit; come luy reciprocrement donnoit à icelle* (if he should dy) *les droits qu'il y pretendoit.*[87] That the dutchess, being then but 14 years of age, with the advice of her councell should irrevocably give, when she attained unto 30 years, unto the king and his successors, kings of France, her dutchy, with all the rights whatsoever belonging; and likewise the king reciprocally should give to her, if he should dy, all the rights, titles and interest whatsoever he pretended thereunto. Now because this guift, in case she should dy before the king, did a plain wrong to the prince of Orange, her next heir, he made also a cessation of his right unto the king, the king promising him, if ever his time of title came, to make him a full recompense elsewhere.

The second treaty and capitulation was between Lewis the 12th and the same Dame Anne, being then 21 years old, when she could better make a bargain for herself, and it was far more for her advantage, for in case they had children, the second son or first daughter was to be duke or duchess of Britany, and if they had none, the king surviving, he should enjoy it only during his life, and then to return to the next heir of the said

---

[86] 1 Philip and Mary, Statute 3, c. 2
[87] Argentré, *Historie de Bretaigne*, fo. 791. The quotation is not exact

lady. In both which cases it appeareth there was no union at all of the dutchy of Britany to the crown of France longer then the mariage indured, which yet might by succession have so happened, as to have bin perpetuall.

Now between the king and the subjects of Britany upon this second mariage the articles of the union were these:

1. *De conserver les privileges de touts estats, libertes, franchises, custumes et stile du pays.*

2. *De ne faire ordonance que par deliberation de barons et seigneurs du pays.*

3. *Que les offices de Bretagne devoyent etre pourveus a la nomination de la dite dame, et les lettres seeles en Bretagne.*

4. *Que les levees de fouages, impositions et subsides seroient levees les estats appellez.*

5. *Que le roy mettroit en ses titres, Duc de Bretagne, en affairs du pays.*

6. *Que les gentilshomes ne seroient contraintes servir hors du pays, si non par consentiment des estats.*

7. *Que le monoye d'or et d'argent seroyent forgez sous le nom du roy et la duchesse.*

8. *Que les benefices du pays ne seroyent baillez a autres qu'aux naturales du pays, ny par lettre naturalite ni autrement*; which article the king by the advice of his councell after his wive's death, who indeed passed all things of the dutchy by herself during her life, revoked, making all French without letters of denization capable.

9. *Que les subjects du Bretagne ne seroyent citez hors du pays.*[88]

1. To observe and keep all priviledges, libertys, immunities and customes whatsoever of all manner of estates, as also the common stile of the country.

2. To make no laws but with the consent and councell of the lords and barons of the country.

3. That all the offices of Britany shall be bestowed upon no other but upon such as the said Lady Dutchess shall appoint and approve, and that all letters patents shall be sealed in Britany

[88] *Ibid.*, fos. 107v-108. The quoted text differs in a number of respects from both the original source and B. The spellings of '*fouage*', '*ordonance*', '*libertes*', and '*naturalite*' have been corrected on the basis of B

which do concern any ways the said dutchy of Britany or the inhabitants thereof.

4. That the taxes upon fires and all other impositions and subsidies shall be rated and imposed by the generall estates there.

5. That the king shall insert in his titles the Duke of Britany, especially in all matters appertaining to the country.

6. That no gentleman shall be forced against his will to serve out of that country but by the assent of the estates there.

7. That the monys of gold and silver shall be stamped jointly with the names of the king and the dutchess.

8. That all benefices and benefits of the country whatsoever shall not be bestowed upon others but upon the naturall born of the country, yea and not by way of charters of naturalization or free denization nor otherwise.

9. That the subjects of Britany shall not be cited nor summoned out of the country.

The third and last union was between Francis, the king of France, and the estates of Britany, by which treaty issued the perfect union of these two estates, the which was made, the king and the estates being present, at Vannes in Britany, anno 1532. In the which assembly we find passed as followeth:

1. That the king by the assent of the estates did unite and conjoin the country and dutchy of Britany with the realm and crown of France *perpetuellement, de forte qu'ils ne puissent entre separez ni tomber en divorce par quelque chose qui se puisse etre.*

2. *Que les droits, privileges et libertes de touts estats, tant de nobless que de l'esglise et du tiers estat, qu'ils avoyent au par a devant et ont à present, leur soyent gardées et observées et que les lettres patentes en forme de chartres en soyent expediment deliverez.*[89]

1. In such sort that they may perpetually so remain and be not severed nor suffer a divorce by what meanes soever.

2. That the rights, privileges and immunities of all manner of estates whatsoever, as well of the nobility and clergy, as of the comminalty which they either have had heretofore or have at this present be duly observed and kept, and that all letters

---

[89] *Ibid.*, fo. 823. For '*par a devant*' B and original read '*par cy devant*' and for '*expediment deliverez*' they read '*expediees et delivrees*'

patents in the form of charters be without delay delivered to them.

3. That no man of what degree soever shall bear the name of count or duke of Britany but the king, nor any bastard of that house, as John and Francis of Britany, the armes without a bar.

Notwithstanding which union, yet were not the Britons united in all things, nor are at this day the customes upon merchandizes brought from Britany into France, imposed in the time of the separation, being not yet taken away, saith my author, which is a thing well worthy to be noted.

Chapter 27

Articles upon the union of Portugal and Castile

My seventh example and my last, and in mine opinion the likest to ours, is that of the union between Portugall and Castile in the year 1580.

The articles of this union (albeit ther be many different circumstances offered by King Philip before the war and in effect performed afterward in part) reported by Jeronimo de Franche, Commissionario[90] Genouese are as followeth:

1. That all customes, priviledges and liberties granted by former kings of Portugall shall be preserved.

2. That the vice-roy or governour (but only to honour the nation by sending one of the king's blood) shall be upon all changes and remooves a naturall Portuguez.

3. That all charges, places of justice, all offices of receipt of the crown, all offices as well of the king's court as of the kingdome, shall be supplyed and bestowed only upon naturall Portuguez, and upon none other, and the same to serve in their places, as well when the king shall come into Portugall in person as in his absence.

4. All secular charges by land or sea, which now are or hereafter shall be erected, all garrisons of fortresses, all prelacyes, abbies, benefices, pensions, orders of knighthood, commanders

[90] For 'Commissionario' read 'Conestaggio', as in B

and all other ecclesiasticall places shall be supplyed with naturall Portuguez only.

5. That the East Indies, Æthiopia and all other foreign places under their regard and obedience shall not be dismembred from the kingdom of Portugall, but that both their officers and lieutenants-generall shall be Portuguez.

6. That the gold and silver currant in Portugal and in all the regions depending upon the same shall be only stamped with the armes of Portugal.

7. That no city, town, fortressed place, jurisdiction nor right devolved to the crown of Portugall whatsoever shall be given to other then to naturall Portuguez, and that all confiscations and casualties whatsoever shall not be kept in the king's hands, but be all bestowed either upon some of the kindred of the family of the former possessor, or upon any other Portuguez which shall have at the least lived in Portugal under the service of the late kings.

8. That the king and his successors shall yearly take and maintain 200 Portuguez for his service in the wars, giving them honourable entertainment.

9. That the king and the queen shall admit for their ordinary attendance in court Portuguez indifferently as well as Castilians.

10. That the king coming into the kingdome of Portugal shall not take up lodgings by harbingers in Portugal, as he doth in Castile.

11. That the king, in what place soever he shall be resident with his court shall continually have about his person a councell of naturall Portuguez only, for the dispatch of the affaires of Portugal; and that all dispatches whatsoever any way concerning Portugal shall be done and written in the Portugall tongue (differing only in dialect from the Castilian as ours and the Scottish).

12. All judgments in matters of justice whatsoever to be executed and ended there, without any appeal.

13. That all dutyes and customes imposed upon merchandizes transported by land from the one kingdom to the other shall be abolished on both sides.

14. That the king shall give all possible furtherance and

assistance for the promotion and the Portugal-Indian fleet, and for all means of defence of the kingdom and conservation of the frontiers of Africk.[91]

Hope was given them, before the war, of free trade into the West Indies, '*e di participar delle cose di Castilia, come i naturali*', and to participate of all the commodities of Castile as the naturall born themselves, but after the victory he demurred upon that point, alledging that he was first to treat with his subjects of Castile about it, because they were grants that would be much prejudiciall to them.[92]

One more thing I will adde, how in their *cortes* (for so they call their assemblies of estates) held by the king at Tomar in Portugall in April 1581, the deputies or burgesses of townes desired expressly there, '*che gli stati di Portugallo restassero sempre separati da Castiglia con moneta da se*', that the estates of Portugal (which is as our parliament) might forever remain separated and divided from Castile, and use and enjoy their own coyn.[93]

Chapter 28

Nine results arising out of the former examples, whereupon may be framed our form of union

Now out of these seven examples, perchance truely, *quia quod exemplo fit jure fieri videtur*, because whatsoever is done by example seems to be justly done; perchance falsly, for *non quid Romae fiat, sed quid fieri debeat spectandum est*, not what is done at Rome, but what ought to be done is to be regarded, a man might make many results, and many more queries concerning this our question in hand:

1. As first, that estates elective may be perpetually united, as appears by the 2nd and 3rd example.

2. Secondly, that estates meerly successive cannot be perpetually united, as appears by the 4th and 5th example, of Isabel and Queen Mary, though not for lack of love to their husbands.

3. Thirdly, that in states which will not admit a perpetuall

[91] See G. F. Conestaggio, *Dell' Unione del Regno di Portogallo alla Corona di Castiglia* (Venice, 1592), Bk. 8
[92] *Ibid.*, fo. 202
[93] *Ibid.* The quoted text is corrected on the basis of B

union, all fortresses, shipping, artillery, etc. are to be maintained still in the same state, as they were found at first in the hands of the naturall born subjects. Example 5th, article 9th and 10th.

4. Fourthly, that between nations where hath bin a long and antient enmity, a straight union and amity will be very hardly at the first taken on both sides, which in time may come on well enough, if the prince carry himself indifferent and without partiallity between the two nations, as appears by the appendix to the article by the motion of the Portugal deputies of estate. And not only is the prince to bear himself indifferently but must deal more respectively and more tenderly with the nation where he was not born, for they will naturally stand more jealous of all his actions then his own countrymen. Example 7th, where King Philip offered to the Portugall nation the same priviledges which the Castilian had in the West Indies, and denyed to his Castilians the priviledges which the Portugals had in the East Indies, article 5th and in the appendix to those articles.

5. Fifthly, that it is indifferent whether the coine be kept severall, as in the 7th example and the 6th article, or the same be made currant in both nations, as in the 2nd and 4th example, provided that the allay of both nations be of equall goodness; else they of the baser will rob the finer of all their good bullion (reciprocall transportation not being forbidden, which could hardly be convenient) and send it home imbased, and so destroy the allay of both nations, to the great dishonour of the kingdomes and decay of traffick. And that I take to have bin the cause why the Portuguez were so earnest to have their own coyn, because the Castilian allay was baser then theirs.

6. Sixthly, that in an union the king is to have allwaies about him, in his service in court and abroad in his warres, of both nations alike. Example 5th, article 6th and example 7th, article 8th and 9th.

7. Seventhly, that in all other places of honour and proffit, especially in all the great offices of justice and revenews, none to be imployed and placed but the naturall born of the country. Example Macedony, article the 1st. Example England, article the 2nd, 3rd and 7th. Example Portugal, article the 2nd, 3rd, 4th and 7th. Example Britany, article the 3rd.

8. Eigthly, that in all benefices and ecclesiasticall livings the same is to be observed. Example Britany, article the 9th, which is so strict that it prohibiteth there in that case all letters of naturalization to have any force. And yet I take it, by the law of England now in force, a stranger (yea without letters of naturalization) is and alwaies hath bin capable of an ecclesiasticall living, by reason as it seems of the universallity of the Church of Rome or the universallity of Pope's power, who would have none of his to be excluded from the fat of any land, be it never so far off.[94] And yet of this result inquire further.

9. Ninethly, that the king after an union is to have perpetually about him two severall councells, for the honour and for the dispatch of affaires of both the two nations, each councell consisting of the naturall born only. Example Portugal, article 5th. A good caution[95] indeed to avoid jealousy, and for the major part of the councell true, but I hold it far better for a king to take one or two of the most considerate, in whom he putteth most confidence, of each nation – a like number of both in both or else no bargain – and make them councellours in both councells; for that the nations being now united in one kind, and having a great sympathy together, it were hard for the best physician in the world to apply a fit medicine to the one member without knowing the estate of the other. For the actions of a great prince have, as I imagine, such a linking and chaining together as they are best understood alltogether, or else they may soon commit that errour which Aristotle[96] findeth fault with in book learning, *respicientium ad pauca*, regarding the fewest, as commonly our Acts of Parliament are made, which bring two faults for mending one, as tinkers mend kettles.

Chapter 29

Queries about the conformity in laws

Now to say somewhat in breif of the three heads before specified, which are laws, liberties and burdens. For laws, let our

[94] See 3 Richard II, c. 2; 7 Richard II, c. 12
[95] Supplied by B. A reads 'conjunction'
[96] Supplied by B. A reads 'Arley'

first quaere be whether in a union there can conveniently be an unity in parliament. The Polonian example, article the 3rd, saies yea, and I think it is true. Now in Britany that they are called as the member alike with the rest, when the king assembleth the estates, time hath brought it to pass, for in the treaty between King Lewis and them it is otherwise. Example Britany, article the 2nd and 4th. Yet the wisedom of our state here at home hath in England and Ireland said no. The wisdome of Spain in Portugal and Castile saith likewise no. The like may be said also of Aragon and Castile, which to this day have their severall *cortes* and *fueros*, parliaments and places of justice, howsoever they have lost some of their liberties in their late troubles which Antonio Perez had better ability to stir up then sufficiently to conduct to a prosperous end.

And if anywhere in the world it be hard to be done, that *concilium unum sit ambobus populis*, I hold it here with us to be most impossible to be done to make one and the same lawmakers for both these nations, whose laws are *toto genere*, in all things different, ours municipall and theirs civil.

Now that our laws and theirs, notwithstanding an union, may stand as they are to both nations, leaving unto our common lawyers the infinity of inconveniences which from their art they alledg,[97] and no man's wit (as far as I can see) is able to remedy, we have all our examples concurring: the Macedonian, article the 1st, that they should live after their own laws; the Polonian example, which is the straightest of all others, article the 9th of the treaty 1501; our own English example, article the 4th and 5th; the Portugal example, article the 1st and 12th; the Aragon example, and what not.

For we are to understand that albeit the kingdomes in Spain, France and the civil world besides ours are said to be governed by the civill law, and so this article of laws may somewhat seem idle at the first sight where England is a party, it is no further but that by the generall grounds and maximes of the civil law they argue, dispute and interpret their own customes and customary

---

[97] The word 'and' is accidentally inserted before 'alledg'. C reads 'leaving an infinite of inconveniences for our common lawyers to alleadge'

bookes.[98] As in Spain they have their *Quintos Partidos*, and in France every several province have their severall customes, upon which they wrangle out of the learning of the civil law, as our common lawyers do upon the unwritten maximes and grounds (if they have any) of their common law and upon our statutes. In France it was by an old constitution very penall for an advocate to alledg any text out of civil law, because it was *Jus Cesareum vel Imperiale*, Cesar's law or the law of the empire, unto which they did ow no recognition.

Chapter 30

Queries about the conformity in Liberties and customs

Our next querie shall be about liberties: whether in an union the same and the like liberties are to be granted to both the nations, I mean to the church, the nobility and the third estate, all after one manner respectively, or each to enjoy severally those which they had before. In which most of our examples concur: example Britany, article the 1st; example Portugal, article the 1st; example England, article the 4th. In the former kind there may be another querie, whether the straighter priviledg shall rise to the larger, as it did in the Lithuanian nobility. Example the 2nd, article the 4th of the treaty 1412, and article the 8th in the treaty 1501 (which no doubt will be more plausible, but prejudiciall for the most part to the crown, as it happened in Lituania, the king loosing by that means his provision of oates and other royal prerogatives); or whether the larger shall fall to the straighter, which cannot be done without great discontentment. Of which latter kind my first querie shall be as followeth:

Chapter 31

Queries about the non-indifferency of grants, and whether the king may not dissolve former liberties, being against the form of an union

Whether in new grants upon a union the king may grant a liberty to one nation and deny it to another, which upon good

---

[98] Savile is arguing here that the laws of various European states are not as similar as they appear to be, despite their common acceptance of the civil law. European difficulties in bringing about legal union are, therefore, still relevant

consideration I make no doubt but he may, as well he may in one nation grant that to one shire there which he denyeth to another. But in that case he must be very circumspect to avoid jealousy or opinion of partiallity between the two nations.

Another querie shall be, and that wherein there is some feeling, whether a king may not in either of his kingdomes at his pleasure before the union casheer and disolve any liberty whatsoever which shall be essentially and formally contrary and opposite to the nature of a union, although after the union it may be inconvenient, yea and pernicious to the king and his estate, to do it. As for example, the Scottish nation, as I have seen in a collection of treaties between Scotland and France, demanded,[99] as I have heard by way of information, some 4 or 5 years agoe to the Duke of Lenox, going into France from the king, the continuance[100] of certain liberties and priviledges they have at this present and a great while have had in France. The speciall prerogatives of which are:

[1] An ordinary guard of Scotts about the king of France his person, instituted by Charles the 7th, and a company of an 100 men at armes instituted by Charles the 6th and confirmed by Charles the 7th before named.

[2] That all Scottish merchants in France should pay no custome but the antient impost foreign, being a matter of nothing, the which was granted them by charters from King Francis the 1st, *anno* 1518, and from Henry the 2nd, *anno* 1554 and 1555. Likewise it was granted by them of Scotland to the French, that the French in Scotland should pay no custome inward and outward but twopence in the pound (whereas other nations pay four times as much) and have free liberty of fishing upon the coast of Scotland.

[3] Thirdly, the whole Scottish nation in the year 1548, at which time the Scottish guards were first instituted, had their charters of naturalization and were afterwards in a larger manner naturalized by the letters patents of Henry the 2nd of France bearing date in the month of June *anno* 1558. '*Par*

---

[99] B, C, and D read 'delivered'

[100] B, C, and D omit 'continuance' and read: 'the Scottish nation I say in France hath at this present and a great while have had 3 speciall prerogatives'

lesquelles', (saith the collection) '*le dit Roy Henry a declaré vouloir gratifier et favoriser les Escosses des graces et privileges dont jouissent ses propres subjets, leur permettant de habiter et resider en son royaume, et accepter tenir et posseder toutes benefices, dignités et offices ecclesiastiques et autres proffits et commodités dont ils se puissent etre induits et nomement purveus a bon titre, suivant les saincts decrees, privileges et libertes de l'Eglise Gallicane, et recevoir les fruicts et proffits a quelque somme que ce foit ou puissent monter et acquirer touts biens tant meubles que immeubles en quelque sorte que ce soit; brief, que les heritiers leur puissent succeder et jouir de leur biens tout ainsi qu'ils estoient originellement natifs du Royaume sans que le procurer general du roy ni autres ses officiers puissent pretender á iceur biens acquis par droit d'Aubien ni que les subjects du royaume d'Escosse soient troublez en tout ce qu'ils sont faits abilles et dispensés, soyent qu'ils soyent habitans en France ou en Escosse, sans qu'ils soyent tenus par raison de ce payer aucun finance ou endeucment; dela quelle, a quelque somme, valeur et estimation qu'elle soit ou puisse monter, ils sont dischargez et acquittez par les dits lettres patentes'.*[101] The said King Henry hast declared that to favour and gratify the Scottish nation, he is content and pleased to give and bestow upon them such graces and priviledges as his own free people enjoy, suffering them to dwell there and to reside in his kingdome, and to buy and possess all manner of benefices, dignities and ecclesiasticall promotions and others wherewith they may be indowed and by name provided and presented unto by any good lawfull and sufficient title, according to the sacred decrees, priviledges and liberties of the Gallican church, and to receive and gather up the fruits and proffits thereof, to what sum and what value soever, and that they may likewise compass and enjoy all manner of goods and proffits, as well moveables as immoveables, in what sort soever. Briefly, that their heires may succeed them and enjoy after them all their goods and proffits, as amply as if they were natives and born within the kingdom of France, the king's advocate generall nor any other officer by any pretence whatsoever making claim to the said goods gotten as

---

[101] The spellings of '*permettant*', '*favoriser*', '*libertes*', '*eglise*' and '*fruicts*' have been corrected on the basis of B. The major deviations of A from B, which include extensive paraphrasing, have been preserved in the text

by aliens, nor that the subjects of the kingdome of Scotland shall be in any way troubled or molested for any thing whatsoever wherein they are made able and capable, and are dispensed with all, whether they be dwelling in France or in Scotland, without being bound by reason of their aboad, be it in France or Scotland, to pay any proffit or duty of the same, what sum or value soever it may amount unto, being thereof discharged by the said letters patents.

In requitall of which favour the like was granted in September by the Queen dowager and the three estates to the French nation, of which favour I hope they have made proffit.

Chapter 32

Querie, whether in this our union the league between France and Scotland, and the liberties granted, may safely stand and not be dangerous either now or hereafter.

Let another of our queries be, whether the first of the third points granted to the Scottish nation by the King of France can any way stand. I say not with this intended union, but with the safety of the king, his posterity and kingdom, a point in part touched before.

Let us also make another quere, whether if the second point granted them by France do stand, the Scots, if the union proceed, making all the Scots naturall English and so not bound to pay customes as merchants and aliens, and all transportations from Scotland to England not customeable otherwise but as from one point to another in England, I say whether the Scots may not thereby put down and mar all other French merchants here who pay in France excessive customes, and also thereby notably diminish the king's revenews, if they, paying little in France and less in Scotland, transport it hither without customes at all.

The only remedy of these two mischeifs as far as I can see (that liberty to the Scots in France standing) will be that all Scots pay custome alien. For my own part, I find no example in my reading howsoever a king may in liberties and burdens within his kingdomes favour, upon just causes, the one more and the other less; yet that he shall not contract with a foreign prince and state that there his subjects shall not be equally respected nor under one and the selfesame condition, I say again I find no example.

As in our late treaty, I think the king of Spain would have found it very strange if we had granted free traffick to an Arragonian and not to a Castilian, or that we should have required of the said king one kind of liberty for an Englishman and another for an Irishman. Besides that, I hold it as I said to be an essentiall and formall contrariety to the nature of an union. I do think it would not stand with the capitulation but of a league,[102] where every part hath reason to make his bargain as broad[103] as he can.

Chapter 33

Of burdens

I will now end this book with burdens, which is the last of the three heads before specifyed. Burdens be, as in our state, wardships, the teddar we are tyed unto for not travelling out of our country without leave, fines upon alienations, forfeitures upon many penall statutes, taxes, subsidies, tenths, fifteenths, etc.; wherein I will say no more then I have said in the other chapter of liberties, for *contrariorum eadem est disciplina*, contraries receive one reason and rule. My seventh example, article the 10th, sheweth a precedent that every horse is to bear his own burden, and seeing we must carry our own burdens, it is good reason we have our own furniture.

And so, *deliratum est satis superque*, I have raved enough and too much.[104]

Finis

[102] B reads: 'of an union, how unperfit soever, so it be an union, not a league'

[103] B, C, and D read 'abroad' for 'as broad'

[104] D, like B and C, concludes: 'by one much lesse in his occupation then Phormio, before one much greater in his then Annibal, this only difference, that he was a voluntary foole, and I a foole by commandment'. *Phormio* was a comedy by Terence based on a play by Apollodorus of Carystus produced in 161 B.C.

APPENDIX

The six tracts printed in this volume constitute only a small part of the total printed and manuscript literature written about the union during the early years of James VI and I's joint reign. The other main treatises written in the two countries are briefly described below.

A. Scottish Tracts

1. Sir Thomas Craig, *De Unione Regnorum Britanniae Tractatus*, ed. C. S. Terry, Scottish History Society, 1909.

Craig, the great Scottish feudalist who pursued a long and successful legal career in Edinburgh, was nominated at the king's request to sit on the Anglo-Scottish Union Commission of 1604. He probably began this work before the Commission met, but he did not complete it until after its last session. Until its twentieth-century translation and publication, *De Unione* existed only in the original manuscript (National Library of Scotland, Advocates MS 24.1.1). It was, however, frequently cited in the union debates of the early eighteenth century. *De Unione* is generally pro-union in stance. Craig supports the change in the royal style, a union in trade and the participation of offices, but opposes alterations in the government and institutions of Scotland. Regarding the union of laws Craig is ambivalent. After going to great lengths to show that such a union was possible, he concludes his treatise with a strong recommendation against the same.

2. John Gordon, *EnΩtikon or A Sermon of the Union of Great Brittannie, in antiquitie of language, name religion, and Kingdome*, London, 1604 (STC 12059). 52 pp.

Gordon was a renowned Scottish cleric and scholar who, after serving as Bishop of Galloway from 1564 to 1572, spent most of the following three decades in France. In 1603 James secured his appointment as Dean of Salisbury and in 1604 Gordon was naturalised as an Englishman by Act of Parliament. On 28 October 1604 he preached this sermon before the King at Whitehall. The tract is notable chiefly for its cabalistic arguments on the meaning of such words as 'union' and 'Britania'. These speculations support a strong assertion of the divine origins of unity, and of James's project in particular. Gordon also stresses the need for a mutual participation of offices.

3. John Gordon, *A Panegyrique of Congratulation for the Concord of the Realmes of Great Britaine in Unitie of Religion, and under One King*, London, 1603 (STC 12061), 47 pp.; republished as *England and Scotlands Happinesse in being reduced to unitie of Religion*, London, 1604 (STC 12058) and as *The Union of Great Brittaine, or England and Scotlands Happinesse in being reduced to unitie of Religion*, London, 1604 (STC 12062).

This tract, which was dedicated to James, was originally written in French but was translated into English by E. Grimston. Gordon uses the tract to present England and Scotland as a united, Elect Nation with a mission to restore purity and unity to the rest of Christendom. Depicting James as the successor to both the legendary Lucius and Constantine, Gordon claims that James was the instrument of God and the union God's work.

4. David Hume, *De Unione Insulae Britanniae Tractatus 1*, London, 1605 (STC 13952). 24 pp.

Hume, a Scottish Presbyterian minister, dedicated this tract to James. It strongly favours union, but one in which the two countries would stand as equal partners. Most of the tract consists of answers to objections against the union. Some, but not all, of these deal with the adoption of the name of 'Britain'; others are concerned with a set of 'Scottish objections' against the union.

5. David Hume, 'De Unione Britanniae, Vincula Unionis, sive Scita Britannica, Liber seu Tractatus Secundus', National Library of Scotland, Advocates MS 31.6.12; British Library, Royal MS 12A.53; Edinburgh University Library, MS Dc.5.50, MS Dc.7.46, and MS Laing III, 249. 64 pp.

Hume's second treatise, also written in Latin, was composed in 1605. Five years later he attempted to publish it in France, but its publication was stopped because of its support for a union of the two churches on the model of the Scottish kirk. Hume appeared to be claiming that 'the union of Scotland with England has no uther end then to make Scotland equal to ingland in al and superiour in sume pointis' (P.R.O., S.P. Dom. 14/57/104). Hume's real purpose, however, was to bring about a just and equitable union in which the best features of each country would be emphasised. The union was to extend to the councils and parliaments of both countries and was to be strengthened by the education of the sons of the nobility of each country at the universities of the other. Inspired by the publication of Cowell's *Institutiones Juris Anglicani* (1605), Hume recommended the establishment of a ten-man commission to consider the possibility of legal union. For the time being, however, the laws of both countries were to remain unchanged.

6. James Maxwell, 'Britaines Union in Love', British Library, Royal MS. 18A.51. 5 fos.

This is in fact not a tract as such but a 'grossed-out shaddow' of a treatise Maxwell intended to write. Maxwell sent this plan to James for his approval in 1604. Having come south to England at the Union of the Crowns, Maxwell, a young scholar whose interest in mathematics, astrology, prophecy and the apocalypse linked him with Pont, Hume and Napier, was seeking a position at Chelsea College. The proposal for the tract follows the favourite Scots theme of divine providence, seeing the union as God's work and the first step in the bringing of concord to

Christendom. As a Scot Maxwell condemns the 'contumelious carping' of the English Commons and strongly favours participation of offices.

B. English Tracts

1. [Anon], 'A Briefe Replication to the Answers of the Objections Against the Union', British Library, Stowe MS 158, fos. 34-39.

The tract lists individually the objections of the Commons to the change in name, together with Thornborough's answers to the same. It then examines these answers and finds them inadequate. The author's deferential servility towards James, and his frequent protestations of loyalty suggest that he intended the tract for public consumption.

2. [Anon], 'A Discourse Against the Union', P.R.O., S.P. Dom. 14/7/65-66.

This tract makes the most extensive use of historical precedents in arguing against a perfect union. After examining nineteen Continental and British unions, the author concludes that only in one, that of Poland and Lithuania, had the union extended beyond the person of the prince to include the laws and institutions of the state. The discourse did admit, however, that in certain unions there had been a union in royal styles and outward marks of government.

3. [Anon], 'A Discourse on the Proposed Union between England and Scotland founded on the opinions of historians ancient and modern', BL, Harleian MS 6850, fos. 35-43; P.R.O., S.P. Dom. 14/9/37.1.

Thomas Hayes sent one copy of this work to King James with a letter in September 1604, but Hayes does not appear to have been its author. The 'Discourse' is a learned disquisition in which the names of Cicero, Tacitus, Cassius Dio and other Roman historians spring from every paragraph. Its main brunt, however, is very limited, showing only that unity is strength and division misery.

The author does, however, justify the name of Britain on grounds of its antiquity and its use by Anglo-Saxon kings of England to express their feudal superiority over the Scots. He also rejects legal union as unprecedented.

4. [Anon], 'A discourse on the Union as being triple-headed: in head, in laws, and in privileges', BL, Harleian MS. 292.59; P.R.O., S.P. Dom. 14/7/61-62. 1 fo.

The author uses historical precedents to oppose a union in laws and trade, but to justify participation in offices and employments.

5. [Anon], 'The Divine Providence in the misticall and reall union of England and Scotland both by nature and other coherences with motives for reconcilinge such differences as may now seeme to hinter the same', BL, Additional MS. 38139, fos. 42-5; Beaulieu Palace House Library, Papers on Scotch Affairs, III, 1.

Despite its title, this tract was not written primarily to support the union as the work of God, or even to justify unity as a divine principle. Instead it makes some radical suggestions for the union, including the organisation of ecclesiastical and temporal government (i.e., parliaments, privy councils and convocations) on a federal basis. The author opposes a union in laws on the grounds that neither country would allow alteration of its own laws. His most entertaining proposal is for the change of the name of Britain to 'Trianglia', a name denoting the shape of the island, the 'Anglian' origins of the English, and the triad of united nations (England, Wales and Scotland).

6. [Anon], 'Pro Unione', Gonville and Caius College, Cambridge, MS 73/40, fos. 183-194.

This tract, written between April and October 1604, argues strongly for the union, predicting great civil discord if the name of Great Britain were not taken. It provides answers to some of the Commons objections, particularly those of utility, precedency, and the legal pretext concerning the erection of a new estate. Like Russell and Pont, 'Pro Unione' asserts an existing religious unity between the nations and calls for a campaign against Papists.

7. [Anon], *Rapta Tatio: The mirrour of his Maiesties present governement, tending to the Union of his whole Iland of Brittonie*, London, 1604 (STC 23705). 58 pp.

The authorship of this tract has been attributed to either Sir J. Skinner or N. Douglas. It was written sometime between April and October 1604. Like Cornwallis's tract, *Rapta Tatio* is long on rhetoric (chiefly about James's impartiality and the advantages of unity as a principle) and short on concrete arguments and proposals. The treatise does, however, advise the establishment of legal union after an interim period in which both nations would be able to study the legal system of the other.

8. [Anon], 'Union by Concurrency of the Homager State with the Superiour. Effects of such union', P.R.O., SP 14/7/80X. 2 fos.

This tract is all that survives of what was once a much larger treatise. It comes from the Conway Papers and is headed 'Cap. 29'. The chapter examines the effect of union by consolidation of an inferior state with a superior state, in terms very similar to those of Savile. The author, however, recommends that James declare Scotland a 'Dependent Diadem', held of England by homage, and so achieve a perfect union without parliament.

9. Sir Francis Bacon, *A Brief Discourse touching the Happy Union of the Kingdoms of England and Scotland*, London, 1603 (STC 1117); reprinted in *The Letters and Life of Lord Bacon*, ed. J. Spedding, 7 vols., London, 1861-74, iii, 89-99.

At the time he wrote this treatise, Bacon was desperately seeking favour and suffering from the predominance of his old rival, Cecil. Writing as a scholar rather than counsellor, Bacon uses an analogy between the political world and the world of nature to make a number of suggestions regarding the union. He argues strongly for a union in name, in the principal and fundamental laws, and in employments. Bacon also defends England's primacy in the union, suggesting (with Henry VII) that 'the greater draw the less'.

10. Sir Francis Bacon, 'Certain Articles or Considerations

touching the Union of the Kingdoms of England and Scotland', in Spedding, *Letters and Life of Bacon*, iii, 217-47.

Bacon's treatise was written between June and October 1604, specifically in preparation for the Anglo-Scots Union Commission, and was submitted to the King. Although it was not printed until the nineteenth century, it existed in numerous manuscript copies in the early seventeenth century. Some of its proposals, such as union in the outward signs of government, the adoption of the British style by proclamation, and the abolition of hostile laws, became part of the government's policy. Other proposals, such as the union of parliaments and public law, were not implemented until the early eighteenth century, while his proposals for the establishment of a special Border court, the institution of a British court of appeal similar to the 'Grand Council' of France, and the expansion of the English nobility in 'proportion' with the Scots were never realised.

11. William Clerk, 'Ancillans Synopsis: Such an additional to that answere of the Reverend B. to certaine objectiones against the happie and desired union of the two famous kingdomes England and Scotland', Trinity College Library, Dublin, MS 635. 20 fos.

Clerk, a legal scholar who was knowledgeable in both civil and common law, drafted this treatise in order to resolve the controversy engendered by Thornborough's answer to the objections against the change in name. The treatise provides additional support for the Bishop.

12. Sir William Cornwallis, *The Miraculous and Happie Union of England and Scotland*, London and Edinburgh, 1604 (STC 5782). 35 pp.

Cornwallis sat as an M.P. from 1597 to 1614 but was known mainly as a minor essayist. His tract, which was published in March 1604, was markedly pro-union in tone, but it lacked a close examination of what union really meant. The tract does, however, favour a union in laws and offers an able, if possibly time-serving defence of James against accusations of partiality in his bestowal of favours.

13. Alberico Gentili, 'De Unione Regnorum Britanniae', in *Regales Disputationes Tres*, London, 1605 (STC 11741), pp. 39-98.

> Gentili, an Italian civilian who served as Regius Professor at Oxford from 1598 until 1608, included this Latin and Greek tract in a collection of disputations which greatly exaggerated the power of the king. Drawing on the work of Continental civilians, especially Bartolus, and appealing to the *jus gentium* as the guiding principle of the union, Gentili answers a number of objections against the union, and in particular those against the union in name. Whether Gentili composed this tract before the assumption of the royal style cannot be determined. The tract makes a strong case for the necessity and advisability of perfect union and attacks 'men who are unwilling for sheer perversity to undertake any common enterprise or to mingle their affairs with adjacent lands so as to provide mutual benefit'.

14. John Hayward, *A Treatise of Union of the Two realmes of England and Scotland*, London, 1604 (STC 13011). 58 pp.

> Hayward was an ambitious civil lawyer who had suffered imprisonment for the publication of a book on Henry IV at the time of Essex's rebellion. Although he published this tract in November 1604, he undoubtedly began it before the royal proclamation of October. Hayward's defence of the royal project is able and convincing, especially with respect to the change of style. Hayward is mainly notable for his civil-lawyer stance on the union of laws. He condemns English beliefs in the superiority and immemorial antiquity of the common law and calls for a genuine but nonetheless limited fusion of the two laws. Hayward opposes participation in offices (and therefore by implication naturalisation) because of the jealousies it would raise among the English.

15. John Thornborough, *A Discourse plainely proving the evident Utilitie and urgent necessitie of the desired happie Union of the two famous Kingdomes of England and Scotland*, London, 1604 (STC 24035). 35 pp.

> Published in May 1604, the *Discourse* was written in

reply to the objections of the Commons to the change in the royal style. It lists the objections individually, and then gives answers to each, pressing at the same time for wide-ranging union in other fields, including the law and participation of offices. Thornborough also emphasises the theme of divine providence, with James as the instrument of God and union as His work. The *Discourse* was the earliest of the answers to the objections and led to allegations by the Lower House that Thornborough had breached parliamentary privilege. The tract was suppressed. See *CJ*, i, 226; HMC, Hastings MSS, iv, 2.

16. John Thornborough, *The Joiefull and Blessed Reuniting the two mighty and famous kingdomes, England and Scotland, into their ancient name of Great Brittaine*, Oxford, n.d. (STC 24036). 80 pp.

Thornborough's second tract is devoted to justifying the Proclamation of October 1604, and to praising the general principle of unity in public and human affairs. It stresses the theme of divine providence and cites precedents for the union in name, laws, and participation of offices. The publication of this tract violated Thornborough's promise not to venture into print on the union again. See *LJ*, ii, 5.

INDEX

INDEX 257

English people, opposition of to union, lviii; religion of, 7, 26, 29-31; lost in the plague, 9; reception of James, 20, 21; name of, 136

Entichians, 113
Eric, king of Norway, 222
Erskine, John, 2nd or 7th earl of Mar, xiii, xxv, xxvi
Erskine, Sir Thomas, xiii
Esau, 183
Esk (Eske), river, 7
Essex, county of, 217
Essex, earl of, see Devereux, Robert
Ethiopia, 230
Eton College, lxxiv, lxxvi
Euclid, 104
Eusebius of Caesaria, 114
Eustathius, archbishop of Thessalonica, 209
Exeter College, Oxford, lxi
Ezechias, 16
Ezekiel, 48, 132

FACULTY of Advocates, lv
Fasciculus Temporum, 113
Ferdinand I, Holy Roman Emperor and king of Bohemia and Hungary, 39
Ferdinand I, king of Naples, 195
Ferdinand II, king of Aragon, 40, 41, 41, 46, 63, 64, 70, 190, 195, 202, 203, 204, 223, 224
Ferdinand III, king of Leon and Castile, 40, 63, 64, 190
Ferrara, house of, 193
Fitzgerald, James, 'the Tower Earl' of Desmond, 174
Five Knights' Case, lxii
Flaminius, Titus Quinctius, 217
Flanders, 40, 54, 57, 123, 140
Foix, earls of, 57
'Form of Apology and Satisfaction', see 'Apology'

Foxe, John, xxx
France, Scottish alliance with, xxvi; Scottish trading privileges with, xli, lxxix; annexations to, lxxi; relations with England, lxxv-lxxvi, 52, 118, 119, 158; religion in, 15; laws in, 30; unions within, 40-41, 97; at time of Roman Empire, 42, 51; kings of, 45, 121, 163, 186-8; usurpations in, 65; English dominions in, 68, 145; inclusion in English royal style, 77, 166; religious wars in, 112; crown of, 158, 165; name of, 167; laws of, 180; see also unions of states and kingdoms, France and Brittany, France and Navarre, France and Normandy
Francis I, king of France, 193, 228
Francis of Brittany, 229, 236
Frederick, Holy Roman Emperor, 159
free trade, xl, lxxii, 51-52, 71, 142; see also commercial union
free will, doctrine of, 112
French language, 212
Frenchmen, 167, 171, 174, 176, 206, 236
Fuller, Nicholas, MP, xx
Furnival's Inn, lxviii

GALICIA, 41, 66
Garibay (Gavarra) y Zamalloa, Esteban, 202
Gascony (Gascoigne), 148
Gaul (Gallia), 64, 159, 167
Gelasius, 115
General Assembly, xlv
Gentiles, 13, 48, 109, 113, 115, 215, 216
Gentili, Alberico, 248
Genoa (Genua), republic of, 97, 205

MEMBERSHIP

*Membership of the Scottish History Society
is open to all who are interested in the history of Scotland.
For an annual subscription of £12.00
members normally receive one volume each year.
Enquiries should be addressed to
the Honorary Secretary or the Honorary Treasurer
whose addresses are given overleaf.*

REPORT

of the 97th Annual Meeting

The 97th Annual Meeting of the Scottish History Society was held in the rooms of the Royal Society of Edinburgh, on Saturday, 10 December, 1983, at 11.15 a.m. Professor Rosalind Mitchison, President of the Society, was in the Chair.

The Report of Council was as follows:

The eighteenth volume of the Fourth Series, *Government under the Covenanters, 1637–1651*, edited by Dr David Stevenson, was issued to members at the beginning of this year, and the next volume, *The Knights of St John*, edited by Rev. P. H. R. Mackay, Professor I. B. Cowan and Dr Alan Macquarrie, should be distributed early in the new year. As indicated in last year's report, the volume for 1984 will be *A Scottish Firm in Virginia: William Cuninghame and Co., 1767–1777*, edited by Dr T. M. Devine; and this will be followed in 1985 by the *Jacobean Union: Six Anglo-Scottish tracts of 1604*, edited by Dr Brian Levack and Dr B. R. Galloway.

In the course of the year the Council has accepted one new proposal for a volume for future publication. Dr Ian Levitt will edit a volume of documents on Government and Social Conditions, 1845–1945, surveying changing attitudes to such matters as poverty, poor relief, public health, unemployment, housing and vagrancy, and growing concern that Scotland was lagging behind England in many fields. With this volume the Society's chronological coverage of Scottish history will take a major leap forward to the mid-twentieth century.

In its Report last year the Council made it clear that subscriptions would have to rise, but some members may be concerned at the size of the increase the Council has had to make. The cost of producing our publications has continued to rise much more sharply than the rate of inflation. *Stirling Presbytery Records* was a very expensive volume on account of its length; but the cost of the much shorter *Government under the Covenanters* was almost as high, and the cost of volumes is now almost 50% greater than the Society's income from subscriptions. Thus the increase in subscriptions to £12 is a realistic response which the Council held to be essential if the Society was to look forward to surviving in a healthy state up to and beyond its centenary in 1986. As well as increasing subscriptions the Council has begun active consideration of alternative production methods to achieve substantial savings in costs. Such economies, so far as possible maintaining the quality of production for which the Society is well known, should enable the Society to maintain the subscription rate now being introduced into our second century.

In order to spread publication costs as widely as possible the Society needs to enlist new members. This makes Council's regular appeal for suggestions as to prospective new members or ways of publicising the Society more urgent than ever. Any suggestions will be welcomed by the Hon. Secretary, Department of History, University of Dundee, and copies of a new publicity leaflet may be obtained from her.

The Council has begun to give consideration to appropriate ways of marking the Society's centenary in 1986. It has been decided that the volume issued to members in 1986 should be *The Charters of the Lords of the Isles*, edited by Mr and Mrs R. W. Munro, and that the main celebration should be combined with the biennial Scottish Historical Conference, which will meet in Edinburgh in September 1986. The theme of the week-end conference would be 'Scottish History: the past, the present and the future', to combine a celebration of the Society's work (and a formal centenary dinner) with a wider consideration of Scottish history which would be of general public interest. Strictly speaking, the centenary of the Society falls in April, and it is proposed that that should be marked by a major effort to get media coverage for the Society to aid recruitment, together with a Scottish Record Office exhibition on the Society's history. But such plans are only provisional at present, and comments or suggestions by members as to marking the centenary will be welcomed by Council.

The Council has noted with great regret the death in the past year of a distinguished member, Dr Eric Cregeen, Reader in the School of Scottish Studies, University of Edinburgh, and editor of the first volume of the Society's Fourth Series publications, *Argyll Estate Instructions*.

The three members of Council due to retire by rotation are the Rev. Mark Dilworth, Mr John di Folco, and Dr Alastair Durie. The following will be proposed to the Annual Meeting for election to Council: Dr John Durkan (a senior research fellow in the University of Glasgow); Dr Norman A. T. Macdougall (lecturer in the Department of Scottish History, University of St Andrews), and Mr William W. Scott (an under-secretary in the Scottish Office).

During the past year 5 members of the Society have died, 11 have resigned and 12 have been removed from membership for non-payment of subscription. Forty-two new members have joined. The total membership, including 212 libraries, is now 792, compared with 778 in 1982.

The Chairman of Council, Mr A. D. Cameron, presented the Annual Report, surveying current and future publications and, in justifying the rise in subscription, asserted the determination of Council to achieve savings in the cost of production of volumes. He outlined some of the ways in which the Society would celebrate its centenary in 1986. The Treasurer then presented his accounts.

On the motion of Mr David Sellar, seconded by Rev. Ian Dunlop, the Report and Accounts were approved; Dr Durkan, Dr Macdougall and Mr Scott were declared elected to membership of Council.

The President delivered an address entitled 'Foundlings and orphans under the old Poor Law'. Dr Jenny Wormald proposed a vote of thanks.

3

ABSTRACT ACCOUNT OF CHARGE AND DISCHARGE OF THE
INTROMISSIONS OF THE HONORARY TREASURER
from the
1st October 1982 to 30th September 1983

GENERAL ACCOUNT

CHARGE

I. Cash in Bank at 1st October, 1982:

    1. Sum at Credit of Savings Account with Bank of
       Scotland   £6,834·59

    2. Sum at Credit of Current Account with Bank of
       Scotland   483·19

    3. Sum at Credit of Special Investment Account with
       Trustee Savings Bank   724·37

                                 £8,042·15

II. Subscriptions received   6,304·89

III. Past Publications sold   545·03

IV. Reprints sold   17·50

V. Royalties on reprints   26·53

VI. Interest on Savings Accounts with Bank of Scotland and
    Trustee Savings Bank   825·96

VII. Income Tax Refund, 1981/82   370·66

VIII. Donations   60·00

IX. Prepublication orders (*Knights of St. John*)   61·00

X. Carnegie Trust Grants   1,000·00

XI. Payment made in error   605·00

XII. Sums drawn from Bank Current Account   £12,441·50

XIII. Sums drawn from Bank Savings Account   £3,500·00

                                 £17,858·72

DISCHARGE

I. Cost of publications during year
    (*Government under the Covenanters*)   £8,578·05
    Cost of printing Annual Reports, Notices and
    Printer's Postage etc.   483·16

                             £9,061·21

II. Insurance   42·19

III. A.G.M. (North British Hotel)   94·50

IV. Refund   605·00

V. Bank charges   115·90

VI. Miscellaneous Payments   417·67

VII. Sums lodged in Bank Current Account   £12,973·80

VIII. Sums lodged in Bank Savings Account   £2,930·99

IX. Funds at close of this account

    1. Balance at credit of Savings Account
       with Bank of Scotland   £6,200·00

    2. Balance at credit of Current Account
       with Bank of Scotland   532·30

    3. Balance at credit of Special Investment
       Account with Trustee Savings Bank   789·95

                             7,522·25

                             £17,858·72

GLASGOW, *27 October 1983.* I have examined the General Account of the Honorary Treasurer of the Scottish History Society for the year from 1st October 1982, to 30th September 1983, and I find the same to be correctly stated and sufficiently vouched.

                                   JOHN A. SMITH
                                   Auditor